Lecture Notes in Computer S

Commenced Publication in 1973
Founding and Former Series Editors:
Gerhard Goos, Juris Hartmanis, and Jan van Leeuwen

Sigmar-Olaf Tergan   Tanja Keller (Eds.)

Knowledge and Information Visualization

Searching for Synergies

 Springer

Volume Editors

Sigmar-Olaf Tergan
Tanja Keller
Institut für Wissensmedien/Knowledge Media Research Center
Konrad-Adenauer-Str. 40, 72072 Tübingen, Germany
E-mail: {s.tergan, t.keller}@iwm-kmrc.de

Library of Congress Control Number: 2005928159

CR Subject Classification (1998): H.2.8, H.3, H.4, I.2, H.5.4, H.5, I.7, F.2.2, K.3.1

ISSN   0302-9743
ISBN-10   3-540-26921-5 Springer Berlin Heidelberg New York
ISBN-13   978-3-540-26921-2 Springer Berlin Heidelberg New York

Springer is a part of Springer Science+Business Media

springeronline.com

© Springer-Verlag Berlin Heidelberg 2005
Printed in Germany

Typesetting: Camera-ready by author, data conversion by Scientific Publishing Services, Chennai, India
Printed on acid-free paper   SPIN: 11510154   06/3142   5 4 3 2 1 0

Editors' Note

Until now, knowledge visualization and information visualization investigated the question of visualization from different perspectives. However, as there are some common areas of interest, synergy effects can be expected. In an international workshop titled "Visual Artefacts for the Organization of Information and Knowledge. Searching for Synergies" held in May 2004 at the Knowledge Media Research Center in Tuebingen (Germany), leading-edge researchers tackled the problem of looking for synergies. This book explores the approaches of most of the workshop participants, as well as other invited experts.

The intention of the book is to advance current research and development in the fields of knowledge and information visualization, to push the borders of what is now feasible and applicable to develop synergistic approaches that may represent both knowledge and information in a comprehensive manner.

The editors are indebted to the authors who contributed to the book, to Margot Stoll, who did the layout and formatted the papers, to Waltraud Lenz who checked the references, and to Sebastian Groteloh who assisted in solving technical problems.

March 2005

Tanja Keller
Sigmar-Olaf Tergan

Table of Contents

Knowledge-Oriented Organization of Information for Fostering Information Use

Visualizing Knowledge and Information: An Introduction

Tanja Keller and Sigmar-Olaf Tergan

Institut für Wissensmedien (IWM), Konrad-Adenauer-Str. 40,
72072 Tübingen, Germany
{t.keller, s.tergan}@iwm-kmrc.de

Abstract. Visualization has proven to be an effective strategy for supporting users in coping with complexity in knowledge- and information-rich scenarios. Up to now, however, information visualization and knowledge visualization have been distinct research areas, which have been developed independently of each other. This book aims toward bringing both approaches together and looking for synergies, which may be used for fostering learning, instruction, and problem solving. This introductory article seeks to provide a conceptual framework and a preview of the contributions of this volume. The most important concepts referred to in this book are defined and a conceptual rationale is provided as to why visualization may be effective in fostering, processing and managing knowledge and information. The basic ideas underlying knowledge visualization and information visualization are outlined. The preview of each approach addresses its basic concept, as well as how it fits into the conceptual rationale of the book. The contributions are structured according to whether they belong to one of the following basic categories: "Background", "Knowledge Visualization", "Information Visualization", and "Synergies".

1 Introduction

Our present-day society is witnessing an explosion of information and knowledge and an increasing complexity of subject matter in many domains. Influenced by the changes in the amount and complexity of knowledge and information, as well as changes in requirements for coping effectively with increasingly complex tasks, a change in the culture of learning and working is taking place (e.g. Schnurer, Stark & Mandl, 2003). Traditional strategies of learning for comprehension and retention are no longer the central goals in learning and instruction. Learning content is often complex, ill-structured, represented in different information repositories, not pre-selected and pre-designed, and sometimes has to be searched for by the learners themselves (Rakes, 1996; http://stauffer.queensu.ca/inforef/tutorials/rbl/). Having information "at your fingertips" has become a crucial issue. The workflow of receiving, structuring, using, creating, and disseminating information requires information, as well as knowledge management techniques. In order to make a large amount of information easily accessible by users, the information has to be pre-structured. The structure itself has to be communicated to the users. Visualizations of the structures inherent in large amounts of information may help in understanding relations between informa-

S.-O. Tergan and T. Keller (Eds.): Knowledge and Information Visualization, LNCS 3426, pp. 1 – 23, 2005.

tion elements and visually searching relevant information. Visualizations of knowledge are needed to make knowledge explicit and better usable, as well as to make sense of information structures. Visualizations concerning structures of knowledge and information are suggested to help learners coping with subject-matter complexity and ill-structuredness (Holley & Dansereau, 1984; Jonassen, Reeves, Hong, Harvey & Peters, 1997). They may help students to elicit, (co-)construct, structure and restructure, elaborate, evaluate, locate and access, communicate, and use ideas, thoughts and knowledge about relevant content and resources (Jonassen, Beissner & Yacci, 1993). There is a need for cognitive tools aiming at supporting cognitive processing in generating, representing, structuring and restructuring, retrieving, sharing, and using knowledge. Therefore, there is a need for visualization techniques for making structures of information in large repositories apparent and for helping users in effectively searching and locating task-relevant information elements while coping with large amounts of information in learning and problem solving.

Visualizations of knowledge and information are widely applied in the fields of education and knowledge management to help users in processing, getting access, and dealing effectively with complex knowledge and large amounts of information. Although visualization has been proven to be an effective strategy for supporting users in coping with complexity in knowledge- and information-rich scenarios, knowledge and information visualization have historically been treated as two distinct areas of research, each being developed independently from the other. Whereas knowledge visualization has its origin in the social sciences, particularly in the field of learning and instructional science, information visualization primarily belongs to the field of computer science.

This situation of two research domains developing independently, but nonetheless being heavily interrelated in processes of working, learning, and problem solving, motivated the authors to ask leading edge researchers of both domains to contribute to this book. The authors were challenged to elaborate on their personal view of knowledge visualization and information visualization. At the same time, they were inspired to combine views and approaches from both domains and to look for synergies to enhance cognitive processing and knowledge and information in knowledge- and information-rich scenarios by means of visualization. The idea for this book is based on the rationale and results of the International Workshop on Visual Artifacts for the Organization of Information and Knowledge, which was held at the Knowledge Media Research Center (http://www.iwm-kmrc.de/) in Tübingen in May 2004. The workshop was intended to bring together researchers from both fields knowledge visualization and information visualization - to think about potential synergies by integrating ideas and approaches and to initiate a discussion on synergistic approaches. Selected participants of this workshop as well as renowned international visualization researchers have been invited to contribute to this book. It is hoped that these presentations will contribute to a mutual understanding of the research questions, the common interests, and to an advancement in both the conceptualization and development of synergistic approaches that may improve visualization practices in fields like education and knowledge management.

In the following introductory chapter, the most important concepts referred to in this book are defined. A conceptual rationale is provided detailing why visualization may be effective in fostering the processing and management of knowledge and information. The basic ideas underlying knowledge visualization and information visualization are outlined. In a short preview of the contributions of this volume, the idea behind each approach and its contribution to the goals of the book are outlined.

2 The Basic Concepts of the Book

Three basic concepts are the focus of this book: "data", "information", and "knowledge". There have been numerous attempts to define the terms "data", "information", and "knowledge", among them, the OTEC Homepage "Data, Information, Knowledge, and Wisdom" (Bellinger, Castro, & Mills, see http://www.systems-thinking.org/dikw/dikw.htm):

Data are raw. They are symbols or isolated and non-interpreted facts. Data represent a fact or statement of event without any relation to other data. Data simply exists and has no significance beyond its existence (in and of itself). It can exist in any form, usable or not. It does not have meaning of itself.

Information is data that has been given meaning through interpretation by way of relational connection and pragmatic context. This "meaning" can be useful, but does not have to be. Information is the same only for those people who attribute to it the same meaning. Information provides answers to "who", "what", "where", "why", or "when" questions. From there, data that has been given meaning by somebody and, hence, has become information, may still be data for others who do not comprehend its meaning. Information may be distinguished according to different categories concerning, for instance, its features, origin, status of cognitive manipulation, or format, for example, "facts", "opinions" (present some kind of analysis of the facts), "objective information" (are usually based on facts), "subjective information" (presents some kind of cognitive analysis of the facts), "primary information" (is information in its original form), "secondary information" (is information that has been analyzed, interpreted, translated, or examined in some way). Information may also be distinguished according to its representational format, for example, verbal, print, visual, or audio-visual. Web-based information is often represented in a mixture of different codes and presented in different modes catering to different senses. Information may be abstract or concrete. In the context of information visualization, abstract non-physically based information with no natural visual representation is in focus. Most articles in this book focus on abstract non-physically based information for the representation of subject matter as potential resources to be used in working and instructional scenarios.

Knowledge is information, which has been cognitively processed and integrated into an existing human knowledge structure. Knowledge is dynamic. Its structure is constantly being changed and adapted to the affordances in coping with task situations. The most important difference between information and knowledge is that information is outside the brain (sometimes called "knowledge in the world") and knowledge is inside. Cognition may be based both on "knowledge in the head" and "knowledge in the world." Knowledge in the head refers to different types of knowledge that are represented in different representational patterns (Rumelhart & Ortony, 1977). Knowledge in the world may be both (1) external representations reflecting aspects of knowledge in the head and (2) cultural and cognitive artefacts appearing as sensory stimuli and perceptual inputs, which are automatically processed and interpreted by the cognitive system in terms of knowledge. Knowledge is owned by a person, a group of persons, or by society. Aspects of knowledge may be externalized, for example, its structure by means of structure visualizations. For other people, externalized knowledge is nothing but information. To become knowledge, it has to be processed, furnished with meaning, and integrated into their mental knowledge structure. Even people owning the externalized knowledge have to reconstruct its meaning and reintegrate it into an existing mental structure according to the affordances of a particular task (Bransford, 1979). Based on knowledge, answering "how"-questions is possible. If knowledge is used for synthesizing new knowledge from the previously held knowledge, understanding may result. Understanding builds upon currently held information, knowledge, and understanding itself. Based on understanding, "why"-questions may be answered.

There is one major distinction between knowledge types referring to the cognitive accessibility of knowledge: knowledge may be explicit or tacit. Explicit knowledge can be expressed either symbolically, e.g. in words or numbers, or pictorially, and can be shared in the form of data, scientific formulas, product specifications, visualizations, manuals, universal principles, and so forth. This kind of knowledge can be readily transmitted among individuals, formally and systematically. Tacit knowledge is highly personal and hard to formalize, making it difficult to communicate or share with others. Subjective insights, intuitions, and hunches fall into this category of knowledge. It consists of beliefs, perceptions, ideals, values, emotions, and mental models. Furthermore, tacit knowledge is deeply rooted in an individual's action and experience (Edvinsson & Malone, 1997).

Cognitive scientists (a.o. Rumelhart & Norman, 1983) discriminate between different aspects of domain knowledge: conceptual knowledge (propositional representation of abstract concepts and their semantic relation), episodic knowledge (mental representation of audio-visual perceptions of realistic events, situations, objects), analogical representations (mental models, images that preserve structures of realistic subject matter in an analogical manner), procedural knowledge (represented as condition-action pairs), enactive knowledge (knowledge, which is bound to the action to be performed), and situated knowledge. Situated knowledge is related to and embedded into a socio-cultural context of everyday activities. Knowledge is termed "situated" if it takes account of the social interaction and physical activity in the learning situation where the knowledge was acquired. The importance of learning episodes within everyday work for acquiring knowledge in communities of practice has been noted by Jean Lave and Etienne Wenger (Lave & Wenger, 1991). Recently, it has been suggested that knowledge may not be restricted to "know-what" and "know-how" but has to be supplemented with "know-where" (Siemens, 2005). Know-where means the understanding of where to find knowledge. This notion of know-where is tantamount to the notion of resource knowledge, the knowledge of where to find information, which may be used as a knowledge resource (Tergan, in this book). Most of the contributions of this book dealing with knowledge visualization focus on structures of conceptual knowledge. However, some authors also address episodic, situational, and analogical knowledge (e.g. Alpert, Cañas et al., Coffey, Tergan, in this book).

3 Why Visualization?

Visualizations of knowledge and information may play an important role as methods and tools. One central reason is that visualizations capitalize on several characteristic features of the human cognitive processing system. According to Ware (in this book), the "power of a visualization comes from the fact that it is possible to have a far more complex concept structure represented externally in a visual display than can be held in visual and verbal working memories". In this regard, visualizations are cognitive tools aiming at supporting the cognitive system of the user. Visualizations can make use of the automatically human process of pattern finding (Ware, 2004). They can draw both on the visual and the spatial working memory system (Baddeley, 1998; Logie, 1995). It is suggested that using multiple codes involves cognitive processing in different subsystems of the human working memory and therefore supports processes of learning (Mayer, 2001). External representations visualizing inherent structures of an individual's knowledge and of great amounts of information can help people in the searching and cognitive processing of the structured elements (Potelle & Rouet, in this book; Wiegmann, Dansereau, McCagg, Rewey & Pitre, 1992).

During the process of learning and problem solving, a visualization may help the learner overcome problems that are due to the limitations of working memory in both capacity and duration of stored information. Thus, visualizations may reduce cognitive load (Sweller & Chandler, 1994) and expand the capability of an individual's memory for coping with complex cognitive task requirements (Cox & Brna, 1995; Larkin, 1989; Larkin & Simon, 1987). Combining a computer-based information system with flexible human cognitive capabilities, such as pattern finding, and using a visualization as the interface between the two is far more powerful than an unaided human cognitive process (Ware, in this book). In an educational context, learner-generated visualizations may foster constructive cognitive processing and visuo-spatial strategies (Holley & Dansereau, 1984). This is particularly true for students preferring a visual instead of a verbal learning strategy (Dansereau, in this book).

A further reason why visualizations may help users in processing the visualized elements is suggested by Cox (1999). Visualizations can enhance our processing ability by visualizing abstract relationships between visualized elements and may serve as a basis for externalized cognition (Scaife & Rogers, 1996; Cox, 1999). External representations may also help in "computational offloading" (Rogers & Scaife, 1997). Compared with an informationally-equivalent textual description of an information a diagram may allow users to avoid having to explicitly compute information because users can extract information 'at a glance' (p. 2). "Such representations work best when the spatial constraints obeyed by representations map into important constraints in the represented domain in such a way that they restrict (or enforce) the kinds of interpretations that can be made" (Rogers & Scaife, 1997, p. 2). They can help to exploit the rapid processing capabilities of the human visual system and very easy perceptual judgements are substituted for more difficult logical ones (Paige & Simon, 1966). Thus, external representations can expand the capability of an individual's memory for coping with complex cognitive task requirements (Larkin, 1989). However, particularly with complex subject matter, a visualization alone may not provide sufficient clues for users in sense-making. Often, visual semantics must be augmented with verbal clues to help users fully exploit the meaning of a visualization (Sebrechts, in this book) and use it in an educational context (Keller & Grimm, in this book).

In many cases it is reasonably to assume advantages from using visualizations because of a 'distributed' representation, the internal and external being coordinated in an 'abstract problem space' (Zhang & Norman, 1994). Chabris and Kosslyn (in this book) suggest the principle of 'representational correspondence' as a basic principle of effective diagram design. According to this principle visualizations work best if they depict information in the same way that our internal mental representation do.

3.1 The Idea of Knowledge Visualization

Spatial strategies are needed to help individuals in acquiring, storing, restructuring, communicating, and utilizing knowledge and knowledge resources, as well as overcoming capacity limitations of individual working memory (Holley & Dansereau, 1984; Novak & Gowin, 1984). In order to cope effectively with complex cognitive task requirements, techniques for the external representation of individual knowledge in a visual-spatial format are suggested to facilitate "the coherent representation of new information in semantic memory" (Holley & Dansereau, 1984, p. 14) and acquiring and conveying structural knowledge (Jonassen, Beissner & Yacci, 1993). Helping students to organize their knowledge is as important as the knowledge itself, since knowledge organization is likely to affect student's intellectual performance (Bransford, Brown & Cocking, 1999). Knowledge visualization may help students to organize and reorganize, structure and restructure, assess, evaluate, elaborate, communicate, and (co-)construct knowledge, and to utilize ideas and thoughts, as well as knowledge, about relevant contents and resources (Holley & Dansereau, 1984; Jonassen, Beissner & Yacci, 1993; Tergan, 2003).

Visual external representations of knowledge are often processed more effectively than propositional ones because they "support a large number of perceptual inferences, which are extremely easy for humans" (Larkin & Simon, 1987, p. 88). In mapping approaches, this is accomplished, for example, by means of the spatial layout and highlighting of elements signifying contextual relationships and their relative importance. Spatial representations are often directly related to spatial mental processes, for example, in mathematics and physics (Larkin, 1983; Young & O'Shea, 1981). In this way, visualizations play an important role in "external cognition" during problem solving (Larkin, 1989; Scaife & Rogers, 1996). As Zhang (1997) points out, externalization is beneficial if the cost associated with the externalization process is outweighed by the benefits of using the external representation.

Jonassen (1991) and Jonassen et al. (1993) have described a variety of visualization methods for fostering spatial learning strategies and technologies used for the visualization of knowledge. The most often used methods are mind mapping and concept mapping methods. Mind maps were suggested as a spatial strategy that uses only key words and images to aid students in structuring ideas and taking notes (Buzan, 1995). Visualizations of knowledge based on concept mapping technology may be used for mapping, managing, and manipulating conceptual knowledge (Cañas, Leake & Wilson, 1999). Tergan (2003; in this book) outlines a conceptual model for the implementation of digital concept maps as tools for managing knowledge and information resources.

According to Dansereau, the concept of "knowledge visualization" in a strict sense is restricted to externalizing aspects of knowledge by the individual herself or himself in a "freestyle mapping mode" (Dansereau, in this book). In literature, the term "knowledge visualization" is, however, also used if a knowledge structure of an expert is presented to students as a means for self-assessing knowledge and for aiding comprehension and navigation. Up to now, "knowledge visualization" has been focused on structures of conceptual knowledge. Knowledge visualization methods in the educational context have been used for fostering idea generation, learning, assessment, and instruction. Reviews on the effectiveness of concept mapping have been published a.o. by Bruillard and Baron (2000), Jonassen et al. (1993), and O'Donnell, Dansereau and Hall (2002). The results of empirical research provide evidence that concept mapping bears a high potential in fostering "external cognition" (Scaife & Rogers, 1996) depending on the task requirements, the domain knowledge of the users, and their spatial learning literacy.

We will use the term "knowledge visualization" with a focus on structure visualizations for the representation of conceptual knowledge. Some authors also address the problem of how subject matter knowledge (like episodic knowledge, images, and analogical representations, as well as resource knowledge) is related to conceptual knowledge, and how different knowledge elements may be integrated into a structure visualization in a coherent manner (e.g. Alpert, 2003, in this book; Tergan, in this book). Except for the technologies used for visualization, knowledge visualization differs from information visualization in a variety of aspects, as, for example, goals, benefits, content, or recipients, which are described in more detail by Burkhard (in this book).

3.2 The Idea of Information Visualization

According to the literature, the term "information visualization" is referred to in a variety of contexts of meaning. In general, psychologists use the term to signify a representational mode (as opposed to verbal descriptions of subject-matter content) used to illustrate in a visual-spatial manner, for example, objects, dynamic systems, events, processes, and procedures. In this regard, the term "information visualization" is an umbrella term for all kinds of visualizations. Here, the term is used in the context of processing, comprehension, and retention of information in static, animated, dynamic, and interactive graphics (Ploetzner & Lowe, 2004; Schnotz, Picard & Hron, 1993). However, computer scientists define the term in a more narrow sense and referred to it as "the use of computer-supported, interactive, visual representation of abstract non-physically based data to amplify cognition" (Card, Mackinlay & Shneiderman, 1999, p. 6). In computer science, information visualization is a specific technology. According to Carr (1999), information visualization of abstract data is of particular importance for information retrieval if the underlying data set is very large (e.g. like in the case of searching for information on the World Wide Web) and the goals of the user with regard to information retrieval are not easily quantifiable. Research in this context refers to information visualization as a technology for fostering the recognition of structures in abstract data and supporting information retrieval.

The articles in this book dealing with the topic of information visualization mainly focus on the notion of information visualization in terms of computer science, that is, as a technology for visualizing abstract data structures. The term "information visualization" as a technology for visualizing abstract data structures can be traced back to the Xerox Palo Alto Research Center in Palo Alto (USA) at the beginning of the nineties (cf. Däßler & Palm, 1998). Since then, information visualization has become an autonomous research field in information science and is growing increasingly important (Schumann & Müller, 2004). Endeavors in information visualization generally aim at facilitating the utilization of the information included (Card et al., 1999).

According to Shneiderman (1996), the type of information visualization depends on both the underlying data type and the demands of the users. In his *task by data type taxonomy,* he differentiates between both seven data types and seven tasks. With regard to the data types, he differentiates between one-dimensional, two-dimensional, three-dimensional, temporal, multi-dimensional, tree, and network data. With respect to the tasks that an information visualization has to support, he differentiates between overview, zoom, filter, details-on-demand, relate, history, and extract (see Jäschke, Leissler & Hemmje, in this book, for an overview of the classifications of information visualizations).

Up to now, information visualizations had been developed for utilization by an individual. However, there is a current trend toward collaborative information visualizations (e.g. Mark, Carpenter, & Kobsa, 2003; Mark, Kobsa & Gonzalez, 2002). As to empirical research, there is a current trend toward usability research, a research field, which had not attracted much attention in the past (cf. Schuhmann & Müller, 2004).

4 Shortcomings

From a representational perspective, knowledge visualization and information visualization in the sense of Card et al. (1999) have one feature in common: They aim at *visualizing structures.* The structures refer to either elements of knowledge or information. Both research domains - information visualization and knowledge visualization - have reached high technological standards and offer a variety of useful applications in different working, learning, and problem solving scenarios. However, there are still shortcomings in visualizing information and knowledge. The shortcomings refer to insufficiencies inherent in the single approaches.

4.1 Shortcomings in Knowledge Visualization

Shortcomings in knowledge visualization relate to representational facilities of the visualization tools. In the following we will concentrate on concept maps. In reviewing the potential of concept mapping tools for the representation of knowledge, Alpert and Gruenenberg (2001) ascertain that "existing concept mapping tools are, indeed, very good at visually representing propositional statements - but not necessarily other forms of information in people's heads". Concept maps "are rooted solely in a propositional knowledge representation scheme in which concepts are often described by verbal means alone via textual labels" (Alpert & Gruenenberg, 2001, p. 316). In effect, focusing on conceptual knowledge is a leftover concept of traditional approaches when concept maps were used for visualizing conceptual structures inherent in texts (see Novak & Gowin, 1984; Jonassen et al., 1993). Content knowledge is fully represented with an abstracted knowledge layer. The restriction on mapping conceptual knowledge only conflicts with cognitive theories of information processing and mental representation of knowledge, stressing that knowledge in the head is also coded non-verbally, including visual imagery, analogous representations, sounds, and other sensory information (Kosslyn, 1980; Johnson-Laird, 1983; Baddeley, 1985; Paivio, 1986; Chabris & Kosslyn, in this book).

Due to the shortcoming of traditional concept maps in also representing visual elements of an individual's domain knowledge, there is a "need for imagery-based elements in conceptual maps if we wish to more comprehensively represent one's knowledge of a domain, or use maps to convey new information to (the) learner" (Alpert & Gruenenberg, 2000, p. 316). "The ability to incorporate static and dynamic imagery, as well as sound, in knowledge maps also allows users to portray concrete instances of concepts, adding significantly to the representational and instructional potential of such maps." "When used as a knowledge elicitation tool, wherein students create their own maps to demonstrate their knowledge of a domain, showing their knowledge of examples of a concept provides a more elaborated and complete representation of the student's knowledge of a domain" (Alpert & Gruenenberg, 2000, p. 318).

Another representational shortcoming of traditional concept maps is pointed out by Siemens. He suggests that knowledge may not be restricted to "know-what" and "know-how" but has to be supplemented with "know-where" (Siemens, 2005). Know-where means the understanding of where to find knowledge. This notion of know-where is tantamount to the notion of resource knowledge, the knowledge of where to find information, which may be used as a knowledge resource in resource-based learning (Neumann, Graeber, & Tergan, in this book; Tergan, in this book).

With the help of digital concept maps the representation of "know-where" knowledge as well as the representation of the respective information as a potential knowledge resource is no longer a problem. Knowing where to find information relevant for a concept may be represented by means of interactive links leading the user to the information which is associated with a particular concept (Cañas, Carff, Hill, Carvalho, Arguedas, Eskridge, Lott & Carvajal, in this book). For example Coffey (in this book) outlines how digital concept maps could be used for both the representation of knowledge by visualizing different types of knowledge, the semantic relations of concepts, as well as for the information related to the concepts, by linking a concept the information to the concepts, which are used to describe the abstract information structure. It is this functionality of concept maps, which is the focus of contributions aiming at using digital concept maps as the main vehicle for the storage of information in a repository for providing easy access (Weideman & Kritzinger, 2003) and suggesting concept maps as cognitive tools for the management of knowledge and information (Tergan, in this book).

There is another shortcoming of concept maps referring to representational features. Traditional concept maps have been used to describe, define and organize static knowledge for a given domain. The representation of dynamic relationships between concepts was not possible because of the predominance of hierarchical and static relations used for mapping. Hence, for any two concepts how the change in one concept affects the other concept could not be represented. This representational shortcoming prevents concept maps from being used for visualizing for example scientific knowledge, which is based on both static and dynamic relationships among concepts. Only recently Safayeni, Derbentseva & Cañas, in press) suggest cyclic concept maps for representing dynamic relations and hybrid maps for representing both the concept map and the cyclic concept map portion of a knowledge representation in an aggregated map.

Shortcomings of traditional paper and pencil concept maps also refer to usability features. Only computerized concept-mapping tools provide typical office-software usability facilities, e.g. free editing to be used for (re)constructing, (re)organizing, and (re)representing mapped knowledge. They allow for storing, printing, representation in different formats (outline, graphic), e-mailing and web-implementation of concept maps in html format. Only digital concept mapping tools provide facilities suited for the above mentioned kinds of use (Alpert, Cañas et al., Coffey, in this book). These tools are increasingly applied for supporting individuals in navigating databases, communicating ideas and collaborative learning. Many of these tools also offer facilities to represent multiple coded subject matter content knowledge in a map (e.g. text, sketches, diagrams, audio, and video). They make information stored on a PC, in a digital library, and on WWW-servers accessible by means of hyperlinking concepts and information (see Alpert; Cañas et al.; Coffey, in this book). Mapping tools used in this way fulfill requirements necessary for coping effectively with knowledge and information in contexts of knowledge management and may overcome shortcomings inherent in traditional technologies when used in resource-based learning and working scenarios (Cañas, Leake & Wilson, 1999; Dansereau, in this book; Tergan, 2003; in this book).

4.2 Shortcomings in Information Visualization

Shortcomings in information visualization relate to both the technical facilities used for visualizing features inherent to large data structures and the rationale for also taking into account the knowledge needed for making sense of an information visualization. As to the visualization of data structures there are some basic problems: Information visualizations cannot compensate for a deficient data structure with a well-designed visualization (Däßler, 1999). Therefore, information visualizations require well-prepared and well-structured data. Due to the fact that - contrary to hierarchical data structures – network data structures do not have a simple structure, the visualization of this data is still very difficult.

In addition, the visualization of very large data sets is still difficult, as well (e.g. Herman, Melançon & Marshall, 2000). The difficulty is that a computer display is limited in its size. Due to this limitation, it is difficult to visualize a large data set in such a manner that the user can perceive all data elements and can understand the data structure. For an efficient utilization of data included in the visualizations, an understanding of the user with regard to the information visualizations is important. In general, it has to be remarked that it is a big challenge for developers of information visualizations to find a well-suited metaphor or abstraction for a visualization of the abstract data (Le Grand & Soto, 1999), because the metaphor or the abstraction have to map the correct data structure, as well as convey the correct meaning of the data to the users.

Another shortcoming of information visualizations refers to technical problems in information presentation. Due to the limited size of the computer display and on account of the limitations of representing structures of information in a two-dimensional space only, there is a trend in computer science to develop information visualizations that use three dimensions for data representation (cf. Wiss & Carr, 1998). There are a lot of ambitious approaches to advancing information visualization. There is, however, a lack of empirical research showing the advantages of highly sophisticated information visualization approaches. For example, research results are lacking showing an advantage of the inclusion of a third spatial dimension for users (Cockburn & McKenzie, 2001; Hicks, O'Malley, Nichols & Anderson, 2003; Keller & Grimm, in this book). There are different reasons for this, among others, that it is hard to navigate in three-dimensional information visualizations, because three-dimensional information visualizations cause more orientation demands (Keller & Grimm, in this book).

A general shortcoming is that, up to now, mainly technical issues have been the focus of discussion. The prerequisites of the user for dealing adequately with information visualizations and making sense of visualizations have not gained much attention in the past. It is important to develop new technologies in alignment with the changing demands of the user, because the user is the one who has to interact with the information visualizations. Therefore, it is necessary to include the experience and know-how of more user-oriented sciences, like Psychology. According to Marshall (2001), information visualizations often lack comprehensibility. Generally, it is necessary to include textual elements in information visualizations to enhance visual semantics (Sebrechts, in this book) and to assure understanding, because symbols or other graphical object attributes could not mirror the complexity of the data units underlying an information visualization. Without textual additions, the users may have difficulties in getting the correct meaning of the data included. However, reading of texts in graphical displays is difficult for users (Däßler, 1999). As a result, it is important in the context of developing information visualizations to find a suitable trade-off with regard to the amount of textual elements included in the information visualization, because too many textual elements will cause too much extraneous cognitive load for information processing and too few textual additions may cause misunderstandings.

5 Need for Synergistic Approaches

The idea behind all visualization methods is that orientation, visual search, and cognitive processing of complex subject matter may be enhanced if structures behind ideas, knowledge, and information, as well as their relevance for coping with a particular task, are made explicit. Researchers in the fields of information visualization and knowledge visualization are trying to develop and use tools for fostering access to information and knowledge resources. Although there is a common interest in facilitating content accessibility and making sense of represented knowledge and information elements by developing visual artefacts, there are hardly any attempts to search for synergies for enhancing learning. Today, the possibilities inherent in knowledge visualization by means of modern digital mapping tools are still unused in the context of teaching and learning and their potential still uncovered. There is a need for a systematic investigation of their potential, for both supporting self-controlled learning and facilitating individual organization, representation and localization, as well as the use of knowledge and knowledge resources, in self-regulated, resource-based studying and problem solving.

One focus of information visualization and knowledge visualization is to organize information and knowledge in such a way that it may be accessed easily and comprehensively. Up to now, both research approaches have investigated the question of visualization from different perspectives. However, there are some common interests, so that synergy effects can be expected. Synergy effects may result with respect to the user-centeredness of visualizations. For example, both research approaches are concerned with questions of information visualization in the new field of dynamic-interactive visualizations. They both use comparable techniques and methods of visualization and aim to support visual searching, localization, and individual utilization with concise, psychologically reasonable, and functional visualizations. Therefore, they both have to focus on psychological questions of design and utilization of visualizations. Furthermore, synergy effects may be expected with respect to the kind of visualizations used. Information visualization focuses on two-dimensional, as well as three-dimensional (or multi-dimensional), visualizations, whereas knowledge visualization restricts itself mainly to two-dimensional visualizations. However, for knowledge visualizations, there is a current trend to integrate representations of concept knowledge, content knowledge and resource knowledge. Thus, multi-dimensional representations and visualizations of knowledge may sometimes be appropriate. As far as information visualization is concerned, the consideration of knowledge mapping as an add-on or integral part of information visualization may be envisaged as a possible way out (cf. Novak & Wurst, Burkhard, in this book).

This book will contain contributions that focus from different perspectives on how synergy effects may be attained. Starting with contributions, which outline theoretical background information, two perspectives of visualizations are addressed in two coherently interrelated chapters dealing with developments and research on knowledge and information visualization. Synergistic approaches are then presented. These approaches aim at integrating knowledge and information visualization in a coherent manner. We discriminate two kinds of approaches, dealing with visualizations of knowledge and information for fostering learning and instruction on the one hand, and visualizations of knowledge-oriented information organization for fostering information use on the other.

It is our intention that research and development in the field of knowledge and information visualization will get new impulses and the contributions may push the borders of what is feasible now and applicable in resource-based learning scenarios of the future.

6 Preview of the Contributions

Contributions outlining theoretical background information. There are two contributions outlining theoretical background information concerning cognitive processing of visualizations.

In his contribution titled "Visual Queries. The foundation of visual thinking", Colin **Ware** outlines basic insights concerning perceptual processing of visualizations. He presents a model of visual thinking based on current theories of visual perception. The basic assumption of Ware is that humans do not have a visual model of the world in their heads. He claims that with some problems, the solution could be found within the problem itself, and that it is up to visual queries and processes of pattern matching to find elements relevant for solving a problem. In his contribution, Ware provides a theoretical grounding for most of the contributions of this book. Due to the fact that visual pattern matching can be faster and more effective than queries to assess data in the brain, visualizations are suggested to enhance cognitive processing. The position of Ware is very much in accordance with a view of ecological psychology held by Zhang (1997) and the position of Jonassen (in this book), who argue that mental problem representations should be made explicit and be visualized, so that processes of pattern finding may apply. In his approach, Ware outlines insights of research into visual working memory, which has focused on simple geometric objects. This is why in order to receive universal validity, the assumptions have to be validated, also for knowledge-rich problems demanding conceptual background knowledge and a problem representation in a problem solver's head (Reinmann & Chi, 1989; Scaife & Rogers, 1996). In their contribution titled "Representational Correspondence as a Basic Principle of Diagram Design", Christopher F. **Chabris** and Stephen M. **Kosslyn** focus on the question "What qualities make a diagram an effective and efficient conduit of information to the human mind?". The authors argue that the best diagrams depict information the same way that our internal mental representations do. They discuss several examples that illustrate this "Representational Correspondence Principle" as a central principle for visual thinking and consider its implications for the design of systems that use diagrams to represent abstract, conceptual knowledge, such as concept networks, social networks, chess diagrams, or web content hierarchies. The basic assumption that there are "visual images in the brain" reflects results of empirical research. However, it does contradict the assumptions of Ware. Thus, the contribution of Chabris and Kosslyn opens up a principled discussion on the characteristics of visual thinking and the level of cognitive processes involved in processing and using visual representations, which is a central topic that draws through all the articles in this book.

Contributions with a focus on knowledge visualization. Three approaches give an overview of how the concept mapping approach, as a knowledge visualization approach, may be applied for fostering knowledge-based cognitive processing in different contexts.

In his article on "node-link mapping principles for visualizing knowledge and information", Donald **Dansereau** describes the Texas Christian University Node-Link Mapping (TCU-NLM) system, and traces its empirical and applied history from 1972 to the present. The TCU approach is an extension of the traditional concept mapping approach aimed at visualizing knowledge. Concept maps are used to represent a person's (a user's/learner's, or an expert's) structure of ideas, thoughts, concepts, and content knowledge about a domain in a visual-spatial format. The terms "information visualization" and "knowledge visualization" in the TCU approach are used to discriminate different kinds of maps from the perspective of the users/learners. The term "information" refers to data, which are presented to the users'/learners' as external stimuli, which have not yet been cognitively processed more deeply and integrated into the users'/learners' knowledge structure. This meaning is different from the information visualization approach and its focus on the visualization of structures inherent in abstract data.

The focus of David **Jonassen**'s paper - titled "Tools for representing problems and knowledge required to solve them" - is on cognitive tools, which may be used to help learners in solving ill-structured problems and to transfer knowledge to different problems. According to Jonassen, problem solving may be fostered when both the relation between information that is inherent in a problem statement and the knowledge needed to make sense of it, is made explicit by using problem representations. The author distinguishes three types of problem representations: semantic network tools (concept maps), production rule models for representing procedural knowledge, and system modeling tools. The problem representation tools share a common characteristic: they simultaneously represent the information inherent in the problem and the particular background knowledge needed for applying a problem solving procedure appropriately. The term "information" refers to conditions, objects, or relations inherent in a situation, for example, in a problem statement. Abstract data, examples of similar problems, and problem solutions, etc., are not referenced. Jonassen argues that once visualized, information from problem representations can be perceived directly from the problem without mediation from memory, inference, or other cognitive processes. With this argumentation, Jonassen is very much in accordance with the position of Ware (in this book), who focuses on pattern matching as a central perceptual process in dealing with visualizations.

In their paper titled "Collaborative knowledge visualization for cross-community learning", Jasminko **Novak** and Michael **Wurst** describe the conceptual rationale and a prototypical realization of a sophisticated knowledge visualization approach aimed at enabling knowledge exchange between heterogeneous communities of practice. The authors discuss a concrete knowledge visualization model and describe its prototypical realization in the Knowledge Explorer. The Knowledge Explorer is an interactive, semi-intelligent, agent-based tool for both supporting users in generating and using personal and collaborative knowledge maps, as well as sharing knowledge between heterogeneous communities with multiple knowledge contexts and "thought worlds". The authors outline and implement ideas of a synergistic approach. Their conceptual model of a knowledge-based approach of sense-making, structuring, accessing, evaluating and sharing content knowledge and information resources satisfies the discrimination requirement between different aspects of knowledge made in the first part of this article. It also satisfies many features of a concept map-based approach of managing knowledge and information (Tergan, in this book).

Contributions with a focus on information visualizations. The following three contributions focus on information visualization. They give the reader an impression of ongoing research. Some authors also address the question of how knowledge visualizations may complement an information visualization approach.

In the contribution of Gerald **Jäschke**, Martin **Leissler**, and Matthias **Hemmje** titled "Modeling Interactive, 3-Dimensional Information Visualizations Supporting Information Seeking Behaviors", a very convincing approach for the topic of this book is developed: Based on the analysis of the differences and similarities of information visualization and knowledge visualization, the authors derive an idea of how to bring both techniques together. They developed the IKVML – information and knowledge visualization modeling language that is an extension of IVML, an information visualization modeling language. This language is a formal and declarative language for describing and defining techniques of information visualization. It provides "a means to formally represent, note, preserve, and communicate structure, appearance, behaviour, and functionality of information visualization techniques and their applications in a standardized way". In their contribution, they also explain the roots, the development, as well as the specifics of IVML, and outline the application of I(K)VML for educational scenarios.

The contribution of Marc **Sebrechts** titled "Visualizing Information in Virtual Space - Prospects and Pitfalls" discusses the potential advantages and disadvantages of using virtual realities to represent either information visualizations or knowledge visualizations. After an introduction to virtual realities (VR) as visualization tools, he presents different empirical evidence concerning the specific reasons for the benefits of these virtual reality systems for visualization. VR provides a model for learning, in which the target knowledge can be presented by interactive modification of the visualization, as well as integration of non-visual material. Sebrechts discusses the kinds of interactions that are possible with virtual realities and that could be applied to learning scenarios in information visualizations and knowledge visualizations. He presents NIRVE, an information retrieval visualization engine that combines a visual aspect (i.e., dimensional layout) referring to information visualization, as well as a conceptual aspect (i.e., grouping of terms into concepts) referring to knowledge visualization. Sebrechts doubts the general adequacy of pure visual semantics for making sense of information visualizations. He claims that sometimes the incorporation of non-visual, textual semantics in VR may be necessary.

In the contribution of Tanja **Keller** and Matthias **Grimm** titled "The Impact of Dimensionality and Color Coding of Information Visualizations on Knowledge Acquisition", a new application field for information visualizations is discussed. The authors investigated in an experimental study whether and under which conditions, with regard to the factors dimensionality and color coding, information visualizations are suited to support processes of knowledge acquisition in the sense of memorizing and understanding large sets of abstract data and their structures. They could in fact show that some kinds of information visualizations are able to foster knowledge acquisition. With their approach, they take leave of the traditional use of information visualizations for information access and information exploration only. Their approach to information visualizations converges to the learning context that is also the frame of reference for knowledge visualizations. The authors try to outline how information visualizations for knowledge acquisition could benefit from the field of knowledge visualizations.

Synergistic approaches. The synergistic approaches aim at integrating knowledge and information visualization in a coherent approach. Two kinds of approaches may be discriminated:

- Visualization of knowledge and information for fostering learning and instruction
- Visualization of knowledge-oriented information organization for fostering information use

The approaches aiming at *visualizing knowledge and information for fostering learning and instruction* are mainly based on concept mapping technology. Information is conceived as a knowledge resource and associated with the conceptual knowledge represented in the map. In general, information has been pre-selected from a broad range of resources, for example, stored on the Web, on the PC, or in a digital library, and has been evaluated as relevant for backing, verifying, elaborating, and extending the meaning of a particular concept. The map is functioning as a personal repository that has been constructed for facilitating visual search and access to knowledge elements and associated resources. Concept maps in approaches for *knowledge-oriented information organization for fostering information use* focus on a spatial structuring of information elements. They may serve as a developmental aid for course designers or as an information basis for students engaged in self-regulated learning in a resource-based learning environment (Rakes, 1996). Concept maps functioning as organizational tools may also be used as navigational aids for fostering knowledge-based use by providing facilities for the visual search of documents in broad information repositories, for example, the World Wide Web, digital libraries, or hypermedia environments.

Visualization of knowledge and information for fostering learning and instruction. The contribution of Sigmar-Olaf **Tergan** titled "Digital concept maps for managing knowledge and information" aims to open up a new perspective of using concept maps in educational scenarios. The potential of digital concept maps for supporting processes of individual knowledge management is analyzed. The author suggests digital concept mapping as a visual-spatial strategy for supporting externalized cognition in resource-based learning and problem solving scenarios (Rakes, 1996). In fact, many of the contributions of this book, dealing with cognitive demands inherent in a variety of educational, social, and workplace scenarios, refer explicitly to concept maps as a means for bridging the gap between knowledge visualization and information visualization (see the contributions of Alpert, Cañas, Carff, Hill, Carvalho, Arguedas, Eskridge, Lott, & Carvajal Coffey, Dansereau, Novak & Wurst, Fiedler & Sharma). A conceptual model of concept map-based representation and access of domain knowledge and related information is outlined. Based on the model, Tergan analyzes the particular contribution digital concepts maps would have for the processes of knowledge management outlined in the model. The paper is meant as a conceptual framework for synergistic approaches aiming at integrating both knowledge and information in a coherent visualization approach.

In their contribution titled "Concept maps: Integrating knowledge and information visualization", Alberto **Cañas,** Roger Carff, Greg Hill, Marco Carvalho, Marco Arguedas, Thomas C. Eskridge, James Lott, & Rodrigo Carvajal outline in detail the IHMC CmapTools approach. Conceptual knowledge represented in a Cmap may be linked with content knowledge and information resources coded as text, images, sound clips, or videos accessible in personal or public repositories. In CmapTools, the use of concept maps has been extended beyond knowledge representation to serve as a browsing interface to a domain of knowledge and associated information. The authors outline special features of the approach for integrating, making accessible, and using knowledge and information. The basics of the CmapTools approach of Cañas and associates are very much in accordance with the conception of using concept maps used for purposes of managing knowledge and information (see Tergan, in this book). The rationale for knowledge visualization resembles the rationale of Webster, a concept mapping tool described by Alpert (in this book). CmapTools in general is a powerful software package with facilities that make the tool attractive not only for knowledge visualization, but also for information visualization approaches looking for supplements for aiding users in sense-making. Its facilities also make it attractive as a tool for incorporating synergistic approaches integrating both knowledge and information visualization (see Coffey, as well as Ware, in this book).

In his contribution titled "Comprehensive mapping of knowledge and information resources: The case of Webster", Sherman **Alpert** describes a computer-based concept mapping tool aimed at both tapping the full potential of the representational capabilities of digital concept maps, as well as satisfying psychological and pedagogical requirements for a more comprehensive representation of knowledge and information associated with it. The paper proposes a cognitive and educational rationale for the hypothesis that traditional concept maps fall short with respect to representing knowledge comprehensively, because they focus on abstract conceptual knowledge only, leaving content knowledge and associated information unconsidered. The author presents Webster, a Web-based concept mapping tool that permits broad flexibility in terms of the kinds of knowledge and information that may be represented, as well as the codes and modes used for representation. The approach fits well with the rationale of the book. It is an implementation of the idea of bringing together knowledge and information visualization into one single visualization approach. In addition, it draws attention to the fact that human knowledge is more comprehensive than conceptual knowledge, which has long been neglected, not least because of lacking facilities for representing content knowledge and resources associated with it. The rationale of Webster has many features in common with the IHMC CmapTools approach presented by Cañas (in this book) and ideas concerning the integration of knowledge and information in a synergistic manner as outlined by Tergan (in this book).

In his article titled "Towards a Framework and a Model for Knowledge Visualization: Synergies between Information and Knowledge Visualization", Remo **Burkhard** examines the research areas information and knowledge visualization from both a business knowledge management and a communication science perspective. The article presents a theoretical framework and a model for the field of knowledge visualization. The chapters deal with an outline of differences between information visualization and knowledge visualization from an organizational perspective of how information visualization may learn from knowledge management and how both principles of knowledge and information visualization may be integrated in complementary visualizations. The presented framework aims at mediating between different research areas and illustrating how information visualization and knowledge visualization complement one another. Burkhard deals with the central goal of the book "searching for synergies" in close relation to knowledge visualization in the field of organizational knowledge management. The outline of principles for designing effective knowledge visualizations satisfies expectations of how to complement knowledge visualization with ideas and techniques from information visualization. Guidelines for applying the complemented knowledge visualization model may help users to successfully implement principles of the synergistic approach into learning and workplace environments.

Anja **Neumann**, Wolfgang **Graeber** and Sigmar-Olaf **Tergan** present a contribution on "Visualizing ideas and information in a resource-based learning environment. The case of ParIS". ParIS is a learning environment that aims at fostering the development of competencies for self-regulated learning and media competencies as central components of scientific literacy. In ParIS, students solve everyday authentic problems by using Mind Mapping, a visual-spatial strategy to assist planning, gathering, generating, organizing, and using knowledge and knowledge resources. The paper describes the rationale for the design and implementation of ParIS in a 10th grade chemistry class of a German Waldorf school. Preliminary results of a pilot study focussing on acceptance and usability of the instructional approach are outlined. The presented instructional design approach transforms ideas of supporting resource-based learning by helping students visualize their knowledge and relate it to information associated with it. It is a synergistic approach in the sense that it uses a Mind Managing tool for both representing knowledge and related information. The tool supports visualizing the structure of knowledge and provides knowledge-based access to specific data and information as potential knowledge resources.

Visualization of knowledge-oriented information organization for fosterin. information use. Approaches that focus on the visualization of a knowledge-oriented information organization aim at fostering an intelligent information access and information use.

John W. **Coffey** describes in his contribution titled "LEO: A Concept Map Based Course Visualization Tool for Instructors and Students" a learning environment organizer (LEO) that provides students and instructors with information and knowledge visualization capabilities. LEO serves as a meta-cognitive tool for course designers and an advanced organizer for students. It is an extension of the CmapTools developed by Cañas and associates (see above). LEO helps to visualize and plan a course organization by using a concept map. The concept map itself is used as a knowledge-based visualization of the structure of course components and provides interactive access to the materials. The contribution of Coffey meshes well with the goals of this book. It presents an approach integrating both fields of research knowledge and information visualization in a synergistic manner.

In their contribution titled "Navigating Personal Information Repositories with Weblog Authoring and Concept Mapping", Sebastian **Fiedler** and Priya **Sharma** describe the tool "Weblog authoring". It enables the user to represent information spontaneously and to maintain it in personal repositories, as well as to generate a social network and collective information filtering and routing. The authors indicate how the structure and practices of Weblog authoring support the construction of a personal repository of information, as well as the ability to engage in shared dialogue about artefacts. They point out the possibility and the benefits of using concept mapping to make sense of the Weblog representations. In this respect, they make use of a technique of knowledge visualization to handle a problem of information visualizations, which is a good example of how to integrate both perspectives in a synergistic approach.

The contribution of Young-Lin **Lee** titled "Facilitating Web-Search with Visualization and Data Mining Techniques" focuses on design rationales and implementations of an alternative Web search environment called "VisSearch". The author points out its advantages, particularly with regard to cognitive processes, in dealing with ill-structured, open-ended research questions, as compared to conventional Web-search environments. The VisSearch environment facilitates information searching in dealing with such problematic search questions by means of visualizing the knowledge and associated Web resources of both the user and other users looking for useful Web-based information on the same or similar topics. VisSearch employs a single, reusable concept map-like knowledge network, called search-graph for a variety of purposes, for example, visualizing Web search results, the history of Web search engine hits of a variety of iterative Web searches of different users, as well as user comments to Web sites and search queries. The search-graph provides interactive access to all Web resources linked with the elements in the graph. The approach outlined by Lee represents a synergetic approach in the sense of the rationale of this book: It brings together both aspects - information visualization and knowledge visualization - in one coherent approach. The approach picks up and extends a topic also dealt with by Cañas et al. (in this book): Visualizing Web-search results using a map that helps to make sense of the semantic relation between them and that provides a knowledge-based access. Further, it closely matches ideas concerning the relation of information and knowledge as outlined by Tergan (in this book).

In their contribution titled "The Role of Content Representations in Hypermedia Learning: Effects of Task and Learner Variables", Jean-Francois **Rouet**, Hervé **Potelle**, and Antonine **Goumi** point out the significance of content representations in hypermedia documents as means for supporting orientation and navigation. Content representations refer to different kinds of visualizations of the main concepts, for example, global representations as topic lists, outlines, and concept maps that describe the structure of a compilation of information (e.g. in a hypertext). The authors review empirical studies investigating different types of global representations in the context of comprehension and information search tasks. The results of two empirical studies provide evidence that the choice for a specific content representation should depend on both the kind of user and the kind of task that should be solved. The results suggest that networked concept maps are most effective for users with some level of prior knowledge in non-specific task contexts. They show that the effectiveness of visualization may depend on variables inherent in the user, as well as in the contexts in which they are used. This result is of importance for all approaches on visualizations presented within this book.

In his contribution on "Supporting Self-Regulated E-Learning with Topic-Map Navigation", Andreas **Rittershofer** describes Topic maps as a means to convey knowledge about resources. Looking for a visualization of the relevant parts of the topic maps to guide the students through huge amounts of information led the author to the development of the LmTM-server, an e-learning server for students at school to support resource-based learning. The information stored in the topic maps is represented in several ways, for example, by means of a concept map-like graph, which is created dynamically out of the topic map. The graph enables the user to visually navigate within the topic map-based information and provides access to information resources associated with the map. The approach is a synergistic approach in the sense that it enhances sense-making of information represented in Topic maps, enables a visual search for information, and provides knowledge-based access to the information represented. It is because of these functions that the approach is suggested to support self-regulated, resource-based learning in e-learning environments.

Like Andreas Rittershofer, Hans-Juergen **Frank** and Johannes **Drosdol** also outline a strictly application-oriented approach. The focus of the contribution is on the visualization of knowledge and information management activities underlying the development of the Management Information System (MIS) at DaimlerChrysler. The MIS is for the leaders of the department of research and technology, the central department for technical innovations and the management of technology. It is used not only as a tool with a controlling function, but as a general homogenous information and dialogue platform of high actuality and flexibility, serving as a knowledge and information space. The aim for developing the system was to match the users needs, processes and visions as closely as possible. The authors show how complex processes and problem solutions in the development and maintenance of a MIS may be visualized and used for facilitating dialogue and for working with a large number of content elements, highly complex information structures and large knowledge networks. This contribution opens up a perspective of how visualizations may be used on a large-scale basis for knowledge and information visualization in the application context.

References

Alpert, S.R. (2003). Abstraction in Concept Map and Coupled Outline Knowledge Representations. *Journal of Interactive Learning Research, 14*(1), 31-49.

Alpert, S.R., & Gruenenberg, K. (2000). Concept mapping with multimedia on the web. *Journal of Educational Multimedia and Hypermedia, 9*(4), 313-330.

Baddeley, A. D. (1998). *Human memory.* Boston: Allyn & Bacon.

Bellinger, G., Castro, D., & Mills, A. (2004). *Data, Information, Knowledge, and Wisdom.* Online available February 7: http://www.systems-thinking.org/dikw/dikw.htm).

Bransford, J.D. (1979). *Human cognition. Learning, understanding, and remembering.* Belmont, CA: Wadsworth.

Bransford, J.D., Brown, A.L., & Cocking, R.R. (Eds.). (1999). *How people learn: Brain, mind, experience, and school.* Washington, D.C.: National Academy Press.

Bruillard, E., & Baron, G.-L. (2000). Computer-Based Concept Mapping: a Review of a Cognitive Tool for Students. In D. Benzie, & D. Passey (Eds.), *Proceedings of Conference on Educational Uses of Information and Communication Technologies* (ICEUT 2000) (pp. 331-338). Beijing: Publishing House of Electronics Industry (PHEI).

Buzan, T. (1995). *The Mind Map book.* 2 ed. London: BBC Books.

Cañas, A.J., Leake, D.B., & Wilson, D.C. (1999). Managing, mapping and manipulating conceptual knowledge. *AAAI Workshop Technical Report WS-99-10: Exploring the synergies of knowledge management & case-based reasoning.* Menlo Park, CA: AAAI Press.

Card, S. K., Mackinlay, J. D., & Shneiderman, B. (1999). Information visualization. In S. K Card, J. D. Mackinlay, & B. Shneiderman (Eds.), *Information visualization. Using vision to think* (pp. 1-34). San Francisco: Morgan Kaufmann.

Carr, D. (1999). Guidelines for Designing Information Visualization Applications. In *Proceedings of ECUE'99, Ericsson Conference on Usability Engineering*. Available online March 16, 2005: http://www.ida.liu.se/~davca/postscript/VizGuidelines.pdf

Cockburn, A., & McKenzie, B. (2001). 3D or not 3D? Evaluating the effect of the third dimension in a document management system. In M. Tremaine (Ed.), *Proceedings of CHI'01, ACM Conference on Human Factors in Computing Systems* (pp. 434-441). New York: ACM Press.

Cox, R. (1999). Representation, construction, externalised cognition and individual differences. *Learning and Instruction, 9*, 343-363.

Cox, R., & Brna, P. (1995). Supporting the use of external representations in problem solving: The need for flexible learning environments. *Journal of Artificial Intelligence in Education, 6*(2/3), 239-302.

Däßler, R. (1999). Informationsvisualisierung: Stand, Kritik und Perspektiven. In *Methoden/Strategien der Visualisierung in Medien, Wissenschaft und Kunst*. Trier: Wissenschaftlicher Verlag. Available online March 16, 2005: http://fabdp.fh-potsdam.de/daessler/paper/InfoVis99.pdf.

Däßler, R., & Palm, H. (1998). *Virtuelle Informationsräume mit VRML: Informationen recherchieren und präsentieren in 3D*. Heidelberg: dpunkt-Verlag.

Edvinsson, L., & Malone, M.S. (1997). *Intellectual Capital*. New York, NY: HarperBusiness.

Herman, I., Melançon, G., & Marshall, M. S. (2000). Graph visualization and navigation in information visualization: A survey. *IEEE Transactions on Visualization and Computer Graphics, 6*, 24-43.

Hicks, M., O'Malley, C., Nichols, S., & Anderson, B. (2003). Comparison of 2D and 3D representations for visualising telecommunication usage. *Behaviour & Information Technology, 22*, 185-201.

Hill, J.R., Hannafin, M.J., & Domizi, D.P. (in press). Resource-based learning and informal learning environments: prospects and challenges. In R. Subramaniman (Ed.), *E-learning and virtual science centers*. Hershey, USA: Idea Group Publishing.

Holley, C.D., & Dansereau, D.F. (1984). The development of spatial learning strategies. In C.D. Holley & D.F. Dansereau (Eds.), *Spatial learning strategies. Techniques, applications, and related issues* (pp. 3-19). New York: Academic Press.

Lave, J., & Wenger, E. (1991). *Situated Learning: Legitimate Peripheral Participation (Learning in Doing: Social, Cognitive and Computational Perspectives)*. `Cambridge, UK: Cambridge University Press.

Johnson-Laird, P.N. (1983). *Mental models. Towards a cognitive science of language, inference, and consciousness*. Cambridge, UK: Cambridge University Press.

Jonassen, D.H. (1991). What are cognitive tools? In P.A. Kommers, D.H. Jonassen, & J.T. Mayes (Eds.), *Cognitive tools for learning*. NATO ASI Series F, Computer and Systems Sciences, Vol. 81 (pp. 1-6), Berlin/Heidelberg: Springer.

Jonassen, D.H., Beissner, K., & Yacci, M. (1993). (Eds.). *Structural knowledge. Techniques for representing, conveying, and acquiring structural knowledge*. Hillsdale, NJ: Lawrence Erlbaum Associates.

Jonassen, D.H., Reeves, T.C., Hong, N., Harvey, D., & Peters, K. (1997). Concept mapping as cognitive learning and assessment tools. *Journal of Interactive Learning Research, 8*(3/4), 289-308.

Kosslyn, S.M. (1980). *Image and mind*. Cambridge, MA: Harvard University Press.

Larkin, J.H. (1983). The role of problem representation in physics. In D. Gentner, & A. Stevens (Eds.), *Mental Models* (pp. 75-98). Hillsdale, NJ: Lawrence Erlbaum Associates.

Larkin, J.H. (1989). Display-based problem solving. In D. Klahr, & K. Kotovsky (Eds.), *Complex information processing. The impact of Heribert Simon* (pp. 319-342). Hillsdale, NJ: Lawrence Erlbaum Associates.

Larkin, J.H., & Simon, H.A. (1987). Why a diagram is (sometimes) worth 10.000 words. *Cognitive Science, 11*, 65-100.

Le Grand, B., & Soto, M. (1999). Navigation in huge information hierarchies. Application to network management. In *Proceedings ACM Workshop on New Paradigms in Information Visualization and Manipulation (NPIVM'99)* (pp. 56-61). Kansas. ACM Press.

Logie, R. H. (1995). *Visuo-spatial working memory*. Hove: Lawrence Erlbaum Associates.

Mark, G., Carpenter, K., & Kobsa, A. (2003). A model of synchronous collaborative information visualization. In E. Banissi (Ed.), *Proceedings of the Seventh International Conference on Information Visualization* (pp. 373-383). Washington: IEEE.

Mark, G., Kobsa, A., & Gonzalez, V. (2002). Do four eyes see better than two? Collaborative versus individual discovery in data visualization systems. In E. Banissi (Ed.), *Proceedings of the Sixth International Conference on Information Visualization (IV'02)* (pp. 249-255). Washington: IEEE.

Marshall, C.C. (2001). *The haunting question of intelligibility. Paper presented at the eleventh Hypertext '01* (Aarhus, Denmark, August 14-18, 2001) (Online available: http://www.csdl.tamu.edu/~shipman/SpatialHypertext/SH1/marshall.pdf).

Mayer, R. E. (2001). *Multimedia learning*. Cambridge, UK: Cambridge University Press.

Novak, J.D., & Gowin, D.B. (1984). *Learning how to learn*. Cambridge, UK: Cambridge University Press.

O'Donnell, A.M., Dansereau, D.F., & Hall, R.H. (2002). Knowledge maps as scaffolds for cognitive processing. *Educational Psychology Review, 14*(1), 71-86.

Paige, J.M., & Simon, H.A. (1966). Cognitive processes in solving algebra and word problems. In B. Kleinmuntz (Ed.), *Problem solving: Research, method and theory* (Chap. 3). New York, NY: Wiley.

Paivio, A. (1986). Mental representations. *A dual coding approach*. New York, NY: Oxford University.

Plötzner, R., & Lowe, R. (Eds.). (2004). Special Issue: Dynamic visualisations and learning. *Learning and Instruction, 14*, 235-357.

Rakes, G.C. (1996). Using the internet as a tool in a resource-based learning environment. *Educational Technology*, September-October, 52-56.

Reimann, P., & Chi, M.T.H. (1989). Human expertise. In K.J. Gilhooly (Ed.), *Human and machine problem solving* (pp. 161-191). New York: Plenum.

Rogers, Y., & Scaife, M. (1997). *External cognition*. Retrieved February 10, 2005 from http://www.sv.cict.fr/cotcos/pjs/TheoreticalApproaches/ExtCogandRepr/ExtCogandReppaperRogers.htm#

Rumelhart, D.E., & Ortony, A. (1977). The representation of knowledge in memory. In R.C. Anderson, R.J. Spiro, & W.E. Montague (Eds.), *Schooling and the acquisition of knowledge* (pp. 99-133). Hillsdale, NJ: Lawrence Erlbaum Associates.

Safayeni, F.N., Derbentseva, A.J., & Cañas, A (in press). A theoretical note on concepts and the need for cyclic concept maps. *Journal of Research in Science Teaching*. Online available February 20, 2005: http://cmap.ihmc.us/Publications/ResearchPapers/Cyclic%20Concept%20Maps.pdf.

Scaife, M., & Rogers, Y. (1996). External cognition: how do graphical representations work? *Int. J. Human-Computer Studies, 45*, 185-213.

Schnotz, W., Picard, E., & Hron, A. (1993). How do successful and unsuccessful learners use texts and graphics? *Learning and Instruction, 3*, 181-199.

Schnurer, K., Stark, R., & Mandl, H. (2003). Auf dem Weg in eine neue Lehr-Lern-Kultur. Gestaltung problemorientierter Lernumgebungen. *Erziehungswissenschaft und Beruf, 2*, 148-161.

Schumann, H., & Müller, W. (2004). Informationsvisualisierung: Methoden und Perspektiven. *it - Information Technology, 46*(3), 135-141.

Shneiderman, B. (1996). The eyes have it: A task by data type taxonomy for information visualizations. In *Proceedings IEEE Visual Languages* (pp. 336-343). Available online March 16, 2005: http://citeseer.nj.nec.com/shneiderman96eyes.html.

Siemens, G. (2005). Connectivism. A learning theory for the digital age. *International Journal of Instructional Technology & Distance Learning, 2*(1), 3-10. (Available online: January 20, 2005: http://www.itdl.org/Journal/Jan_05/article01.htm).

Sweller, J., & Chandler, P. (1994). Why some material is difficult to learn. *Cognition and Instruction, 12* (3), 185-233.

Sweller, J., van Merriënboer, J.J.G., & Paas, F.W.C. (1998). Cognitive architecture and instructional design. *Educational Psychology Review, 10*, 251-296.

Tergan, S.-O. (2003). Managing knowledge with computer-based mapping tools. In D. Lassner, & C. Mc Naught (Eds.), *Proceedings of the ED-Media 2003 World Conference on Educational Multimedia, Hypermedia & Telecommunication* (pp. 2514-2517). Norfolk, VA, USA: AACE.

Ware, C. (2004) *Information Visualization: Perception for Design* (2nd Edition). San Francisco, CA: Morgan Kaufman.

Weideman, M., & Kritzinger, W. (2003). *Concept Mapping - a proposed theoretical model for implementation as a knowledge repository.* Working paper from the "ICT in Higher Education" research project. University of Western Cape - South Africa. Available on-line: January 20, 2005: http://www.uwc.ac.za/ems/is/hicte

Wiegmann, D.A., Dansereau, D.F., McCagg, E.C., Rewey, K.L., & Pitre, U. (1992). Effects of knowledge map characteristics on information processing. *Contemporary Educational Psychology, 17*, 136-155.

Wiss, U., & Carr, D. (1998). *A Cognitive Classification Framework for 3-Dimensional Information Visualization.* Research report LTU-TR--1998/4--SE, Luleå University of Technology.

Wiss, U., Carr, D., & Jonsson, H. (1998). Evaluating Three-Dimensional Information Visualization Designs: A Case Study of Three Designs. In E. Banissi (Ed.), *Proceedings IEEE International Conference on Information Visualization* (pp. 137-145). Washington: IEEE.

Young, R.M., & O'Shea, T. (1981). Errors in children's substraction. *Cognitive Science, 5*, 153-177.

Zhang, J. (1997). The nature of external representations in problem solving. *Cognitive Science, 21*(2), 179-217.

Zhang, J., & Norman, D.A. (1994). Representations in distributed tasks. *Cognitice Science, 18*, 87-122.

Background

Visual Queries: The Foundation of Visual Thinking

Colin Ware

Data Visualization Research Lab, Center for Coastal and Ocean Mapping,
University of New Hampshire, Durham, NH 03924, USA
colinw@cisunix.unh.edu

Abstract. There is no visual model of the world in our heads. Over the past few years the phenomena of change blindness and inattentional blindness as well as studies of the capacity of visual working memory all point to the fact that we do not retain much about the world from one fixation to the next. The impression we have of a detailed visual environment comes from our ability to make rapid eye movements and sample the environment at will. What we see at any given instant in time is determined by what we are trying to accomplish. We see what we need to see. If we need to find a path through a crowd we see the openings. If we are trying to find a friend we see the faces. We can think of this process of seeing as the execution of a continuous stream of visual queries on the environment. Depending on the task at hand the brain constructs a visual query and we execute a visual search to satisfy that query. Making visual queries a central concept opens the door to a theory of how we think visually with interactive displays. The process can be thought of as constructing and executing queries on displays. Problem components are formulated into questions (or hypotheses) that can be answered (or tested) by means of pattern discovery. These are formulated into visual queries having the form of search patterns. Visual eye-movement scanning strategies are used to search the display. Within each fixation, active attention determines which patterns are pulled from visual cortex subsystems that do pattern analysis. Patterns and objects are formed as transitory object files from a proto-pattern space. Elementary visual queries can be executed at a rate of 40 msec per simple pattern. Links to non-visual propositional information are activated by icons or familiar patterns, bringing visual information simultaneously into verbal working memory.

1 Introduction

How is it that we have the compelling illusion that we are aware of the visual complexity of the world? Make no mistake, this is an illusion, any numbers of experiments have shown it to be so. The studies of change blindness suggest that we hold only about three objects in our visual working memories from one second to the next (Vogel, Woodman & Luck, 2001). Studies of inattentional blindness show that we simply do not register things even though we may be looking right at them, if we are attending to some other visual patterns (Rock & Gutman, 1981). Studies using unsuspecting subjects in the real world show that people are unaware of 99% or more of what is in the visual field (Simons & Levin, 1998).

S.-O. Tergan and T. Keller (Eds.): Knowledge and Information Visualization, LNCS 3426, pp. 27–35, 2005.
© Springer-Verlag Berlin Heidelberg 2005

So we have an apparent contradiction. On the one hand we subjectively think we see everything; on the other, it seems, we see almost nothing.

The resolution is that in the words of Kevin O'Regan "the world is its own memory" (O'Regan, 1992). We do not need to have the world in our heads because it is out there in all its glorious detail and by making rapid eye movement, as soon as we think we would like to know about something, we have it. It is subjectively instantaneous, although it actually takes about one tenth of a second. The brain is a slow machine, at least compared to modern computers, and so the time-to-execute the query is not noticed. Although we can fully process only very little information, we have sufficiently rapid access to any part of the visual field that we feel we are instantaneously aware of all of it. What we actually do see is determined by attention and the task at hand. Seeing can thus be thought of as a series of visual queries on the world. We are not consciously aware that our eyes are darting to and fro, gathering information, but they are. Most of the visual queries we make of the world seem literally effortless, so much so that we are not even aware that we are making them.

Understanding the process of seeing as a series of visual queries on the world provides a basis for a cognitive systems approach to visual thinking. Visual queries on displays can be faster and more effective than queries to access data in the brain and this is the reason why we think best with the aid of cognitive tools (Hutchins, 1995). Visualizations can be powerful tools. A visual query is executed through a search for a pattern and it is the pattern finding capacity of the visual system that makes visual displays so powerful. In many cases, to perceive a pattern is to solve a problem, and the human visual system is an extraordinarily flexible and adaptive pattern finding system.

This paper outlines the nature of visual thinking with the idea of the visual query as a core concept. First, we briefly review the evidence that there is no model of the world in the head. Next the core functional cognitive components are described and the visual thinking process is outlined.

1.1 The Evidence

There are three major lines of evidence supporting the idea that we do not have a visual model of the world in out heads. First, we are only sensitive to detail in the center of the visual field. At any instance we cannot be aware of detail anywhere except for where we are fixating. Second, there is no evidence that we store more than a minimal amount from one fixation to the next. Indeed the best estimates are that the most we can store are three very simple colored shapes (Vogel et al., 2001). Third, the inattentional blindness studies of Mack and Rock (1998) show that people focusing on a task are generally unaware of visual events that are not relevant to that task, even though these events can be occurring right next to the point of fixation. In the absence of a detailed visual model of the environment in our heads, the most plausible explanation for our conscious feeling of awareness of visual detail is that eye movements are rapid enough that we only have to think we need something and we have it, seemingly without delay. This process can be thought of as the execution of a task-related visual query on the world.

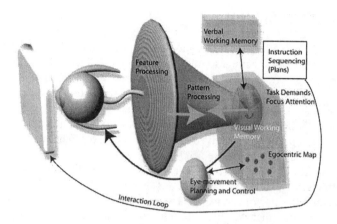

Fig. 1. The major system components involved in visual thinking

1.2 The Power of a Visualization

A visualization consists of both a visual structure and a set of symbols. Structures are embedded in maps, and various types of node-link diagrams. The symbols can be of various types: words, symbolic shapes, icons, glyphs. If the symbols are already familiar they automatically excite the corresponding concepts and cause them to be loaded into verbal working memory. Kahneman, Triesman and Gibbs (1992) coined the term "object file" to describe a short-term linking device that can hold together visual structures in visual working memory together with concepts in verbal working memory. Data structures expressed through effective layout and graphical design can make relationships between concepts readily accessible.

The power of a visualization comes from the fact that it is possible to have a far more complex concept structure represented externally in a visual display than can be held in visual and verbal working memories. People with cognitive tools are far more effective thinkers than people without cognitive tools and computer-based tools with visual interfaces may be the most powerful and flexible cognitive systems. Combining a computer-based information system with flexible human cognitive capabilities, such as pattern finding, and using a visualization as the interface between the two is far more powerful than an unaided human cognitive process.

The remainder of this chapter presents a high-level overview of visual query construction. The three component model illustrated in Fig. 1 is a useful simplification to illustrate the different visual subsystems involved. At the lowest level information is processed through massively parallel feature finding mechanisms. Pattern finding occurs in the mid level; patterns are constructed from low level features according to the top down demands of attention operating in the context of a temporary store called *visual working memory*. Queries are executed by means of eye movements and a focusing of attention on task-relevant patterns so that patterns are held briefly in working memory. In the following sections we consider the critical cognitive subsystems in more detail beginning with the central role of pattern finding.

2 Visual Query Patterns

Visual thinking is, to a large extent, synonymous with pattern finding. In many cases to perceive a pattern is to have a solution to a problem and this is done through visual queries tuned to specific patterns. Visual attention acts as a filter, influencing the middle layer pattern forming mechanisms of vision, so that only the current search pattern, if present, is brought into working memory (Baddeley & Logie, 1999). This process can be thought of as a mechanism whereby competing bottom-up forces are modified by the top down task driven attentional processes. The net result is that we only see what, for the most part, we need to see.

Fig. 2 illustrates how we can focus attention to pull out different parts of a pattern. In this figure three sequences of symbols are encoded: one in fine lines, the second in blurred lines and the third in transparent yellow lines. If you try to read the blurred symbols you will find that you tune out the other patterns. Alternatively you can attend to the thin lines or the broad yellow lines and tune out the others.

Fig. 2. Three symbol sequences are encoded in different ways. Through attention we can tune our mid-level pattern finding machinery allowing us to read off either the fine-line symbol set, the yellow symbol set, or the fuzzy-grey symbol set

The patterns we can easily tune for are by no means universal. Indeed, understanding which patterns are easily discriminated and which are not is an invaluable tool for the designer. The rules for easy-to-see patterns are complex and difficult to summarize (see Ware, 2004 for an overview). However we can say that the major function of the pattern finding mechanism is to segment the visual world into regions based on some combination of contour, color, motion and texture. The extraction of contours and the connections between objects is critical. Organizing information by regions and contours is, unsurprisingly, critical in display design.

The patterns that can be formed as queries are infinitely diverse: a major highway on a map winding though a number of towns, the pattern of notes on a musical score that characterizes an arpeggio, or the spiral shape of a developing hurricane. For a display to be effective such data patterns must be mapped into visual patterns in such a way that they are visually distinct.

The studies of Triesman (1985) and others showed that we process simple visual patterns serially at a rate of about one every 40-50 msec. Since each fixation typically will last for 100-300 msec. this means that our visual systems process 2-6 objects within each fixation, before we move our eyes to visually attend to some other region.

3 Visual and Verbal Working Memories

The most critical cognitive resource involved in visual thinking is visual working memory. Theorists disagree on details of exactly how visual working memory operates but there is broad agreement on basic functionality and capacity, enough to provide a solid foundation for a theory of visual thinking. Visual working memory can be roughly defined as the visual information retained from one fixation to the next. A list of some key properties follows.

- There is not a single working memory supporting cognition; rather there are several limited-capacity systems for processing auditory, visual and haptic information (Baddeley & Logie, 1999; Baddeley & Hitch, 1974) and there may be additional stores for sequences of cognitive instructions.
- Visual working memory capacity is limited to a small number of simple visual objects and patterns, perhaps 3-5 simple objects (Rensink, O'Reagan & Clark, 1997).
- Kahneman et al. (Kahneman et al., 1992 coined the term object file to describe the temporary grouping of a collection of visual features together with other links to verbal-propositional information. They hypothesized that an object file would contain the neural equivalent of pointers reaching into the part of the brain where visual features are processed as well as pointers to verbal working memory structures and to stored motor memories needed to generate an appropriate response. Rensink (2000, 2002; Rensink et al., 1997) coined the term nexus to describe this instantaneous grouping of information by attentional processing. The semantic meaning or gist of an object or scene (related more to verbal working memory) can be activated in about 100 msec.
- Positions of objects are stored in an egocentric map. This stores some information about approximately nine locations (Postma & De Haan, 1996); three of these may contain links to object files, while the remaining locations code that there is something at a particular region in space, but very little more.
- Deeper semantic coding is needed for items to be processed into long term memory.

4 Eye-Movement Strategies

In a visual search task the eye moves rapidly from fixation to fixation. The dwell period is generally between 200 and 600 msec and the saccade takes between 20 and 100 msec. A simple heuristic strategy appears to be employed by the brain to plan a sequence of eye movements (Wolfe & Gancarz, 1996). The egocentric map is weighted according to the current task. For example, if we are scanning a supermarket to look for oranges, regions of space with the color orange will be set up for searching. Next, eye-movements are executed in sequence, visiting the strongest possible target first, and proceeding to the weakest. Once each area has been processed it is cognitively flagged as visited.

5   Problem Solving with Visualizations

We are now in a position to discuss how thinking can be augmented with visualizations of data. Fig. 5 provides an overview of the various components. This borrows a great deal from Rensink (2000; Rensink et al., 1997) as well as earlier theorists (Baddeley & Logie, 1999; Jonides, 1981; Triesman, 1985). The whole process can be thought of as a set of embedded procedures:

1. Problem components that have potential solutions based on pattern discovery are identified. These are formulated into visual queries consisting of simple patterns.
2. Visual eye-movement scanning strategies are used to search the display for patterns.
3. Within each fixation, the query weights attention and determines which patterns are pulled from the pattern analysis subsystems to answer the queries.
   a. Patterns and objects are formed as transitory object files from a proto-object and proto-pattern space.
   b. Only a small number of objects or pattern components are retained from one fixation to the next. These object files also provide links to verbal propositional information in verbal working memory.
   c. A small number of cognitive markers are placed in a spatial map of the problem space to hold partial solutions where necessary. Fixation and deeper processing is necessary for these markers to be constructed.
4. Links to verbal/logical complex information are activated by icons or familiar patterns, bringing in other kinds of information.

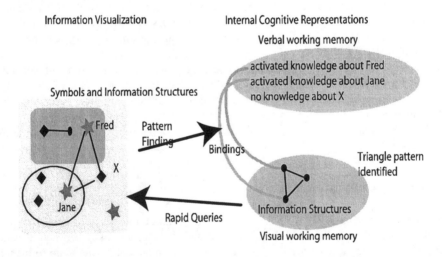

Fig. 3. A snapshot of a cognitive system in action

Fig. 3 illustrates a snapshot of the cognitive system in operation. The cognitive tool is a visualization representing various people in an organization. Visual pattern elements show subgroups and connecting lines show various kinds of working relationships. Visual queries result in different sets of relationship loaded into visual working memory at the same time as corresponding knowledge structures are activated in verbal working memory. For example, the high-level query "Who works with Fred?" might result in a series of visual-pattern queries; one of them focused on the green sub region enclosing Fred and other workers, another focused on the triangular structure. One answer is that Fred works with Jane. Of course this is a very simple example constructed for the purpose of illustration. The power of visualizations, especially if they are interactive front ends to databases, is that they can provide rapid querying on very complex structures.

6 Visual Query Costs

For non-interactive displays, such as maps, eye-movements are the main way of obtaining more information. We simply point our foveas (the high-resolution area in the center of vision) and tune for the required patterns. With computer-based visualization, interactive techniques can be used to increases the size of the information space that can be obtained by means of visual queries. It is useful to compare eye movements with other navigation techniques.

Eye movements allow us to acquire a new set of informative visual objects in 100-200 msec. Moreover, information acquired in this way will be readily integrated with other information that we have recently acquired from the same space. This suggests that the ideal visualization is one where all the information for visualization is available on a single high-resolution screen.

It is instructive to compare the cost of getting information through an eye movement with other methods for getting new information into the visual field. For example, walking across a room, opening a filing cabinet and extracting a document can take minutes, a hugely costly query. Clicking on a hypertext link involves a 1-2 sec guided hand movement and a mouse click to generate an entirely new screenful of information. However, the entire information context typically has changed and the new information may be presented using a different visual symbol set and different layout conventions. Thus several seconds of cognitive reorientation may be required.

There are rapid interactive techniques that bind the human and the computer into a tightly coupled system. Both *brushing* (Becker & Cleveland, 1987) and *dynamic queries* are techniques that allow information to be revealed on some data dimension by making a continuous mouse movement. Hover queries cause extra information to rapidly pop-up as the mouse is dragged over a series of data objects (Munzner, Guimbretière & Robertson, 1999). All three of these require a mouse movement to get started, typically taking about 2 seconds, but after this initial setup time every change in mouse position changes the information visually available resulting in a tight exploratory visual feedback. The data is continuously modified and this may enable an effective rate of several queries per second, similar to the rate for eye movements. However this rate is only possible for quite specific kinds of query trajectories; we cannot jump from point to point in the data space as we can by moving our eyes.

The MEGraph System of Ware and Bobrow (Ware & Bobrow, 2004) provides an example of how a highly interactive node-link visualization can provide views a very complex semantic network, far larger than can be displayed using a static map. ME-Graph supports queries in allowing for rapid highlighting of subsets of the graph by setting them in motion. This made it possible for users to rapidly explore a node link diagram that was essentially illegible because of the large number of links. We have recently extended this system to show graphs having up to 3200 nodes. This is more than two orders of magnitude greater than the typical node-link diagram which usually has fewer than 20 nodes.

7 Conclusion

The purpose of this paper has been to present a model of visual thinking based on current theories of visual perception. The model describes how visual queries can be executed with a combination of eye movement scanning patterns and attentional processes within each fixation. Visual working memory retains a small amount of object and location information from one fixation to the next, and this, for many tasks, is a major factor limiting the effectiveness of the visualization. One of the implications of this theory is that the cognitive cost of navigation in visual data spaces will be critical in determining the effectiveness of a particular interactive visual display. In a cognitive systems approach, what matters is how quickly and easily information can be acquired. This will be particularly true when more complex patterns are being sought and where it is necessary to integrate information across several screens. Indeed, the theory suggests that large high-resolution screens should be very effective for complex tasks because they can be navigated by means of eye movements, thereby reducing the need for cognitively disruptive screen changes. When screens are small, or information spaces are very large, the various alternative navigation methods should be weighed in terms of their cognitive load and time requirements. In general, rapid fluid access to information is likely to win out over attractive but slow to navigate 3D spaces.

The model suggests a significant research agenda since it is far from complete. Most of the underlying theory has been developed in vision research laboratories, and not with the goal of understanding and improving information visualizations. Much of the research into visual working memory has focused on simple geometric objects, such as those used by Vogel et al. (2001). Research is needed to understand the visual and cognitive resources needed to support common visual queries on information displays. For example many visualizations consist of node-link diagrams of one form or another. Common queries are "Which nodes are connected?", "What is the shortest path between two nodes?" and "Is there a path between two particular nodes?" If we can understand the cognitive processes involved in these queries then we can optimize for them. Research is also needed to improve our understanding of how complex queries can be decomposed into simpler ones.

Acknowledgements. This research was supported from Grants from NSF 0081292 and NOAA. Discussions with Ron Rensink have helped refine some of the ideas.

References

Baddeley, A.D., & Logie, R.H. (1999). Working Memory: The Multiple-Component Model. In A. Miyake, & P. Shah (Eds.), *Models of Working Memory* (pp. 28-61). New York: Cambridge University Press.

Baddeley, A.D., & Hitch, G.J. (1974). Working memory. In G.H. Bower (Ed.), *The psychology of learning and motivation: Advances in research and theory*, Vol. 8 (pp. 647-667). Hillsdale NJ.: Erlbaum.

Becker, R.A., & Cleveland, W.S. (1987). Brushing scatterplots. *Technometrics, 29*(2), 127-142.

Hutchins, E. (1995). *Distributed Cognition*. Cambridge, MA: MIT Press.

Jonides, J. (1981). Voluntary versus automatic control over the mind's eye. In J. Long, & A.D. Baddeley (Eds.), *Attention and Performance*, Vol. 9 (pp. 187-203). Hillsdale, NJ.: Erlbaum.

Kahneman, D., Triesman, A., & Gibbs, B.J. (1992). The reviewing of object files: Object-specific integration of information. *Cognitive Psychology, 24*, 175-219.

Mack, A., & Rock, I. (1998). *Inattentional Blindness*. Cambridge, MA: MIT Press.

Munzner, T., Guimbretière, F., & Robertson, G. (1999). Constellation: A Visualization Tool for Linguistic Queries from Mindnet. In D. Keim, & G. Wills (Eds.), *Proceedings of the 1999 IEEE Symposium on Information Visualization* (pp. 132-135). Washington, DC: IEEE CS Press.

O'Regan, J.K. (1992). Solving the "real" mysteries of visual perception: The world as an outside memory. *Canadian Journal of Psychology, 46*, 461-488.

Postma, A., & De Haan, E.H.F. (1996). What was where? Memory for Object locations. *Quarterly Journal of Experimental Psychology, 49A*(1), 178-199.

Rensink, R.A. (2000). The dynamic representation of scenes. *Visual Cognition, 7*, 17-42.

Rensink, R.A., O'Reagan, J.K., & Clark, J.J. (1997). To see or not to see: The need for attention to perceive changes in scenes. *Psychological Science, 8*(5), 368-373.

Rensink, R.A. (2002). Change Detection. *Annual Review of Psychology, 53*, 245-277.

Rock, I., & Gutman, D. (1981). The effect of inattention on form perception. *Journal of Experimental Psychology: Human Perception and Performance, 7*(2), 275-285.

Simons, D.J., & Levin, D.T. (1998). Failure to detect changes to people during a real-world interaction. *Psychonomic Bulletin and Review, 5*, 644-649.

Triesman, A. (1985). Preattentive processing in vision. *Computer Vision, Graphics and Image Processing, 31*, 156-177.

Vogel, E.K., Woodman, G.F., & Luck, S.J. (2001). Storage of features, conjunctions and objects in visual working memory. *Journal of Experimental Psychology: Human Perception and Performance, 27*(1), 92-114.

Ware, C. (2004). *Information Visualization: Perception for Design* (2nd Edition). San Francisco, CA: Morgan Kaufman.

Ware, C., & Bobrow, R. (2004). Motion to support rapid interactive queries on node-link diagrams. *ACM Transactions on Applied Perception, 1*(1) 3-18.

Wolfe, J.M., & Gancarz, G.G. (1996). Guided Search 3.0. A model of visual search catches up with Jay Enoch 40 Years Later. In V. Lakshminarayanan (Ed.), *Basic and Clinical Applications of Vision Science* (pp. 189-192). Dordrecht, Netherlands: Kluwer Academic.

Representational Correspondence as a Basic Principle of Diagram Design

Christopher F. Chabris[*] and Stephen M. Kosslyn

Department of Psychology, Harvard University,
Cambridge, MA 02138, USA
{cfc, smk}@wjh.harvard.edu

Abstract. The timeworn claim that a picture is worth a thousand words is generally well-supported by empirical evidence, suggesting that diagrams and other information graphics can enhance human cognitive capacities in a wide range of contexts and applications. But not every picture is worth the space it occupies. What qualities make a diagram an effective and efficient conduit of information to the human mind? In this article we argue that the best diagrams depict information the same way that our internal mental representations do. That is, "visual thinking" operates largely on relatively sketchy, cartoon-like representations of the physical world, translating sensory input into efficient codes before storing and manipulating it. Effective diagrams will assist this process by stripping away irrelevant detail while preserving or highlighting essential information about objects and their spatial relations. We discuss several examples that illustrate this "Representational Correspondence Principle," and we consider its implications for the design of systems that use diagrams to represent abstract, conceptual knowledge, such as social networks, financial markets, or web content hierarchies.

1 Introduction

Diagrams are uniquely powerful tools for communication. Everyone has heard the adage that a picture is worth a thousand words (or ten thousand, according to the Chinese version), and this adage bears repetition because it so often is correct. Diagrams, which we take to include information graphics and all other non-photographic forms of visual communication, are usually good examples of this adage at work—but not simply because they save time or space. Rather, diagrams are useful because they make explicit and accessible *to human users* patterns among facts. Our brains have particular properties that must be respected if a diagram (or anything else) is to communicate effectively, and a good diagram exploits our strengths and does not fall prey to our limitations.

Conceptual maps, such as systems of labeled nodes and links used to represent the relationships between individuals, ideas, or other abstract content, are becoming increasingly common as the computing power and tools needed to design them become more available. Indeed, the power of software to implement increasingly

---

[*] Corresponding author.

S.-O. Tergan and T. Keller (Eds.): Knowledge and Information Visualization, LNCS 3426, pp. 36–57, 2005.
© Springer-Verlag Berlin Heidelberg 2005

complex, colorful, and rapidly accessible knowledge visualizations may encourage researchers and information designers to develop representational schemes that will overwhelm, or at least unduly tax, the cognitive powers of the very users they are supposed to be serving. In this chapter we first discuss diagrams as general tools for representing information, and propose a principle of effective diagram design. After explaining the key to this new principle, we illustrate its force with examples drawn from different domains, and then apply this principle to the design of conceptual maps and similar knowledge visualization tools.

1.1 The Power of Diagrams

Tufte (1983) describes an early example of the power of diagrams that is still very relevant today: the solution of the September 1854 cholera epidemic in London. The epidemic showed no signs of abating, and many people puzzled over its causes and possible solutions. Dr. John Snow (along with others) pondered tables of data that

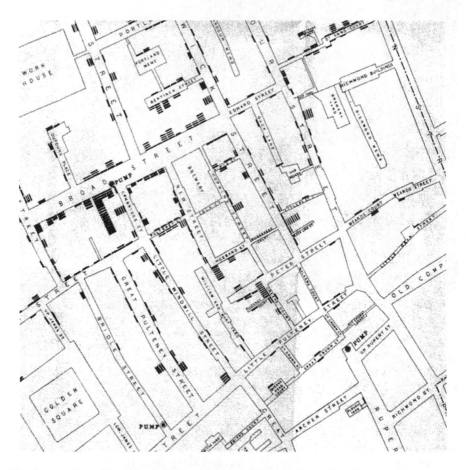

Fig. 1. A portion of Dr. John Snow's original map of the 1854 London cholera epidemic. Note the clustering of cases near the Broad Street pump

Fig. 2. Visual stimulus used by Bransford & Johnson (1972; redrawn from original)

described the locations of victims, and then hit on the idea of converting these data into a graphical display, as shown in Figure 1. Once he displayed them as symbols on a map, Dr. Snow noticed a pattern in the data: the deaths clustered around the location of a particular water pump, which he inferred was the most likely source of the infection. This sort of diagram can help the user discover spatial patterns that otherwise are extraordinarily difficult to discern, and today this form of graphic display is implemented in many database software packages and is seen widely in all types of publications, from epidemiology journals to the popular press.

In addition to such dramatic anecdotal evidence of the power of diagrams in visual communication, there is a longstanding and overwhelming confluence of quantitative research on the topic. Bransford and Johnson (1972) provided a now-classic illustration, if you will, of the power of diagrams in a study that relied on the picture shown in Figure 2. They showed this picture to participants along with a printed story that included sentences like "If the balloons popped, the sound wouldn't be able to carry since everything would be too far away from the correct floor," "Since the whole operation depends on a steady flow of electricity, a break in the middle of the wire would also cause problems," and "With face to face contact, the least number of things could go wrong." They also asked other, less fortunate, participants to study the text without ever seeing the picture. All were later asked how well they understood the story and tested to see how much of it they could recall. The results were clear: adding the picture improved comprehension and memory by over 50%, and showing the picture before the text was over 100% better than giving the text alone.

This experimental situation relied on unusually ambiguous text, but we can still learn valuable lessons from it. First, pictures can be useful in helping readers to interpret and remember text. Indeed, Levie and Lentz (1982) surveyed 46 experiments comparing text with pictures to text alone and found that 45—all but one—showed that pictures did in fact improve memory or comprehension. In one case, a group following directions in text illustrated with diagrams did an amazing 323% better than a group following the same directions without the illustrations. Second, to be maximally effective, the diagram should be examined *before* the reader encounters the relevant text, in part because the diagram helps to organize the text and in part because the reader may try to visualize what the text is describing, and the results may not match the diagram. However, adding pictures to prose is not a panacea. Levie and Lentz found that whereas illustrations that were merely "vaguely related" to accompanying text led readers to score 25% better on later tests of understanding and memory than text alone, truly irrelevant illustrations had a minimal effect (5% improvement). Worse yet, pictures serving a purely decorative purpose actually cause readers to perform more poorly than those who received unadorned text.

1.2 Understanding Effective Diagrams

In short, it's not that all diagrams are inherently good: some are, but some are not. But why? What makes one diagram the key to good comprehension, but another a puzzle in its own right? Research that shows the value of adding illustrations to text does not reveal the design characteristics that make some illustrations more effective than others.

We have argued elsewhere that research in cognitive psychology and neuroscience yields principles of display design that play to the strengths of human perception, memory, comprehension and reasoning while avoiding their weaknesses (Kosslyn, 1985, 1994a; Kosslyn & Chabris, 1992, 1993; Kosslyn, Chabris, & Hamilton, 1990). We could present here a long catalogue of facts about how the mind and brain work that are relevant to diagram design. On the one hand, many of these facts point out specific weaknesses in human information processing, such as our notoriously poor abilities to hold information in short-term memory or to discriminate subtle changes. Clearly, good displays should not require that the user have super-human abilities, and thus designers should eschew displays that are too complex or that don't have good contrast among separate portions. On the other hand, relevant features of our information processing systems can be used to overcome its limitations. For example, the Gestalt Laws of organization dictate how perceptual units are formed, and the limits of short-term memory are defined in terms of such units. Symmetrical shapes, for example "[ ]", are organized into a single unit, whereas asymmetrical ones, such as "_ l", are not. Thus, by cleverly organizing a display to minimize the number of perceptual units, a designer can pack a lot of information into it. Similarly, by using contrast to define a "foreground" (such as a line in a graph that specifies data from a country of interest) and "background" (all other lines), a designer can direct the viewer's attention to the most important features, thereby not requiring him to understand everything else in detail.

Such facts are useful, and can lead to nuts-and-bolts recommendations for how to produce comprehensible displays (e.g., see Kosslyn, 1994a). We expect principles based on such facts to be developed as more researchers study the anatomy of effective displays. However, there is another approach to understanding the "cognitive ergonomics" of effective diagrams, which we develop in the following section.

2 The Representational Correspondence Principle

Rather than focus on particular characteristics of our information-processing systems for vision, memory, comprehension and reasoning, in this article we describe a more general principle of graphic communication. This principle may help designers, software developers, and researchers to take advantage of psychological research in a novel way. We call this principle the *Representational Correspondence Principle,* which states that *effective diagrams depict information the same way that our internal mental representations do.* This principle is rooted in the observation that all visual input is translated into internal codes before it is operated on by reasoning processes. Although these translation steps seem effortless in many everyday situations (for example, we are typically completely unaware of all the brain activity going on in the split-second before we recognize a familiar face), they can require a surprising amount of effort in other situations, such as when we must decode a confusing diagram in order to install a new component in a computer. Here's our crucial idea: Information will pass through the translation bottleneck faster and less painfully if it starts out in a form that corresponds as closely as possible to the one in which it eventually will be specified.

Depending on one's point of view, the Representational Correspondence Principle may seem obvious or vacuous. We argue that it is neither: First, if it were obvious, then we wouldn't expect to find that other principles have been proposed that are inconsistent with it. In fact, such inconsistent principles have been seriously proposed. Tufte (1983, p. 93) offered a salient example when he suggested that "a large share of the ink on a graphic should present data-information, the ink changing as the data change. *Data-ink* is the non-erasable core of a graphic, the non-redundant ink arranged in response to variation in the numbers represented." He went on to argue that the best graphic maximizes the ratio of "data-ink" to "total ink used to print the graphic," and that "most important … is the idea that other principles bearing on graphical design follow from the idea of maximizing the share of data-ink." Notice that this principle suggests that instead of showing a complete bar in a bar graph, the designer would be best advised simply to present one side of the bar and a line demarcating its top. Never mind that the resulting bracket would not be symmetrical, and thus would involve two perceptual units instead of the one that is formed by a complete bar; and never mind that thin lines are more difficult to detect and discriminate from the background than are bars. We will revisit Tufte's specific recommendations that flow from his data-ink principle later. For now it should be clear that Tufte's principle, which has had wide influence, says nothing about human internal representations of information or the limitations on how human beings process information; instead, it addresses itself exclusively to the ink on the page (or, nowadays, the pixels on the screen).

Second, could the Representational Correspondence Principle be vacuous? If one believes that it is impossible or currently beyond science's reach to understand how the mind and brain represent information, then one would conclude that there cannot be any way to implement the principle in practice. Or, one might readily concede that science is revealing properties about how information is represented in the human mind and brain, but be skeptical (as Tufte himself was) that it can teach us any lessons about how to design effective diagrams. In our view, both concerns are misguided. Although it is true that there are many unsolved problems in neuroscience (as in every other branch of science), there is more than enough knowledge about how information is represented to give us detailed guidance in how to design effective diagrams. In the following section, we will hint at some of these discoveries and the various methods that have been developed to plumb the workings of the mind and brain.

2.1 Visual Images in the Brain

Although we cannot yet say definitively how visual information is stored and processed in the brain, considerable progress has been made in such research. One line of research hinges on the idea that much of the visual information we store in memory can be recalled in the form of visual mental images, and thus the study of visual mental imagery can reveal the nature of internal visual representations. This hypothesis is supported by many forms of research. For example, for well over 100 years researchers have reported that visual imagery interferes with visual perception —as expected if the same system is used in both cases. For instance, researchers showed that visualizing impairs the ability to see (Perky, 1910; Segal & Fusella, 1970). Later researchers documented that people falsely remember having seen an object when they in fact only visualized it (e.g., Johnson & Raye, 1981). And yet other researchers focused on functional similarities between imagery and perception (for reviews, see Finke & Shepard, 1986; Kosslyn, 1980, 1994b). For example, objects in mental images require more time to imagine rotating greater amounts, as if the images were literally rotating about an axis (Shepard & Cooper, 1982). Similarly, people require more time to scan greater distances across imagined objects, as if the imagined objects are arrayed in space. Moreover, they require more time to "zoom in" greater amounts when "viewing" imagined objects (Kosslyn, 1980).

With the advent of modern brain-scanning technologies, researchers moved beyond purely behavioral studies of imagery and perception to studies of the underlying neural mechanisms (e.g., Kosslyn et al., 1997). The results are remarkable: At least two-thirds of the same brain areas are used in visual imagery and visual perception—which is a far greater amount than either shares with language or memory processing. Visual imagery isn't called "seeing with the mind's eye" only for poetic reasons; it really does use most of the neural machinery used in actual seeing.

Although many brain areas are shared by visual imagery and perception, of particular importance is the fact that imagery usually recruits the first parts of the brain to register visual input from the eyes (Kosslyn et al., 2001; Kosslyn & Thompson, 2003; Thompson & Kosslyn, 2000). During perception, light strikes the retinas and neural signals are sent back into the brain. These signals in turn evoke a pattern of activation on the surface of the cerebral cortex (the thin outer covering of the brain, where most of the neural cell bodies are located). In the first areas to receive such input, the pattern of activation is literally spatial: It preserves the layout of the pattern of activity on the retina itself, which is why these areas are said to be *retinotopically mapped*. There actually are "pictures in the head."

This sort of code has several important properties. For example, it uses space on the cortex to represent space in the world. As such, it makes explicit and accessible *shape* and the *spatial relations* among shapes and parts of shapes. In addition, the code is tailor-made to function well within the brain's processing system. This is a crucial point, so we need to emphasize it: The properties of any representation can only be understood in the context of the systems in which it is embedded. If there were no processes that could interpret shapes (e.g., ^ is readily seen as pointed and U as rounded), the representations would have no impact on the rest of the system—and for all intents and purposes would not exist. Thus, when we evaluate properties of a representation, we need to consider them in the context of the types of processes that operate on them. Specifically, some aspects of representations will be easily operated upon by the extant processes, whereas others will not be. For example, it would be easy to *draw* a rounded point, but the brain might find it difficult to *verbally label* such a shape.

The fact that the initial input to the visual system is picture-like is convenient for those who want to use diagrams to convey information, but if we want our diagrams to correspond as closely as possible to the representations used by the brain itself we need to know more about those representations. The patterns of activation in the first visual areas are just the beginning. These representations are converted to a series of other representations as processing continues. We focus on one fact about these conversions: The brain is often in danger of being overwhelmed by too much information, and thus a crucial aspect of processing involves stripping down representations to their core, preserving some aspects and discarding others.[1] An effective diagram should not only map neatly into the representations used early in processing, but also facilitate the processing such representations evoke. In the next section we unpack this idea.

---

[1] Although the abstraction of relevant information, or "gist," is a critical component of human perception, there are in fact some individuals who are able to suppress this tendency, or who even have difficulty *not* being overwhelmed by visual detail. Autistic savants with artistic ability are able to draw surprisingly detailed, naturalistic pictures, unlike all normal children their age (e.g., Snyder and Thomas, 1997), who tend to draw schematically, showing the general shapes of critical parts and their spatial relations, but not the visual details.

2.2 Chess Diagrams

An elegant illustration of representational correspondence is found every week in hundreds of newspapers: chess diagrams. As shown in Figure 3, the configuration of pieces on a three-dimensional chess board can be represented by an array of symbols in a two-dimensional diagram. Indeed, this type of diagram is used throughout the world, in virtually every country and culture where the Western form of chess is played. In particular, all chess publications aimed at expert players use this type of diagram, and have for over a century. Internet chess services, computer chess software, and video projection systems at public chess events use the same format. In fact, even though they could easily have realistic three-dimensional displays, chess professionals prefer to use this format to study the game on their computers. And this diagrammatic representation has even yielded an international convention for a notation to communicate the moves of chess games: the symbols used for the different pieces replace the initials of the piece names in the local language, making it possible for literature produced in one country to be read and understood in many others regardless of language differences.

How does this format demonstrate representational correspondence? To answer this question, we must discover how chess experts internally represent the locations and identities of the pieces on the board when they are playing chess. Again, we can appeal to visual mental imagery as a way to study the nature of the internal representations used to this end. The easiest way to begin this process is simply to ask players what they "see in their mind's eye" when they visualize a chess position or "think ahead." Is it a veridical, three-dimensional image of a particular chess board and set of pieces (perhaps the ones currently being played on, or the ones the player most often uses)? Taine (1875), based on the report of one amateur player, believed that it was, and characterized the type of imagery used in chess as an "internal mirror" that reflected the precise state of the thing(s) being imagined.

Fig. 3. A photograph of a chess position on a standard board and set, viewed from a player's visual perspective (*left*); a standard symbolic diagram of the same chess position (*right*)

But further examination of the chess literature suggests a different conclusion. Reuben Fine (1965), a psychoanalyst and former world championship contender, said that "the visualization that takes place must emphasize the chess essentials and must eliminate accidental factors, such as size or different colors [of the board and pieces]." Commenting on the qualities of the chess player's internal image, the chess master Jacques Mieses (1940) wrote that "it is not a planimetrical or stereometrical picture that appears before the mind's eye of the chess player ... His task lies rather in mentally picturing the constantly changing formations of the pieces ... This process is indeed more closely allied to the department of 'topographic sense'." Alfred Binet (1894), the father of modern intelligence testing, surveyed many experts who engaged in simultaneous blindfold chess, a popular public "stunt" in the late 19th century in which the performer played several games at once, entirely without sight of a board. One of Binet's participants, a young master named Goetz, reported that he was "aware only of the significance of a piece and its course ... to the inner eye, a bishop is not a uniquely shaped piece, but, rather, an oblique force" (Binet, 1893).

One of us (CFC) recently asked American grandmaster Sergey Kudrin to reconstruct chess positions with a standard set and board after five seconds of viewing them as printed chess diagrams. Afterwards, he asked this player how he remembered where the pieces were located. The response: "I visually remembered the diagram, but [the pieces] were on this diagram, which for me is almost the same as the board, but in my mind they stayed as the pieces of this diagram." Did he have any problems in translating between his memory of the diagram and the three-dimensional board and pieces? "It seemed natural, although maybe I lost it somewhere because I didn't get this [particular] position exactly. Although at the moment when I stopped looking at [the diagram], I was sure I would remember everything, but I didn't remember, and I knew I was doing something wrong," he replied. That is, Kudrin formed some sort of visual image of the chess position with the same characteristics as the two-dimensional diagram he studied, and when the stimulus was removed he had a clear image. But as he began to construct the position on the (three-dimensional) board, the image faded, and he could not complete the task as accurately as he initially expected.

A common thread running through these descriptions, and many others in the literature, is that all players denied using a representation of the three-dimensional qualities of the board or pieces, and instead emphasized that the spatial relationships among pieces are more important than their particular shapes, colors, and so on. Chess diagrams discard all the superfluous detail of the chess board and pieces (and the player's particular perspective), and in the process make more salient the identities of the pieces (high-contrast black and white symbols, instead of lower-contrast dark- and light-brown woods) and their spatial relationships (each piece's location is clearly visible, instead of occluding nearby pieces as on a real board).[2]

Further introspective accounts of chess masters suggest uses to which diagrams are put in visual thinking. Binet's subject Goetz drew a diagram showing what he "saw" when thinking ahead about a particular chess position, as illustrated in Figure 4; note

---

[2] Indeed, the diagram seems so optimal for visual thinking about chess that one might ask why (beyond for historical reasons) three-dimensional sets are still used. They are superior to diagrams for actually grasping and moving the pieces with the hands, and for face-to-face interaction. But chess competition is conducted increasingly via the Internet, and there players find it faster to use a diagram depiction and move pieces by clicking with a mouse.

that some squares are highlighted and movements between squares are also shown. According to Steiner (1972, p. 66), "the great chess player does not see squares and pieces as discrete units, or even abstract counters. He internalizes a very special sense of 'fields of force,' of regions characterized, differentiated by the fact that certain events can or cannot take place in them. What matters, thus, is not the particular square, or even piece, but a cluster of potential actions, a space of and for evolving events." The chess diagram, of course, does not represent these "fields of force" explicitly; they are the phenomena that occur during visual "thinking ahead" by chess masters, whereas diagrams are meant to represent snapshots of a game in progress. What is critical is that none of these aspects of chess thinking revealed by these reports depend on a photograph-like representation of the chess board; indeed, they would apparently be impaired if they had to perform in such a cumbersome, overly detailed arena instead of the simplified two-dimensional diagram.

Thus, chess diagrams appear to capture what is important about a board configuration, and strip away the irrelevant details. Moreover, because the diagram has a 1:1 correspondence with the actual board, it captures all of the possible relations among pieces. This representation is easily internalized, given what we know about how visual information is stored.

Note that we are not claiming that modern chess diagrams and notation systems were developed to conform to the Representational Correspondence Principle. They use a convention that evolved over centuries of practice and publishing. We suspect

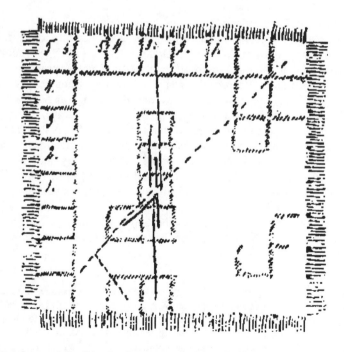

Fig. 4. A drawing made by Binet's chess-master subject Goetz of his internal mental imagery while thinking ahead about a chess position (Binet, 1893)

that they are the product of a kind of Darwinian selection, winning out over other competing schemes, and that their continued success as a representational scheme (and their proliferation in an age when computers can depict three-dimensional scenes and complicated images in video games with lifelike detail) reflects their (inadvertent) adherence to the principle.[3] If so, we are led to suggest that novel diagrammatic schemes in other fields may be developed by carefully debriefing expert practitioners, trying to discover how they convert relevant stimuli into internal representations. Of course, not all aspects of representations are accessible to introspection, but many of the functional properties of visual images are in fact evident to introspection (Kosslyn, 2001), as in the case of chess.

2.3 Caricatures of Faces

We noted earlier that most human beings can effortlessly recognize hundreds of different individual faces. Face recognition is completed in less than one second, usually with no conscious thought, and—unlike the situation in chess—we have no introspective access to the procedures we use to do it or the way that different faces are represented in our memories. Faces themselves are not diagrams, but they can be represented by diagrams—assuming that caricatures of faces are diagrams. Caricatures are drawings that exaggerate distinctive features (as in political cartoons of George W. Bush that emphasize his ears) and de-emphasize nondistinctive features (such as Mr. Bush's chin). What can these illustrations teach us about diagram design in general?

An elegant line of research suggests that faces, despite our ability to recognize them rapidly and seemingly without effort, are not internally represented in a veridical, photograph-like format. Rhodes, Brennan, and Carey (1987) took a set of faces that were familiar to their participants, and used a computer program to generate a caricature for each face. The program generated these caricatures by starting with photographs, extracting key points and lines, and then comparing these features to "average" faces. By stretching the features farther from the average, or moving them closer, caricatures and "anti-caricatures" of the faces could be created (see Figure 5 for an example). Participants were then asked to identify the individuals depicted by veridical, caricature, and anti-caricature drawings as quickly and accurately as possible. The findings were straightforward: Viewers identified the caricatures fastest—even faster than they identified veridical depictions—and the anti-caricatures most slowly. When these researchers later showed the participants a range of caricatures and anti-caricatures and asked them to select the best likeness for each person, the average choice was a caricature that exaggerated the distinctive aspects of the face by about 16%.

---

[3] The Darwinian selection hypothesis is not the only possibility, of course. Simple tradition, ease of production, or cost could also explain why a particular sort of display has persisted. However, we doubt that a truly ineffective display would be retained for long if better alternatives are developed. Consider the case of the dial clock: Many predicted its demise when digital watches and displays became common. But the dial conveys information explicitly that needs to be computed from a digital display: Namely the proportion of the hour that has passed and that remains. Dial clocks do something well that isn't done well by the current alternative, and hence are unlikely to be supplanted by them.

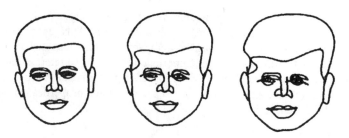

Fig. 5. Caricatures of John F. Kennedy in 0% (*left*), 50% (*center*), and 100% (*right*) exaggeration away from the average face. The exaggerated versions are easier to identify (Rhodes, Brennan, & Carey, 1987; reprinted by permission of Gillian Rhodes)

Accordingly, although we may not be aware of it, our internal representation of a human face appears to magnify what distinguishes it from other faces and minimize what it has in common with them. This makes sense: if the task is to recognize a particular individual's face, the facts that he has a mouth, two eyes, a nose, and so on will not help us much. When presented with a caricature, the unconscious translation process that converts a face into the internal code does not have to work as hard, and we are able to recognize the face faster. Consistent with this view, a subsequent study by Rhodes and McLean (1990) found that people who are expert in identifying birds benefited similarly when they identified caricatures of particular birds compared to when they identified veridical drawings of them.

The lesson for diagram design is clear: Caricatures make use of the Representational Correspondence Principle by matching a stimulus more closely to our internal representation of the represented object, and thereby facilitate our encoding and using the representation. Moreover, our internal representation is not simply a mental photograph; rather, these representations emphasize the most useful aspects of the stimulus and de-emphasize those aspects that will not help us in the most common tasks involving those stimuli.[4] In fact, caricatures appear to resemble our internal representations more closely than veridical drawings of the same objects.

---

[4] How much of what we feel we are seeing at any given time is actually being represented and saved in memory? Recent research on "change blindness" suggests that surprisingly little visual detail, even visual detail we think we must be storing, persists beyond the point when we stop looking at an object or scene. For example, Simons and Levin (1998) conducted a study in which an experimenter approached an unwitting pedestrian and asked for directions to a nearby building on a college campus. While the pedestrian was giving directions to the experimenter, two other experimenters carrying a door passed between the them. As the door passed, the first experimenter switched places with one of the experimenters who had been carrying the door, so that once the door was gone, the pedestrian was now talking to a different person from the one who initially asked for directions. Approximately half of the pedestrians approached in this study did not notice the change at all, and similar results have been obtained many times since in other studies (e.g., Levin, Simons, Angelone, & Chabris, 2002). In general, despite our introspective belief that we perceive the full appearance of someone we are talking to, this line of research suggests that only the most critical information, such as sex, age, and ethnicity, is guaranteed to be stored. Diagram designers should always keep in mind the inherent paucity of detail in human perception and memory.

In general, we propose that diagrams drawn to exaggerate or highlight critical distinctions will be more effective than veridical drawings. This recommendation will apply especially when diagrams must be compared or otherwise differentiated from one another. Note that in this case, the important qualities of an internal representation were only understood through measuring speed of performance in cognitive testing (identification), not through introspection. Representational properties can be revealed by a range of different techniques.

3 Consequences of Violating the Principle

What about traditional information graphics? Does the Representational Correspondence Principle apply to situations in which the constituents of the diagram are purely symbolic representations of quantities rather than depictions? If this principle is in fact general, as we suggest, then violating it should render any sort of diagram difficult to encode and understand. Let's consider some examples.

3.1 Keeping the Bar in Bar Graphs

Tufte (1983, p. 96) attacks the traditional bar graph as wasting ink, and thus violating his data-ink efficiency principle. In particular, he notes that:

> "The labeled, shaded bar of the bar chart ... unambiguously locates the altitude [the quantity represented by the bar] in six separate ways (any five of the six can be erased and the sixth will still indicate the height): as the (1) height of the left line, (2) height of the shading, (3) height of right line, (4) position of top of horizontal line, (5) position (not content) of number at bar's top, and (6) the number itself."

He then redesigns a traditional bar graph from a scientific journal by erasing many of the lines that form the bars, leaving essentially a single vertical line for each bar, and connects the baselines of pairs of adjacent bars, a process that "improves the graphic immensely" (p. 101). Figure 6 shows an example of this process.

Is it true that turning bars into lines or points will make communication more effective? Tufte is correct, of course, that much of the ink used to draw a bar is "redundant" in a mathematical sense. But the visual system does not represent the separate elements of a simple object like a bar. In fact, individual neurons respond to bars of different lengths and orientations, which suggests that the bar itself is one of the fundamental stimuli for the brain to process. Deconstructing a bar into a set of lines or points, as Tufte recommends, *converts it from a single object into multiple objects*, which will actually increase the load on processing and memory. This is because, as recent research in psychology and neuroscience has shown, objects (not pixels or ink) are a fundamental unit of representation (for a review, see Scholl, 2001). For example, viewers habitually register spatial relationships between objects, and can pay attention to an individual object more readily than to its parts. Representational correspondence therefore suggests that if what must be depicted is a single quantity, the diagram component chosen should be an object—which will be encoded into memory with less effort than will isolated parts. In fact, Tufte's redesign rules have created four new objects (connected sets of lines that resemble hooks), which are not easily decomposed by the visual system into their constituent "bars."

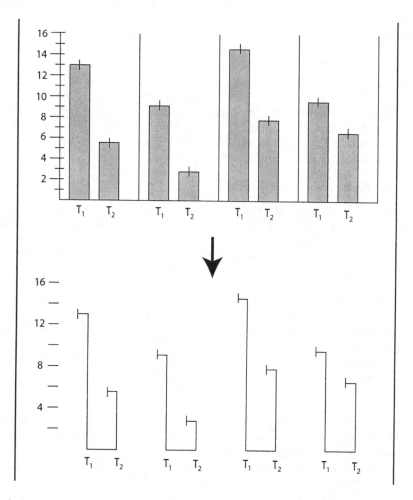

Fig. 6. A bar graph (of fictional data) drawn in the traditional way (*top*) and after applying Tufte's suggested transformations to increase the "data-ink ratio"

In fact, when Gillan and Richman (1994) actually tested Tufte's idea, they did not find that people could interpret simple bar graphs faster or more accurately after they were pared down; even when only two bars were present, participants tended to require more time to use the pared-down bar graphs than the standard ones. Gillan and Richman note that "ink can be helpful or detrimental to a graph reader depending on the function and location of the ink, the user's task, the type of graph, and the physical relations among graphical elements." (p 637). And they continue, "Thus, these data call into question Tufte's general rule that graph designers should maximize the data-ink ratio by eliminating non-data-ink and redundant ink." (p. 638).

A bar is the simplest visual depiction whose properties capture all that we need to know about quantity *in a single object*. Note that a circle at a specified height is not as good as a bar: the viewer must register not only the circle, but also the distance between the circle and the x-axis to estimate the height; in this case, the viewer would need to compare two objects, rather than encode the length of a single object. Also note that making bars appear three-dimensional actually detracts from processing them in bar graphs (Fischer, 2000). Although a 3-D bar is, like a 2-D bar, a single object, it is harder to place these bars properly within the axes, and difficult to avoid making the lines that depict the third dimension seem relevant. Three-dimensional bars also require the reader to ignore truly irrelevant information (such as apparent distance), which taxes processing. Note, however, that the added information is "irrelevant" not in Tufte's sense of quantitative aesthetics, but in the sense of what will optimize our cognitive performance.

3.2 Face Displays and Train Schedules

As a general rule, diagrams that violate the Representational Correspondence Principle are likely to be ineffective or obfuscating. In this section, we note two more examples, also coincidentally endorsed by Tufte as ink-efficient displays. First, as illustrated in Figure 7, the so-called Chernoff faces (Chernoff, 1973; Flury and Riedwyl, 1981) use different facial features to represent different variables: the expression of the eyes, the size of the mouth, the width of the face, the location of the ears, and so on, all may specify the values of different variables, enabling a compact representation of multidimensional information. Unfortunately, these face displays are almost impossible to use for extracting and comparing this information. Why? Human faces are processed primarily as single objects, not as collections of individual features. It is notoriously difficult to recognize individual facial features, and comparing features to one another is difficult when they must be isolated from their facial context. Given all that is known about visual processing of faces (for recent reviews, see Haxby et al., 2002; Rakover, 2002), it is hard to imagine a worse way to communicate multiple variables.[5]

Second, the 1880 Paris–Lyon train schedule designed by Marey (detail shown in Figure 8) is a grid with time along the x-axis, and location (Paris, Laroche, Dijon, etc.) along the y-axis. Each train is represented by a line that starts at the top when it leaves Paris, or starts at the bottom when it leaves Lyon. The line progresses across and down (or up) the grid until it reaches the final destination. When a line intersects a

---

[5] For example, Tanaka and Farah (1993) conducted an experiment in which participants studied labeled pictures of faces and houses (e.g., "this is Bob's face" or "this is Bob's house"), and later were shown individual features from these types of pictures (e.g., a pair of eyes, or a door) and asked to decide whether the feature was part of a named face or house (e.g., "are these Bob's eyes?"). On some trials, the part was shown in isolation, but on others it was shown in the context of the whole studied face or house. Showing house parts in context did not improve accuracy compared to showing them alone, but showing face parts in context helped the participants to decide whether they had seen them before; this finding suggests that individual facial features are not well-processed in isolation from the other facial features or the overall shape and context provided by a face. Perhaps designers who wish to pursue the concept behind the Chernoff faces should consider using houses instead—or just stick with a series of old-fashioned bar graphs.

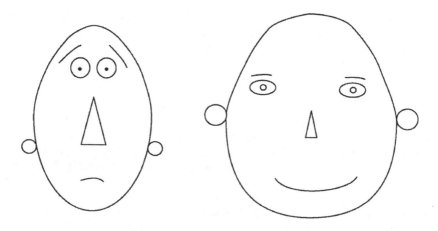

Fig. 7. Two sample "Chernoff faces"

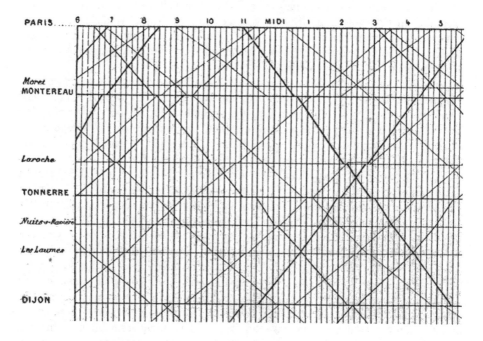

Fig. 8. A detail of Marey's original 1880 Paris–Lyon train schedule diagram

horizontal line representing a city, that indicates a stop. When viewers look at this diagram, however, all they can see is a mass of oriented lines. Orientation is one of the most salient properties of lines, and lines that differ by only a small amount in orientation are readily discriminated (indeed, line orientation is another one of the properties encoded very early in the brain's visual system). In this display, orientation conveys information about the train's *speed,* but the display was constructed to convey information about routes and schedules, so having speed "pop out" of the display is counterintuitive. Travelers are less interested in a train's speed than when it leaves and arrives, but to determine these facts they must compare multiple objects and scan across the chart to find the corresponding point on the axes. It's no wonder that these displays are rarely seen today.

3.3 Conceptual Networks

Our principle also applies to another sort of display, which is gaining increasing currency: conceptual network diagrams. An early use of such diagrams was the semantic network (e.g., Collins & Loftus, 1975). This now familiar type of diagram shows words or concepts as nodes, with links among them representing how strongly the nodes are associated in human memory. Of course, the "closeness" of two concepts in semantic space cannot be observed directly in the mind or brain, but it can be inferred from the results of different kinds of experiments. These experiments can be as simple as word association tasks, in which many people are asked to say the first word they think of when they hear or see a target word; in this case, the frequency of specific word responses determines the strength of their links to the target word. For example, what do you think of when you see "fork"? "Knife" would be a frequent response, which therefore is inferred to be close to "knife" in semantic space. Various methods can be used to converge on a single representation of a particular semantic network for an individual or a group.

An intriguing use of network diagrams developed more recently is social network analysis. For example, terrorist networks can be analyzed by depicting individual members as nodes, with links indicating the strength of the relationships among the individuals. In such cases, the network diagram can increase our knowledge of the underlying facts used to create it because it uses spatial codes to depict properties and patterns in the data that our limited powers of attention and memory impede us from recognizing in masses of individual facts. For example, Fellman et al. (2003) describe a network analysis of the interactions among the hijackers involved in the September 11, 2001 terrorist attacks. The information used to create the network was extracted entirely from public sources, but the network depiction highlights the central roles of the pilots of the four teams in the planning that preceded the attacks. The network can also be a tool for testing hypotheses by manipulating the data that underlies it; in this case, redrawing the network *without* using the data on the most recent contacts among the hijackers before September 11 suggests that one of the non-pilots was a central hub of interaction, and may thus have served a more critical role in planning than he did in operations. This observation in turn suggests possible new avenues of investigation for intelligence and law enforcement, and might stimulate new thinking about the organization of terrorist networks in general. (See Sageman, 2004, for analysis of terrorist networks on a group, rather than individual, level.)

Bar graphs and chess diagrams are obvious examples of representational correspondence; what about semantic and social network diagrams? The network diagram uses a spatial code to depict inherently non-spatial information. The fact that "cat" is more closely related to "dog" than it is to "train" is not a spatial fact in the same sense that the number of squares between two chess pieces is spatial; the fact that Mohammed Atta met with one of his conspirators more often than he met with another one is not spatial in the same sense that the difference between today's temperature and yesterday's temperature is spatial. However, the network diagram does represent information in a cartoon-like code that excludes irrelevant information, and it highlights important distinctions, for example by making obvious the difference between "hubs" and "loners" in social networks. A network diagram of the domestic terrorists involved in the Oklahoma City bombing of 1995 would look much different from the diagram of Al Qaeda, instantly showing that the two events were carried out by much different organizations.

Because the network diagram does not depict spatial information, it cannot match the power of the bar graph, caricature, or chess diagram to convey large quantities of information instantly through the human perceptual systems. Network diagrams are better suited to long-term exploration of complex data sets than to short-term communication of patterns and facts. Nonetheless, designers of knowledge visualization systems should keep in mind the general principle of representational correspondence, as well as the specific strengths and weaknesses of human cognitive architecture, if they want to maximize the satisfaction (and repeat business) of their customers.

Unfortunately, some of the most intriguing visualization systems do not fully succeed in these respects. The "Map of the Market" (updated continuously at www.smartmoney.com/maps) is a case in point. A large rectangular display is broken up into smaller rectangles, each of which represents a specific industry sector. Within each sector, smaller rectangles correspond to individual companies. The size of a rectangle indicates relative market value, and its color indicates daily changes (green for increases, red for decreases). One problem with this display is that the human visual system does not excel at comparing the areas of different objects, especially when they are not presented on a common baseline. General differences are apparent (Microsoft is a very large rectangle, Unisys is a very small one), but a more fine-grained comparison is difficult. Moreover, the spatial layout of the sectors and stocks does not seem to correspond to any "map" observers will have encountered previously. In this case a spatial code is being used when there is no underlying spatial or numerical dimension in the information being depicted.

Contrast this with distorted geographic maps, in which countries or regions are scaled up or down in size to match their share of some quantity, such as economic output, foreign debt, or oil consumption. In such maps two different spatial codes are in competition, but the familiar one (geography) can be used as an index to find the other, unfamiliar one. This is not the case in the Map of the Market, or in similar systems for representing the organization of information available on the web, such as ET-Map (ai3.eller.arizona.edu/ent/entertain1/), in which there is no natural index to help a user search for relevant information. Representational correspondence is not being exploited in these displays because the depiction uses a spatial code that does not match any internal representation that the human mind is likely to use or be familiar with.

Even worse, however, is the situation where a spatial code normally used for another purpose is appropriated for representing an incompatible form of knowledge. For example, NewsMaps (mappa.mundi.net/maps/maps_015/) use the metaphor of a topographic map to organize the news stories from a single time period, resulting in a sort of "representational mismatch" that may do more harm than good relative to a simple grouping of headlines into hierarchical categories.

4 Conclusions

The Representational Correspondence Principle states that to be effective, diagrams should depict information in the same way that our internal mental representations do. These internal representations are not veridical photographs, but instead are sketchy and cartoon-like (in the sense that distinguishing characteristics are emphasized). These internal representations do not include irrelevant detail, but "irrelevant" is defined relative to the task they will be used to accomplish and relative to how information is easily encoded, stored, and used in human cognition. This principle applies to diagrams that are intended to be manipulated by human mental processes, such as chess diagrams, bar graphs, and train schedules, all of which must be studied to extract relevant information.

We have two general concluding observations about the Representational Correspondence Principle. First, it does not trump all other considerations in design; indeed, no single principle could or should. In particular, diagram creators should not overlook longstanding conventions and the individual viewer's practice and experience with specific types of diagrams. For instance, differences in hue are often used to convey variation on a quantitative dimension; images of brain activation, as one example, use different hues to indicate different amounts of activity. However, hue is a so-called "nomothetic" dimension: Variations in hue do not naturally line up with variations along a single quantitative dimension; indeed, psychologically, hue is arrayed as a circle (the famous "color wheel"), not a single continuum. Nevertheless, many users have mastered the conventions (white indicates the largest amount, yellow next, followed by red, and so on). That said, variations in the other two aspects of color—saturation and intensity—do vary psychologically along a continuum. Even for experts, we expect that if these other two variables are manipulated to line up with the information conveyed (e.g., by using brighter colors to indicate the largest amount), and thereby respect representational correspondence, the display will be even more effective than one that follows an accepted but suboptimal convention of representation. Even a two-dimensional chess diagram only demonstrates representational correspondence for viewers who understand the game and are familiar with the symbolic conventions involved; for beginning players or those who have never seen such a diagram before, it may look like nothing more than an overwhelming jumble of odd figurines.

Second, this principle is not set in stone. The implications of the principle will evolve as researchers learn more about how external representations are converted to internal representations, and how internal representations are used in mental processing. Much of this research will focus on basic science, and those researchers will not consider possible applications. But this does not mean that questions that arise from considering diagram design cannot themselves feed into this research. From our perspective, there should be a rich exchange between researchers who study mental processing and those who design diagrams and the systems that create them. We expect such interactions to become especially productive when truly interactive computerized displays become common. According to our principle, such displays will be most effective when they mimic the corresponding mental processes, allowing them to become, in effect, prosthetic devices for the human mind. If well designed, displays can seem like extensions of ourselves, as easy and natural to work with as mental images.

Finally, we have commented on the design of conceptual network diagrams and other knowledge visualization systems in the context of the representational correspondence principle. Our aim was not to criticize or discourage the originators of novel information displays; every diagrammatic convention that is now in widespread use, facilitating human communication and understanding, had to be invented by someone at some point. We do believe, however, that technology has made it easier to invent a new form of display than to determine how effective a display is. The most successful display conventions illustrate the principle of representational correspondence, and although conceptual networks and other new visualization forms have great potential to help us make sense of more and varied types of information, they will succeed or fail in large measure based on how well they adhere to representational correspondence and respect the limitations of human information processing capabilities.

References

Binet, A. (1893). Les grandes mémoires: Résumé d'une enquête sur les joueurs d'echecs. *Revue des Deux Mondes, 117,* 826–859. (Translated by M.L. Simmel and S.B. Barron as "Mnemonic virtuosity: A study of chess players," *Genetic Psychology Monographs, 74,* 127–162, 1966.)

Binet, A. (1894). *Psychologie des grands calculateurs et joueurs d'échecs.* [Psychology of great calculators and chess players.] Paris: Hachette.

Bransford, J.D., & Johnson, M.K. (1972). Contextual prerequisites for understanding: Some investigations of comprehension and recall. *Journal of Verbal Learning & Verbal Behavior, 11,* 717–726.

Chabris, C.F., & Kosslyn, S.M. (1995). Illustrated editorial is value-added text. *Folio,* February, 28–29.

Chernoff, H. (1973). The use of faces to represent points in k-dimensional space graphically. *Journal of the American Statistical Association, 68,* 361–368.

Collins, A.M. & Loftus, E.F. (1975). A spreading activation theory of semantic processing. *Psychological Review, 82,* 407–428.

Fellman, P.V., Sawyer, D., & Wright, R. (2003). Modeling terrorist networks: Complex systems and first principles of counter-intelligence. Presented at "NATO and Central Asia: Enlargement, Civil – Military Relations, and Security," Kazach American University/North Atlantic Treaty Organization (NATO), May 14–16.

Fine, R. (1965). The psychology of blindfold chess: An introspective account. *Acta Psychologica, 24,* 352–370.

Finke, R. A., & Shepard, R. N. (1986). Visual functions of mental imagery. In K. R. Boff, L. Kaufman, & J. P. Thomas (Ed.), *Handbook of perception and human performance* (pp. 37–55). New York: Wiley-Interscience.

Fischer, M.H. (2000). Do irrelevant depth cues affect the comprehension of bar graphs? *Applied Cognitive Psychology, 14,* 151–162.

Flury, B., & Riedwyl, H. (1981). Graphical representation of multivariate data by means of asymmetrical faces. *Journal of the American Statistical Association, 76,* 757–765.

Gillan, D.J., & Richman, E.H. (1994). Miminalism and the syntax of graphs. *Human Factors, 36,* 619–644.

Haxby, J.V., Hoffman, E.A., & Gobbini, M.I. (2002). Human neural systems for face recognition and social communication. *Biological Psychiatry, 51*, 59–67.

Johnson, M.K., & Raye, C.L. (1981). Reality monitoring. *Psychological Review, 88*, 67–85.

Kosslyn, S.M. (2001). Visual consciousness. In P. Grossenbacher (Ed.), *Finding consciousness in the brain* (pp. 79–103). Amsterdam: John Benjamins.

Kosslyn, S.M. (1980). *Image and mind*. Cambridge, MA: Harvard University Press.

Kosslyn, S.M. (1985). Graphics and human information processing: a review of five books. *Journal of the American Statistical Association, 80*, 499–512.

Kosslyn, S.M. (1994a). *Elements of graph design*. New York: Freeman.

Kosslyn, S.M. (1994b). *Image and brain*. Cambridge, MA: MIT Press.

Kosslyn, S.M., & Chabris, C.F. (1993). The mind is not a camera, the brain is not a VCR: Some psychological guidelines for designing charts and graphs. *Aldus Magazine,* September/October, 35–38.

Kosslyn, S.M., & Chabris, C.F. (1992). Minding information graphics. *Folio*, February, 69–71.

Kosslyn, S.M., Chabris, C.F., & Hamilton, S.E. (1990). Designing for the mind: Five psychological principles of articulate graphics. *Multimedia Review, 1*, 23–29.

Kosslyn, S.M., Ganis, G., & Thompson, W. L. (2001). Neural foundations of imagery. *Nature Reviews Neuroscience, 2*, 635–642.

Kosslyn, S.M., & Thompson, W.L. (2003). When is early visual cortex activated during visual mental imagery? *Psychological Bulletin, 129*, 723–746.

Kosslyn, S.M., Thompson, W.L., & Alpert, N.M. (1997). Neural systems shared by visual imagery and visual perception: A positron emission tomography study. *Neuroimage, 6*, 320–334.

Levie, W.H., & Lentz, R. (1982). Effects of text illustrations: A review of research. *ECTJ, 30*, 195–232.

Levin, D.T., Simons, D.J., Angelone, B.L., & Chabris, C.F. (2002). Memory for centrally attended changing objects in an incidental real-world change detection paradigm. *British Journal of Psychology, 93*, 289–302.

Mieses, J. (1940). Psychology and the art of chess. *Chess*, April, 154–156.

Perky, C.W. (1910) An experimental study of imagination. *American Journal of Psychology, 21*, 422–452.

Rakover, S.S. (2002). Featural vs. configurational information in faces: A conceptual and empirical analysis. *British Journal of Psychology, 93*, 1–30.

Rhodes, G., Brennan, S., & Carey, S. (1987). Identification and ratings of caricatures: Implications for mental representations of faces. *Cognitive Psychology, 19*, 473–497.

Rhodes, G., & McLean, I.G. (1990). Distinctiveness and expertise effects with homogeneous stimuli: Towards a model of configural coding. *Perception, 19*, 773–794.

Sageman, M. (2004). *Understanding terror networks*. Philadelphia: University of Pennsylvania Press.

Scholl, B.J. (2001). Objects and attention: The state of the art. *Cognition, 80*, 1–46.

Segal, S.J., & Fusella, V. (1970). Influence of imaged pictures and sounds on detection of visual and auditory signals. *Journal of Experimental Psychology, 83*, 458–464.

Shepard, R.N., & Cooper, L.R. (1982). *Mental images and their transformations*. Cambridge, MA: MIT Press.

Simons, D.J., & Levin, D.T. (1998). Failure to detect changes to people during a real-world interaction. *Psychonomic Bulletin & Review, 5*, 644–649.

Snyder, A.W., & Thomas, M. (1997). Autistic artists give clues to cognition. *Perception, 26*, 93–96.

Steiner, G. (1974). *Fields of force: Fischer & Spassky at Reykjavik*. New York: Viking.

Taine, H-A. (1875). *On intelligence (Vol. I).* New York: Henry Holt. ("Translated from the French by T.D. Haye and revised with additions by the author." First published *as De l'intelligence,* Hachette, Paris, 1870. Reprinted by University Publications of America, Washington, 1977.)

Tanaka, J.W., & Farah, M.J. (1993). Parts and wholes in face recognition. *Quarterly Journal of Experimental Psychology: Human Experimental Psychology, 46,* 225–245.

Thompson, W.L. & Kosslyn, S.M. (2000). Neural systems activated during visual mental imagery: A review and meta-analyses. In: A. W. Toga and J. C. Mazziotta (Eds.), *Brain mapping II: The systems* (pp. 535–560). San Diego: Academic Press.

Tufte, E.R. (1983). *The visual display of quantitative information.* Cheshire, CT: Graphics Press.

Knowledge Visualization

Node-Link Mapping Principles for Visualizing Knowledge and Information

Donald F. Dansereau

Department of Psychology, P.O. Box 298920
Texas Christian University, Fort Worth, Texas 76129, USA
d.dansereau@tcu.edu

Abstract. This chapter describes the Texas Christian University Node-Link Mapping (TCU-NLM) system, and traces its empirical and applied history from 1972 to the present. TCU-NLM, which consists of information, guide, and free-style maps, has been explored in the areas of education, counseling, and business. Principles derived from experiences with this system are presented in four categories: goal specification, node-link infrastructure, spatial organization, and map processing. Implications of these principles for both knowledge and information visualization are discussed.

1 Introduction

In the early 1970's we began developing and evaluating a node-link mapping strategy. This strategy produces spatial arrays of ideas enclosed in boxes (nodes) connected to one another via coded links (lines). The inspiration for this approach was the usefulness of flow diagrams and organizational charts for communication, and the emergence of network models for conceptualizing human memory. At about this same time mind mapping (Buzan, 1974), concept mapping (Novak, 1980), and other node-link systems were being concurrently and independently developed. Consequently, there is now a rich history that can be drawn upon to improve information and knowledge visualization.

This chapter will follow one thread of this history in describing lessons learned from the application of our node-link representations to education, counseling, and to a lesser extent, business. From these lessons certain principles, cautions, and enhancements have emerged that can be used to unify and improve visualization techniques.

2 Texas Christian University Node-Link Mapping (TCU-NLM)

The latest incarnation of the approach begun in 1972 is called Texas Christian University Node-Link Mapping (TCU-NLM). In previous work the term Knowledge Mapping was used to refer to this system. However this label has proved to be too restrictive. Regardless of name, there are three general categories of maps: information, guide, and freestyle, which correspond to different aspects of knowledge and information visualization. It is important to note that in this context, these two forms of visu-

S.-O. Tergan and T. Keller (Eds.): Knowledge and Information Visualization, LNCS 3426, pp. 61–81, 2005.
© Springer-Verlag Berlin Heidelberg 2005

alization are defined with respect to the learner or user. In information visualization the content is presented to the learner/user, while in knowledge visualization the learner generates the content.

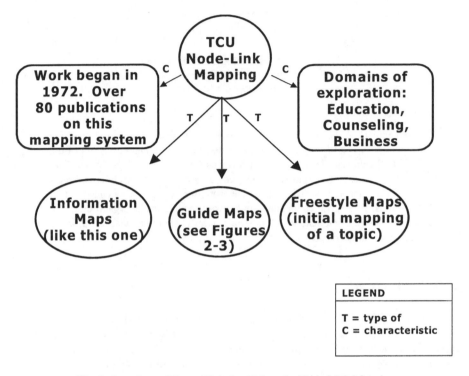

Fig. 1. Overview of Texas Christian University Node-Link Mapping

- *Information maps* are complete node-link maps usually produced by an expert to communicate about a topic. These maps, which can substitute for or supplement other presentation formats (e.g., text), are typically provided to users and/or learners as reference, navigation, and/or learning aids. Fig. 1, which overviews this system, is an example of an information map. In terms of the theme of this book, these types of maps are most closely related to the notion of information visualization.
- *Guide maps* are "fill-in-the-blank" graphic tools that can be used to solve problems (e.g., problems in planning, see Fig. 2) and to promote active learning (e.g., learning about a theory, see Fig. 3). The structure of the map and the questions within the nodes are provided by an expert, the answers to the questions are inserted by a user or learner. These maps are at the interface of information and knowledge visualization.
- *Freestyle maps* are produced by a learner or user (sometimes in conjunction with an expert, teacher, or counselor) to transform material presented in verbal format or to express personal knowledge. A format sheet (see Fig. 4) that provides easy reference to link types, node shapes, and content structures can serve as an aid to free style mapping. This type of mapping is a form of knowledge visualization.

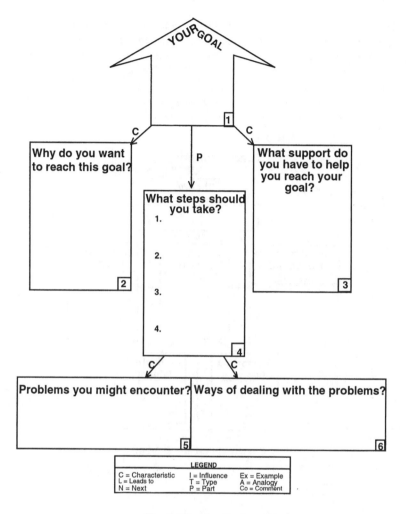

Fig. 2. Planning Rocket

These three mapping types rely on generally the same symbolic infrastructure (node-link) and organizational (spatial layout) principles, and are particularly useful when it is important to communicate relationships between ideas, objects, and actions. The freestyle format sheet (Fig. 4) gives a brief list of some of the links and node types along the left side and bottom, and the spatial structures along the right side. These basic mapping principles can be learned in approximately 2 hours of training and practice. However, expertise continues to grow over months and even years. Part of this growth process is due to individuals developing their own personal styles, in-clud-ing specialized links, nodes, and spatial layouts. TCU-NLM has benefited from feedback provided by users as they have explored new methods of mapping. Because the dispersal of TCU-NLM to different settings has been increasing rapidly over the past few years, there is a substantial amount of user knowledge that needs to be tapped to further expand and improve the system. This evolution of node-link mapping as a communication tool parallels that of written language which has changed over time based on "bottom up" influences from individuals creating new styles and forms. These changes are then incorporated into formal writing courses and textbooks. It seems that node-link mapping has reached a point where the lessons learned need to be codified to create the type of formal training opportunities that have supported the continued evolution of written language.

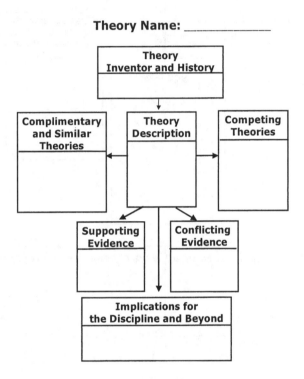

Fig. 3. An example of an Academic Guide Map

The process of codification has been initiated by developing training and transfer principles for TCU-NLM (Dansereau & Dees, 2002). At this point these efforts have been focused on the use of mapping in personal counseling. However, the formalizing of training principles is being expanded to include educational and business use.

The current TCU-NLM system has much in common with the many other node-link approaches (e.g., concept mapping and mind mapping). However, it can be distinguished by its use of the following combination of features: coded links (i.e., letters serving as labels to distinguish types of relationships), the "Gestalt" spatial organizational features of symmetry, similarity, proximity, closures, continuation and common boundary, schematic structures such as hierarchies, chains/loops, clusters, and point-to-point comparisons, and the different types of mapping reflected by information,

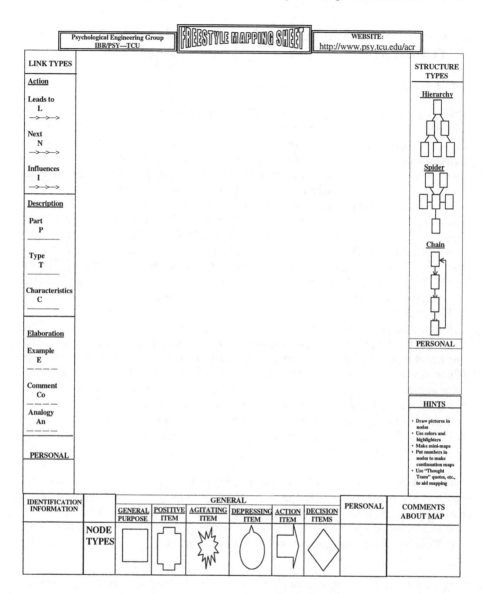

Fig. 4. Freestyle Mapping Format Sheet

guide, and freestyle approaches. Another point of distinction is that the TCU-NLM has been broadly applied to education and to problem solving in both counseling and business. This breadth of application has created positive synergies between domains. The next section will briefly describe some of the general findings from these applications.

3 General Empirical Findings from the Applications of TCU-NLM

3.1 Educational Studies of TCU-NLM

Freestyle mapping. Early work on TCU-NLM involved training college students to use mapping as a note taking method and to compare the use of this technique to typical study approaches (e.g., outlining). In most cases, students were given 2-3 hours of training and practice on making freestyle maps, then a randomly selected subset of them were asked to use this approach in studying text material for approximately one hour. The other students were asked to use their normal study methods. Delayed free recall tests were used to assess performance. Generally, college students using freestyle mapping performed at significantly higher levels than those using their own approaches (Long, 1976; Holley, Dansereau, McDonald, Garland & Collins, 1979; Dansereau, Collins, McDonald, Holley, Garland, Diekhoff & Evans, 1979; Dansereau, McDonald, Collins, Garland, Holley, Diekhoff & Evans, 1979; Dansereau & Holley, 1982). The results and implications of these early studies have been reviewed by Holley and Dansereau (1984) and Lambiotte, Dansereau, Cross, and Reynolds (1989).

Freestyle mapping has also been successfully used as an alternative to traditional writing assignments in undergraduate courses (Czuchry & Dansereau, 1996). Furthermore, it has been shown that exposure to freestyle mapping training itself is sufficient to promote better text learning even when the technique is not explicitly used (Chmielewski & Dansereau, 1998). Taken together these findings suggest that freestyle mapping can serve as an effective note taking technique for learners. However, based on our training experiences we find that many students claim that freestyle mapping is too effortful to be used on a regular basis. Consequently, attention has also been focused on the teaching side of the educational coin with the exploration of information maps.

Information mapping. In this research, experts map text material and the performance of students receiving these maps are compared with that of students receiving the text from which the maps were derived. On some occasions this process has been reversed by having experts make maps of their knowledge and then produce text from the maps for comparison purposes. In summary, the results using this paradigm are as follows:

- Students recall more main ideas from an information map than from corresponding text although there are no significant differences on the recall of details (Hall, Dansereau & Skaggs, 1992; Rewey, Dansereau, Skaggs, Hall & Pitre, 1989; Rewey, Dansereau & Peel, 1991).
- Students with low verbal ability or low prior knowledge often benefit the most from information maps (Lambiotte & Dansereau, 1992; Lambiotte, Skaggs & Dansereau, 1993; O'Donnell & Dansereau, 1992; O'Donnell, Dansereau, Hall, Skaggs, Hythecker, Peel & Rewey, 1990; Rewey et al., 1989; Patterson, Dansereau & Wiegmann, 1993).
- Information maps have a positive impact on cooperative learning activities (Patterson, Dansereau & Newbern, 1992; Patterson et al., 1993; Rewey et al., 1989).

Guide mapping. We have also developed and examined the effects of a set of academic guide maps that represent topics occurring in most of the sciences (Motes, Bahr, Atha-Weldon & Dansereau, 2003). These maps represent the common features associated with: experiments, processes, theories, systems, concepts, and procedures. For example, Fig. 3 is a guide map for the common features of a theory. These types of guide maps help provide students with a more integrative view of complementary disciplines.

3.2 Counseling Studies of TCU-NLM

Freestyle mapping. In one set of studies randomly selected sets of counselors at methadone maintenance treatment agencies were trained in using freestyle mapping with their clients to help them understand and solve their problems by spatially laying out their ideas, feelings, and activities. Clients receiving freestyle mapping counseling were compared to those receiving traditional counseling. Freestyle mapping led to greater client commitment to treatment (as measured by session attendance), to more positive counselor perceptions of the client, and to fewer positive opiate and cocaine urinalysis results during the first 3 months of treatment (Dansereau, Joe & Simpson, 1993, 1995), as well as during later treatment stages (Czuchry, Dansereau, Dees & Simpson, 1995; Dees, Dansereau & Simpson, 1997; Joe, Dansereau & Simpson, 1994). Freestyle mapping is more effective for African Americans and Mexican Americans than for Caucasians (Dansereau, Joe, Dees & Simpson, 1996) and for more difficult clients, such as multiple drug users and those with attentional problems (Czuchry et al., 1995; Dansereau et al., 1995; Joe et al., 1994). Freestyle mapping also is particularly effective for group counseling (Dansereau, Dees, Greener & Simpson, 1995; Knight, Dansereau, Joe & Simpson, 1994).

The use of freestyle mapping in substance abuse treatment centers in the criminal justice system has also been explored. Participants receiving freestyle mapping counseling rated their counselors, group counseling sessions, their fellow residents and their own treatment progress better than those receiving standard counseling (Czuchry, Dansereau, Sia & Simpson, 1998; Czuchry & Dansereau, 1999; Pitre, Dansereau & Simpson, 1997; Pitre, Dansereau, Newbern & Simpson, 1997; Czuchry & Dansereau, 2000; Blankenship, Dansereau & Simpson, 1999). Further, it appears to be especially beneficial for those residents with co-occurring psychological problems (Czuchry & Dansereau, 1996).

Information mapping. Information maps have been used by counselors to effectively communicate information on relapse prevention (Knight, Simpson & Dansereau, 1994) and HIV/AIDS (Bartholomew & Simpson, 1994), improving clients' recall of these materials.

Guide mapping. Approximately 60 guide maps have been created to help clients deal with treatment-related issues (Dees & Dansereau, 2000) see Fig. 2 for an example of a planning guide map. These maps have been shown to have positive impacts on treatment outcomes when cooperatively completed by the client and counselor (Newbern, Dansereau, Czuchry & Simpson, in press; (Czuchry, Dansereau, Newbern & Simpson, 2004).

3.3 Other Applications

TCU-NLM has been used in consulting with businesses (Newbern & Dansereau, 1995) and in creating a "self-exploration" web site (Thinkerer.org).

3.4 Conclusions

Research on TCU-NLM has shown it to be useful in both information and knowledge visualization within education and counseling. The next step is to take a more detailed look at what has been learned about node-link mapping over the course of these studies.

4 TCU-NML Principles

Fig. 5 contains an overview of the sets of principles (goal specification, organizational, infrastructure, and processing) derived from our work with TCU-NLM. Each set will be described separately.

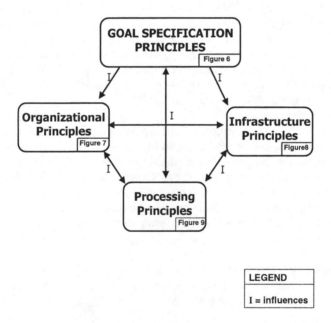

Fig. 5. TCU-NLM Principles

4.1 Goal Specification

Three goals for using node-link mapping (see Fig. 6) have been examined. These include increasing awareness and ability to resolve issues and problems (e.g., within counseling sessions), enhancing the learning of new material, and improving access to information for question answering and direction. Awareness and issue resolution can be aided by knowledge visualization techniques such as freestyle mapping and/or by hybrid visualization techniques that combine knowledge and information such as guide mapping. Learning can be aided by knowledge visualization and hybrid visualization, for example, when the learner creates or fills out a map to reflect understanding of the to be learned material. Learning can also be facilitated by information visualization, for example, when the topic is presented in the form of an information map. Finally, reference and prescription can be enhanced by information and hybrid visualization. In summary, goal specification (awareness, learning, reference) leads to particular node-link mapping options.

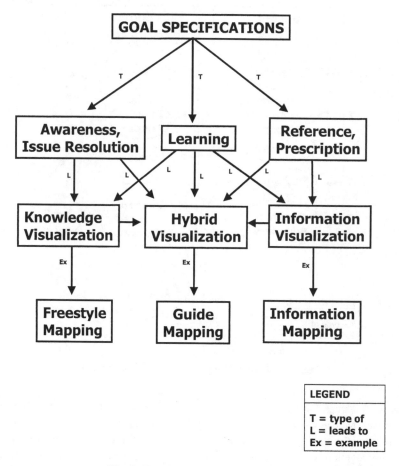

Fig. 6. Goal Specification Principles

4.2 Organizational Principles

Fig. 7 illustrates three classes of NLM organizational principles; "Gestalt" features, amount of material per map, and content-specific structures. The use of these features to create an effective spatial layout is important whether the map is created by an expert, as in the case of information and guide maps, or created by a user/learner in the case of freestyle maps.

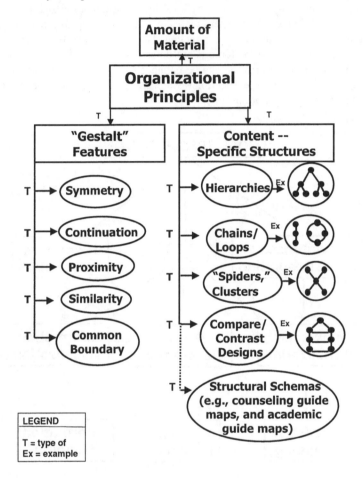

Fig. 7. Node-Link Mapping Organizational Principles

Gestalt features. With regard to research on "Gestalt" features, Wiegmann, Dansereau, McCagg, Rewey and Pitre (1992) constructed two isomorphic maps, (i.e., informationally identical) one followed Gestalt principles and the other was presented in a homogeneous "web" format. The spatial layout of the Gestalt map was symmetrical, related objects were grouped together, similar objects were enclosed in the same node shapes, and sequences of thought and action were visually continuous.

Students who learned from the Gestalt map outperformed those who learned from the web map. These results are consistent with those found by Wallace, West, Ware and Dansereau (1998). In this experiment, three presentation formats were contrasted: text, enhanced map, and unenhanced map. The enhanced map was designed to emphasize the Gestalt principle of similarity (by using shape and color) and proximity (by using spatial grouping). Results show a strong effect for the enhanced map, supporting the results of Wiegmann et al. (1992), who recommended text maps be designed according to Gestalt principles whenever possible (also see Chmielewski, Dansereau & Moreland, 1998).

Amount of material per map. How many nodes and links should appear in a single display? The ability to create cross-referenced sub-maps using hypertext methods in a computer environment or stacking in paper format (Fig. 1-3 are an example), gives the map maker some control over the breadth and depth of the topic presentation and thus some control over the amount of material per display. Wiegmann et al. (1992) ran an experiment in which they compared students who learned from a single whole map on a large sheet of paper (approximately 30 interconnected nodes) with students learning the same material via a series of 5 stacked maps averaging about 6 nodes per map. Because individual differences (IDs) in processing preferences and/or ability often provide clues as to how maps are best structured, Wiegmann et al. (1992) included selected ID variables. Interestingly, performance on the content presented in the two map formats depended on whether the student was field independent (able to disembed simple figures from complex ones) or field dependent (not as easily able to disembed figures from a complex field). Field dependent students did better when they studied the whole map, while field independent students benefited from the stacked maps. In this case, the preferred amount of material per display interacted with the students' individual differences. One possibility for map designers is to offer optional presentation formats, and allow learners to choose which to use.

Content-specific structures. Fig. 7 presents a number of content-specific structures that can be used across domains to provide a common spatial "signature" for particular types of information/knowledge. Learners and users can then recognize these "signatures" and tailor their processing accordingly. Although not conclusive, research by O'Donnell (1994) suggests that hierarchies and chains should be oriented vertically rather than horizontally, especially for those with low verbal ability. Compare/contrast designs seem to work well when oriented vertically with explicit comparison links between relevant nodes (Hall et al., 1992). Guide maps based on derived structural schemas that reflect the common elements across a collection of topics (e.g., the planning map, Fig. 2 and the theory map, Fig. 3) are also effective when organized vertically (Motes et al., 2003).

One of the main lessons learned from work with these content-specific structures is that it is important to carefully match the topic domain to the structure. For example, procedures and processes are typically best represented by chains and loops; trying to force them into hierarchical structures is usually ill-advised. Likewise, forcing a topic hierarchy into a cluster formation will usually produce a less effective display.

4.3 Node-Link Infrastructure Principles

Fig. 8 presents the basic building blocks of NLM: links and nodes.

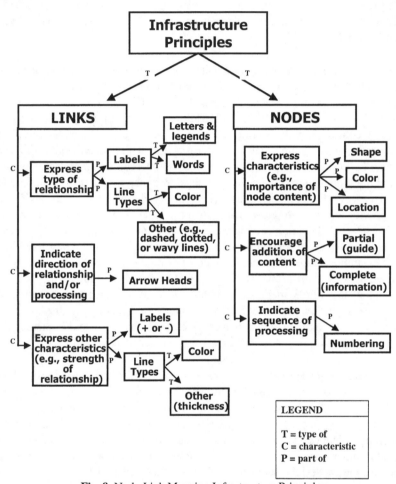

Fig. 8. Node-Link Mapping Infrastructure Principles

Links. The lines connecting the material contained in nodes can express the nature, strength, and direction of interrelationships using color, line style, arrowheads, and labels. The main problems that emerge with designing links are over or under specification of the relationships. Using too much coding to create a more detailed description of the relationships may overwhelm the learner/user with visual complexity, may mask the information communicated by the spatial organization, and may require the learner to expend substantial effort translating the coding. On the other hand, under specification by using plain, homogeneous lines to represent relationships may create confusion and misinterpretation. An appropriate degree of specification is influenced by the complexity of the topic, prior content and mapping knowledge of the learner/user, and the purpose of the display. For example, if the goal of the display is reference or the expressions of personal knowledge, the level of specification can typically be low. However, if the goal is the learning of complex information, the level of link specifications should be relatively higher. In exploring this issue, Wiegmann et al. (1992) did a study on the impact of embellished vs. unembellished links. Students either received maps with links embellished by labels, arrowheads, and configural information (i.e., barbed vs. solid lines) or they received maps with unembellished straight lines. Students with low verbal ability (as measured by a vocabulary test) did better when their maps had plain lines whereas those students with higher verbal ability did better with maps containing embellished links). Apparently, the high verbal ability students were able to make use of the additional coding, while the low verbals were disrupted by it. Clearly the design of links remains very much an art rather than a science. The map creator must balance the importance of relationship specification with the need for visual clarity and processing simplicity.

Nodes. Although there are some common conventions for enclosing information/ knowledge (e.g., a diamond shaped boundary for enclosing decision information), there is little other information to guide the map designer. However, it should be noted that node features such as color and shape can be used to implement the Gestalt principle of similarity (i.e. putting similar material in similar looking nodes and non-similar material in non-similar nodes). As mentioned earlier, the Wallace et al. (1998) study supports this approach to designing nodes. However, as with links, the over or under use of node characteristics to express knowledge/information can result in display processing problems. Further, link and node specification can work synergistically or can further increase confusion and misinterpretation.

4.4 Processing Principles

Fig. 9 illustrates the two major categories of node-link map processing: production and use.

Production. Based on the developer's level of knowledge about the topic, NLMs can be produced deductively (top-down), inductively (bottom-up), or through some combination of the two. Top-down, deductive development is guided by the organization of the topic domain and usually requires the selection of one or more of the content-specific spatial structures (e.g., hierarchy, see Fig. 7). The macro-level information is placed in these structures (structures are of course modified as needed to accommodate the content). Micro-level (detailed) information is then added to the macro nodes to "flesh out" the topic domain. This approach, which typically requires substantial knowledge of the topic, usually produces a well-organized map that needs little revision.

The bottom-up, inductive approach typically starts with a few nodes as "seed" ideas; the developer then links related ideas to these "seeds" and slowly grows a structure in much the same way as a crystal forms. The resulting structure is usually an undifferentiated web that may need re-structuring according to the spatial organization principles described earlier (see Fig. 7) in order to make it useful as a communication device. Bottom-up maps are particularly valuable for exploring new ideas, and in "brainstorming" activities. The use of note cards as portable nodes that can be re-arranged enhance these processes.

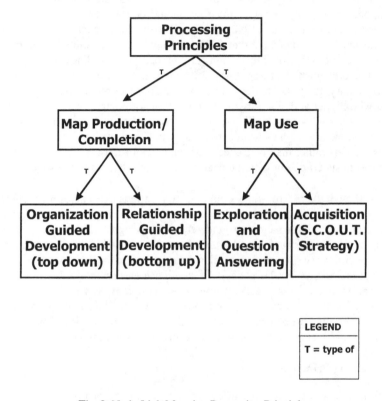

Fig. 9. Node-Link Mapping Processing Principles

Use. A certain degree of NLM literacy is required for individuals to effectively use a map for reference or learning. In essence, it is necessary for learners and users to understand how to read a map, that is, to be able to convert the node-link-node structures into standard verbal sentences. This, of course, requires an understanding of the link and node codes used by the map developer. Legends placed on the maps that define the coding are particularly helpful in this regard. Users must also be able to coherently sequence their movement through the map. This can be aided by the inclusions of numbers in the nodes that illustrate a potential sequence for the map reader to follow. The spatial organization of the map provides additional information to the user. Meta knowledge about the domain such as areas of high complexity and similarity are often communicated by Gestalt features (e.g., maps depicting major divisions of the nervous system, such as the sympathetic and parasympathetic divisions, could make use of proximity and symmetry to highlight similarities and differences between the two). The users can be trained to tailor their processing based on this meta knowledge.

To aid in the processing of maps, a simple strategy labelled by the acronym SCOUT has been developed (Dansereau, 1995). This strategy contains the following steps:

- Survey the map identifying its general organization, main sub-sections, familiar information, and areas of complexity.
- Chart an approach to studying the map by dividing the map into sections or regions using a pencil.
- Operate on the map by translating sections into sentences and/or images.
- Unify related information by marking ideas that should be put together.
- Transform the map into your own words and images. In effect, summarize the content.

With regard to the elements of this strategy, we have found that summarization (Hall, Saling & Cara, 1999; Rewey et al., 1991) and annotation (Moreland, Dansereau & Chmielewski, 1997) are effective map learning techniques. Although SCOUT is primarily a learning strategy, the first step could be used as a prelude to using the map as a reference (question answering) tool.

5   Node-Link Mapping Strengths, Limitations, and Enhancements

This section serves as a summary and extension of what has been presented to this point.

5.1   Node-Link Infrastructure

In Table 1 are the strengths, limitations, and enhancements related to the node-link infrastructure associated with map presentations. NLMs have fewer words than typical text and a consistent, universal node-link-node (simple active declarative) grammar. These characteristics force map creators to be more succinct and organized than traditional writers. On the user side, the lack of word "clutter" and the simple grammar make NLMs particularly effective with low verbal individuals who struggle with traditional language presentations. Because the node-link grammar is interpretable by most cultures, it can serve as a useful bridge between languages. The nodes can be split and different language versions of the content can be inserted. For example, Bahr and Dansereau (2001) found that split node maps containing German and English versions of the information in each node led to superior vocabulary learning than traditional methods. Although untested, expert split node maps could be useful adjuncts in international meetings as a way of providing a shared representation.

Although generally positive, the NL structure may be problematic in two ways: the lack of words may reduce understanding of complex and/or ambiguous material and the consistent node-link-node grammar may negatively affect motivation and interest due to its lack of variety. In addition, as mentioned earlier, when the complexity of node-link coding is increased via labels, arrowheads, line styles, and shapes in order to improve the communication of topic nuances, negative effects on spatial organization may result.

Table 1. Node-Link Mapping Infrastructure: Strengths, Limitations, and Enhancements

NODE LINK INFRASTRUCTURE

	Reduces Word Clutter	Uses Simple Universal Grammar
STRENGTHS	• Force map creators to be succinct and organized • Helpful for people with lower verbal ability	• Valuable for cross-cultural communication and language learning (split nodes containing two or more languages)
LIMITATIONS	• Contain insufficient detail and richness for expressing complex and ambiguous relationships	• Lack of variety may reduce interest and motivation
ENHANCEMENTS	• Provide auditory and pictorial supplements (e.g., "button on" links) • Use maps for higher descriptive levels (macrostructure) and text, pictures, etc. for microstructure	

In order to overcome these problems, NLMs can be enhanced by providing auditory supplements (e.g., via CD) that talk through the map, providing additional topic information as needed. In our experiences maps and spoken lectures can be synergistic, with maps aiding the understanding of the lecture, and the lecture facilitating map interest and interpretation. Combining written topic descriptions with maps can create a similar synergy, but may be less desirable due to the competition for visual resources (e.g., Skaggs, 1988). In both cases using maps for higher descriptive levels macrostructure) and written or spoken text for details (microstructure) is likely to maximize effectiveness (Rewey et al., 1989, studies of map learning support this notion).

In computer environments, more specific map supplementation can be provided. For example, "button on" links can be used to provide quick access to a more detailed auditory or written description of the relationships being illustrated. Similar approaches can also be used to amplify node information, and the content of specific map regions.

In general, experience suggests that there are very few instances where node-link maps can serve as "stand alones." Because of the limitations of a simple node-link infrastructure, typically maps need to be combined with other forms of communication in order to maximize their usefulness.

5.2 Spatial Organization

Table 2 illustrates the strengths, limitations, and enhancements associated with NLM spatial characteristics. The use of space to express relationships of similarity, etc. activates the user's non-verbal processes. Based on Baddeley's (1986) memory model, this inclusion of visual and spatial processing increases working memory capacity, thereby making learning and other cognitive activities more efficient. The use of space also provides landmarks and configurations that are visible from a distance which allow people to easily share the map during collaborative activities. On the other hand, the use of space to simultaneously display large amounts of information can cause what we have termed "map shock," a negative emotional and motivational reaction to visual complexity. In these cases, the topic material appears overwhelming to the user which may cause procrastination, false starts, and subsequent rejection of map displays. In addition, stimulation of visual and spatial processes by map displays may interfere with the imagery required to create mental models of the information being presented. This may be ameliorated by promoting strategies for actively transforming maps into language, pictures, and actions.

Table 2. Node-Link Mapping Spatial Organization: Strengths, Limitations, and Enhancements

SPATIAL ORGANIZATION

	Uses Space to Express Relationships	Illustrates Structure of Topic Domain	Provides Numerous Processing Domains
STRENGETHS	• Expands capacities by encouraging visual processing • Is easily referenced thereby aiding collaborative processing	• Shows higher order relations • Shows knowledge gaps and other meta knowledge information • Aids memory and retrieval	• Allows user to engage in self guided exploration
LIMITATIONS	• May cause "Map Shock," an adverse negative reaction to the visual complexity • May impede mental (situational/model) development by overloading visual channel	• May restrict alternative views of the topic domain • May conflict with prior knowledge of the topic	• Creates confusion and backtracking
ENHANCEMENTS	• Promote strategies for actively transforming maps into language, pictures, and actions	• Create alternative maps to express same content	• Supplement with auditory guided tour • Provide route guidance • Show map development • Provide processing training

The spatial organization can also be used to illustrate the structure and complexity of the topic domain (e.g., hierarchical). This information can be used to guide the user's processing, including the identification of gaps and inconsistencies, and it can enhance memory and retrieval (Newbern, Dansereau & Patteson, 1997). On the other hand, it may restrict alternative views of the domain and conflict with prior knowledge (Rewey et al., 1991). This may require the map developer to create alternative maps to express the same content and to develop "fill-in-the-blank" guide maps that allow learners and users to integrate their prior knowledge with the new material.

The two dimensional organization of maps provides numerous potential processing routes through the topic domain. Map readers are not bound to the strict sequencing inherent in most text; they are free to explore the material in ways that suit their processing styles, interests, and purposes. Although this flexibility can be extremely valuable, it can also cause backtracking and confusion. To alleviate these problems, the map developer can provide an auditory-guided tour, route guidance through the use of numbers placed in nodes to indicate reading sequence, and in the case of computer displays, a sequential presentation of the map components (Blankenship & Dansereau, 2000), found this form of animation very helpful in aiding map processing. However, this route assistance should be optional so that the reader might at any point initiate their own processing pattern.

6 Conclusions and Implications

Exploration with TCU-NLM has shown that information, guide, and freestyle mapping can be useful in improving outcomes in education and counseling, and that they have potential for enhancing business activities such as group meetings. In conducting this research four sets of principles important to map development and use have been identified: goal specification, spatial organization, node-link infrastructure, and processing. Exploration of these principles have led to a number of design notions, a few of which are re-iterated here:

- Node-link visualizations can enhance: (1) awareness and self-exploration, (2) learning, and (3) referencing and prescription/instruction. The specification of these goals lead to the use of different types of mapping. At a broader level, knowledge visualization is reflected in the first two goals and information visualization in the last two. It should be noted that both forms of visualization are relevant for learning activities. From this point of view, node-link mapping provides a general purpose system for both types of visualization when the communication of relationships (links) between ideas, actions, or objects is of paramount importance.
- Gestalt features and content-specific structures should be matched to topic domain characteristics and used to spatially organize the map. In general vertical organization is preferred over horizontal.
- The amount of coding used in presenting nodes and links needs to be minimal to reduce visual clutter, but sufficient to meet the purpose of the display.
- At least two hours of training and experience on developing and using TCU-NLM is needed for individuals to be competent across a variety of mapping episodes.
- NLMs are particularly useful for individuals with low verbal ability and/or prior knowledge. They are also useful as communication aids in group collaborations.
- NLMs can use a split node approach to present information in multiple languages for improving cross-cultural interactions and language learning.
- NLMs typically need to be combined with oral or written language-based presentations in order to capitalize on synergies and compensate for weaknesses.
- Alternate maps of the same domain should be provided to allow users to gain alternative perspectives and/or choose a preferred format.

The major shortcoming of this discussion of the TCU-NLM is the fact that it focuses on only one thread in the rich history of node-link displays. The hope has been to lay out this thread in anticipation of subsequently weaving it together with those of other researchers and developers. The ultimate goal is to create a set of operating and design principles that can inform a wide variety of knowledge and information visualization techniques.

References

Baddeley, A. (1986). *Working memory*. Oxford, UK: Clarendon Press.

Bahr, G. S., & Dansereau, D. F. (2001). Bilingual knowledge maps (BiK-Maps) in second language vocabulary learning. *Journal of Experimental Education, 70*(1), 5-24.

Bartholomew, N., & Simpson, D. D. (1994). *Approaches to HIV/AIDS education in drug treatment*. Bloomington, IL: Lighthouse Institute Publishing.

Blankenship, J., & Dansereau, D. F. (2000). The effect of animated node-link displays on information recall and session evaluation. *Journal of Experimental Education, 68*(4), 293-308.

Blankenship, J., Dansereau, D. F., & Simpson, D. D. (1999). Cognitive enhancements of readiness for corrections-based treatment for drug abuse. *The Prison Journal, 79*(4), 431-445.

Buzan, T. (1974). *Using both sides of the brain*. New York: Dutton

Chmielewski, T. L., & Dansereau, D. F. (1998). Enhancing the recall of text: Knowledge mapping training promotes implicit transfer. *Journal of Educational Psychology, 29*(3), 407-413.

Chmielewski, T. L., Dansereau, D. F., & Moreland, J. L. (1998). Using common region in node-link displays: The role of field dependence/independence. *Journal of Experimental Education, 66*(3), 197-207.

Czuchry, M., & Dansereau, D. F. (1996). Node-link mapping as an alternative to traditional writing assignments in undergraduate psychology courses. *Teaching of Psychology, 23*(2), 91-96.

Czuchry, M., & Dansereau, D. F. (1999). Node-link mapping and psychological problems: Perceptions of a residential drug abuse treatment program for probationers. *Journal of Substance Abuse Treatment, 17*(4), 321-329.

Czuchry, M., & Dansereau, D. F. (2000). Drug abuse treatment in criminal justice settings: Enhancing community engagement and helpfulness. *American Journal of Drug and Alcohol Abuse, 26*(4), 537-552.

Czuchry, M., Dansereau, D. F., Dees, S. M., & Simpson, D. D. (1995). The use of node-link mapping in drug abuse counseling: The role of attentional factors. *Journal of Psychoactive Drugs, 27*(2), 161-166.

Czuchry, M., Dansereau, D. F., Newbern, D., & Simpson, D. D. (2004). *Using free and guided mapping to reduce heroin use*. Manuscript in preparation.

Czuchry, M., Dansereau, D. F., Sia, T. L., & Simpson, D. D. (1998). Using peer, self, and counselor ratings to evaluate treatment process. *Journal of Psychoactive Drugs, 30*(1), 81-87.

Dansereau, D. F. (1995). Derived structural schemas and the transfer of knowledge. In A. McKeough, J. Lupart, & A. Marini (Eds.), *Teaching for transfer: Fostering generalization in learning* (pp. 93-121). Hillsdale, NJ: Lawrence Erlbaum Associates, Inc.

Dansereau, D. F., & Dees, S. M. (2002). Mapping Training: The transfer of a cognitive technology for improving counseling. *Journal of Substance Abuse Treatment, 22*(4), 219-230.

Dansereau, D. F., & Holley, C. D. (1982). Development and evaluation of a text mapping strategy. In A. Flammer, & W. Kintsch, (Eds.), *Discourse processing* (pp. 536-554). Amsterdam: North-Holland Publishing Co.

Dansereau, D. F., Collins, K. W., McDonald, B. A., Holley, C. D., Garland, J., Diekhoff, G., & Evans, S. H. (1979). Development and evaluation of a learning strategy training program. *Journal of Educational Psychology, 71*(1), 64-73.

Dansereau, D. F., Dees, S. M., Greener, J. M., & Simpson, D. D. (1995). Node-link mapping and the evaluation of drug abuse counseling sessions. *Psychology of Addictive Behaviors, 9*(3), 195-203.

Dansereau, D. F., Joe, G. W., & Simpson, D. D. (1993). Node-link mapping: A visual representation strategy for enhancing drug abuse counseling. *Journal of Counseling Psychology,*
40(4), 385-395.

Dansereau, D. F., Joe, G. W., & Simpson, D. D. (1995). Attentional difficulties and the effectiveness of a visual representation strategy for counseling drug-addicted clients. *International Journal of the Addictions, 30*(4), 371-386.

Dansereau, D. F., Joe, G. W., Dees, S. M., & Simpson, D. D. (1996). Ethnicity and the effects
of mapping-enhanced drug abuse counseling. *Addictive Behaviors, 21*(3), 363-376.

Dansereau, D. F., McDonald, B. A., Collins, K. W., Garland, J., Holley, C. D., Diekhoff, G. M.,
& Evans, S. H. (1979). Evaluation of a learning strategy system. In H. F. O'Neil, Jr., & C.
D. Spielberger (Eds.), *Cognitive and affective learning strategies* (pp. 3-43). New York:
Academic Press.

Dees, S. M., & Dansereau, D. F. (2000). *TCU guide maps: A resource for counselors.* Lighthouse Institute Publishing: Bloomington, IL.

Dees, S. M., Dansereau, D. F., & Simpson, D. D. (1997). Mapping-enhanced drug abuse counseling: Urinalysis results in the first year of methadone treatment. *Journal of Substance Abuse Treatment, 14*(1), 45-54.

Hall, R. H., Dansereau, D. F., & Skaggs, L. P. (1992). Knowledge maps and the presentation of
related information domains. *Journal of Experimental Education, 61*(1), 5-18.

Hall, R. H., Saling, M. A., & Cara, B. (1999). The effects of graphical postorganization strategies on learning from knowledge maps. *Journal of Experimental Education, 67*, 101-112.

Holley, C. D., & Dansereau, D. F. (Eds.). (1984). *Spatial learning strategies: Techniques, applications, and related issues.* New York: Academic Press.

Holley, C. D., Dansereau, D. F., McDonald, B. A., Garland, J. C., & Collins, K. W. (1979).
Evaluation of a hierarchical mapping technique as an aid to prose processing. *Contemporary
Educational Psychology, 4*, 227-237.

Joe, G. W., Dansereau, D. F., & Simpson, D. D. (1994). Node-link mapping for counseling cocaine users in methadone treatment. *Journal of Substance Abuse, 6*, 393-406.

Knight, D. K., Dansereau, D. F., Joe, G. W., & Simpson, D. D. (1994). The role of node-link
mapping in individual and group counseling. *The American Journal of Drug and Alcohol
Abuse, 20*, 517-527.

Knight, K., Simpson, D. D., & Dansereau, D. F. (1994). Knowledge mapping: A psychoeduca-
tional tool in drug abuse relapse prevention training for probationers. *Journal of Offender
Rehabilitation, 20*(3/4), 187-205.

Lambiotte, J. G., & Dansereau, D. F. (1992). Effects of knowledge maps and prior knowledge
on recall of science lecture content. *Journal of Experimental Education, 60*(3), 189-201.

Lambiotte, J. G., Dansereau, D. F., Cross, D. R., & Reynolds, S. (1989). Multirelational semantic maps. *Educational Psychology Review, 1*(4), 331-367.

Lambiotte, J. G., Skaggs, L. P., & Dansereau, D. F. (1993). Learning from lectures: Effects of
knowledge maps and cooperative review strategies. *Applied Cognitive Psychology, 7*, 483-
497.

Long, G. L. (1976). The development and assessment of a cognitive process based learning
strategy training program for enhancing prose comprehension and retention (Doctoral dissertation, Texas Christian University, 1976). *Dissertation Abstracts International 38*, 2B.
(University Microfilms No. 77-44, 286).

Moreland, J. L., Dansereau, D. F., & Chmielewski, T. L. (1997). Recall of descriptive information: The role of presentation format, annotation strategy, and individual differences. *Contemporary Educational Psychology, 22*, 521-533.

Motes, M. A., Bahr, S. G., Atha-Weldon, C., & Dansereau, D. F. (2003). Academic guide maps for learning psychology. *Teaching of Psychology, 30*(3), 240-242.

Newbern, D., & Dansereau, D. F. (1995). Knowledge maps for knowledge management. In K. Wiig (Ed.), *Knowledge management methods* (pp. 157-180). Arlington, TX: Schema Press.

Newbern, D., Dansereau, D. F., & Patterson, M. E. (1997). Spatial-semantic display processing: The role of spatial structure on recall. *Contemporary Educational Psychology, 22*, 319-337.

Newbern, D., Dansereau, D. F., Czuchry, M., & Simpson, D. D. (in press). Node-link mapping in individual counseling: Effects on clients with ADHD-related behaviors. *Journal of Psychoactive Drugs*.

Novak, J. (1980). Learning theory applied to the biology classroom. *The American Biology Teacher, 42*, 280-285.

O'Donnell, A. M. (1994). Learning from knowledge maps: The effects of map orientation. *Contemporary Educational Psychology, 19*, 33-44.

O'Donnell, A. M., Dansereau, D. F., Hall, R. H., Skaggs, L. P., Hythecker, V. I., Peel, J. L., & Rewey, K. L. (1990). Learning concrete procedures: The effects of processing strategies and cooperative learning. *Journal of Educational Psychology, 82*(1), 171-177.

O'Donnell, A.M., & Dansereau, D. F. (1992). Scripted cooperation in student dyads: A method for analyzing and enhancing academic learning and performance. In R. Hertz-Lazarowitz, & N. Miller (Eds.), *Interaction in cooperative groups: The theoretical anatomy of group learning* (pp. 120-141). Cambridge, MA: Cambridge University Press.

Patterson, M. E., Dansereau, D. F., & Newbern, D. (1992). Effects of communication aids and strategies on cooperative teaching. *Journal of Educational Psychology, 84*(4), 453-461.

Patterson, M. E., Dansereau, D. F., & Wiegmann, D. A. (1993). Receiving information during a cooperative episode: Effects of communication aids and verbal ability. *Learning and Individual Differences, 5*, 1-11.

Pitre, U., Dansereau, D. F., & Simpson, D. D. (1997). The role of node-link maps in enhancing counseling efficiency. *Journal of Addictive Diseases, 16*(3), 39-49.

Pitre, U., Dansereau, D. F., Newbern, D., & Simpson, D. D. (1998). Residential drug-abuse treatment for probationers: Use of node-link mapping to enhance participation and progress. *Journal of Substance Abuse Treatment, 15*(6), 535-543.

Rewey, K. L., Dansereau, D. F., & Peel, J. L. (1991). Knowledge maps and information processing strategies. *Contemporary Educational Psychology, 16*, 203-214.

Rewey, K. L., Dansereau, D. F., Skaggs, L. P., Hall, R. H., & Pitre, U. (1989). Effects of scripted cooperation and knowledge maps on the processing of technical material. *Journal of Educational Psychology, 81*(4), 604-609.

Skaggs, L. P. (1988). *The effects of knowledge maps and pictures on the acquisition of scientific information*. Unpublished doctoral dissertation, Texas Christian University, Fort Worth, Texas.

Wallace, D. S., West, S. W. C., Ware, A., & Dansereau, D. F. (1998). The effect of knowledge maps that incorporate gestalt principles on learning. *Journal of Experimental Education, 67*(1), 5-16.

Wiegmann, D. A., Dansereau, D. F., McCagg, E. C., Rewey, K. L., & Pitre, U. (1992). Effects of knowledge map characteristics on information processing. *Contemporary Educational Psychology, 17*, 136-155.

Tools for Representing Problems and the Knowledge Required to Solve Them

David H. Jonassen

University of Missouri-Columbia, School of Information Science
and Learning Technologies,
221C Townsend Hall, Missouri, USA
Jonassen@missouri.edu

Abstract. In this chapter, I have shown that problem solving depend on how the
problem is represented to the learners. That representation affects, to some degree, they ways that problem solvers represent problem mentally. A more effi-
cacious way of affecting those internal mental representation is to provide students with a variety of knowledge representation tools, such as concept maps,
expert systems, and systems dynamics tools, to represent the problem space,
that is, their mental representation of the problem and the domain knowledge
required to solve it.

1 Introduction

Problem solving is at the heart of practice in the everyday and professional contexts.
Professionals are hired and retained in most contexts in order to solve problems. In
our everyday lives, we regularly solve problems. What is distinctive about all of these
problems is that they are ill-structured. That is, the problems that we solve in everyday and professional contexts some problem elements are unknown; have unclear
goals; possess multiple solutions, solution paths, or no solutions at all; possess multiple criteria for evaluating solutions, have no general rules or principles for applying to
most cases; and often require people to make judgments about the problem and de-
fend them (Jonassen, 1997). In formal educational contexts, however, students almost
invariably solve well-structured problems that require the application of a finite number of concepts, rules, and principles; possess a well-defined initial state, a known
goal state, and constrained set of logical operators; present all elements of the problem to the learners.

Researchers have long assumed that learning to solve well-structured problems
transfers positively to learning to solve ill-structured problems. Although information
processing theories believed that "in general, the processes used to solve ill-structured
problems are the same as those used to solve well structured problems" (Simon, 1978,
p. 287), more recent research in situated and everyday problem solving makes clear
distinctions between thinking required to solve convergent problems and everyday
problems. Dunkle, Schraw, and Bendixen (1995) concluded that performance in solving well-defined problems is independent of performance on ill-defined tasks, with
ill-defined problems engaging a different set of epistemic beliefs. Hong, Jonassen,
and McGee (2003) found that solving ill-structured problems in a simulation called on

S.-O. Tergan and T. Keller (Eds.): Knowledge and Information Visualization, LNCS 3426, pp. 82–94, 2005.

different skills than well-structured problems, including metacognition and argumentation. Other research has shown that communication patterns in teams differed when solving well-structured and ill-structured problems (Cho & Jonassen, 2002; Jonassen and Kwon, 2001). Clearly more research is needed to substantiate these findings, yet it is reasonable to conclude that well-structured and ill-structured problem solving engage different cognitive skills.

Another problem with school-based problem solving is that a large number of studies have documented learners' inability to transfer problem-solving skills, even for well-structured problems. Numerous studies have shown that students are unable to solve structurally identical problems because learners focus on surface features of the problems rather than developing adequate conceptual understanding of the problem domain (Gick & Holyoak, 1980, 1983; Reed, 1987). Even instructional programs in problem solving and critical thinking have failed to show evidence of transfer (Chipman, Segal & Glaser, 1985; Nickerson, Perkins & Smith, 1985). Why are students unable to transfer skills in problem solving?

The inability of students to transfer well-structured problem-solving skills to novel problems or to ill-structured problems results from a number of conditions. The major claim of this chapter is that problem solving fails because in most educational contexts because learners inadequately represent the knowledge that is required to solve the problems. Simon (1981, p. 303), the undisputed father of problem-solving research, claimed that "solving a problem simply means representing it so as to make the solution transparent." That is, problem representation is central to problem solving. Representing the problem in a coherent way is key to solving problems. Why is problem representation so important?

Experts are better problem solvers than novices for a number of reasons. The most important reason is that they construct richer, more integrated mental representations of problems than do novices (Chi, Feltovich & Glaser, 1981; Chi & Bassock, 1991; de Jong & Ferguson-Hessler, 1991; Larkin, 1983). Experts are better able to classify problem types (Chi, Feltovich & Glaser, 1981; Chi & Bassock, 1991) because their *representations* integrate domain knowledge with problem types. However, researchers and theorists differ in their claims about the forms in which experts represent problems. Anderson (1983) claims that problems are represented as production rules, whereas Chi and Bassock (1991) and Larkin (1983) believe that they are schema-like forms. Whatever form, it is generally accepted that problems solvers need to construct some sort of internal representation (mental model) of a problem (problem space) in order to solve a problem. Personal problem representations can serve a number of functions (Savelsbergh, de Jong & Ferguson-Hessler, 1998):

- To guide further interpretation of information about the problem.
- To simulate the behavior of the system based on knowledge about the properties of the system.
- To associate with and trigger a particular solution schema (procedure).

Knowing that problem representation is so crucial to problem solving, why are student unable to represent problems in a meaningful way?

Most overt problem solving in schools occurs in maths and the sciences. Typically, the kinds of problems that are solve are well-structured, story problems. These problems are normally solved by learners identifying key concepts and values in a short scenario, selecting the appropriate algorithm, applying the algorithm to generate a quantitative answer, and hopefully checking their responses (Sherrill, 1983). This is known as the direct translation strategy, where student directly translate problems into formulas. In this approach to problem solving, the only form of problem representation is quantitative in the form of a formula from which the correct answer can be derived. Research has shown that problem solvers who base their solution plans on the numbers and keywords that they select from the problem are generally unsuccessful (Hegarty, Mayer & Monk, 1995). The underlying assumption of this chapter is that relying exclusively on a quantitative form of representation restricts student's understanding of the problem and its relationship to domain knowledge. This assumption can be generalized: relying on any single form of problem representation restricts student's understanding of the problem and its relationship to domain knowledge. In order to be able to transfer problem-solving skills, students must learn how to represent their conceptual understanding of how problems relate to domain knowledge. In order to do so, it is necessary that students learn to represent their understanding in more than one way. How does this work?

In order to develop conceptual understanding, it is necessary for students to understand the internal connections between problems and domain knowledge in order to transfer skills (Singly & Anderson, 1989). Well-developed mental models of problem states consist of multiple representations including structural knowledge, procedural knowledge, reflective knowledge, images and metaphors of the system, of strategic knowledge as well as social/relational knowledge, conversational/ discursive knowledge and artifactual knowledge (Jonassen & Henning, 1999). The more ways that learners are able to represent the problems that they are trying to solve, the better able they will be to transfer their problem-solving skills. Evidence to support this claim is provided by Ploetzner and Spada (1998), who claim that "the ability to construct and coordinate qualitative and quantitative problem representations is a precondition for successful and efficient problem solving in physics" (p. 96). Qualitative and quantitative representations are complementary. Ploetzner, Fehse, Kneser and Spada (1999) showed that when solving physics problems, qualitative problem representations are necessary prerequisites to learning quantitative representations. Qualitative representation is a missing link in novice problem solving (Chi, Feltovich Glaser, 1981; Larkin, 1983). When students try to understand a problem in only one way, especially when that way conveys no conceptual information about the problem, students do not understand the underlying systems they are working in. So, it is necessary to support conceptual understanding in students before solving problems by helping them to construct qualitative representations of the problems they are learning to solve as well as quantitative representations. Problem representation is the key to problem solving.

2 Problem Representation

Problem representation is the key to problem solving among novice learners as well as experts. Problem representation has been historically addressed in at least three different ways. Most of the research has focused on the ways that information required to solve the problem is represented to learners. The assumption is that the attributes of external problem representations will be mapped onto learners' knowledge representations. So, organizing and displaying problems to learners in ways that enhance their mental representations and engage appropriate problem-solving processes is the goal.

2.1 Representing Problem Information

There are three characteristics of problem information displays: the form of information item, the organization of items into structures, and the sequences of items or groups (Kleinmutz & Schkade, 1993). Problem information can assume three different forms: numerical, verbal, or pictorial. That information can be organized into meaningful structures, including groups, hierarchies, or patterns such as tables or matrices. Schwartz (1971) found that matrix representations of information were substantially superior to groupings, graphs and sentences because they clearly define needed information, suggest orders of operations, and provide consistency checks for partial solutions. Schwartz and Fattaleh (1973) confirmed the efficacy of matrix representations except for problems stated in the negative. When given the opportunity to change the problem representation, most students chose to restructure problems in the form of matrices. Diagrams (flowcharts) have also produced better performance than verbal representations, especially for more complex problems (Mayer, 1976). Carroll, Thomas and Malhotra (1980) found that spatial layouts of isomorphic design problems resulted in better performances and shorter solution times than temporal representations. Mayer (1976) concluded that the more integrated the representations are, the better the learner's performance on problem solving tasks because the degree of structural integration is an important factor in mental representation.

The conceptual rationale for these findings is referred to by Zhang (1997) as representational determinism. He argues that the form of the external representation of problem information determines what information can be perceived, what processes can be activated, and what structures can be discovered from the representation. He believes that, based on principles of ecological psychology, information from problem representations can be perceived directly from the problem without mediation from memory, inference, or other cognitive processes. External problem representations have different affordances. External representations are more than merely inputs (e.g. memory aids) to an internal representation process during problem solving, so care must be exercised in how we represent problems to learners. More systematic research is needed to clarify the relations between problem elements and problem mapping process.

Ultimately the goal of external problem representations is to affect the internal, mental (knowledge) representations constructed by learners. Why? Because "problem solving must begin with the conversion of the problem statement into an internal representation" (Reimann & Chi, 1989, p. 165), and because individuals choose to represent problems in ways that make more sense to them. Problem spaces are mentally constructed by selecting and mapping specific relations from a problem domain onto the problem (McGuinness, 1986). These mappings may facilitate or impede different kinds of processing required to solve the problem. For example, spatial mappings are most effective when memory load is greatest (Potts & Scholz, 1975). Spatial reasoning supports problem solving when used to visually disambiguate problem elements. As the complexity of the problem increases, producing efficient representations becomes more important; and efficiency of representations is a function of organization, integration, or coherence (McGuinness, 1986).

2.2 Supporting Knowledge Representations

The focus of this chapter is how to directly affect learners' abilities to represent problems. The solution that I recommend is to provide learners with tools with which to construct different kinds of knowledge representations of the problems they are learning to solve. Tools that constrain and scaffold students' problem representation performance are more likely to affect the knowledge representations they construct than the ways in which the problems are represented to the learners. The rationale for using tools to scaffold problem representations is artificial intelligence in reverse: rather than having the computer simulate human intelligence, require the human to simulate the computer's unique intelligence and come to use it as part of their cognitive apparatus (Salomon, 1988). When learners internalize the tool, they begin to think in terms of it. So, this paper proposes that we examine the use of three different tools for qualitatively representing problems in the sciences and engineering.

Another rationale for using tools to scaffold problem representations is the distribution of cognitive responsibility. Zhang and Norman (1994) developed a theoretical framework for distributing representations internally and externally. They consider the internal and external representations as equal partners in a representation system, each with separate functions. For example, external information representations, Zhang and Norman claim, activate perceptual processes while internal representations activate cognitive processes. Together, the representations are symbiotic. A key assumption of problem solving, according to Zhang (1997) is that information representations need not necessarily be re-represented as an knowledge representation in order to be used for problem solving.

It is also important to note that using formalisms and tools to represent both the external problem representation as well as the problem solver's knowledge representation goes beyond distributing cognitive tasks. Using problem representation tools begins to integrate internal and external problem representations into a continuous form of representation. The functions of those separate representations begin to blur. How seamless that representation becomes probably depends on the problem solver's comfort and facility with the tool to represent different classes of problems.

3   Tools for Externalizing Problem Spaces (Knowledge Representations)

Successful problem solving requires learners to qualitatively as well as quantitatively represent problems that they are attempting to solve qualitatively as well as quantitatively. The most effective way to support different problem representations by learners is to provide them with different knowledge representation tools for constructing problem spaces (the specific problem embedded in domain knowledge). The use of such tools assumed that people learn more from constructing and justifying their own models of systems than from studying someone else's (Jonassen, 2000). That is, we learn by building models than from using them (Morgan, 1999). I briefly describe a variety of computer-mediated tools that can be used by learners to represent the knowledge required to solve problems.

3.1 Semantic Networks for Modeling Conceptual Knowledge

Semantic networks, also known as concept maps or cognitive maps, are spatial representations of concepts and their interrelationships that are intended to represent the knowledge structures that humans store in their minds (Jonassen, Beissner & Yacci, 1993). These knowledge structures are also known as cognitive structures, conceptual knowledge, structural knowledge, and systemic knowledge. They are useful for our purpose because internal problem representations can be represented as semantic nets (Larkin, 1985).

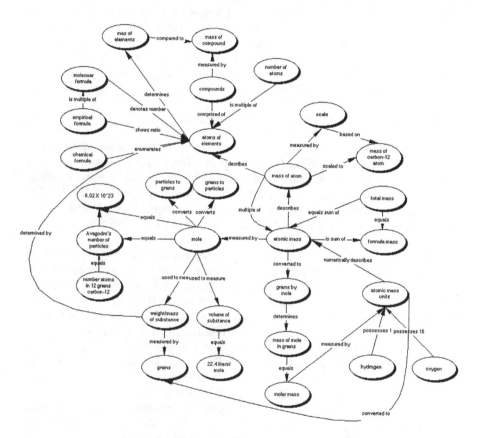

Fig. 1. Semantic network of stoichiometry problem

Semantic networks are graphs consisting of nodes representing concepts and labeled lines representing relationships among them. Fig. 1 illustrates a semantic network about stoichiometry problems that are solved in introductory chemistry courses. When students construct semantic nets, they are required to isolate the most important concepts in a problem domain, assemble those concepts into nodes, and link the nodes and determine the semantic nature of the link between the nodes. Why is it important to externalize structural knowledge? Meaningful learning requires that learners connect new ideas to prior knowledge. Semantic networks help in organizing learners' knowledge by integrating information into a progressively more complex conceptual framework. When learners construct concept maps for representing their understanding in a domain, they reconceptualize the content domain by constantly using new propositions to elaborate and refine the concepts that they already know. More importantly, concept maps help in increasing the total quantity of formal content knowledge because it facilitates learners to use the skill of searching for patterns and relationships among concepts (Slack & Stewart, 1990). Research has shown that well-organized and integrated domain knowledge (as evidenced by integrated semantic networks) are essential for problem solving. It is necessary to understand the conceptual relationships between the concepts in any problem domain in order to be able to transfer any problem-solving skills developed. How much effect the construction of semantic networks will have on problem solving needs to be examined. There are a number of tools available for constructing semantic networks. The most powerful, I believe, is Semantica (SemanticResearch.com).

3.2 Expert Systems for Representing Procedural Knowledge

Expert systems are artificial intelligence programs designed to simulate expert reasoning in support of decision making for any kind of problem. Like a human expert, an expert system (computer program) is approached by an individual (novice) with a problem. The system queries the individual about the current status of the problem, searches its knowledge base (which contains previously stored expert knowledge) for pertinent facts and rules, processes the information, arrives at a decision, and reports the solution to the user.

Building expert systems is a knowledge modeling process that enables experts and knowledge engineers to construct models of causal reasoning processes (Adams-Webber, 1995). Production rule models used in expert system are the best representation of procedural knowledge (Gagne, 1985). That is, the IF-THEN rules that comprise expert systems knowledge bases are regarded as the most accurate representation of the application of knowledge. Table 1 illustrates part of a rule base predicting the results of stoichiometry problems. Externalizing the predictions and inferences of a skilled problem solver requires the learner to think like a skilled agent. Using expert system shell programs to construct the IF-THEN rule bases, novices can easily learn to build expert systems to reflect the procedural knowledge required to solve particular kinds of problems. These rule bases are qualitative representations of the causal reasoning that is implied in the formulae they use to solve the problems. Rather than representing problem solving as a series of steps, building expert systems requires learners to represent the causal (predictive or inferential) reasoning that is required to solve the problem. Lippert (1987) found that the analysis of subject matter that is required to develop expert systems is so deep and so incisive that learners develop a greater domain comprehension which is essential for problem solving. How much effect the construction of expert systems will have on problem solving needs to be examined.

Table 1. Excerpt from expert system rule base on stoichiometry

D1: 'You know the mass of one mole of sample.'
D2: 'You need to determine molar (formula) mass.'
D3: 'Divide sample mass by molar mass.'
D4: 'Multiply number of moles by molar mass.'
D5: 'You know atomic mass units.'
D6: 'You know molar mass.'
D7: 'Divide mass of sample by molar mass and multiply by Avogadro's number.'
D8: 'Divide number of particles by Avogadro's number'
D9: 'Convert number of particles to moles, then convert moles to mass'
D10: 'Convert mass to moles using molar mass, and then convert moles to molecules using Avogadro's number.'
D11: 'Convert from volume to moles (divide volume by volume/mole), and then convert moles to moles by multiplying by Avogadro's number.'

Q1: 'Do you know the number of molecules?'   A 1 'yes'   2 'no'
Q2: 'Do you know the mass of the sample in grams?'   A 1 'yes'   2 'no'
Q3: 'Do you know the molar mass of the element or compound?'   A 1 'yes'   2 'no'
Q4: 'Do you know the number of moles of the sample?'   A 1 'yes'   2 'no'
Q5: 'Do you want to know the number of molecules?'   A 1 'yes'   2 'no'
Q6: 'Do you want to know the mass of the sample in grams?'   A 1 'yes'   2 'no'
Q7: 'Do you want to know the molar mass of the compound?'   A 1 'yes'   2 'no'
Q8: 'Do you want to know the number of moles of the sample?   'A 1 'yes'   2 'no'
Q9: 'Do you know atomic mass units?'   A 1 'yes'   2 'no'
Q10: 'Do you know the volume of a gas?'   A 1 'yes'   2 'no'

Rule1:   IF q2a1 AND q8a1 THEN D2
Rule2:   IF (d1 OR q3a1) AND q2a1 AND q8a1 THEN D3
Rule3:   IF q4a1 AND q3a1 AND q6a1 THEN D4
Rule4:   IF q3a1 THEN D1
Rule5:   IF q3a1 THEN D5
Rule6:   IF q9a1 THEN D6
Rule7:   IF qq3a1 AND q2a1 AND q5a1 THEN D7

Rule8:   IF q1a1 AND q8a1 THEN D8
Rule9:   IF q1a1 AND q6a1 THEN D9
Rule10:   IF q2a1 AND q5a1 THEN d10
Rule11:   IF q10a1 AND q1a1 THEN d11

Expert system shells (editors for constructing and testing expert systems) are not as available as they once were. The easiest is WinExpert, which comes bundled with *How to Model It* (Starfield, Smith & Bleloch, 1990). This tool can be mastered in less than one hour. A search of the World Wide Web will also manifest other shells as well.

Context 'This knowledge base is intended to cognitively simulate the processes of calculating molar conversions.'

3.3 Systems Modeling for Representing

A systems model is a conceptual, conjectural representation of the dynamic relations among factors in a system, resulting in a simulation that imitates the conditions and actions of it. These dynamic simulation models represent the changing nature of systemic phenomena. Systems modeling tools use a simple set of building block icons (stocks, flows, converters, and connectors) to map processes. These tools enable learners to run and test the model that they have created and observe the output in graphs, tables, or animations. Systems modeling tools provide a powerful suite of tools for representing the complexity of dynamic systems. Learners can build models of those systems and test them. Observing the systems that students create is perhaps the most powerful way of assessing the viability and comprehensiveness of learners' knowledge. Fig. 2 illustrates the factors in the creation of smog in cities. This model can be applied to any city by inserting data from that city in order to test the likelihood ofsmog creation. Fig. 3 represents an even more ill-structured and vexing problem: the Palestinian-Israeli conflict. This student created model can be debated and altered based upon that debate, making systems models the most powerful cognitive tool available.

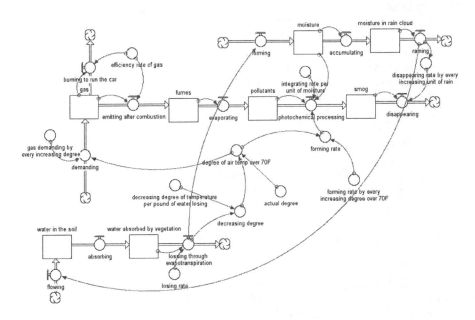

Fig. 2. Systems model of smog creation

There is a small base of literature that describes experiences with systems modeling in high school and college. However, no empirical research has ever focused on the use of systems modeling to support problem solving or higher order thinking. It is obvious from any form of cognitive task analysis that systems modeling necessarily engages causal reasoning about dynamic systems. Because systems modeling supports strategic understanding of a problem, we believe that building systems models of problem types will support problem solving and transfer better than any other kind of tool. How much effect the construction of systems models will have on problem solving needs to be examined.

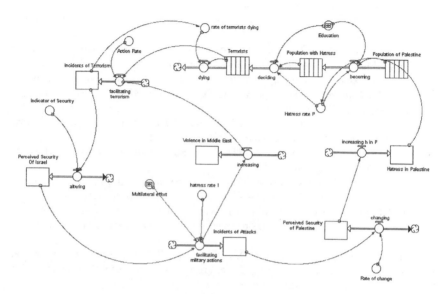

Fig. 3. Systems model of Palestine-Israeli conflict

4 Conclusions

Although no empirical research has examined the effects of using technology tools for representing problem on problem solving performance, there are several good reasons for predicting their efficacy.

External problems will decrease cognitive load in learners, especially while solving complex problems. Sweller and Chandler (1994) showed that limited working memory makes it difficult to assimilate multiple elements of information simultaneously, and multiple elements must be assimilated when the problem components interact, especially when solving complex problems. Providing an external representation of the problem components scaffolds working memory by off-loading the need to simultaneously model multiple problem components.

External problem representations, especially those in the form of dynamic models, enable learners to manipulate and test their models. That is, learners can test predictions of their models as a way of confirming the validity of their assumptions. The problem comes alive when learners can test the assumptions that are conveyed by their model.

Finally, building models of problems is at the heart of scientific thinking and requires diverse mental activities such as planning, data collecting, collaborating and accessing information, data visualizing, modeling, and reporting (Soloway, Krajcik, & Finkel, 1995). The potential for research confirming positive relationships between modeling and problem solving is great.

References

Adams-Webber, J. (1995). Constructivist psychology and knowledge elicitation. *Journal of Constructivist Psychology, 8* (3), 237-249.

Anderson, J.R. (1983). *The architecture of cognition.* Cambridge, MA: Harvard University Press.

Carroll, J.M., Thomas, J.C., & Malhotra, A. (1980). Presentation and representation in design problem solving. *British Journal of Psychology, 71,* 143-153.

Chi, M.T.H., & Bassock, M. (1991). Learning from examples vs. self-explanations. In L.B. Resnick (Ed.), *Knowing, learning, and instruction: Essays in honor of Robert Glaser* (pp. 251-282). Hillsdale, NJ: Lawrence Erlbaum Associates.

Chi, M.T.H., Feltovich, P.J., & Glaser, R. (1981). Categorization and representation of physics problems by experts and novices. *Cognitive Science, 5,* 121-152.

Chipman, S.F., Segal, J.W., & Glaser, R. (1985). *Thinking and learning skills,* Vol. 2. Hillsdale, NJ: Erlbaum.

Cho, K.L., & Jonassen, D.H. (2002). The effects of argumentation scaffolds on argumentation and problem solving. *Educational Technology: Research & Development, 50* (3), 5-22

de Jong, T. & Ferguson-Hessler, M.G.M. (1991). Knowledge of problem situations in physics: a comparison of good and poor novice problem solvers. *Learning and Instruction, 1,* 289-302.

Dunkle, M.E., Schraw, G., & Bendixen, L.D. (1995). *Cognitive processes in well-defined and ill-defined problem solving.* Paper presented at the annual meeting of the American Educational Research Association, San Francisco,

Gagne, R.M. (1985). *Conditions of learning,* 4th Ed. New York: Holt, Rinehart & Winston.

Gick, M.L., & Holyoak, K.J. (1980). Analogical problem solving. *Cognitive Psychology, 12,* 306-355.

Gick, M.L., & Holyoak, K.J. (1983). Schema induction and analogical transfer. *Cognitive Psychology, 15,* 1-38.

Hegarty, M., Mayer, R.E., & Monk, C.A. (1995) Comprehension of arithmetic word problems: A comparison of successful and unsuccessful problem solvers. *Journal of Educational Psychology, 87,* 18-32.

Hong, N.S., Jonassen, D.H., & McGee, S. (2003). Predictors of well-structured and ill-structured problem solving in an astronomy simulation. *Journal of Research in Science Teaching, 40*(1), 6-33.

Jonassen, D.H. (1996). *Computers as cognitive tools: Mindtools for critical thinking.* Columbus, OH: Merrill/Prentice-Hall.

Jonassen, D.H. (1997). Instructional design model for well-structured and ill-structured problem-solving learning outcomes. *Educational Technology: Research and Development 45*(1), 65-95.

Jonassen, D.H. (2000). *Computers as Mindtools in schools: Engaging critical thinking.* Columbus, OH: Merrill/Prentice-Hall.

Jonassen, D.H., & Henning, P. (1999). Mental models: Knowledge in the head and knowledge in the world. *Educational Technology, 39*(3), 37-42.

Jonassen, D.H., & Kwon, H.I. (2001). Communication patterns in computer-mediated vs. face-to-face group problem solving. *Educational Technology: Research and Development, 49*(10), 35-52.

Jonassen, D.H., Beissner, K., & Yacci, M.A. (1993). *Structural knowledge: Techniques for representing, conveying, and acquiring structural knowledge.* Hillsdale, NJ: Lawrence Erlbaum Associates.

Kleinmutz, D.N., & Schkade, D.A. (1993). Information displays and decision processes. *Psychological Science, 4*(40), 221-227.

Larkin, J.H. (1983). The role of problem representation in physics. In D. Gentner, & A.L. Stevens (Eds.), *Mental models* (pp. 75-98). Hillsdale, NJ: Lawrence Erlbaum Associates.

Larkin, J.H. (1985). Understanding, problem representation, and skill in physics. In S.F. Chipman, J.W. Segal, & R. Glaser (Eds.), *Thinking and learning skills (Vol. 2): Research and open questions* (pp. 141-160). Hillsdale, NJ: Erlbaum.

Lippert, R. (1987). Teaching problem solving in mathematics and science with expert systems. *School Science and Mathematics, 87,* 407-413.

Mayer, R.E. (1976). Comprehension as affected by structure of problem representation. *Memory & Cognition, 4*(3), 249-255.

McGuinness, C. (1986). Problem representation: The effects of spatial arrays. *Memory & Cognition, 14*(3), 270-280.

Morgan, M.S. (1999). Learning from models. In M.S. Morgan, & M. Morrison (Eds.), *Models as mediators: Perspectives on natural and social science* (pp. 347-388). Cambridge: Cambridge University Press.

Nickerson, R.S., Perkins, D.N., & Smith, E.E. (1985). *The teaching of thinking.* Hillsdale, NJ: Erlbaum.

Ploetzner, R., & Spada, H. (1998). Constructing quantitative problem representations on the basis of qualitative reasoning. *Interactive Learning Environments, 5,* 95-107.

Ploetzner, R., Fehse, E., Kneser, C., & Spada, H. (1999). Learning to relate qualitative and quantitative problem representations in a model-based setting for collaborative problem solving. *Journal of the Learning Sciences, 8*(2), 177-214.

Potts, G.R., & Scholz, K.W. (1975). The internal representation of a three-term series problem. *Journal of Verbal Learning & Verbal Behavior, 14*(5), 439-452.

Reed, S.K. (1987). A structure mapping model for word problems. *Journal of Experimental Psychology: Learning, Memory, and Cognition, 13,* 124-139.

Reimann, P., & Chi, M.T.H. (1989). Human expertise. In K.J. Gilhooly (Ed.), *Human and machine problem solving* (pp. 161-191). New York: Plenum.

Salomon, G. (1988). AI in reverse: Computer tools that turn cognitive. *Journal of Educational Computing Research, 4*(2), 123-139.

Savelsbergh, E.R., deJong, T., & Ferguson-Hessler, M.G.M. (1998). Competence-related differences in problem representations. In M. van Sommeren, P. Reimann, T. deJong, & H. Boshuizen (Eds.), *The role of multiple representations in learning and problem solving* (pp. 262-282). Amsterdam: Elsevier.

Schwartz, S.H. (1971). Modes of representation and problem solving: Well evolved is half solved. *Journal of Experimental Psychology, 91,* 347-350.

Schwartz, S.H., & Fattaleh, D.L. (1973). Representation in deductive problem solving: The matrix. *Journal of Experimental Psychology, 95,* 343-348.

Sherrill, J.M. (1983). Solving textbook mathematical word problems. *Alberta Journal of Educational Research, 29*(2), 140-152.

Simon, D.P. (1978). Information processing theory of human problem solving. In D. Estes (Ed.), *Handbook of learning and cognitive process* (pp. 271-295). Hillsdale, NJ: Lawrence Erlbaum Associates.

Simon, H.A. (1981). Studying human intelligence by creating artificial intelligence. *American Scientist, 69*(3), 300-309.

Singly, M.K., & Anderson, J.R. (1989). *The transfer of cognitive skill.* Cambridge, MA: Harvard University Press.

Slack, S., & Stewart, J. (1990). Improving Student Problem Solving in Genetics. *Journal of Biological Education, 23*(49), 308-312.

Soloway, E., Krajcik, J., & Finkel, E.A. (1995). *Science project: Supporting science modeling and inquiry via computational media and technology.* San Francisco: American Educational Research Association.

Starfield, A.M., Smith, K.A., & Bleloch, A.L. (1990). *How to model it: Problem solving for the computer age.* New York: McGraw-Hill.

Sweller, J., & Chandler, P. (1994). Why some material is difficult to learn. *Cognition and Instruction, 12*, 185-233.

Zhang, J. (1997). The nature of external representation in problem solving. *Cognitive Science, 21*, 179-217.

Zhang, J., & Norman, D. (1994). Representations in distributed cognitive tasks. *Cognitive Science, 18*, 87-122.

Collaborative Knowledge Visualization for Cross-Community Learning

Jasminko Novak[1] and Michael Wurst[2]

[1] Fraunhofer IMK.MARS, Schloss Birlinghoven,
53754 Sankt Augustin, Germany
j.novak@imk.fraunhofer.de
[2] Dortmund University, FB IV, Artificial Intelligence,
44221 Dortmund, Germany
wurst@kimo.cs.uni-dortmund.de

Abstract. Knowledge exchange between heterogeneous communities of practice has been recognized as the critical source of innovation and creation of new knowledge. This paper considers the problem of enabling such cross community knowledge exchange through knowledge visualization. We discuss the social nature of knowledge construction and describe main requirements for practical solutions to the given problem, as well as existing approaches. Based on this analysis, we propose a model for collaborative elicitation and visualization of community knowledge perspectives based on the construction of personalised learning knowledge maps and shared concept networks that incorporate implicit knowledge and personal views of individual users. We show how this model supports explicit and implicit exchange of knowledge between the members of different communities and present its prototypical realization in the Knowledge Explorer, an interactive tool for collaborative visualization and cross-community sharing of knowledge. Concrete application scenarios and evaluation experiences are discussed on the example of the Internet platform netzspannung.org.

1 Introduction

The concept of knowledge visualization is often interrelated with information visualisation and the problem of organizing and displaying complex information structures with the goal of amplifying cognition of human users (Card, Macinlay & Shneiderman, 1999). In contrast, Eppler and Burkhard (2004) propose the definition of knowledge visualization as being concerned with the "use of visual representations to improve the *creation* and *transfer* of knowledge between people". Such a definition leads to a fundamental insight – while information visualization typically solves problems of complex *information* structures, knowledge visualization is intrinsically connected to the problem of knowledge transfer in *social structures*. The view that "knowledge visualization aims to improve the transfer and creation of knowledge among people by giving them richer means of expressing what they know" (Eppler & Burkhard, 2004) puts emphasis on the relationship between knowledge and human actors - even when designing and developing visual knowledge artefacts, which will inevitably be based on some form of visual presentation of information.

S.-O. Tergan and T. Keller (Eds.): Knowledge and Information Visualization, LNCS 3426, pp. 95–116, 2005.
© Springer-Verlag Berlin Heidelberg 2005

In proposing this perspective on the concept of knowledge visualization, this paper starts with the premise that in order to develop effective knowledge visualization, we need to consider a social context. In a concrete approach, we consider the problem of supporting knowledge exchange between heterogeneous communities of practice, which has been recognized as the critical source of innovation and creation of new knowledge in organizations. We discuss the social nature of knowledge construction in such communities and describe the main problems that need to be solved. We then discuss a concrete knowledge visualization model that we have developed as a possible solution, and describe its prototypical realization in the Knowledge Explorer, an interactive tool for collaborative visualization and cross-community sharing of knowledge.

2 Communities and Social Construction of Knowledge

Social theories of learning (such as constructivism and social constructionism) help us understand how people construct meaning out of information, and how this is related to social interaction and communication with other people. For example, Berger and Luckmann (1966) describe how people interacting in a certain historical and social context share information from which they construct social knowledge as a reality, which in turn influences their judgment, behaviour and attitude. Bruner (1990) shows how the construction of meaning can be related to cultural experiences, in a similar way as Vygotsky (1962) has explained how thought and language are connected and framed by a given socio-cultural context of the learner. The studies of Lave and Wenger (1991) emphasise the role of immediate social context for learning a body of implicit and explicit knowledge through a kind of apprenticeship they call „legitimate peripheral participation".

All these studies demonstrate how the construction of knowledge (learning) is an inherently social process in which the „learner" actively constructs meaning through a process of information exchange and social interaction with other people. Furthermore, both the personal implicit knowledge of the learner (his previous knowledge, interests, values and beliefs), his current context of intention (e.g. a problem or task at hand) and the social and cultural context in which the learning takes place (e.g. team, workplace, community) fundamentally determine the possible meanings that the learner can/will construct in this process. The principal implication of these findings is the notion of a shared cognitive and social context, which has to be established in order for the members of a social group to negotiate, share meanings, and hence construct collective knowledge.

One of the major models of social structures in which knowledge is generated and exchanged in today's so-called knowledge society are technologically supported informal social networks. Such social networks are often referred to as virtual communities (Rheingold, 1993), communities of practice (Brown & Duguid, 1991; Wenger, 1998), knowledge communities (Carotenuto, Etienne, Fontaine, Friedman, Newberg, Muller, Simpson, Slusher & Stevenson, 1999) and business communities. They bring together groups of people based on a shared set of interests or specific concerns (virtual communities, communities of interest), or based on work-related sharing of knowledge and experience (communities of practice). While such social formations have been a major model of knowledge production and dissemination in scientific research even before the Internet, in recent years they have been increasingly acknowledged as major forms of knowledge exchange in professional and work-related settings, both within organisations and across organisational boundaries (Cohen & Prusak, 2001). This class of approaches is based on the social paradigm of knowledge construction: knowledge exists only in a social context and is created by social practices shared by the individual members, e.g. Wenger (1998).

Communities are a special form of such a context that has been increasingly used as an important unit of analysis when considering processes of knowledge construction, sharing and collaboration. In contrast to groups and teams that are defined institutionally, participation in communities is voluntary and typically independent of specific projects and formal organizational processes. Rather, the evolvement of such communities is based on spontaneous participation and self-motivated choice, common goals such as shared needs and problems and on a common repertoire (experiences, places and practices) resulting in common sense-making and a common language. According to this view, knowledge is created and reproduced through social relationships and interaction in communities and makes sense only in relation to such communities. Social interaction between community members and information exchange through shared community repositories facilitate the knowledge flows and the conversions between implicit and explicit forms of knowledge (Nonaka & Takeuchi, 1995).

While much research has been devoted to the development of tools and systems for supporting knowledge creation and sharing in teams and within communities, the problem of supporting cross-community exchanges has been relatively under-investigated. At the same time, a critical requirement for modern organizations and knowledge-intensive work has become the need for supporting cooperation and integration of knowledge between different communities, with highly specialized expertise and activities. Different studies have emphasised cross-community interactions as a critical source of new knowledge and innovation (Swan, 2001; Dougherty, 1992; Brown & Duguid, 1991).

A common approach to this problem has been the establishment of shared community platforms and knowledge portals (Internet/Intranet) aiming at providing one central point of encounter and knowledge workspace for different communities. Examples are corporate knowledge portals in commercial organizations and cross-community platforms in research settings such as netzspannung.org or the EU mosaic-network.org. However, appropriate support for such platforms is still missing. They are typically based on a combination of centralized knowledge bases and standard community-tools that have been developed for supporting exchanges in teams and within communities (e.g. shared workspaces, awareness, online communication). In contrast, Dougherty (1992) and Swan (2001) identify special challenges and requirements that need to be considered in such heterogeneous situations. But the development of appropriate systems and tools incorporating these insights is still lagging behind.

3   Requirements for Supporting Cross-Community Sharing and Creation of Knowledge

As observed by a number of authors, each community develops its own social and interpretative context (genres, repertoires, perspectives), which in turn determines its interpretations of the world. Different communities inhabit different "thought worlds" (Dougherty, 1992) which determine how their members interpret the meaning of information, artefacts, procedures, events and experiences. Different thought worlds then have different funds of knowledge and systems of meaning which means they cannot simply "share" ideas since important issues in one world may be viewed as meaningless in the other (Boland & Tenkasi, 1995).

In other words: knowledge artefacts produced by different communities (documents, emails, forum discussions) are not a neutral organization of information, but reflect perspectives of those involved in the sensemaking process. Thus knowledge cannot simply be passed on by exchanging information between members of different communities. In order to make sense out of information and construct knowledge, one needs to contextualise it within one's own existing knowledge and thought world. What is needed is finding ways for enabling the members of different communities to discover how the knowledge reflected in artefacts of one community, relates to their own knowledge and its context within their own community.

Thus, in order to support the sharing of knowledge between different communities we need to provide a way for members of different communities to establish a „shared context of knowing" as a way of "locating one form of knowledge in the context of another" (Boland & Tenkasi, 1995; Swan, 2001). On one hand, this requires that knowledge perspectives underlying individual communities be captured, represented and visualized. On the other hand, the different knowledge perspectives need to be put in relation to each other. But these perspectives are neither immediately visible nor readily available. They are largely implicit and are normally acquired only through extensive participation in community interactions. This is a requirement congenial with processes of knowledge development and sharing within communities, but not applicable between heterogeneous communities since intensive interactions between members are not given.

3.1   Perspective Making and Perspective Taking

The theoretical foundations for dealing with this problem have been provided by the model of perspective making and perspective taking describing the processes of knowledge exchange between different "communities of knowing" (Boland & Tenkasi, 1995). Perspective making refers to intra-community development and refinement of knowledge, whereas perspective taking refers to making the thought worlds of different communities visible and accessible to each other. Boland and Tenkasi (1995) propose that these processes are intrinsically connected: a community develops new knowledge both through social exchanges and knowledge discourses between its members, as well as by taking on perspectives of others. The interplay of these two processes then provides the ground for allowing knowledge to be exchange between different communities.

This kind of cross-community interaction and integration of knowledge inherently involves two needs. Firstly, the need to share meanings (of information, artefacts, procedures) among a community's members. This occurs through reification of knowledge within physical, mental, and cultural artefacts, that stem from members' participation in the community. Secondly, the need to negotiate and coordinate meanings among different communities, which manage specialized knowledge. Due to local needs, different background, contexts, and artefacts, local knowledge is managed and represented in different ways that are appropriate for different communities' needs. Thus, communities share, convert, negotiate and cooperate only through negotiation of perspectives. These processes are facilitated and mediated by particular artefacts such as boundary objects (Star, 1989) and human knowledge brokers (Wenger, 1998).

3.2 Boundary Objects

In the context of this paper, of particular importance is the proposition that perspective making and perspective taking can be supported technologically by designing systems that allow the construction and discussion of "boundary objects" - such as classification schemes, cognitive maps and narrative structures (Boland & Tenkasi, 1995). The concept of "boundary objects" (Star, 1989) refers to knowledge artefacts that embody different perspectives and can be interpreted in different ways, without the need for prior shared understanding to be established. Thus such boundary objects are seen as essential means for supporting cooperation between different communities in a way, which allows each community to retain local perspectives and yet these perspectives to become interconnected.

3.3 Community Knowledge Repositories and Implicit Knowledge

The exchange of knowledge in communities is commonly reflected in an unstructured repository of knowledge artefacts reflecting community exchanges (e.g. discussion forums, mailing list archives, project repositories.). But, in contrast to formal organizational structures, explicit creation of taxonomies or ontologies to represent local community knowledge is rarely done by informal communities. Moreover, individual communities are by no means homogeneous within themselves. Individual members often have strongly profiled personal views (e.g. communities of experts) and the dynamics of communication constantly shifts between current information need (a problem or opportunity at hand) and long-term information need (interest profiles). Such a decentralised and loosely structured mode of community interaction makes it difficult to express the knowledge contained in the community information space by means of a predefined and unique categorisation.

Furthermore, since in communities knowledge is created and exchanged to a large extent through informal social interactions, the information pool that archives the community exchanges will reflect merely some externalised part of this knowledge. So, even if cross-connected categorisation structures are created by hand through explicit negotiation, they will not capture the highly personal (implicit) knowledge of individual members (Nonaka & Takeuchi, 1995). Thus, supporting cross-community exchanges through visualizing community knowledge perspectives and relating them to each other poses the following challenges: How can we construct artefacts that elicit and visualize the existing, but not explicitly formulated knowledge of a community? And how can we do so in a way, which makes it usable for discovering relationships between perspectives of different communities and domains of knowledge?

4 Existing Approaches to Knowledge Sharing and Collaborative Knowledge Visualization

Existing approaches to knowledge sharing and collaborative knowledge visualization usually cover some of the following aspects: sharing implicit knowledge, mediating between different conceptualisations, eliciting knowledge automatically and visualizing the derived shared structures.

4.1 Sharing Implicit Knowledge: Internalisation, Socialization and Externalisation

Different authors have emphasized the largely tacit nature of human knowledge (Nonaka & Takeuchi, 1995) and the difficulties of codifying and formalizing socially distributed knowledge in communities. Existing solutions to this problem can be roughly classified into three main approaches: the „internalisation" model based on individual reflection on the community discourse, the „socialisation" model based on direct interaction mediated by CMC & CSCW technologies and the „externalisation" model based on the explicit construction of shared conceptualisations.

The internalisation model is the only model supported by basic community technologies such as mailing lists, bulletin boards and discussion forums. The development of a shared context requires members' extensive and active participation in the community exchange. There is no mode for the shared understanding of the community to be expressed, and the repository of the collective memory is an unstructured space of many interrelated but rather isolated pieces of information. Context is very difficult to establish.

The socialisation model is connected to approaches that aim at supporting the sharing of social knowledge through a shared virtual space (e.g. Erickson & Kellogg, 2001). This is the so-called awareness and knowledge socialisation approach, which can be related to two basic premises. The first is that by providing mutual awareness of spatially distributed, but contextually related users (e.g. working on same task, or belonging to same community) by means of a shared virtual space, the cognitive distance between them is bridged. The second is that once this cognitive distance is bridged, the conditions are established for the users to enter into conversations through which they exchange otherwise inaccessible personal knowledge. There are several variants of this basic model. Some of them are for example connected to the constructionist theory of learning (Papert, 1991), others focus on the establishment of identity and the self-organising of social norms (e.g. Turkle, 1995).

The externalisation model is addressed by approaches aiming at supporting the explicit formulation of shared conceptualisations in form of knowledge ontologies. Ontologies represent models for formal descriptions of concepts and named relationships between them, that describe how a given individual or a group of people understands a particular domain of knowledge. Ontologies often have to be created explicitly by hand and require a process of explicit community negotiation for achieving a consensus about the shared understanding that is to be expressed. Once created they can be used to access and navigate the community information pool, as well as to visualise the semantic structure of the shared community understanding. An example of existing efforts for building such ontologies in different disciplines but interrelated to each other is the DublinCore initiative (http://www.dublincore.org). The Open Directory Project aims at a collaborative definition of a somewhat simpler taxonomy for manually mapping the content of the whole Web (http://dmoz.org).

The main shortcoming of computer-mediated socialisation approaches is that the sharing of implicit knowledge requires extensive interaction between individual members, and the resulting exchange still resides only in individual users. There is no possibility to visualise the resulting structure of shared understanding. On the other hand, existing approaches to creating externalised representations of a shared conceptual structure require explicit negotiation for achieving consensus between the members. There is no or little support for expressing the personal points of view of individual users and putting them in relation to the shared structure. At the same time, one of the essential mechanisms of knowledge creation is the ability to change perspective and see the world with „different eyes". Finally, the challenge remains of how to provide insight into the underlying values and beliefs shared by a group of users, as fundamental elements influencing their thinking, judgment and the creation of new knowledge.

4.2 Creating a Shared Structure vs. Mapping Multiple Structures

While the aim of ontologies and other forms of knowledge externalisation usually is to create a formalized common understanding, a radically different approach is to allow different knowledge structures to co-exist and to mediate between them automatically by means of a mapping between different taxonomies, categorization structures or ontology schemes (see Lacher, 2003 for a survey). These approaches offer the benefits of allowing a decentralized creation and maintenance of knowledge (and thus personal views on a domain) with little explicit coordination. But finding an intentional mapping between conceptualisations is far from being trivial and usually depends on a logical description of concepts. Thus ontology mapping also depends on the assumption that the meaning of concepts and thought worlds of communities can be codified in a formal representation and therefore suffers from the same basic problem as the other knowledge externalisation approaches.

4.3 Knowledge Elicitation and Knowledge Discovery

While explicit externalisation is often costly and unsuitable for capturing tacit and social knowledge, an alternative is to infer the common understanding of groups of users from their interactions. On the one hand, this reduces the amount of work for the users. On the other hand, it is often acknowledged that knowledge is created through interaction. An example is the paradigm of information access (Pirolli & Card, 1995), that emphasizes the need to understand the process of information retrieval as a knowledge acquisition and sense-making process – i.e. a process in which people through their interaction with information develop and internalise new knowledge. While there are several approaches following this paradigm that help individual users to elicit their personal implicit knowledge, such as information interfaces with sense-making support (e.g. Baldonado & Winograd, 1997), the problem of the social context of individual users and the problem of eliciting the common knowledge of a group of people is usually not supported by such systems.

Analysing the interactions of users among each other and the interactions of users with information spaces therefore provides a means of eliciting tacit knowledge of individual users and groups of users in an unobtrusive and intuitive way. On a technical level, many of the approaches that follow this basic idea are based on Data Mining and Knowledge Discovery (Fayyad, Piatetsky-Shapiro & Smyth, 1996) techniques. They try to find structures in given sets of interaction data, from which the common understanding of the participants can be inferred (semi-)automatically.

Two approaches that explicitly support elicitation of this kind of knowledge are Cognitive Maps and Collaborative Filtering. Previous experiments on cognitive maps include the use of methods inspired by personal construct psychology (Kelly, 1955) such as the repertoire grid elicitation, for extracting conceptual structures of individuals and groups of users (Shaw, 1995). For an overview of different methods and applications in the context of knowledge management see also (Huff & Jenkins, 2002).

On the other hand, the approaches of collaborative filtering and recommender systems (Resnick et al., 1994; Shardanand & Maes, 1995) provide a way for putting in relation perspectives of different users, based on explicit expression of their judgment and preferences (e.g. ranking) or on implicit statements such as bookmarks or patterns of interaction with information. Typically, they allow the identification of members with similar interests and can recommend items of relevance to a given user based on the fact that they have been highly rated by other users with similar interests.

A special form of automatic knowledge elicitation is text mining. By analysing a corpus of documents that represents parts of the knowledge of a given community (e.g. publications on human genetics), it is possible to derive a common understanding in the corresponding field to the extent to which it is encoded in these documents. Text-mining techniques have been used for constructing semantic overviews of complex information spaces and for computer-supported social network analysis based on statistical and linguistic analysis (Sack, 2001). In scientific communities, a frequently used technique has been the author co-citation analysis (Chen, 1999b). This method extracts patterns of relationships that show how scientists in a particular subject domain are intellectually interrelated as perceived by authors in their scientific publications.

4.4 Knowledge Visualization

Typical structures extracted from data by techniques of knowledge discovery or knowledge elicitation include hierarchies, networks and graphs, matrices or multidimensional tables and vector spaces (e.g. see Andrews, in this book). In our application context, these structures typically represent connections between documents, topics, concepts and users. They are organized and visualized through knowledge representation models such as ontologies, semantic nets, concept and topic maps, based on different forms of graph-based models, hierarchical trees or concept networks. Here techniques from information visualization are often used to solve the problem of displaying complex and high-dimensional structures. Information visualization techniques attempt to solve this through the use of appropriate visual metaphors, mapping algorithms or special interaction paradigms, which reduce the complexity by allowing the user to manipulate the visualization. Examples of popular information visualization techniques include hierarchical trees and Tree Maps, and focus+context techniques for graph visualizations such as FishEye Views or Hyperbolic trees (see Card et al., 1999 for an overview). Hence, developing effective models for knowledge visualization intrinsically depends on the combination and integration of techniques from knowledge discovery, knowledge elicitation and information visualization.

5 Our Approach

The main idea of our approach is to develop a model of dynamic knowledge artefacts that support users' access to community information spaces, in a way, which enables the discovery of relationships between knowledge of different communities. The assumption is that by mediating users' access to community repositories through interactive knowledge maps, which enable them to see the information contained in the repository from different semantic perspectives, we can qualitatively enhance the processes of knowledge construction that occurs during information access. This approach is related to the view that understands information access as a process of sensemaking and knowledge acquisition in which people through their interaction with information develop and internalise new knowledge (Pirolli & Card, 1995). Accordingly, incorporating the ability to explore the community repositories not only from a predefined community perspective, but through the perspectives of members of different communities, is a way of supporting the sharing and creation of knowledge that crosses boundaries of individual communities (Boland & Tenkasi, 1995).

5.1 The Knowledge Map Metaphor

In developing this approach we use the knowledge map metaphor as a vehicle for describing the idea of a visual structuring of information in a way, which provides insight into contexts and relationships between semantically related information. The crucial difference to existing approaches from knowledge management and knowledge visualisation is thereby that the point of departure for constructing such maps is the personal, highly implicit knowledge of individuals and communities of users, rather than explicitly predefined taxonomies or ontologies. Since knowledge in communities is highly implicit and socially constructed (Chapter 2) such knowledge maps cannot be static representations which "codify" knowledge. Rather they are conceived as interactive visual artefacts that can be interactively manipulated and discussed by the community members in order to get an understanding of different mental models and interpretative schemas underlying different communities: e.g. by exploring maps of different users, applying them to different situations, comparing personal concept structures to those of others. Hence, such interactive knowledge maps could support the processes of perspective making and perspective taking that have been recognized as critical means of cross-community exchange of knowledge (Chapter 3).

Framing the problem in this way shifts the focus away from the problem of appropriate formal models of knowledge representation addressed by taxonomy and ontology approaches. Rather, the focus becomes the need for constructing models and tools for dynamic knowledge visualization that provide contextualised views of information, showing its relationships to the knowledge perspective of a given community and supporting the discovery of relationships to potentially relevant knowledge perspectives of others. The question is then, how can we construct and visualize such knowledge maps so that they reflect personal, implicit knowledge of individuals and communities of users? How can we design an intuitive interface that enables the users to apply them easily and to interactively manipulate the criteria determining their behaviour? And how can we visualize the resulting new cross-community knowledge structures created through such exchanges?

6 Conceptual Model for Collaborative Elicitation and Exchange of Knowledge

As a practical context we consider the everyday practice of information seeking and access to the community information space as a process of knowledge acquisition and sensemaking (Pirolli & Card, 1995). The users' interaction with information both reflects their interpretation of the meaning of information, their personal knowledge perspectives and their creation of new knowledge structures. Thus, it can be taken as a point of departure for uncovering and visualizing community perspectives in a way which incorporates personal viewpoints of individual users, and hence the shared

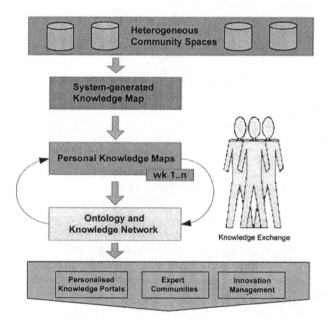

Fig. 1. The Collaborative Knowledge Elicitation and Exchange Model

implicit knowledge. In order to develop a practically feasible solution for capturing and visualizing implicit knowledge structures of human users based on their interaction with information, two basic problems need to be solved:

1. A context for user actions has to be created in order to be able to interpret the meaning of user interaction with information items. The lack of a sufficiently clear interaction context is the main difficulty of general "user-tracking" and interaction mining approaches.
2. A form of visual representation has to be found that communicates to the user both the semantics of the information space in itself (content, structure and relationships) and relates this to the meaning of his actions.

To this end we have developed a model for creating and visualizing personalised learning knowledge maps and shared concept networks based on user interaction with information (Novak, Wurst, Fleischmann & Strauss, 2003). This chapter presents the main elements of this model and the technical foundations for its realization based on the integration of methods from knowledge discovery, information access and knowledge visualization.

6.1 Eliciting Individual Points of View Through Personalised Learning Knowledge Maps

In our model a knowledge map consists out of two main elements: the Document Map and the Concept Map. The Document Map (Fig. 1, left) presents the knowledge artefacts from the community space (e.g. documents, emails, forum postings, project descriptions) structured into clusters of semantically related objects. This provides an overview of topics and relationships in the community information space. The Concept Map (Fig. 1, right) displays a network of terms that represents groups of different words used in similar contexts and the relationships between them. It provides insight into criteria determining the structuring of the Document Map and serves as a navigation structure.

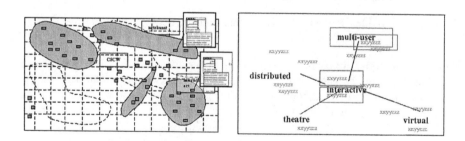

Fig. 2. The Knowledge Map Model

To construct such maps based on a users' personal points of view we combine methods for statistical text-analysis and self-organised clustering with methods for supervised learning of user-induced templates (for details refer to Novak et al., 2003) The user is presented with a system-generated structure that provides an initial context for accessing the community information space. In doing so, the user can explore and rearrange the system-generated structuring as part of her normal access to information (moving documents between groups, creating new groups and adding new cluster labels). In this way the user creates personal DocumentMaps that reflect her personal point of view and the insights she discovered and internalised as knowledge. Such personal maps serve as templates that are learned by the system and can be used as personalised semantic filters to automatically classify information into user-defined clusters.

Based on the statistical analysis of the users' personal DocumentMaps, for each user the system also extracts a personal Concept Map, which displays a network of most relevant terms and connections between them, as „seen" from a user's perspective. The most relevant terms for the document clusters from all personal maps of a given user are put in relation to user-defined labels of the clusters in question. In this way a personal knowledge perspective is created. It consists of conceptual structures represented in the personal Concept Map and a series of personal DocumentMaps that present specific contexts of user's knowledge. The documents, which are contextualized and labelled in clusters of the user's personal DocumentMaps, are also connected to corresponding concepts in the personal Concept Map. Hence, they represent concrete instances and examples of concepts defining a user's knowledge perspective.

6.2 Constructing Community Perspectives

In a similar way, an overall structure of relationships between words and concepts based on personal maps of all users is created. The inference of relations between concepts from personal maps is based on the fact that by labelling clusters, the users draw a connection between a term and a set of objects. Two concepts to which related objects are assigned by many users can be considered to be related. Using this kind of relationships, a collaborative Concept Map is created that represents a shared community perspective (Novak et al., 2003).

6.3 Supporting Collaborative Discovery and Sharing of Knowledge

This model provides several ways for collaborative discovery and sharing of knowledge.

Applying personal maps for "seeing with different eyes". Firstly, a map can be called up explicitly by another user and applied to classify an information space from the viewpoint of the map author. This supports learning by providing a contextualised view on a possibly unfamiliar knowledge domain. Not only can relevant documents be discovered but also relationships between topics, concepts and documents in the resulting map provide a way for developing an understanding of the other user's knowledge. In this way personal maps support "seeing through different eyes" and facilitate knowledge sharing between members of different communities.

Contextualised search and matchmaking. Secondly, the results of users search queries can be automatically contextualised in the personal maps of different users. The idea is that while the query expresses the user's current information need, the long-term information need (interest profile) can be extracted from the maps a given user has created so far. The search results can then contain both the list of retrieved objects based on full-text keyword match, as well as a ranked list of most relevant personal maps of different users. Search result objects can then be, for example, highlighted within thematic groups represented in the most relevant map. Hence, the user can identify related documents, which a normal, match-only search query would not have retrieved. At the same time, based on document-concept relationships, the corresponding concepts can be marked in the appropriate Concept Map. This supports the discovery of unfamiliar concepts that describe related knowledge perspectives. In this way users can enter queries in their own community vocabularies and discover possibly related artefacts, concepts and people (map authors) from other communities and areas beyond one's own expertise.

Navigating through cross-community concept networks. Through the above describe ways, users from different communities can discover relevant objects and concepts from unfamiliar domains of knowledge. By adding the found objects to their own maps and clusters they express relationships between concepts and documents from different communities. Based on such similarity of objects and similarity of concepts a Concept Map emerges that connects concepts from different communities. This structure can then be used as a means of navigation across different domains of knowledge.

Reflective awareness as a means of constructing new knowledge. Another important aspect is what we call „reflective awareness". The basic idea here is that one of the critical elements influencing the potential for the construction of new knowledge is the existing knowledge of individuals and groups of people. Thus becoming aware of this knowledge is a prerequisite for processes involving the creation of new knowledge. In other words, one of the critical aspects of learning is the ability to change perspective and discover hidden assumptions and mental models underlying a given point of view. From this aspect the personalised knowledge maps can also be seen as a kind of knowledge artefacts that can be interactively manipulated and discussed by the community members (exploring maps of other users, applying them to different situations, comparing a personal concept structure to other individual and shared concept maps) in order to get an understanding of different mental models and interpretative schemas. The idea is that rather than just through automatic inference of relationships, it is through one's interaction with the maps that one can develop an awareness of and insights into implicit structures - such as mental models, values and beliefs - of one's own or shared by the community. The hypothesis is that by achieving this kind of reflective awareness the processes of communication and sharing of knowledge especially in heterogeneous communities can be qualitatively improved to stimulate the emergence of new knowledge.

7 Visualization Model for Interactive Cross-Community Knowledge Artefacts

The task of the visualization model is to present the elicited knowledge structures to the user, in a way which allows her to discover and learn from relationships between different perspectives on community knowledge. As noted in Chapter 5.1 the constructed knowledge maps cannot be considered as static representations, which "codify" knowledge that merely needs to be "presented". Rather we need to visualise dynamic artefacts that can be interactively manipulated by the community members in order to get an understanding of different perspectives.

To achieve this we have developed an interactive visualization model for representing multiple perspectives and relating them to each other. A particular requirement has been that the visualization model needs to be appropriate for embedding it into an exploratory information interface for access to community knowledge repositories. The developed model enables simultaneous visualization of 1) document-topic relationships that can be inferred from heterogeneous community document collections, 2) personal ontologies representing views of individual members, 3) shared ontologies and concept networks representing a community perspective, and 4) relationships between concepts, topics and artefacts used in different communities.

7.1 The Multiple-Perspectives Visualization Model

We employ a multiple coordinated views concept (similar to Becks & Seeling, 2004) for simultaneously providing different visualizations of knowledge structures and information in the community space. Rather than a fixed, predefined semantic structuring of information, the multiple views concept allows us to simultaneously present views of different users and communities in relation to each other.

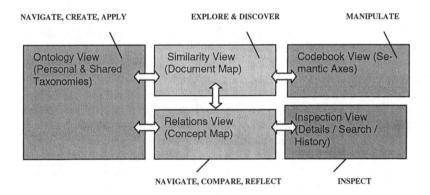

Fig. 3. The Multiple Perspectives Visualization Model

To this end the multiple perspective visualization model (Fig. 3) consists of the following components:

- *Similarity View.* The task of the similarity view is to enable the user to *explore and discover* possible relationships between documents from information spaces of different communities. To achieve this, this view is conceived as a spatial visualization of semantically related document clusters based on inter-document and inter-cluster similarity. Different ways for realizing this view exist, such as methods for clustering textual collections and multidimensional scaling (Card et al., 1999). Such techniques commonly support the construction of visual maps where similar documents and groups of documents are positioned close to each other, and the document groups can be characterized by characteristics concepts that describe their semantics.

- *Codebook View.* This view complements the similarity view, by displaying the main semantic criteria that determined the presented structuring of the document collection. These criteria are represented by a set of principal concepts that best characterize the document collection, such as the most frequent terms in the document pool and the sets of terms that have been used to encode the semantic properties of documents into text vectors used for the mapping. Understanding and manipulating these criteria is a critical requirement for making sense of the visualization and gaining a deeper understanding of implicit knowledge structures contained in the collection. To communicate this to the user we introduce the metaphor of *semantic axes* to describe the "meaning" of the concepts and terms presented in this view.

- *Ontology View.* The ontology view enables the user to *navigate* a document pool based on a predefined semantic structure. This structuring can represent personal views of individual members or shared community views, as well as taxonomies representing formal knowledge domains or organizational structures. As the ontology view represents an explicitely expressed and edited externalisation of a semantic structure (by individuals or groups of users) it provides an insight into explicit knowledge of communities and individual users. But, since the personal ontologies in our model have been created by a method similar to perceptual mapping, they also reflect implicit knowledge of the individual users. Different techniques for visualising ontological structures, such as hierarchical trees, tree maps or graph networks can be used.

- *Relations View.* This view allows the user to visualize and explore relationships between concepts used by different individuals and communities of users. It presents relationships between concepts and groups of concepts, based on inter-concept relationships. Two concepts are defined as related if they are used by the user (or community) in similar contexts. This view maps the patterns of language use in different communities and relationships between them. In contrast to Ontology View where conceptual structures are created manually by the users themselves, the concept maps of the Relations View are extracted by the system. The system thereby combines the relations extracted from word usage in texts with the relations that can be induced from the comparison and analysis of user's personal and shared ontologies (Novak et al., 2003).

- *Inspection View.* This view accommodates the display of object details, the formulation of search queries and the visualization of the history of user actions (e.g. inspected maps, search queries etc.).

7.2   User Interaction with Visualizations

The main modalities of user interaction with the visualizations are selection, navigation and drag&drop interaction. The user can select individual documents or sets of documents in the Similarity View, as well as topics, concepts or documents in the Ontology View and concepts in the Relations View. Selecting an item in a particular view causes related items in other views to be highlighted. For example, the Similarity View might be presenting a system generated structuring of the document collection from a user's community. In the Ontology View, a user's personal Document Map as well as his personal Concept Map might be open. In the Relations View a collaborative Concept Map that represents the relationships between perspectives of all users might be shown. Selecting a document in the Similarity Map would highlight similar documents in the user's personal Document Map and related concepts in his personal Concept Map (Ontology View). At the same time, related concepts stemming from maps of other users would also be highlighted in the collaborative Concept Map. In this way, by simply selecting a document that spurred his interest, a rich context of relationships to different knowledge perspectives is presented to the user. In a similar way, the user might have selected an unfamiliar but interesting concept in the Relations View and would have discovered example documents in the Similarity View - both those directly highlighted by the system as well as those positioned in the same thematic clusters. The discovered relationships can then be incorporated into the personal or community structure by dragging&dropping the documents or concepts in question into the Ontology View. Finally, selecting a particular personal map in the Ontology View as a dynamic semantic template for a given document collection, causes the relevant documents in the Similarity View to be classified into topics defined by the map in question.

7.3 View Coordination

The different views are coordinated between each other according to the "navigational slaving" principle (Baldonado, Woodruff & Kuchinsky, 2000): effects of user actions in one view are immediately reflected in dependent views. In our case, we have two main couplings of dependent views. Firstly, the Codebook view is directly coupled to the Similarity View. As the user explores the document clusters and relationships presented in the Similarity View, she can select individual clusters or sets of documents from different clusters for closer inspection. The visualisation in the Codebook view is updated accordingly, to present only concepts relevant for the clusters and documents in the user's selection. In this way the user can explore the details of the semantic structure of a document collection representing one or more community repositories. The user can also select a subset of concepts presented in the Codebook View and define them as new semantic axes. As a result, the cluster structure presented in the Similarity View will be recalculated by the system, based on the user-defined concepts. Dragging & dropping an individual document, a set of documents or a whole cluster into the inspection view displays details of the documents in question.

A second coupling connects the Similarity View, the Relations View and the Ontology View with each other. Conceptually, this coupling is represented by associations between documents and clusters, documents and concepts, and between concepts themselves. Technically, the coordination is modelled by the star-schema layout with the Similarity View acting as the coordinating view (see also Becks & Seeling, 2004). Whenever the user performs a selection in one view, the corresponding set of documents is determined and the other views are updated appropriately. This is possible because the data-models underlying all views, associate documents as concrete instances of knowledge resources to corresponding concepts, and vice-versa.

8 Prototypical Realization: The Knowledge Explorer

A prototypical realization of the described model for collaborative elicitation and exchange of knowledge and of the related interactive multi-perspective visualization is presented by a multi-agent system and an interactive interface, the Knowledge Explorer (Fig. 4)[1].

8.1 The Multi-agent System

Our prototypical system consists of two groups of agents that together provide a set of services to the client applications. One group of agents is concerned with responding to user requests (e.g. visualization and interactive tasks). These agents have to work very efficiently, as interactive work requires very short respond times. To achieve this, we use a second group of agents, which asynchronously pre-process data and store it in intermediate structures. These agents take much of the workload from the first group of agents. Using this strategy we can use sophisticated and costly data and interaction analysis methods and even so have short respond times. Please refer to Novak et al. (2003) for a more detailed description of the underlying agent system.

8.2 The Knowledge Explorer Interface

The principal goal of the Knowledge Explorer prototype is to realize a tool that incorporates the described model of collaborative knowledge elicitation and multiple perspective visualization into an exploratory information interface for cross-community access to knowledge repositories (Fig. 4).

In the concrete implementation, the Similarity View has been realized by a clustering and visualization method based on the Kohonen's self-organised network. The resulting Document Map presents clusters of related documents based on inter-document similarity. By displaying the distribution of all documents and their grouping in semantically related clusters, such a Document Map (top left) presents the user with a quick overview of the topics and relationships in the community document pool. The semantic space of each cluster is described by the most representative keywords. The corresponding Concept Map (top right), realizing the Relations View is displayed to the right of the Document Map.

The current system distinguishes between three different kinds of Concept Maps: 1) the system-generated Concept Map related to the system generated Document Map, 2) the personal Concept Map is based on term usage in personal maps of a given user, and 3) the collaborative Concept Map presents relationships between terms and concepts used by different users and communities. The user can switch between these different visualizations at will by selecting the appropriate interface icon in the Concept Map window (Fig. 4, top right). Multiple Concept Maps can be visualized by simply dragging the Concept Map icon into another window.

The system-generated Concept Map is realized using a Kohonen self-organized network to determine clusters of words used in similar contexts and their relationships

---

[1] Developed in the project AWAKE – Networked Awareness for Knowledge Discovery, http://awake.imk.fraunhofer.de

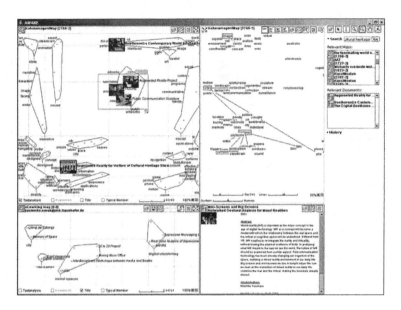

Fig. 4. The Knowledge Explorer Prototype

to principal concepts characterizing the document collection. In this way, the system-generated Concept Map also serves as the Codebook View visualization. The main concepts displayed in red (Fig. 4, top right) present the most characteristic concepts that have determined the clustering in the related Document Map. The user can select any set of terms as new semantic axes and invoke the reclustering of the Document Map based on these new criteria. The construction of personal and collaborative ConceptMaps is based on a variant of the "nearest neighbour" collaborative filtering method. The visualization of the resulting graph network uses a spring-based algorithm for two-dimensional layout of graph structures (Chen, 1999a).

The Ontology View is realized in two ways. On one hand the collaborative Concept Map presents the shared structure, although in the current version it cannot be manually edited and is rather complex due to the large number of connections. The latter problem is addressed by interactive sliders that allow the user to adjust the maximum number of nodes and connections displayed. On the other hand, the personal maps represent user-defined ontologies. They are currently visualized as groups of labelled document clusters on a two-dimensional surface (bottom left). The user can position the documents and the clusters on the 2D surface of the personal map at free will.

The Inspection View has been realized by simply dragging an object into any free window (bottom right). The search query, the interaction history and search results have been accommodated in the rightmost interface column.

9   Application and Evaluation

The practical test bed and an application context of the described work is the Internet platform netzspannung.org (Fleischmann, Strauss, Novak, Paal, Müller, Blome, Peranovic, Seibert & Schneider, 2001). netzspannung.org aims at establishing a knowledge portal that provides insight in the intersections between digital art, culture and information technology. Typical netzspannung users are artists, researchers, designers, curators, journalists and interested public. By using the system in the way described in previous chapters, such a heterogeneous user group is enabled not only to construct an information pool in a collaborative way but also to interactively and collaboratively structure this pool, to visualize and explore it by the means of personalized knowledge maps. Furthermore, the user group sets up a shared navigational structure, which combines different points of view on the semantics of the information. This allows them to explore possible relationships between work in different topics or fields of profession (e.g. for finding projects from different disciplines relevant for one's own work). Another scenario is comparing sets of projects against one's own personal point of view and against views of other experts (e.g. for discovering contexts and hidden assumptions). Finally the general public could use the knowledge maps of experts as a guide for navigating the information space of netzspannung.org.

Following the methodologies of participatory design an early proof-of-concept prototype has been evaluated in a netzspannung.org workshop with a heterogeneous group of target users: curators, artists, information technology researchers, media designers and representatives from museums, cultural institutions and media industries[2]. The users reacted very well to the exploratory interface for discovering relationships between different thematic fields. In particular the idea of an initial system-generated map serving not only as an overview, but also as a means of inspiration for discovering unexpected relationships between different thematic fields has been appreciated. A very much discussed issue has been the users' need to understand the criteria of the system functioning. This is incorporated in the current model by the system-generated Concept Map that provides insight into the clustering criteria of the Document Map and enables its interactive parameterization by the users. The users also highlighted the importance of the support for expressing personal views and relating them into a shared but multi perspective structure. This was seen as an essential feature for supporting the exchanges between such heterogeneous and loosely connected communities as theirs. Finally, they received enthusiastically the envisioned possibility of publishing and exchanging their personal maps with each other.

The developed system has also been internally deployed as information access interface to the submissions of the cast01 conference and of the competition of student projects digital sparks. This simulates the use scenario in which users can explore possible relations between information usually isolated in separate archives of different communities in the fields of media art, research and technology. The results can be tried out in the guided tour and partially online available interactive demos[3]. An early visualization prototype for browsing system generated maps is still in day-to-day use as a public information interface in netzspannung.org[4].

A usability evaluation of the current prototype of the Knowledge Explorer with 12 test persons has proven good acceptance of the main use cases. In particular the fol-

---

[2] This very early proof-of-concept workshop took place in 2001. See http://netzspannung. org/workshops/knowledgemaps
[3] http://awake.imk.fhg.de/guided_tour.html, http://awake.imk.fhg.de/prototypen.html
[4] http://netzspannung.org/cast01/semantic-map

lowing functions were considered very helpful: applying maps of other users for discovering new knowledge, the contextualization of search results and the topic-based navigation across different fields of profession. At the same time the variety of the available interaction and navigation methods was also perceived as a source of complexity that requires a noticeable learning curve. We are currently addressing this by optimising the navigational ways to optimal paths identified in the trial.

10   Concluding Remarks

In this contribution we have discussed the problem of cross community knowledge sharing and visualization, as well as several requirements to successfully enable it.

We have presented an approach based on the construction of personalised knowledge maps and shared concept networks in a way which is unobtrusively embedded in the users everyday activity of access to the community information space. In the described way, a semantic representation of shared understanding of the community can be constructed, which presents the main concepts and relationships describing both the community knowledge and incorporating personal views of individual users. As the collaborative structure is created dynamically based on user interaction with information it will evolve together with the patterns of the community development and interaction. The members of the community can share knowledge through exchanging their personal maps or by navigating the shared concept structure. This is enabled by a multi-perspective knowledge visualization model that has been prototypically realized in the Knowledge Explorer tool. We described how this supports cross-community access to knowledge repositories and outlined the results of an application and evaluation of the prototype to the Internet platform netzspannung.org.

We are aware of several critical issues of the presented model. One is the classical problem of collaborative aggregation methods, which tend to suppress minority views. In consequence only mainstream patterns of relationships might emerge in the shared concept structure, hiding more interesting ones. In an extension to the current model, this problem is addressed explicitly.

Another critical point is also the question of privacy. Since our concrete application context is an interdisciplinary professional community of experts (netzspannung.org), the assumption is that the users will be willing to share their maps, as a motivation for gaining expert reputation within the community. But in other cases this might be a non-trivial problem to consider.

References

Baldonado, M.Q., Woodruff, A., & Kuchinsky, A. (2000). Guidelines for using multiple views in information visualization. In V. di Gesù, S. Levaldi, & L. Tarantino (Eds.), *Proceedings of ACM Advanced Visual Interfaces Conference* (pp. 110-119). New York: ACM Press.

Baldonado, M.Q., & Winograd, T. (1997). SenseMaker: An Information-Exploration Interface Supporting the Contextual Evolution of a User's Interest. In S. Pemberton (Ed.), *Human factors in computing systems: CHI 97 conference proceedings* (pp. 11-18). New York: ACM Press.

Becks, C., & Seeling, C. (2004). SWAPit - A Multiple Views Paradigm for Exploring Associations of Texts and Structured Data. In M.F. Costabile (Ed.), *ACM Proceedings of the 9th International Working Conference on Advanced Visual Interfaces (AVI'2004)* (pp. 193-196). New York: ACM Press.

Berger, P., & Luckmann, T. (1966). *The Social Construction of Reality: a Treatise in the Sociology of Knowledge.* Garden City, NY: Doubleday.

Boland, J.R., & Tenkasi, R.V. (1995). Perspective Making and Perspective Taking in Communities of Knowing. *Organization Science*, 6(4), 350-372.

Brown J.S., & Duguid P. (1991). Organizational Learning and Communities-of-Practice: Toward a Unified View of Working, Learning and Innovation. *Organization Science*, 2(1), 40-57.

Bruner, J. (1990). *Acts of Meaning.* Cambridge, MA: Harvard University Press.

Card, S.K., Mackinlay, J.D., & Schneiderman, B. (1999). *Readings in Information Visualization; Using Vision to think.* Los Altos, CA: Morgan Kaufmann.

Carotenuto, L., Etienne, W., Fontaine, M., Friedman, J., Newberg, H., Muller, M., Simpson, M., Slusher, J., & Stevenson, K. (1999). Community space: Towards flexible support for voluntary knowledge communities. In T. Rodden, & K. Schmidt (Eds.), *Online Proceedings of Workshop on Workspace Models for Collaboration.* London, UK: Springer. Online available: http://www.dcs.qmw.ac.uk/research/distrib/Mushroom/workshop/final-papers/lotus.pdf.

Chen, C. (1999a). *Information Visualisation and Virtual Environments.* London, UK: Springer.

Chen, C. (1999b). Visualizing Semantic Spaces and Author Co-Citation Networks in Digital Libraries. *Information Processing and Management*, 35(3), 401-420.

Cohen, D., & Prusak, L. (2001). *In Good Company: How Social Capital Makes Organizations Work.* Boston: Harvard Business School Press.

Dougherty D. (1992). Interpretative barriers to successful product innovation in large firms. *Organization Science*, 3(2), 179-202.

Eppler, M., & Burkhard, R. (2004). *Knowledge Visualization: Towards a New Discipline and its Fields of Applications.* Working Paper, Wirtschaftsinformatik. Retrieved from http://www.wirtschaftsinformatik.de/wi_arbeitsberichte.php?op=anzeigearbeitsbericht&abid=142.

Erickson, T., & Kellogg, W.A. (2001). Knowledge Communities: Online Environments for Supporting Knowledge Management and its Social Context. In M. Ackerman, V. Pipek, & V. Wulf (Eds.), *Sharing Expertise: Beyond Knowledge Management* (pp. 299-326). Cambridge, MA: MIT Press.

Fayyad, U.M., Piatetsky-Shapiro, G., & Smyth, P. (1996). From data mining to knowledge discovery: An overview. In U.M. Fayyad, G. Piatetsky-Shapiro, P. Smyth, & R. Uthurusamy (Eds.), *Advances in Knowledge Discovery and Data Mining* (pp. 1-34). Cambridge, MA: AAAI/MIT Press.

Fleischmann, M., Strauss, W., Novak, J., Paal, S., Müller, B., Blome, G., Peranovic, P., Seibert, Ch., & Schneider, M. (2001). netzspannung.org : an internet media lab for knowledge discovery in mixed realities. In M. Fleischmann (Ed.), *Proceedings of cast01 - living in mixed realities* (http://netzspannung.org/version1/journal/special/index.html). Sankt Augustin: Fraunhofer IMK.

Huff, A.S., & Jenkins, M. (2002). *Mapping Strategic Knowledge.* London, UK: SAGE Publications.

Kelly, G.A. (1955). *The Psychology of Personal Constructs.* New York: Norton.

Lacher, M. (2003). *Supporting the Exchange of Knowledge in Communities of Interest via Document Catalog Mediation.* PhD Thesis, Technical Univ. Munich.

Lave, J., & Wenger, E. (1991). *Situated Learning: Legitimate Peripheral Participation*. New York, NY: Cambridge University Press.

Nonaka, I., & Takeuchi, H. (1995). *The Knowledge-Creating Company*. Oxford, UK: Oxford University Press.

Novak, J., Wurst, M., Fleischmann, M., & Strauss, W. (2003). Discovering, visualizing and sharing knowledge through personalized learning knowledge maps. In L. van Elst, V. Dignum, & A. Abecker (Eds.), *Agent-mediated Knowledge Management: Papers from the AAAI Spring Symposium* (pp. 101-108). Menlo Park, CA: AAAI Press.

Papert, S. (1991). *Introduction*. In I. Harel, & S. Papert (Eds.), *Constructionism* (p. 1). Norwood, NJ: Ablex Publishing Corporation.

Pirolli, P., & Card, S. (1995). Information foraging in information access environments. In I.R. Katz, R. Mack, L. Marks, M.B. Rosson, & J. Nielsen (Eds.), *Proceedings of the SIGCHI conference on Human factors in computing systems* (pp. 51-58). New York: ACM Press.

Resnick, P., Iacovou, N., Suchak, M., Bergstrom, P., & Riedl, J. (1994). GroupLens: An Open Architecture for Collaborative Filtering of Netnews. In J.B. Smith, D.F. Smith, & T.W. Malone (Eds.), *Proceedings of the 1994 ACM Conference on CSCW* (pp. 175-186). New York: ACM Press.

Rheingold, H. (1993). *Virtual Communities: Homesteading on the Electronic Frontier*. Cambridge, MA: MIT Press.

Sack, W. (2001). Conversation Map: An Interface for Very Large-Scale Conversations. *Journal of Management Information Systems*, *17*(3), 73-92.

Shardanand, U., & Maes, P. (1995). Social information filtering: algorithms for automating "word of mouth". In B. Nardi, G.C. van der Veer, & M.J. Tauber (Eds.), *Proceedings of the SIGCHI Conference on Human factors in computing systems* (pp. 210-217). New York: ACM Press.

Shaw, M.L., & Gaines, B.R. (1995). Comparing Constructions through the Web. In J.L. Schnase, & E.L. Cunnius (Eds.), *Proceedings of CSCL95: Computer Supported Cooperative Learning* (pp. 300-307). Mahwah, NJ: Erlbaum.

Star, S.L. (1989). The Structure of Ill-Structured Solutions: Boundary Objects and Heterogeneous Distributed Problem Solving. In L. Glaser, & M.N. Huhn (Eds.), *Readings in Distributed Artificial Intelligence, Vol. II* (pp. 37-54). San Mateo, CA: Morgan Kaufman Publishers Inc..

Swan, J. (2001). Knowledge Management in Action: Integrating Knowledge Across Communities. In R.H. Sprague, Jr. (Ed.), *34th Annual Hawaii International Conference on System Sciences HICSS-34* (p. 7017). Maui, Hawaii: IEEE Computer Society Publications.

Turkle, S. (1995). *Life on the Screen: Identity in the Age of the Internet*. New York: Simon and Schuster.

Vygotsky, L. (1962). *Thought and Language*. Cambridge, MA: The MIT Press (republished 1986).

Wenger, E. (1998). *Communities of Practice: Learning, Meaning and Identity*. Cambridge, MA: University Press.

Information Visualization

Modeling Interactive, 3-Dimensional Information Visualizations Supporting Information Seeking Behaviors

Gerald Jaeschke[1], Martin Leissler[2], and Matthias Hemmje[1]

[1] FernUniversität Hagen, Universitätsstr. 1,
58097 Hagen, Germany
{gerald.jaeschke, matthias.hemmje}@fernuni-hagen.de
[2] Brainmelt GmbH, Hugenottenallee 15,
63263 Neu Isenburg, Germany
martin@brainmelt.com

Abstract. Information visualization and knowledge visualization use comparable techniques and methods. Based on mapping rules, resource objects are translated into visual objects as meaningful representations, offering easy and comprehensive access. Whereas information visualization displays data objects and relations, knowledge visualization maps knowledge elements and ontologies. Bridging this gap must start at concept level. Our approach is to design a declarative language for describing and defining information visualization techniques. The information visualization modeling language (IVML) provides a means to formally represent, note, preserve, and communicate structure, appearance, behavior, and functionality of information visualization techniques and applications in a standardized way. The anticipated benefits comprise both application and theory.

1 Introduction

Knowledge visualization and information visualization have progressed independently of one another. But there are endeavors to bring these research fields together. Modern, computer-based mapping tools are capable of displaying both content and conceptual knowledge at the same time. In the predominant approach, conceptual maps structure the domain and serve as navigational tool that provides knowledge-based access to information. Links in the map attached to concepts reference underlying information and allow to immediately access that information. Information, also referred to as content knowledge, comprises, for example, personal notes, sketches, and example instances of concepts. With this linking feature, this kind of mapping tools could serve as an interface between knowledge visualization and information visualization when the content knowledge consists of abstract mass data. In such alliance, information visualization and knowledge visualization can collaborate side by side.

Information visualization and knowledge visualization can further mutually enrich each other beyond this scope. Today, both disciplines endue strong conceptual foundations. At the same time, information visualization and knowledge visualization

S.-O. Tergan and T. Keller (Eds.): Knowledge and Information Visualization, LNCS 3426, pp. 119–135, 2005.
© Springer-Verlag Berlin Heidelberg 2005

employ comparable techniques and methods: Based on mapping rules, resource objects are translated into visual objects as meaningful representations, offering easy and comprehensive access to the subject matter presented. Whereas information visualization displays data objects and relations, knowledge visualization maps explicate knowledge representations, e.g. concepts.

Under these circumstances, knowledge visualization should be able to adopt achievements that emerged from information visualization research and vice versa. Mapping tools then could display conceptual knowledge and content knowledge within one and the same visual environment. Moreover, mapping tools could visualize knowledge applying (parts of) information visualization techniques and the other way round, provided that setting up a common basis is successful.

Bridging this gap must start at concept level. We tackle this challenge from the information visualization perspective. Our approach is to design a declarative language for describing and defining information visualization techniques. The information visualization modeling language (IVML) provides a means to formally represent, note, preserve, and communicate structure, appearance, behavior, and functionality of information visualization techniques and their applications in a standardized way.

The anticipated benefits comprise both application and theory. Standardized models allow for the specification and implementation of diverse interpreters serving various target platforms. Graphical user-interfaces deploying information visualization techniques can be described and dynamically generated on-the-fly, also by machines. More importantly, the underlying formal model underlying the dynamic generation also renders possible analysis and reasoning, in turn supporting the detection of (information) visualization design flaws.

Such a language needs to rest on solid foundations. The information visualization modeling language puts into practice a formal model that reflects the concepts and relationships of information visualization as it is understood today. To the best of our knowledge, no such integrated model exists. Research on information visualization has so far established an outline of the information visualization process and shed light on a broad range of detail aspects involved. However, there is no model in place that describes the nature of information visualization in a coherent, detailed, and well-defined way.

In order to mutually open-up the treasure chests of visualization techniques for knowledge and information, information visualization and knowledge visualization must base on a joint visualization model. Or at least, they must share a significant amount of visualization model. Integrating the principles of knowledge visualization techniques, such information and knowledge visualization modeling language (IKVML) could provide the means to represent both information and knowledge visualization techniques.

On our way towards the information visualization modeling language, first we survey and discuss extant models of which each covers selected facets of (information) visualization (section 2). The survey focuses on work that devised classification schemas. Our supposition that the presence of classifications indicate an elaborated level of formalization is the rationale behind this selection. Second, we provide an overview of the entire set of models under investigation and discuss the coverage of and the relationships between the models (section 3). Next, we present computational requirements as well as requirements imposed by the application the information visualization modeling language has to fulfill (section 4). We conclude by sketching application scenarios that illustrate the language's benefits within resource-based e-learning scenarios (section 5). Throughout this paper, we will refer to the visualization reference model in order to organize our investigations.

2 Information Visualization Models

"Classification lies at the heart of every scientific field." (Lohse, Biolsi, Walker & Rueter, 1994) In striving for a better understanding of information visualization, a variety of classification schemes have been proposed over the past years. Depending on provenance and intention, they shed light on the information visualization process, its application, or its utility. Information visualization techniques, applications, systems, and frameworks can be classified according to the data types they can display, user tasks they support, characteristics of visual representations they deploy as well as cognitive aspects of their visual appearance.

Reference model for visualization. Card, Mackinlay and Shneiderman (1999) introduced a reference model for information visualization (Fig. 1), which provides a high-level view on the (information) visualization process.

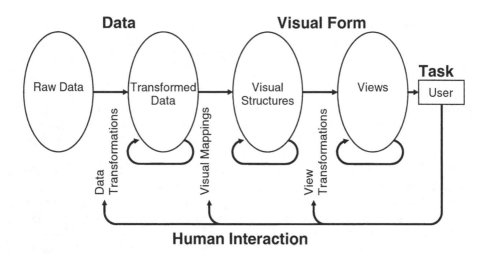

Fig. 1. Reference model for visualization

The model assumes a repository of raw data, which exist in a proprietary format, be it structured or unstructured. To get to a visualization of this data, data have to first undergo a set of transformations. Data transformations comprise filtering of raw data, computation of derived data as well as data normalization. These steps result in a set of transformed data in a unified structure. Visual transformations map the transformed data onto a corresponding visual structure. From this visual structure, a set of views can now be generated, which allow users to navigate through the display. User interactions can influence the transformation process at different stages. Users can adjust their view on the data, change the visual structure, or even affect the data transformation. The cyclic arrows in the diagram refer to the fact that the processes involved in the distinct steps are of an iterative nature and can occur repeatedly before the next step follows.

Data type. Shneiderman (1996) suggested a taxonomy for information visualization designs built on data type and task, the type by task taxonomy (TTT). He distinguished seven data types. High-level abstractions and specific data-types are treated as subordinates of the types presented. In this model, Shneiderman assumes that all data in information space are collections of items, where items have multiple attributes.

- *1-dimensional*
  Text files and alphanumeric list of names
- *2-dimensional*
  Geographic map or book layout
- *3-dimensional*
  Real world objects and chemical molecules
- *Temporal*
  Time-series and scientific measurement rows
- *Multi-dimensional*
  Relational database content
- *Tree*
  Structured data collections with hierarchy constraints
- *Network*
  Structured object sets which do not apply to tree constraints.

Shneiderman (1996) deployed the type taxonomy to sort-out research prototypes of that time and point towards new opportunities. He himself considered the classification incomplete and forecast that upcoming applications would require novel and, respectively, specialized data structures.

A variety of consecutive taxonomies proposed extensions to the TTT, but were never as widely adopted as Shneiderman's work. In his summary, Keim (2002) discards 3-dimensional data and temporal data as data-types on their own. In contrast to the TTT, temporal data is a peculiarity of one-dimensional data. Text in turn becomes promoted a data type, whereas Shneiderman considered it one-dimensional. Hypertext joins text. Central information objects in text as well as in hypertext are documents. As outlined in (Keim, 2002), documents themselves are not atomic but, more often than not, internally are of complex structure and most standard visualization techniques cannot be applied right away. First a transformation of the text data into description vectors is necessary. In the last decade, hypertext has certainly become a widely available and significant data repository. Yet, as hypertext can be considered a directed network structure of documents, considering it a data-type opens up ambiguity in the model. Extending the TTT, Keim introduces software and algorithms as new data types that could be visualized.

Visual representations. Visual representations, in general, are structures for expressing knowledge. Long before computer technology emerged, visualizations were well-established and widely used. In their empirical study Lohse et al. (1994) investigate how people classify two-dimensional visual representations into meaningful categories. From this survey, a structural classification of visual representations became apparent.

- *Graphs* encode quantitative information using position and magnitude of geometric objects; graphs typically deploy a Cartesian coordinate or polar coordinate sys-tem
- *Tables* are an arrangement of words, numbers, signs, or combinations of them to exhibit a set of facts or relationships in a compact format
  - *Graphical tables* use color to encode numerical data
  - *Numerical tables* show numeric data in text format
- *Time charts* display temporal data; they differ from tables in their emphasis on temporal data
- *Network charts* show the relationships among components; symbols indicate the presence or absence of components; correspondences among the components are shown by lines, arrows, proximity, similarity, or containment
- *Diagrams*
  - *Structure diagrams* are a static description of a physical object
  - *Process diagrams* describe the interrelationships and processes associated with physical objects
- *Maps* are symbolic representations of physical geography; maps depict geographic locations of particular features using symbols or lettering
  - *Cartograms* are spatial maps that show quantitative data
  - *Chloropleths* use color, grey scale, or texture to code areas of equal value
  - *Isopleths* use lines to join points with the same quantity of value
  - *Dot maps* use points or symbols to show the location of individual points on a map
  - *Flow maps* show direction of movement by the number, width, and direction of lines and arrows
- *Icons* impart a single interpretation or meaning for a picture; each icon provides a unique label for a visual representation
- *Photo-realistic pictures* are realistic images of an object or scene.

The visual artifacts under examination originated from the domain of static, two-dimensional graphic representations. Hence, no statement can be made to what extent the classification also covers three-dimensional or interactive displays. Lohse et al. (1994) themselves mention as a caveat that their classification schema structures the domain of visual representations at a high level. As yet, no deep, hierarchical struc-tures within clusters have been identified. Moreover, the study focuses on perceived similarity among the visual artifacts that were inspected. Instead, a classification must represent structure that is used by people in interpreting graphs.

Visualization techniques. The classification identified by Lohse et al. (1994) distinguishes itself by clear terminology. Common terms like diagrams, or specialized terms, like chloropleths, indicate classes of visual representations that deploy a well-defined set of visualization techniques that are already established. More importantly, visual representations often get associated with scenarios in which they are deployed regularly.

Keim (2002) concentrates on the design of the visual environment and suggests a classification of visualization techniques that takes into consideration recent developments in information visualization.

- *Standard 2D/3D displays* deploy traditional visual encodings.
- *Geometrically transformed displays* find appealing and useful geometric transformations of visualizations of multidimensional data sets.
- *Icon-based displays* map the attribute values of a multidimensional data item to the features of an icon.
- *Dense pixel displays* map each dimension value to a colored pixel and group the pixels belonging to each dimension into adjacent areas.
- *Stacked displays* present data partitioned in a hierarchical fashion.

Wiss and Carr (1998) intuitively grouped information visualization designs according to their presentation.

- *Node-link style designs* typically support networks and tree data types.
- *Raised surface designs* display information on surfaces (horizontal or vertical) that gets distorted.
- *Information landscapes* support a variety of data types; they all share 2.5D appearance with information plotted as shapes on a surface.
- *Other designs* that do not fall into previous classes.

The classifications of Keim (2002) as well as of Wiss and Carr (1998) describe high-level procedures for the construction of visual environments.

All classifications of visualization techniques examined are concerned with visual attributes like color (texture, shading), shape, size, position, and (semantic symbols). In dynamic systems, however, time can serve as additional dimension for display. With this approach, all visual attributes can alter in time. The change of position during time is also known as animation.

In the last decades, a large number of novel information visualization techniques have been developed. Good overviews of the approaches can be found in a number of recent books (Card et al., 1999; Ware, 2000; Spence, 2000).

Tasks. Bundled with the type taxonomy, Shneiderman (1996) enumerated seven tasks users could perform on the data. Complex tasks, e.g. focus & context, can be described as a combination of tasks presented, in this case overview, relate, and zoom.

- *Overview* Gain an overview of the entire collection.
- *Zoom* Enlarge items of interest.
- *Filter* Filter out uninteresting items.
- *Details on demand* Select an item or group and get details when needed.
- *Relate* View relationships among items.
- *History* Keep a history of actions to support undo, replay, and progressive refinement.
- *Extract* Take out sub-collections of data or history to save and communicate.

Interaction. The information visualization process of transforming data into visual representations is a one-way street unless the human perceiver is given the opportunity to intervene. Human interaction completes the loop between visual forms and control of the visualization process. It includes controlling the mappings performed in the visualization process (Card et al., 1999): data transformations, visual mappings, and view transformations.

Although interactive techniques and metaphors differ in design, Chuah and Roth (1996) have identified primitive interactive components visualization systems have in common. Composing these primitives can model the complex behavior of visualization system user-interfaces at the semantic level of design. The functional classification distinguishes between three main types of basic visualization interactions. Each main type ramifies to a hierarchy of more specific interaction types.

- *Graphical operations* affect the graphical representation of data.
  - *Encode data* operations modify visual mappings (Fig. 1).
    - *Change mapping* operations alter existing or create new mappings between data and visual representations.
    - *Transform mapping* operations manipulate the encoding range of mappings, allowing the magnification of differences between values or separate sets of objects.
  - *Set graphical value* operations alter visual representations of selected entities by directly specifying the new value. Hence, the appearance of the affected visual objects no longer solely depends on the underlying data.
    - *Constant* operations set the graphical attribute to a constant.
    - *Graphical transform* operations determine the values of visual attributes through formulas.
  - *Manipulate objects* operations treat graphical objects as building blocks and modify the visual scene independent of underlying data and mappings.
    - *Copy* operations instantiate new graphical objects.
    - *Delete* operations remove graphical objects from the visual representation.
- *Set operations* refer to all those operations that act on or form sets. Sets provide users with the capability to collect and assemble objects that belong together. The underlying data gets enriched with new classification information.
  - *Create set* operations establish new object sets.
    - *Enumerate* operations let users individually pick objects to accommodate from the visualization.
    - *Express membership* operations express conditions for set membership through a formula or constraints. All objects that meet these criteria are automatically added to the set in bulk.
  - *Delete set* operations dissolve sets whereas objects formerly included persist.
  - *Summarize set* operations perform aggregation operations on set members.
- *Data operations* directly affect the data presented by the visualization. In contrast to all other interactions, data operations promote visualizations. Visualizations become a means not only to retrieve but also to input and change data.
  - *Add* operations create new data elements.
  - *Delete* operations destroy data elements.
  - *Derived attributes* operations augment data with new attributes.

Compared to the reference model for visualization (Fig. 1), this classification sprawls beyond the traditional limits of information visualization. In addition to presenting, retrieving, and exploring data, data operations also allow the manipulation of underlying (raw) data. This feature is required for visualizations in order to grow to full-fledged application system user-interfaces.

Set operations also contribute to this development. Although not in the center of the information visualization process, set operations reflect today's code of practice. Theus (2003) adds that setting up complex selection sets usually is achieved by stepwise refinement. Boolean operators combine subsets derived by enumeration or membership rules, creating unions, intersections, and complements.

Interactions to geometrically navigate within the view presented are not considered in that work.

View transformations. The visual mapping process results in graphical structures that represent information. In a final step, views render these graphical structures and make them accessible to the human perceiver, on computer screens, for example. View transformations specify graphical parameters that influence the view such as position, scaling, and clipping. Varying view transformations can reveal more information from one and the same graphical structure than static visualizations possibly could. Card, Mackinlay and Shneiderman (1999) distinguish three common view transformations.

- *Location probes* are view transformations that expose additional information based on the position within the graphical structure. When triggered by the human perceiver, location probes could also be referred to as details-on-demand. For display, location probes can either augment the visual structure in the selected region or create additional views.
- *Viewpoint controls* are pure geometrical transformations to zoom, pan, and clip the viewpoint.
- *Distortion techniques* help to maintain orientation during the exploration process (Keim, 2002). Meanwhile the focus is displayed in great detail, the surrounding context remains visible. Distortion techniques graphically transform the visual structure to render focus and context combined within one single view.

Since location probes can, and often do, result in additional views, it is critical to classify them as view transformations. Moreover, location probes also do influence the visual mapping, in case they trigger the enrichment of the visual structure for details-on-demand.

Scales, as introduced by Theus (2003), encompass location probes and viewpoint controls. The former is referred to as logical zoom, whereas the pure graphical operational performed by viewpoint controls is a simple zoom.

Leung and Apperley (1994) introduce transformation and magnification functions for various distortion-oriented presentation techniques. Different classes of functions refine the classification of distortion view transformations.

Multiple view coordination. Multiple view systems "use two or more distinct views to support the investigation of a single conceptual entity." (Wang Baldonado,

Woodruff & Kuchinsky, 2000) To fully exploit the potential of multiple views, sophisticated coordination mechanisms between views are required.

- *Navigational slaving*
  Movements in one view are automatically propagated to another view.
- *Linking*
  Connects data in one view with data in another view.
- *Brushing*
  Corresponding data items in different views are highlighted simultaneously.

Views are distinct, if they reveal dissimilar aspects of the conceptual entity presented. Roberts (2000) identified three ways in which multiple views may be formed according to stages in the information visualization process comparable to the reference model (Fig. 1). Multiple views from the filter level branch during the data mapping step. Multiple views from different mappings emanate from varying visual mappings. Finally, display-level multiple views arise due to altering the viewport or projection specification.

Multiple views perfectly join with the reference model (Fig. 1), which did consider sequential presentation of views, but no coordination of parallel views.

Theus (2003) reports about the most common use of multiple views.

Cognition. By definition, the purpose of information visualization is to "communicate properties of information to a human". The research on information visualization must not stop at producing and designing visualization but must also consider how visualizations affect the human observer. Wiss & Carr (1998) propose a framework for classification of 3D information visualization designs based on three cognitive aspects.

- *Attention* denotes how designs draw attention to certain elements of the visualized data.
  Focus on certain elements of the visualized information. Differences in visual appearance, movement, location, and metaphors can be used to attract human attentions.
- *Abstraction* indicates how designs support information structuring and information hiding.
  Clustering or grouping parts of the information to form higher-level elements.
- *Affordances* measure how designs show to the users what they can do with them.
  The visual cues that a visual element gives to indicate what can be done with it.

Any of these aspects allow for a multitude of peculiarities. A survey revealed that information visualization systems have come up with a variety of solutions in order to guide user attention, abstract from complex data and indicate available functionality and interaction modes. Introducing their solutions as second level classes would turn the current framework of aspects into a classification.

Information visualization operating steps. The data state reference model (Chi, 2000) describes visualization techniques with a focus on data and its transformations. The model breaks down the information visualization process into four data stages:

value, analytical abstraction, visualization abstraction, and view. Three types of data transformation operators carry over into states.

- *Data transformation* operations generate some form of analytical abstraction from the raw data values.
- *Visualization transformation* operations further transform analytical abstractions into visualizable content. The visualization abstractions resulting from this are not visual structures yet.
- *Visual mapping transformation* operations map visualizable content into graphical structures.

Another four types of operators cater for data transformation within data stages. Based on the data state model, Chi decomposed the data processing pipelines of visualization techniques and identified operating steps they share.

3   Information Visualization Model Consolidation

With our approach, we do not intend to substitute information visualization models and classifications that have evolved so far. Instead, best-of-breed will be selected and combined into one consolidated formal model describing information visualization.

3.1   Information Visualization Model Space

All the classification models presented describe selected subsets of the complex area of information visualization. Our attempt to arrive at a consolidated model for information visualization starts out with the analysis of what areas these discrete models cover and how they are mutually related (Fig. 2). To answer that question, we locate information-visualization models within *model space* for information visualization. There are two axes that span model space. The first dimension reflects the processing pipeline for (information) visualizations as introduced by the reference model for visualization (Fig. 1). Roughly speaking, three sections subdivide this pipeline. Beginning with the data section, data is transformed and mapped into graphical objects in the visualization section. Of course, models describing data properties, for example, are located to the left whereas multiple views and their coordination cover the area from the middle to the right. The second dimension expresses dependencies between models as well as the level of abstraction from the actual task of handling (computer) data. On the lowest level, models deal with data properties and visual attributes, whereas at the upper levels, models such as cognition abstract away from implementation details. Upper level models depend on their subordinates. The absence of visual objects and their properties would render talking about cognition futile.

Of course, as information visualization model space lacks metrics, positions and borderlines get blurred. So far, the diagram reflects our subjective assessment. Furthermore, drawing rectangles is a simplification. More often than not, single models

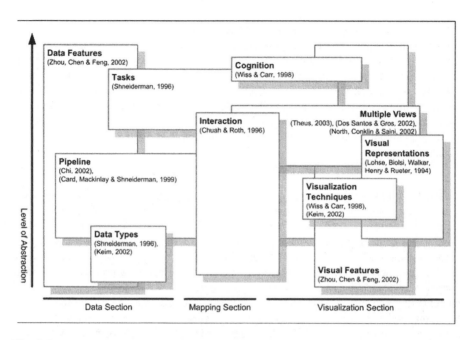

Fig. 2. Interrelationship of information visualization models in information visualization model space

do not handle all aspects at one constant level of abstraction and vice versa. This holds true especially for substantial models. Hence, the areas in the diagram depict an approximation of the real state of affairs.

3.2 Coverage and Ambiguity

The first overview reveals that there is little white space in the diagram. Judging from that, the extant models in total cover nearly all facets of information visualization as we know it today.

The frayed right side of the visualization section indicates that information visualization model space has no clearly marked border in this direction. Multiple views, visual representations, cognition, and interaction not only apply to information visualization exclusively. Partially, these models belong to visualization in general. From our point of view, visualization model space begins in the visualization section and extends beyond the diagram.

The next observation is that rectangles in the diagram overlap. If this occurs within one section, the models involved compete. Such conflict can be observed, for example, between data types, as introduced by Shneiderman's (1996) TTT, and the data features invented by Zhou et al. (2002). Sorting out the differences and matching concepts are the anticipated tedious tasks required in order to arrive at a joint model. The above presentation of information visualization models discusses corresponding models. Note that the collection of models portrays selected samples. Less important items have already been omitted.

Sections cannot always be clearly separated without ambiguity. Cross-section over-lapping arises when one and the same phenomenon of information visualization is covered by various models starting out from different perspectives. For instance, in-teraction and the processing pipeline are closely interwoven. From the standpoint of the reference model, view transformations are modifications that are likely to be trig-gered by human interaction. Conversely, interaction claims that location probes and viewpoint controls are their terrain, and terms them interactive filtering, interactive zooming, interactive distortion, and interactive linking and brushing.

3.3 Quality and Level of Granularity

As the diagram suggests, the area of information visualization has been thoroughly re-searched and only few white spaces remain. Yet the stake the various models claim reflects neither the model quality nor its level of detail. There are always two sides to quality: correctness and completeness. Before they can be integrated into the coherent model, extant models need to be assessed with care. More easy to judge is the model's level of granularity. Classification systems vary in how detailed a way they have been conceived. Generally, coarse models leave space for alternatives and variations, whereas in depth models provide better guidance. To illustrate the difference, the in-teraction model with three hierarchy levels of classes is far more detailed than the data types according to the TTT. Then again, not all facets of information visualiza-tion share the same level of complexity. It is natural that different areas feature differ-ent numbers of classes.

4   Information Visualization Modeling Language

Current practice in information technology favors the use of formal languages as rep-resentation formalisms which abstract away from details of specific realization. The information visualization modeling language enables the declarative description of an information visualization need or solution in preference to describing the steps re-quired in order to realize the visualization process. It is a formal language; it has a set of strings which can be derived from a (formal) grammar consisting of a deductive system of axioms and inference rules (Partee, ter Meulen & Wall, 1990). We give the term information visualization modeling language *blueprint* to the formal description of an information visualization technique or application expressed by the language. A blueprint is composed of a number of sections. Blueprint sections are legal combina-tions of language elements derived from the grammar.

Conceiving the information visualization modeling language may follow two sim-ple rules of thumb. First, concepts identified within the model constitute the vocabu-lary. Secondly, relationships between concepts determine the grammar. Presumably, however, relationships from the model will also contribute to the language vocabu-lary. The information visualization modeling language will constitute a specific en-coding of the consolidated information visualization model. In order to be useful, its design has to meet requirements for both computation and application.

4.1 Computational Desiderata

The information visualization modeling language (IVML) carries knowledge about information visualization within its schema. Moreover, information visualizations denoted in the language are formal structures which represent knowledge about information visualization techniques, applications, and requirements, respectively. Hence, the information visualization modeling language can be considered a meaning representation language. Meaning representation languages need to meet a number of practical computational requirements (Jurafsky & Martin, 2000).

Verifiability is the most basic requirement for a meaning representation: "it must be possible to use the representation to determine the relationship between the meaning of a sentence and the world as we know it." In the case of the IVML, it can (say) describe information visualization techniques and data types these techniques are capable of displaying. These descriptions establish knowledge. Demands for visualization of data of a specific type can be considered a question expressed in IVML. If there is no visualization technique that can handle the requested data type, matching will fail. In general, sentences can have different meanings depending on the circumstances in which they are uttered. Since the IVML is intended to be the means we reason about and act upon, it is critical that blueprint sections expressed in the language (analogous to natural language sentences) have single unambiguous interpretations. The IVML is required to be an *unambiguous representation*. Conversely, distinct sentences in general may have the same meaning. Such a situation is highly problematic, since it hinders verification and adds complexity to reasoning. Therefore, the IVML should follow the doctrine of *canonical form*: Sentences that mean the same thing should have the same representation. More complex requests cannot be answered solely on the basis of verification and canonical form. Let's agree that whilst traditional diagrams in general are suitable for presentation purposes, they are not a good choice to pursue data exploration. Pie charts belong to this class of traditional visualization techniques. To meet the demand for visualization of data for presentation purposes using pie charts, *inference* is required. It must be possible to draw conclusions about propositions that are not explicitly represented, but are nevertheless logically derivable from the knowledge available. Finally, in order to be useful, the IVML must be *expressive* enough to treat a wide range of the subject matter of information visualization. But, since research in this area is ongoing, the IVML cannot be expected to be complete.

4.2 Applicational Desiderata

By analogy with design criteria that underlie related modeling languages (Web3D Consortium, 1997), the information visualization modeling language should meet a set of requirements in order to be useful in application.

Information visualization is a multifaceted subject matter. The formal description of information visualization techniques and applications using the IVML will be accordingly complex. *Composability* provides the ability to use and combine information visualization objects, like data sources, mapping formulas, or view definitions, within an IVML application and thus allows reusability. Depending on the application, the complete set of constructs is not always required. In a single-view application, for example, multiple-view coordination is pointless. The design of the IVML must permit the omission of constructs which are not essential for the given situation. The notion of language constructs which are independent by design is known as *orthogonality*. Since the IVML is anticipated not to cover all future inventions in the area of information visualization, the language has to be *extensible*, allowing the introduction of new concepts. Wherever concepts are missing in the language, *bypasses* help to fill the gaps with alternative solutions. Bypasses also stand in when IVML design does not meet particular requirements. In the case of parsers interpreting the IVML in order to render information visualizations, the bypass addresses purpose-built implementations. The IVML needs to be *authorable*: Computer programs must be capable of creating, editing, and maintaining IVML files, as well as automatic translation programs for converting related data into IVML. More generally, the language must be *capable of implementation* on a wide range of systems. Considering the implementation of software systems, language design must foster the development of scalable high-*performance* implementations. Finally, IVML must *scale* and enable arbitrarily large dynamic information visualization applications.

5   Modeled Information Visualizations in Education

The characteristics of the IVML can greatly contribute to the field of education. Today, mapping tools for visualizing conceptual knowledge are broadly available and so are mapping tools for visualizing content knowledge. Out of these mapping tools, a large number allow for designing and utilizing visualizations in a quick and efficient manner. Modern, computer-based mapping tools are capable of handling both content and conceptual knowledge at the same time. In the majority of cases, however, mapping tools are not capable of externalizing the knowledge implicitly embedded in the design of the visualization of content knowledge. This was, however, essential for the application of mapping tools in education. Imagine tutors designing lectures or self-driven students generating individual maps while learning. The tutor notes the created map so that students later can recall and use it. Students in turn conserve their individual map. Or, for sharing their experience, communicate it to peers. In all these scenarios, the modeling language captures structure, appearance, behavior, and functionality of the visualization. In fact, IVML stores knowledge about the mappings.

5.1   Peer Students Scenario

Imagine a student investigating in a self-regulated fashion, being engaged in an information retrieval dialogue with a computer-based interactive information visualization system, seeking to meet an information need he cannot fully specify. Hence, it is impossible for him to formulate a question and have the system answer in a targeted way. Instead, the dialogue is of an exploratory nature. During a series of iterative steps the student learns about the data source, locates relevant information, and refines his information need. This process is put into practice by human actions demanding the system to adapt in return. Beginning with an initial setup, interactions manipulate data transformations, visual mappings, and view transformations. Finally, if the dialogue succeeds, the student will have come to a relevant data set answering his information needs.

So far, the mapping tool and its functionality supported the student in primarily one out of a variety of knowledge management processes (Tergan, 2003): The student *localized* content knowledge and the corresponding knowledge resources. But there is more to it. At the end of the dialogue, the student will not only have come to a relevant data set answering his information needs, but moreover end up with an information visualization application tailored to the task performed. During the dialogue, knowledge has been *generated*. On the one hand, the student gained new insights. On the other hand, the mapping tool configuration reflects how the knowledge has been derived and justifies the new knowledge.

Imagine the system was able to export its final state as a blueprint. The information visualization modeling language would then be deployed to formally *represent* the knowledge about the information visualization technique that has evolved, allowing it to be noted down (electronically). Usually, only content retrieved is retained as a result of the dialogue, discarding the history and the supporting tool's setup. With the various blueprint sections, all these facets of the information retrieval dialogue can be preserved. Furthermore, the knowledge captured using the information visualization modeling language can be re*used* in similar tasks or applied to diverse data sources. With the blueprint the information visualization technique can be *communicated* in its entirety to third parties, particularly to peer students.

5.2 Tutor Scenario

Imagine the lecturer creating a new tutorial. Unlike in traditional lectures, students are expected to study in a self-regulated fashion, investigating given resources utilizing an interactive information visualization system. Basically, the tutor needs to decide what resources to base the tutorial on. More challengingly, he must come to a decision what presentation styles and what investigation tools are most appropriate to support the students in achieving the intended learning outcome. In the case of information visualization techniques, this design task implies the definition of data transformations, visual mappings, and view transformations. Depending on the learning outcome, the tutor will choose proper mappings, multiple view constellations and available interactions in order to enable the students to reveal patterns, clusters, gaps, or outliers, for instance. The resulting information visualization techniques then get distributed to the students as teaching aids who in turn apply them to the resource data and, hopefully, gain new insights.

Again, the information visualization blueprint gets deployed to store and distribute all facets of information visualization applications, thus *representing* and *communicating* knowledge about the information visualization technique and its application. Beyond applying blueprints prepared by the tutor, students may compare the encoded experts' knowledge with blueprints they created themselves and *evaluate* their own knowledge this way. The information visualization modeling language also may support the tutor in authoring appropriate blueprints. Blueprint sections may capture the tasks and goals established visualization techniques serve best. With this knowledge, the language may help the tutor to select and adapt appropriate techniques and foster the re*use* of knowledge this way.

6 Summary and Conclusion

This article outlines our approach towards the information visualization modeling language (IVML). To lay a sound foundation, we survey the state-of-the-art of information visualization, assess the coverage and relationships between extant models, and identify potential obstacles in the process of setting up an integrated formal model that reflects the concepts and relationships of information visualization as it is understood today. Finally, we present computational requirements as well as those imposed by the application the information visualization modeling language has to fulfill.

The survey focuses on work that devised classification schemas. To assess which facets of information visualization these discrete models cover and how they are mutually related, we established the notion of information visualization modeling space. The analysis suggests three findings. First, the extant models in total cover nearly all facets of information visualization as we know it today. Secondly, areas of information visualization model space are described by rival models, leading to ambiguity. Third, the models vary in the level of detail in which they have been worked out.

In order to mutually open-up the treasure chests of visualization techniques for knowledge and information, information visualization and knowledge visualization must share, at least to a significant amount, a joint visualization model. Achievements in information visualization then could get applied to knowledge and vice versa.

The information visualization modeling language constitutes a specific encoding of the consolidated information visualization model. Its design has to meet requirements for both computation and application.

Two scenarios suggest how the information visualization modeling language could contribute to the field of education, supporting students studying in a self-regulated fashion. The benefits arise from the language's capability to formally represent, note, preserve, and communicate structure, appearance, behavior, and functionality of information visualization techniques and their applications. In combination with interactive mapping tools, the modeling language assists students and tutors in the evaluation, localization, generation, representation, communication, as well as the use of knowledge.

References

Card, S., Mackinlay, J., & Shneiderman, B. (1999). Information Visualization. In: S. Card, J. Mackinlay, & B. Shneiderman (Eds.): *Readings in Information Visualization* (pp. 1-34). San Francisco, CA: Morgan Kaufmann.

Chi, E.H. (2000). A Taxonomy of Visualization Techniques Using the Data State Reference Model. In S.F. Roth (Ed.), *Proceedings of the IEEE Symposium on Information Visualization (InfoVis 2000)* (pp. 69-76). Washington, DC: IEEE Computer Society Press.

Chuah, M.C., & Roth, S.F. (1996). On the Semantics of Interactive Visualizations. In S. Card, S. Eick, & N. Gersham (Eds.), *Proceedings of the IEEE Symposium on Information Visualization (InfoVis'96)* (pp. 29-36). Washington, DC: IEEE Computer Society Press.

Jurafsky, D., & Martin, J. (2000). *Speech and Language Processing*. Upper Saddle River: Prentice Hall.

Keim, D.A. (2002). Information Visualization and Visual Data Mining. *IEEE Transactions on Visualization and Computer Graphics*, 8(1), 1-8.

Leung, Y., & Apperley, M. (1994). A Review and Taxonomy of Distortion-Oriented Presentation Techniques. *ACM Transactions on Computer-Human Interaction, 1*(2), 126ff.

Lohse, G.L., Biolsi, K., Walker, N., & Rueter, H.H. (1994). A Classification of Visual Representations. *Communications of the ACM, 37*(12), 36-49.

Partee, B., Ter Meulen, A., & Wall, R. (1990). *Mathematical Methods in Linguistics.* Dordrecht, The Netherlands: Kluwer Academic Publishers.

Roberts, J.C. (2000). Multiple-View and Multiform Visualization. In R.F. Erbacher, P.C. Chen, J.C. Roberts, & C.M. Wittenbrink (Eds.), *Visual Data Exploration and Analysis VII, Proceedings of SPIE*, Volume 3960 (pp. 176-185). Bellingham, WA: SPIE The International Society for Optical Engineering.

Shneiderman, B. (1996). The Eyes Have It: A Task by Data Type Taxonomy for Information Visualizations. In *Proceedings of the IEEE Symposium on Visual Languages 1996* (VL '96) (pp. 336-343). Washington, DC: IEEE Computer Society Press.

Spence, R. (2000). Information Visualization. Harlow, England: Addison-Wesley.

Tergan, S.-O. (2003). Managing Knowledge with Computer-Based Mapping Tools. In D. Lassner, & C. McNaught (Eds.), *Proceedings of the World Conference on Educational Multimedia, Hypermedia & Telecommunication (ED-Media 2003)* (pp. 2514-2517). Charlottesville, Country: AACE Press.

Theus, M. (2003). Navigating Data – Selections, Scales, Multiples. In C. Stephanidis, & J. Jacko (Eds.), *Human-Computer Interaction - Theory and Practice (Part II). Proceedings of HCI International 2003 (HCII 2003)* (pp. 1323-1327). Mahwah, NJ: Lawrence Erlbaum Associates.

Wang Baldonado, M.Q., Woodruff, A., & Kuchinsky, A. (2000). Guidelines for Using Multiple Views in Information Visualization. In V. Di Gesù, S. Levialdi, & L. Tarantino (Eds.), *Proceedings of the Working Conference on Advanced Visual Interfaces (AVI'00)* (pp. 110-119). New York: ACM Press.

Ware, C. (2000). Information Visualization: Perception for Design. San Francisco, CA: Morgan Kaufmann.

Web3D Consortium (1997). Information Technology - Computer Graphics and Image Processing - The Virtual Reality Modeling Language (VRML) - Part 1: Functional Specification and UTF-8 Encoding (VRML97), ISO/IEC 14772-1:1997.

Wiss, U., & Carr, D. (1998). *A Cognitive Classification Framework for 3-Dimensional Information Visualization.* Research report LTU-TR-1998/4-SE. Luleå, Sweden: Luleå University of Technology.

Zhou, M.X., Chen, M., & Feng, Y. (2002). Building a Visual Database for Example-based Graphics Generation. In P. Ch. Wong, & K. Andrews (Eds.), *Proceedings of the IEEE Symposium on Information Visualization 2002 (InfoVis'02)* (pp. 23-30). Boston, MA: IEEE Computer Society Press.

Visualizing Information in Virtual Space: Prospects and Pitfalls

Marc M. Sebrechts

Department of Psychology, The Catholic University of America,
4001 Harewood Rd, N.E., Washington DC 20017, USA
sebrechts@cua.edu

Abstract. This paper suggests how virtual reality (VR) may be a fruitful means to analyze potential synergies of information visualization and knowledge visualization in a learning context. Emphasis is placed on VR as a spatial context and as an interaction model. Three example cases from our laboratory highlight different approaches to VR visualization: a human-computer interaction approach examines spatial dimensions in information retrieval; a transfer of learning approach explores "navigation" using typical and transformed virtual environments; and an experiential learning approach describes development of an environment to evaluate and improve social skills.

1 Introduction

Evolutionarily, knowledge and perception have been closely linked. We acquire knowledge of the world through our senses, primarily by seeing the world and the constant correlation that serves as a basis for causal inference (Locke, 1964). When we come to understand something, we often utilize the expression "I see" to signify that it is as though we have seen the relationships.

Over time, more and more of what we know has become abstract, related in language or symbolism rather than through the concrete aspects of reality. One way in which we can enhance our ability to "know" is by making it possible to visualize these otherwise abstract relationships. Information and knowledge visualization are focused on that goal, on the ability to comprehend through visual display.

The strategy of using spatial layout for organization and retention dates back at least to the time of the ancient Greeks. The poet Simonides is said to have left a celebration shortly before the building's roof collapsed. He was subsequently able to identify the bodies by the location where people had been just prior to his leaving the building. The utility of this approach for memory has become a standard memory technique referred to as the method of loci (Yates, 1966). Since that time, the notion of spatial layout as an adjunct to thinking and memory has become commonplace while myriad techniques have amply demonstrated the utility of visual display (Tufte, 2001).

The emergence of print media was accompanied by improved strategies for representing information. However, the limited data capacity and static character of fixed print media constrained their significant contribution to learning. Computer

S.-O. Tergan and T. Keller (Eds.): Knowledge and Information Visualization, LNCS 3426, pp. 136–166, 2005.
© Springer-Verlag Berlin Heidelberg 2005

technology provided the means to analyze more data, dramatically expanding on the static character of print. The ability to visualize and manipulate this data emerged as a potentially workable concept about half a century ago (Baecker, Grudin, Buxton & Greenberg, 1995), although it is only within the last decade or so, that these ideas became commonplace reality. Information visualization techniques enable the display and manipulation vast amounts of data that could not otherwise be processed or subsequently assimilated. Knowledge visualization provides a means to display and manipulate relationships among concepts in real time (see Tergan, in this book).

Virtual reality (VR) is among the most recent approaches to visualization. It includes a set of techniques and tools that facilitate the dynamic interactive potential in visualizations based on real world experiences. Most typically, VR is thought of as a means to replace an actual physical setting, but it also provides a framework for thinking about the problem of visualization more broadly. As a model of human-computer interaction, VR may also help advance our thinking about information and knowledge visualization.

2 Virtual Reality as Visualization Tool

VR is one of many ways to characterize the current highly interactive tools for manipulation of information. It thereby shares many of the characteristics of other tools, although it focuses on the use of more complex higher order interaction based on typical unmediated interactions in the world. Virtual Environment (VE) typically emphasizes the properties of the display rather than tools for constructing them, although many authors use VR and VE interchangeably.

The exact nature of VR is fixed neither by definition nor by consensus. There are many types of virtual display, ranging from 3D desktop visualizations to CAVEs in which one can walk in large spaces with minimal constraint. However, in general, these various VR strategies attempt to change the interaction in such a way as to allow the user to have many points of view, including one internal to the viewed scene, that are under the user's control. Some authors (e.g., Chen, 1999) even include text-based communication as VEs; such communication can exploit the notion of a virtual context for interaction and exchange of information. In this paper, however, the focus is on VR as an interactive methodology with three-dimensional spatial properties. Emphasis is placed on the "reality" of the interactive model, and the "virtual" construction of the display. It is argued that one of the principle contributions of this model is that interaction is described in terms that fit with "natural" perceptual, cognitive, and motor abilities that have evolved to cope with the real world. This is a primary source of the power of these environments.

At the same time, these highly overlearned real-world skills can be applied in virtual contexts in which the spatial and temporal dimensions are revised and adjusted to fit the demands of data display and associated semantics. The domain of application and its characteristics need not be familiar, but the tools for manipulation should be.

The emphasis on the user characteristics here minimizes boundaries between information visualization and knowledge visualization. The goal in both cases is design that minimizes the use of mental resources for the interaction, so that more resources can be devoted to the underlying semantics. As with most effective interface designs, the goal is for the tools to "get out of the way" of achieving the task.

VR is not a comprehensive solution to visualization issues, but it provides a conceptual framework for thinking about visualization in ways that might promote development of visualizations for learning. This paper focuses on three aspects of VR visualization that may help in this framework: (1) as a human-computer interaction (HCI) model for structuring interactive visualizations; (2) as a way to characterize alternate "worlds" that can be used in transfer of learning; (3) as a means to extend visualization into experiential learning. "VR-Vis" is used as a shorthand to reference this framework; it does not imply a specific tool or development.

3   VR-Vis as HCI: Person-Task-Interface Interaction

Thinking of VR as a context for visualization poses many useful prospects. Some of these are based on the benefits that derive from aspects of human-computer interaction related to reality constraints and conceptions. Others emerge from the virtual character of the interaction.

3.1   Human-Computer Interaction and Processing Characteristics

User-centered design. Since VEs build on real-world environments and interaction, they can foster a user-centered approach, capitalizing on individuals' extensive prior learning and knowledge about the world. The development of "immersive" environments begins with user characteristics and attempts to match aspects of the virtual world to those characteristics.

Model human processor. Basic computer user activities depend upon a similar underlying set of processes that have been characterized by a "model human processor" (Card, Moran & Newell, 1983). Interaction depends on a cycle of perceiving a state of affairs, interpreting that state within a context of memories and goals, and generating action to modify the given state (Norman, 1986).

As Hutchins, Hollan, and Norman (1986) pointed out, the effectiveness of an interactive paradigm depends on the relative ease of appropriately perceiving the state of affairs (gulf of evaluation) and implementing the desired action (gulf of execution). Information visualization and knowledge visualization approaches are likewise built on an attempt to minimize these gulfs, with primary emphasis on "evaluation" or perceiving the state of affairs. Whereas individuals cannot simultaneously process thousands of data points, they can understand the relationship if expressed as a graphical form. VEs provide a special case of minimization of these gulfs by optimal use of human processor characteristics as described here briefly.

Perception: High throughput vision. One goal of human-computer interaction is to provide a means to effectively acquire information with minimal effort. Card, Pirolli, and Mackinlay (1994) described the effectiveness of such information acquisition as a "cost of knowledge characteristic function."

The human system is designed in a way that can provide a low "cost" for data acquisition. Using relatively small changes in motor output (low bandwidth), the visual system can acquire substantial amounts of visual data (high bandwidth). In natural settings and learning contexts this amounts to being able to absorb large amounts of information with relatively little change in the control mechanism (Ware, 2000). Virtual environments take advantage of precisely these properties, by providing the user with high input transformations for low output change.

Small eye movements can identify new regions of space either in the physical or in the virtual world. Head rotation in the physical world or in a head-mounted display in the virtual world can result in rich new views being made available with little effort.

Both information visualization and knowledge visualization attempt to take advantage of these perceptual properties by "concretizing the abstract." Information that is not otherwise spatial in character is given visual embodiment. The underlying assumption is that this will provide a lowered "cost of knowledge" because we can then manipulate substantial amounts of information with limited effort.

Such perceptual benefits have been found even for novel spaces. One of the first instances of interactive 3D information visualization was SemNet (Fairchild, Poltrock & Furnas, 1988). This system addressed strategies for representing large knowledge bases, by using spatial layout to structure a network of nodes and relations. Rather than using a known space, this system focused on how the syntax would influence the positioning and management of nodes and links. At the same time, their approach demonstrated how spatial layout of information enabled known perceptual processes to be used for comprehension and navigation.

Cognition: Decreased processing and memory load. The perceptual properties of a VE also impact the cognitive demands. Our problem solving ability is best thought of as the knowledge space that includes both internal and externalized representations (Sebrechts, Enright, Bennett & Martin, 1996). During problem solving the ability to annotate, to draw, to manipulate an image are all part of what constitutes our cognitive ability. It is in large part these forms of externalized knowledge that, according to Norman (1994) can help to "make us smart." By creating a visual information space for person-computer interactions, resources that would otherwise need to be allocated to data assimilation can be used for analysis and problem solving. If a series of numeric data points are presented as a terrain, for example, it is possible to literally see the structure that otherwise might take very substantial cognitive resources to extract. In addition, the ability to store the image in memory far exceeds the capacity for storing numbers.

Of course, in order for a visualization to work, the selected display must capture a useful underlying semantics. In a document retrieval context, for example, visualizing keyword search results would be pointless if the keyword extraction failed to capture the essential aspects of the database. In this sense, information visualization and knowledge visualization need to go hand in hand. Chen (1999) describes this process as requiring "structural modeling" that captures the underlying relationships before the "graphical representation" that transforms those structures into visualizable representations. The representation is only as useful as the underlying structures and relationships that are displayed. In some cases, the particular factors that need to be extracted, as in a simple correlation of smoking and lung disease can be very straightforward. In other cases, as in document content analysis, there may be no simple structure. In those cases, an extraction technique such as latent semantic indexing (Deerwester, Dumais, Landauer, Furnas & Harshman, 1990) might be needed to extract statistical commonalities among documents before any sensible display is possible.

A synergistic relationship between information visualization and knowledge visualization captures the need to take the perceptual and provide a cognitive framework, i.e., a means to structure, to organize, to modify it. In a sense, the perceptual to cognitive link is just what constitutes a VE; it is a means for treating the perceptual as a world within which to navigate and manipulate. Of course, there are many steps to making this happen, but a VE provides a metaphor within which we can envision a perception-cognition bridge.

One of the best-known examples of using a familiar structure to organize information is WebBook™ (Card, Robertson & York, 1996). In this case a virtual book is used to embody information from a collection of web pages. The disparate semantic aspects are restructured into a more manageable visual space. Known affordances of a book minimize the cognitive requirements in training and use. At the same time, since the book is virtual, it can easily be restructured to capture diverse organizing principles.

Motor Control: Mapping actions to visualization. In contrast to our extensive ability to assimilate vast quantities of visual information, our motor control is of relatively low bandwidth. However, we have developed a series of interactions that are again highly overlearned. We are able to grasp objects, to reposition them in space, or to rotate them, as well as to reposition ourselves.

In a VE context, we can use these abilities to dynamically modify the visual display either by manipulating it or manipulating our position with respect to the objects of interest. Interestingly, since the world is virtual, we can sometimes shift from our own motion (egocentric) to world motion (exocentric) more easily than in a physical space.

3.2 NIRVE: An Empirical Assessment of Visualization Dimensionality

Although many VR systems have demonstrated the potential of visualization techniques, there is relatively little empirical data supporting the specific reasons for the benefits of these systems. These visualizations typically add a range of functionalities to the available information in addition to the spatial visualization itself. So for example, a 3D visualization might also add color-coded links that relate information, whereas a text equivalent has no such coding. Items might be spatially grouped in a 3D display, but simply listed, without grouping, in a text version. Alternatively, the forms of access might be enhanced, so that you can zoom in on an item in a 3D display, but you cannot manipulate those items in a traditional 2D map.

Many such changes often accompany the design of a new visualization technique, but it is not clear what role they play in improved performance. In our laboratory, for example, we have found that 3D VEs can lead to enhanced performance compared to more typical 2D "maps" for wayfinding. However, when we augmented the map and provided interactive motion in two dimensions, the 3D VE advantage was substantially reduced. Presumably, the interaction provided a learning advantage independent of the dimensionality of the representation.

A more recent information retrieval study (Sebrechts, Vasilakis, Miller, Cugini & Laskowski, 1999) attempted to systematically dissociate the spatial properties of the

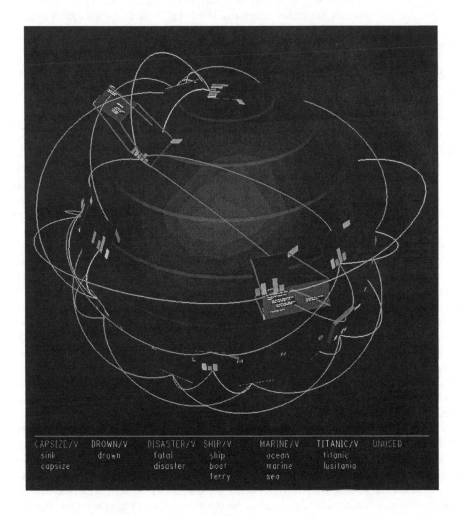

Fig. 1. 3D-globe version of NIRVE. Color-coded concept names are in color at bottom above keywords. Concept clusters are shown on globe surface as bargraphs with concept frequency. Colored arcs show association of concept clusters. Title windows from two selected clusters are projected out from globe

visualization from the associated functionality by comparing performance using three functionally parallel document displays – textual (1 dimension), map (2D), and globe (3D VE).

The domain of study was comprehension of a set of retrieved documents using NIRVE (NIST Information Retrieval Visualization Engine), a set of tools developed by the Visualization and Virtual Reality Group at the National Institute of Standards and Technology (NIST). A set of documents was retrieved based on a keyword search. The various keywords were then grouped into "concepts" with associated colors. So, for example, the keywords "burglar," "robbery," "steal," "theft" might all indicate the concept "theft" and be color-coded as green. (Note that the concept can but need not be one of the keywords.) Groupings of concepts then form "concept clusters" or sets of concepts that go together. For example, one set of documents might include the concepts "theft" and "banking," whereas another might include "banking," "foreign," and "fraud." Each document is then identified as belonging to the concept cluster that best identifies its contents according to these groupings.

The 3D version of the retrieved information was represented as a virtual globe, as shown in Fig. 1. Each concept cluster was displayed as a box on the surface of the globe with colored bars indicating the average frequency of occurrence of the related keywords for all the documents in that cluster. The thickness of the box indicated the number of documents in that cluster. Cluster boxes were placed so that clusters with the fewest concepts were towards the "south pole," and the cluster with the maximum number of concepts was placed at the "north pole." Clusters that differed by only one concept were linked by arcs, color-coded to match the differentiating concept.

When a cluster was selected, a listing of all the contained documents would be projected forward from the surface of the globe. Documents were listed vertically according to their relevance rating from the initial retrieval. Horizontal placement grouped articles by similarity of title. Selection of a document displayed it in a separate text window with keywords highlighted with the associated concept color. Documents or document clusters could be marked with a flag.

It is important to note that the design here entails what might otherwise be considered knowledge visualization (data structuring) in addition to information visualization (spatial layout of data). The way in which concepts are identified and colored and subsequently grouped into clusters specifies a semantics that enables certain interpretations and interactions with the data. (The specific knowledge visualization can be changed dynamically in NIRVE, but here only the access not the restructuring was examined.) The merging of the display properties with the chosen concept structure facilitates direct access to certain types of questions: What are the various groupings (as boxes)? How are they related (as arcs)? How many documents are there with a particular set of concepts (as density)? In many cases of visualization it is difficult to separate the change in spatial dimensionality from what are perceived as "incidental" modifications in functionality, so it could be the functionality rather than the visualization that improves the exploration and learning potential.

In order to isolate the visual rather than the semantic properties, parallel 2D and 1D (text) displays were constructed, mimicking as much as possible the 3D functions. The 2D version was a flattened globe that maintained the properties of concepts and clusters (Fig. 2). Arcs became lines, and cluster box depth was coded by the thickness of a gray bar. When clusters were selected, document titles were presented as an overlay rather than as a projected surface. For the 1D condition, documents were organized as a list that was grouped into color-coded concept clusters (Fig. 3), starting with the clusters with most concepts and working towards the least. There were no arcs, and cluster box depth was replaced by a list of the number of articles at the beginning of each cluster. Documents titles were presented sequentially and were accessed by scrolling.

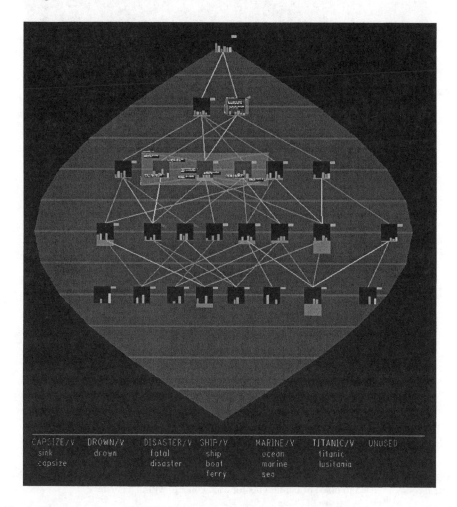

Fig. 2. 2D-map version of NIRVE. Flattened version of Fig. 1. Cluster box depth is indicated by gray bars under clusters. Expanded cluster windows appear as overlays rather than projections

Fifteen participants completed a range of tasks using one of the three interfaces. Over six sessions, using a series of different topic areas, participants were asked to locate, describe, and compare documents or clusters given specific types of information such as content, title, or key concepts.

Interface properties. As expected, the use of a familiar globe structure enabled the participants to engage in the task with relative ease. Of course, the relative familiarity with text and 2D approaches meant that there was no compelling 3D advantage.

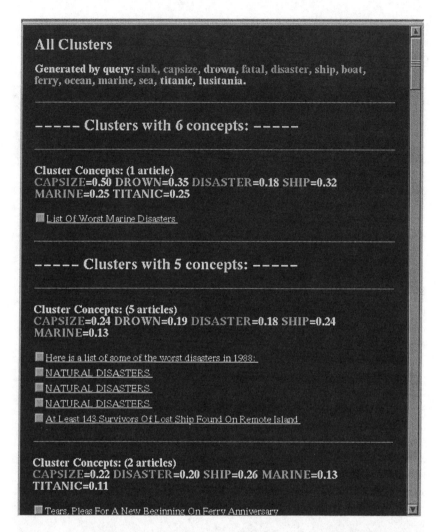

Fig. 3. 1D-text display of NIRVE. Clusters are listed by keyterms with appropriate color. Numeric codes are used in place of bar heights for each concept within a cluster

"Natural" interaction can be matched by highly learned interaction. In addition, variations from the normal interaction had some associated costs. Use of a spaceball was moderately intuitive for rotation of the globe. However, pulling up or pushing down on the spaceball as a zoom tool, did not always work seamlessly. Combining the more natural spaceball rotation with the use of a mouse selection tool, however, proved to be complicated for many users. Adding a more "natural" interface tool (the spaceball) may not be advantageous if it has to be combined with other interaction models (the mouse). The influence of lags in the system were especially noticeable.

Once individuals assumed the mapping of the "normal" world, they appeared to have the expectation that the transitions would be relatively instantaneous. When the globe did not rotate fast enough, users adopted the intuitive notion that more force would increase speed; this approach often resulted in a subsequent overshoot which could disorient users. Those users with more computer experience (including with other visualization software) demonstrated faster performance with the 3D than with the 2D interface, whereas the opposite was true for those with less experience.

Conceptual grouping. The grouping of clusters was seen as an advantage in a search that required knowing the concepts. This was particularly the case in searching for "similar" articles. However, the utility of the clusters did not necessarily produce a benefit for the 3D visualization, since all three interfaces provided some cluster grouping functionality. The arcs provided a means to visualize a path among related sets of concepts and occasionally served as one means to construct an ordered document search. Only 2D and 3D had "arcs," and in general the 2D static arrangement was faster, since no time was needed to rotate to the appropriate clusters.

Color coding. Scanning of color served as an especially useful way in which to examine the document space. Since this process occurs with little effort, it is faster and less effortful than scanning for words. The use of color was evident for all the different interfaces, but was especially helpful for the text list, where other spatial organizing cues were lacking. As the number of concepts increased, the identification of concept clusters by their sets of colors became more difficult. About five color bars appeared to be the maximum useful number. So, in this case, a very useful coding is bounded by the ability to grasp multiple instances simultaneously. It is at that point that the spatial display of relationships becomes especially important.

Screen real estate. One of the tradeoffs that was evident in this study is the screen real estate for visualization as opposed to text presentation. In many instances, there were difficulties with legibility of cluster information at the bottom of the 2D and 3D screens as well as the article titles that popped up. This is an issue for focus and context approaches. Full screen text seemed to work best, but that approach comes at the price of losing context.

User experience. The effectiveness of a visualization depended on the experience of the user and the task. One of the benefits of a "virtual globe" was that it presented a known framework for users, with little need for training. At the same time, those who had previously used visualization tools showed relatively faster performance using the 3D visualization than those who had not. For the less experienced users, there was a learning curve. Performance with 2D and 3D interfaces improved over time compared to search, presumably a function of familiarization with both the tool and the knowledge base. As in the real world, performance in a virtual world is dependent on prior knowledge.

Task dependence. The specific tasks also influenced the ability to effectively utilize the alternative visualizations. For example, searching for a specific title turned out to be easiest for the 1D group because they could simply scroll through the list. Those in the 2D or 3D conditions needed to figure out the appropriate cluster based on the title, open up the appropriate cluster, and then find the title. In this instance, the knowledge grouping was not helpful. This is a case when a simple title search would work. Of course, this is not a scalable solution. Scrolling through the 100 documents that were displayed is relatively straightforward. As that number increases to thousands, the scrolling strategy becomes more time-consuming and error-prone.

Functionality over dimensionality. Both information and knowledge visualization work by making the display space decrease mental workload by assuming some of the mental cost. Our study of information display suggested some ways in which that impact depends on the interaction of the user, the interface, and the task. It was the functionality rather than the dimensionality that primarily determined functionality. The added dimensions were helpful only insofar as they contributed to decrease in resources needed for a given task. In fact, when there was a cost to a dimension, users tended to accommodate their performance strategies. For example, when the zooming on an article title was slow, users would simply click to open the document in a separate window, thereby losing the contextual information, but substantially increasing the response time.

This study was focused on comparative assessment of dimensionality. In part, the results indicate that integration of different dimensions, depending on function, may be optimal. Andrews (1995) provides an interesting example of how these different dimensional approaches, including basic VR, can be integrated into strategies for web visualization using the Harmony Internet browser.

3.3 GOMS Analysis: Functional Bases of Visualization Effects

The arguments for a VR approach to visualization is that known real-world activity can be readily translated to virtual contexts. The study described above, suggests that such "translation" is contingent on a match between the interactive task requirements and the functionality provided by the specific visualization. To assess this hypothesis, following the reasoning from the model human processor described previously, we conducted a study to determine if a detailed task analysis using the alternative visualizations could provide a reasonable account for our data (Vasilakis, 2000; Sebrechts, Vasilakis & Miller, 2000).

Based on the CPM-GOMS (cognitive, perceptual, motor-goal, operator, method, selection rule) approach (Card, Moran & Newell, 1983), three types of information retrieval tasks from the visualization study were broken down into a detailed set of perceptual, cognitive, and motor steps. The tasks were to locate an article by (1) title, (2) concepts, or (3) content description. Cognitive steps included reading, generating concepts from titles, and generating concepts from content descriptions. Perceptual steps included matching words to concept colors, scanning for colors on the screen, and visually skimming target articles for appropriate terms. Motor steps included mouse movements, vocal repetition, and scrolling, zooming, and rotating. The steps for each task and visualization were structured into a scheduling chart with critical path and parallel steps as illustrated in Fig. 4 for finding an article by title. Note that the 2D and 3D conditions require generating concepts in order to identify the cluster for search as well as marking the cluster for later identification of article location.

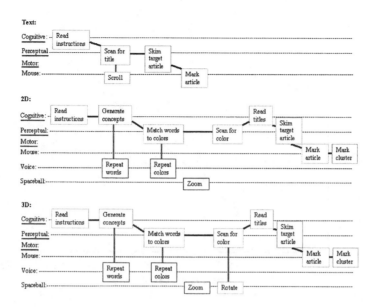

Fig. 4. Task analysis scheduling charts of cognitive, perceptual, and motor steps involved in finding an article by title for text-1D (top), map-2D (middle), globe-3D (bottom). Black lines indicate critical path. Red lines indicate activities conducted in parallel. "Generate concepts" is a key source of time and errors.

The time required for each identified step was determined by recording data from six participants who performed each individual step multiple times. These data were used to determine parameters associated with each step. These parameters were multiplied by factors that indicated the number of repetitions in the actual retrieval tasks. The resultant step times were then combined following the scheduling charts, with some activities such as scrolling and scanning occurring simultaneously. This provided a total estimate of time for one of three visualization tasks using each of the three visualization approaches (1D-text, 2D-map, 3D-globe).

Fig. 5 illustrates the relationship between the constructed GOMS scheduling chart times and the data from our information visualization study for three search questions (by name, by title, and by content), and the three interactive tools (text, map, globe). The Pearson correlation coefficient (r = .92, p < .01) indicated that the model of the critical perceptual-cognitive-motor path for that task captured a significant amount of the variance in visualization performance. Of course the model is an idealized, error free, model so it doesn't capture many of the system constraints or errors present in the actual information retrieval study. As a consequence, the times are very much lower for the predicted than the real task.

The results of the visualization study thus seem consistent with what we would expect based on an underlying model of cognitive activities. The more effort involved in the task, the longer the task takes. Interestingly, the cognitive costs were especially

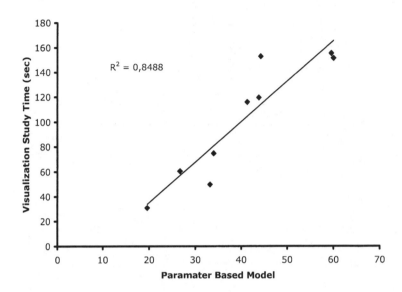

Fig. 5. A depiction of the relationship between the parameter-based model constructed with the CPM-GOMS study and the information visualization data from actual task performance in the previous study

significant. When the concepts were given in the task, the cognitive demands were limited because the concepts could be matched to colors and then color could be used as a search mechanism. Although it might appear that this is a knowledge based task, once the match was completed, scrolling while scanning for color (1D) was still faster than zooming in and then scanning (2D) or zooming, rotating, and scanning (3D). Finding an article by content was more difficult (time-consuming) because the content had to be mapped into a concept cluster. Since the visualization did not do that mapping, all three approaches required the same added cognitive load.

In this limited domain, a familiar 3D spatial model worked well and users learned it quickly. It is a reasonable presumption, that a comparison with a typical textual list model would have shown the superiority of the globe. Concepts would have had to be inferred, color scanning would not have been an option, and there would have been no perceived grouping of titles. However, both our empirical study and the analysis of an underlying model indicated that the utility of visualization is based on how the interactive environment reduces the workload for relevant functional objectives.

4   VR-Vis as Learning Transfer: Simulation and Transformation

The previous sections emphasized how VR can focus attention on the way in which visualizations take account of human-computer interface characteristics. By building on the models of real world interaction, visualization tools can be designed to optimize reduction of physical and mental workload. At the same time, by focusing on the interface functionality, we can redesign even basic text and 2D systems in ways that can enhance their utility.

Building on interface issues, more generally VR studies have highlighted how the activity in a virtual world can be useful for a variety of learning circumstances. Most research has focused on *simulative* worlds that mimic reality by providing comparable visual stimulation without the spatial or temporal constraints. Alternatively, VR can provide non-existent, *transformative* worlds in which many of the properties of the physical world are modified or deliberately violated. Both approaches may have utility for information and knowledge visualization and the associated learning.

4.1 Simulative VR

The more typical use of VR is to simulate or to represent aspects of the world with varying degrees of fidelity. Thus, one can learn about any place or time by becoming virtually immersed in the space. In this context, VR provides simulations that support training in those environments. A measure of effectiveness of such simulation for learning is the degree of transfer to the physical context, and there is ample evidence that presenting a high-fidelity VR shows transfer to the actual environment (e.g., Witmer, Bailey, Knerr & Parsons, 1996).

Of course, the perceived transfer may be task dependent. Somewhat surprisingly, early research suggested that learning and transfer in a variety of contexts could be very specific. Thorndike (1906) argued that transfer occurred when tasks shared identical elements not some strength in general reasoning. This notion of very specific learning was supported much later by examples such as the finding that increasing short-term recall of digits did not generalize to letters (Chase & Ericsson, 1982). More recently, Singley and Anderson (1989) have argued that an identical elements viewpoint is too restrictive. Learning occurs with respect to the underlying logical structure, and transfer can be achieved if that structure is preserved. One of the challenges in developing simulative visualizations is to determine how specific the learning is and how general the transfer might be.

There are several variants to the use of simulative visualization, which still work on the assumption that the physical world provides the knowledge-based context for learning, but which deviate from full replication. These include diminished fidelity, partial task visualization, and structural visualization.

Diminished fidelity. As described above, stimulus fidelity appears to be important for a spatial visualization to be effective. This is made even more compelling by the suggestions that event learning makes everything relevant, even the learning context (Tulving & Thompson, 1973; Tulving, 1983). This appears problematic for simulation since a perfect correspondence with reality may be unachievable (Stoffregen, Bardy, Smart & Pagulayan, 2003).

At the same time, there is reason to suspect that exact replication may not always be necessary or desirable for learning. If everything were relevant to learning, then any minor changes between training and performance would interfere with performance. There are, however, instances where this does not appear to be the case. Moroney, Hampton, Biers and Kirton (1994), for example, found comparable flight skills for participants trained with a desktop or an FAA flight simulator, which differed dramatically in their realism. Of course, the performance measures may not have identified the relevant differences. Although learning may be optimal for the "exact" circumstances and context of learning, learning is generally targeted at providing the greatest possible generalization.

Identifying the consequences of diminished fidelity for learning remains an open question. Instead of focusing just on the stimulus fidelity or high quality of the visualization, we needed to identify those factors that influence how the visualization influences the target learning, what has been called functional fidelity (Moroney & Moroney, 1998) or action fidelity (Stoffregen et al, 2003).

Partial-task visualization. One specific way in which VEs can deviate from reality is by representing only portions of the relevant environment. Although visualizations can serve as spaces for direct interaction, they can also serve as placeholders for some aspects of a task during which the learning is focused on other aspects. A VE can be used to isolate relevant aspects for learning, while controlling other aspects of the interaction. Applying this to the learning of a medical procedure, for example, can enable a user to work on one aspect of the task, while other aspects are virtually controlled and displayed (see Sebrechts, Lathan, Clawson, Miller & Trepagnier, 2003). This enables a person to develop knowledge about a task in manageable pieces, referred to as part-task or part-whole training. This is a critical component of the general notion of focus plus context used widely in a variety of visualization techniques. A VR approach highlights the notion that the "context" may be dynamically updated rather than just serving as a static framework.

Structural visualization. Many, if not most, visualizations do not mimic the details of a real environment. They do frequently, however, borrow a known real-world framework. This is perhaps most evident in visualizing information that is geographically distributed. For example, Munzer, Hoffman, Claffy and Fenner (1996) use a globe for visualizing topology of the multicast backbone of the Internet. Here the globe is a representation of the actual 3D world on which non-spatial information relations can be superimposed. Many other cases use the geography or a geographic metaphor of a globe, star patterns, or other known layouts as the basis for visually organizing non-spatial information (VR-VIBE: Benford, Snowdon, Greenhalfh, Ingram, Know & Brown, 1995; Starfield: Ahlberg & Shneiderman, 1994; SPIRE (Spatial Paradigm for Information Retrieval and Exploration): Hetzler, Harris, Havre & Whitney, 1998; StarWalker: Chen, Thomas & Chennawasin, 1999). Our document visualization study described previously used the globe surface as a structural visualization on which was imposed a knowledge framework for document search.

4.2 Transformative VR

The previously described simulative VEs and their variations capture or preserve some aspects of reality as a visualization strategy. VEs can also be "magical" or transformative, by deliberately violating or modifying properties of the world. (In the limit case, these are differences in emphasis since every VE has a range of relationships to real environments.)

Some transformations introduce new behaviors on known structures. For example, gravitational and other physical properties can be changed to provide insight into how those changes modify object behavior (Dede, 1995; Dede, Salzman, Loftin & Ash, 1999). Presumably the variation from known properties provides a better sense of how such properties function. In another context, designers often deliberately restrict stimulus fidelity (Stappers, Gaver & Overbeeke, 2003). Presumably, excessive realism tends to impose more constraint than is desired at early visualization stages, so tools for "expressive" rather than photorealistic rendering have been developed.

Physical structures can be changed in relative size or made transparent (see below). Transformative VR can also change the temporal scale as well as the visual properties, making it possible for search activities through a space to occur much faster than in real situations. Simulated real-world navigation in a virtual environment is important if (1) knowing the specific path is informative or (2) navigation is the basis on which information is located (e.g., it provides the basis for the semantic structure). In many hypermedia systems or web-based applications, the linking structure is not conceptually relevant to the target task. In those cases movement should violate the sequential conventions of typical navigation.

4.3 An Empirical Study of Simulative and Transformative VR for Navigation

Several of our studies have focused on a better comprehension of the utility of visualization in virtual environments, especially with respect to understanding the aspects of spatial layout. These approaches can have implications for how spatial layout can serve as a variable for the display of a variety of informational properties, although the specific focus is on the ability to use the VE for learning navigation.

A series of studies in our laboratory (Clawson, Miller, Knott & Sebrechts, 1998; Miller, Clawson & Sebrechts, 2000; Miller, 2001; Mullin, Sebrechts & Clawson, 2000) have demonstrated that virtual environments of moderate environmental fidelity (Fig. 6 and 7) can lead to effective learning and transfer of spatial layout. However, there are a number of constraints on the learning, and a VE may induce certain types of visual learning.

Specificity. One study compared VE route learning with learning from a map or learning in the actual environment. When subsequently tested on following that route in the actual building, VE and map were comparable to having learned in the actual building. However, when the testing route was reversed from the learned route, performance on the VE route took substantially longer, and pointing to alternative locations in the building was substantially less accurate, suggesting that VE learning may be quite specific to the particular visual representations. We examined the possible role of restricted field of view in a virtual space by using restricted FOV while learning in the actual space (Piller, Miller & Sebrechts, 2003). This study suggested that some but not all of the VE specificity is due to limitations in field of view.

This also raises the more general concern that any aspects of a visual representation may be "perceived" as important. For example, in our early explorations of NIRVE for document visualization, a spiral layout was used moving from the highest relevance documents in the middle through lower relevance documents as the spiral expanded.

Fig. 6. An image of the virtual building used in several of our studies on transfer of training. Inset is photo of actual building

Fig. 7. A screenshot of the interior of the building used in the exploratory navigation studies. The green sphere is used to indicate one of a number of locations that need to be identified

There were many interaction tools to rotate and zoom the spiral, to explore and flag item clusters, etc. However, at the same time, depending on the rate of spiral looping,patterns would emerge along one or more axes of the spiral. There was a tendency to interpret these as meaningful, even though they were spurious effects of using a spiral with a certain periodicity of item placement.

Exploratory learning. In another series of studies (Sebrechts, Mullin, Clawson & Knott, 1999; Mullin, 2002; Mullin, Sebrechts & Clawson, 2000; Mullin & Sebrechts, 2003), participants were able to explore the environment. In this condition, piloting testing demonstrated that users of the VE do not explore all of the visually available spaces. This is a common difficulty with providing exploratory learning environments; a companion target task is needed to ensure that the visualized properties are adequately explored. In this case spheres were added (Fig. 7) to enable participants to determine that they had adequately explored the space. Identifying the spheres became a measure of exploration of the space. In addition, the spheres would change color from green to red once they had been encountered as a means to visualize which aspects of the space had already been explored. This VE was compared to training with a map of the building. When tested in the actual building, those who had learned with the VE could navigate in the real building more directly than those who had learned with the map.

In addition, after having explored the space, participants were asked to identify the location of objects they had seen. Placement was more accurate for those who trained and tested with a VE than with those who had used a map for training or testing. This may be a positive aspect to the specificity of visualization. Although having seen a particular representation may foster the development of specific representations, those can be useful when precise location is important.

Flexibility. The results from specificity suggest that the learning from a visual representation may be specific to the route followed or the pattern of interaction. Although not specifically tested, our more exploratory approach suggested that variation in paths may help in developing a general model of the space. We assessed this experimentally (Miller, 2001) by comparing performance with multiple trials on a single route versus a single trial on each of several different routes. The model was modified so that parts of the building would match the single route, whereas other parts of the building would match none of the presented routes. Single route participants navigated more quickly through the unaltered portion of the building, whereas multiple-route participants navigated more quickly through the altered portion. Examining the environment from multiple paths decreased the specificity and increased the flexibility in the environment.

Transparency. The descriptions of the virtual space here have focused on simulative VR with some modifications to routes or cues (spheres). Other studies have examined how these same environments can be transformed by making them transparent (Sebrechts & Knott, 1998; Sebrechts, Knott & Clawson, 1998; Knott, 1999; Piller 2001; Piller & Sebrechts, 2003). In these studies, a typical opaque VE was transformed so that participants could see through the walls and floors, which could still be identified and which had virtual solidity, i.e., participants could not pass through them (Fig. 8).

Following learning the placement of objects within rooms to criterion, participants were required to draw maps of the buildings they had learned. As shown in Fig. 9,

Fig. 8. Screenshots illustrating a scene from the opaque (top) and transparent (bottom) versions of the building used in the transparency studies

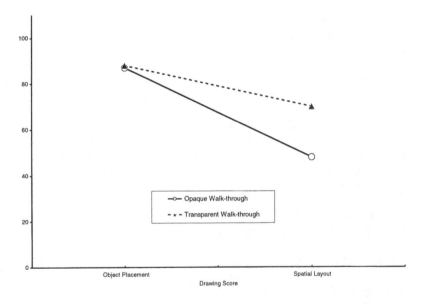

Fig. 9. Percent correct placement of objects and spatial structures after training in opaque and transparent VEs

although participants in either training knew the object locations very accurately, they differed greatly in their understanding of the structural layout of the building, with the transparent participants showing a better representation of the relative scale and placement of rooms.

In a related study, after similar learning conditions, participants were asked to indicate the relative position of two locations in the building. A regression model indicated that the route distance between objects predicted the time required for identifying relative locations for those in the opaque condition, whereas Euclidean or straight line distance better predicted the identification times for those in the transparent condition. In addition, the opaque condition resulted in a higher rate for objects from different rooms than for same rooms; the transparent condition produced no such distinction between objects in same versus different rooms. These results support the notion that the specific VE played a role in determining the type of mental representation that individuals had of a space. The particulars of the visualization as well as the character of the interaction influence how the space is conceived.

4.4 Direct Perception of Transformed Space

Although transparency is a transformative VR, the foregoing example still focuses primarily on understanding the actual spatial properties. This model can be extended to other kinds of informational space in which the properties of the space directly influence perception. Take for example, imperfect monitoring of air traffic as illustrated in Fig. 10. The geographic space replicates the physical space. However, the information that is available is specified perceptually.

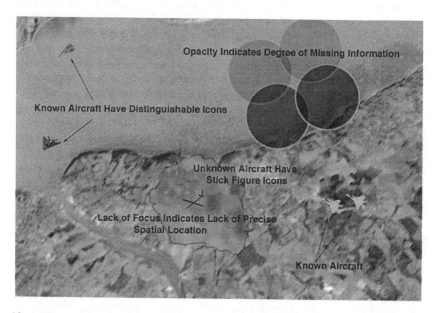

Fig. 10. A VE can have geographical properties as well as transformations in which information is represented as a way of perceiving the space with degrees of specificity and clarity directly conveying the known as seen

Planes that are of a known type are represented by clear images; planes that are of unknown type are represented as stick-figure planes, indicating no known type. Similarly information on placement is represented by either clear, in-focus, geographic indicators, or fuzzy, out-of-focus indicators. The former indicates that the location is known, the latter that the location is vaguely within the specified fuzzy area. In some instances, the available information will be only partially available. This is signaled by the clarity of the view; the greater the opacity of a region, the less the information that is available. These approaches again try to capture the analogous aspects of perception. When trying to determine an aircraft location, the inability to see what is in a given location reflects perceptually the state of information.

Information states are reconstructed into a dynamic VE that combines simulative with transformative approaches. Again, the use of the perceptual processes can be extended metaphorically into the design of the virtual space.

5   VR-Vis as Experience-Based Learning

Previous sections have suggested how VR provides some useful ways to think about interaction that could be applied to learning issues in information and knowledge visualization. This section focuses on how VR emphasizes alternative ways of thinking about visualizations, as interactive tools for experience-based learning.

5.1   The (Partial) Myth of Abstraction

One motivation for visualization is "concretization of the abstract," taking data that is numerical or symbolic in character and rendering it in spatial terms. This is an important aspect of information visualization since there are many instances in which data is provided initially in abstract form. In other instances, however, the division between abstract and concrete is at least in part a function of the limits on our ability to render what is to be learned in visual form.

Methods of instruction and assessment often use "proxies" for the actual target task. Instructions in a variety of domains ranging from political processes to surgical procedures are often conveyed by textual description. Examinations often ask question about how one would do a task, rather than examining that person's ability to perform the task. In part this has been due to a lack of options, but VR and other technologies have made it possible to examine the target performance directly.

One of the benefits of a VR approach is that it helps place the focus on task rather than tool. Information need not be characterized solely as data points, and knowledge need not be tightly linked to the extraction of textual knowledge. Of course, this is a suggestion for how VR can augment learning; it cannot substitute for either data visualization or the extensive use of language.

5.2   Constructivist and Procedural Approaches

A more interactive approach to learning has been the focus of many efforts to change education. Contructivist theories have argued that learning occurs as a building of mental models (Duffy & Jonassen, 1992) not an assimilation of facts. The related constructionists have argued that it is the actual process of building those models that provides the critical basis for learning (Papert, 1980). Closely aligned with these views is an emphasis on training and assessment that focuses directly on performance of the target activities of interest under realistic conditions (Gardner, 1998). This emphasis on alternative learning strategies has given additional impetus for exploring how visual approaches may be especially helpful to some students with limited verbal skills.

VR provides a particularly good match between constructivist learning and visualization tools. With its interactive focus, VR emphasizes procedural over declarative knowledge, activity more than description. This interactive model of learning is applicable to the exploration of information and knowledge spaces, but has been made most evident in experience-based learning contexts. Examining these contexts focuses attention on how to assess the relevant aspects of visual fidelity.

5.3 Fidelity Revisited

Experience-based learning is in part a construction of the situations of actual practice. However, an effective VE design, as any effective visualization, requires not just a spatial display, but an organization and selection that extract the relevant characteristics. In experience-based learning, the functional fidelity, the match of VE and task requirements, should also guide the stimulus or environmental fidelity, the match between the VE and the physical or conceptual entities.

If, for example, the task is to group a series of paintings by their size for storage purposes, then the environmental fidelity can be low, since the functional fidelity is only with respect to distinguishing among sizes. If, however, the task is to organize the same paintings by subject matter, then experiential fidelity depends on greater environmental fidelity. Note that either of these tasks demands a certain amount of organizational structure, even just deciding on groupings, which could be completed with manipulation of item identifiers and structured concept maps. However, we would have to translate the visual aspects into size and subject matter categories for subsequent manipulation. Alternatively, the grouping can be done by manipulation of visual images of the virtual paintings that capture relevant properties.

5.4 Applications of VR to Experiential Learning

Although it is highly plausible that constructing VEs will enhance learning, the associated costs in time and money are still very substantial. In addition, mimicry is not sufficient for success, and identifying the appropriate functional characteristics and levels of abstraction remains a challenge. The design of various VEs for learning about physics, gorilla behavior, garden design, spherical character of the earth, all have experienced significant limits on their effectiveness, but they have provided information on identifying aspects of functional fidelity (Moshell & Hughes, 2002). In addition, there is substantial information on how these environments need to be integrated into learning contexts; so far they are not freestanding training tools. In many cases the need for associated non-visual information as part of the learning context was noted.

In other contexts, virtual learning environments have already shown educational utility (Cobb, Neale, Crosier & Wilson, 2002). The Virtual Life Skills project has provided a useful framework for training basic life skills for those with learning disabilities. The Virtual RadLab, developed in cooperation with teachers, has been distributed to a number of English schools to help teach radioactivity to secondary school level. In these instances, the target users were identified as critical in determining what needed to be represented and how, an strong example of user-centered design.

The field of medicine is perhaps the area where acquisition of procedural knowledge through VE has been most studied (Satava & Jones, 2002). Visualization of many different surgical procedures allows experiential learning without risk to patients. Of course, in this domain functional and environmental fidelity are often strongly linked. In the health domain, part whole learning has also become important, with the virtual world assuming a portion of a procedure, while the learner focuses on learning another aspect of that procedure. In some cases, this shared virtual-real activity then becomes part of the actual experience. For example, the telesurgery system, Zeus (Satava & Jones, 2002), is designed for remote surgery; the system augments performance by removing tremors and scales hand motion.

There are also arguments in favor of using VE to extend learning to teams that are at distributed locations. Salas, Oser, Cannon-Bowers and Daskarolis-Kring (2002) show how a VE provides the sense of a common environment with virtual team members. In order to be successful, they argue, the VE must be part of an event-based approach to training which provides strategies, methods and tools that can train and test knowledge, skills, and attitudes. Shared visualization space will require additional interaction tools that have been less fully explored.

5.5 Virtual Buddy: An Example of Experience-Based Learning

The highly interactive character of VR suggests that it may be especially useful in training that requires interaction. Based on its potential for event-based learning, we are using VR principles as a means to address social interactions in persons with autism.

Autism is generally characterized by severe impairments in social and communicative domains, together with repetitive behaviors and restrictive interests. Early development is characterized by lack of typical interaction, including absence of expected monitoring of and reaction to facial expressions (Klin, Volkmar & Sparrow, 1992; Klin, Sparrow, de Bildt, Cicchetti, Cohen & Volkmar, 1999). Atypical face gaze persists in young adults with autism (Trepagnier, Gupta, Sebrechts & Rosen, 2000; Trepagnier & Sebrechts, 2002), and it has been hypothesized that if responding to facial cues is one of the sources of diminished social functioning (Trepagnier, 1996; Phillips, Baron-Cohen & Rutter, 1992; Parritz, Mangelsdorf & Gunnar, 1992), perhaps improving the use of those cues could in turn improve social interaction.

The Autism Intervention Project and the Cognition and Virtual Reality Laboratory are designing and evaluating an environment to test that hypothesis which incorporates and expands on a number of interactive virtual components. A display screen is embedded within a helicopter kiddie ride (Fig. 11).

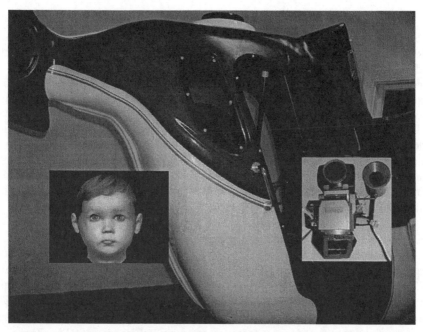

Fig. 11. A depiction of the 'kiddie-ride' training environment for the Autism Intervention Project. A camera inside the helicopter (inset on right) tracks eye-gaze as a child observes the screen. Interaction will take place with a 'virtual buddy' (inset on left) whose image is used to detect the child's eye-gaze resulting in appropriate feedback

In addition to displaying videos, a virtual character (buddy) is introduced into the scenario. This character and other aspects of the environment are programmed to respond based on the looking behavior of the child. Depending on determined sequences, the child will receive different video presentations, or be given a ride or other rewards. The goal is for the child to learn that looking at and extracting facial information can be rewarding. Over time, virtual images of other known characters or environments can be introduced into the VR context. Changes in social interaction in real situations will then be assessed.

This ongoing research project is an example of how the interactive conceptions of visualization in VR can be used in order to provide learning of complex behaviors, in this case social interaction. It is an instance of what may be a more general trend to incorporate eye-input, visual display, motion, and avatars in a rich learning context. The goals here are largely procedural, so the match of an environment and the task may be especially apt.

Some have argued that such integrative "learning by doing" is also a model for revolutionary change in education (Schank, 1997). While the merging of conceptual knowledge and skills can certainly be improved, the scope of application of the revised learning approaches as well as the role of VR in this context remain open questions.

6 Conclusions

VR-Vis suggests the extensive interactive possibilities of information visualization and knowledge visualization. VR is neither a replacement for other techniques, nor necessarily an improvement. Instead, as a conceptual approach it helps to clarify some important issues in visualization more broadly that may help in thinking about bridges between available alternative techniques for learning.

In combination the virtual and real properties can foster a different way of learning, where emphasis is on the interaction rather than the representation, on information rather than stimulation (Stapper et al., 2003), on task completion rather than task decomposition. VEs also help draw attention to the ways in which visualization can be a learning tool for procedural knowledge and/or cognitive strategies as well as for factual knowledge.

6.1 Challenges to VR Learning

Mental Effort and Attention. Not everyone finds the notion of highly visual learning compelling. For example, by focusing on the concrete, visual images may diminish the ability to deal with verbal communication or abstraction (Mitchell, 1994). Furthermore, by minimizing the need for mental effort during learning, certain visual representations could reduce subsequent retention (Wickens, 1992). These are legitimate concerns that need to be incorporated into VEs. Experience alone is an inadequate model of learning; extraction of relevant information from the environment (real or virtual) can be a long and complicated process, and the goal of education is in part to decrease the length and complexity of the process. So, as indicated earlier, VEs need to be tailored and augmented to focus attention on the relevant information. This includes specific modifications to the visualization as well as incorporation of non-visual, textual semantics; there are many abstract concepts that have not been and may not be well captured in visual form. VR provides a model for learning in which the target knowledge can be presented by interactive modification of the visualization as well as integration of non-visual material.

Fidelity limits. Virtual environments extend common prospects and constraints of visualization technologies. The principles of user-centered design remain critical. Just as VE shows the HCI benefits, it shows limitations. User experience, user-ability, and task-relevance provide core criteria in realizing effective visualizations. Current VEs often fall short of desired simulation, and there is no fully compelling unencumbered visualization. The same characteristics that set real world expectations and facilitate learning can become confused when those expectations are violated. Lag in updating displays or other visual and motion discrepancies, for example, can lead to cybersickness (Prothero & Parker, 2003; Harm, 2002). When the visual field is restricted, as is the case in most VR systems, users may be unaware of relevant information in the periphery.

Visual semantics. Of course, not all of reality as we know it can be captured in visual form. VEs to date do not provide any privileged way to capture textual information, which is often used as part of knowledge visualization. Of course, textual information can always be added to a visual setting, and it may be that any visualization of this type will need some accompanying text. It is an interesting theoretical question as to how much of our semantics can be captured in visual form. VEs can depict a number of relational properties of containment, contiguity, and other spatial properties. Arnheim (1969) makes an interesting case for how we can engage in "visual thinking," allowing perceptual aspects to engage a variety of thought processes, including selection and abstraction. Images can depict instances of a category, as a means to illustrate a concept, but the relation of such images to the underlying semantics has not been fully worked out. It is perhaps here that lays the greatest challenge for information visualization, finding the optimal mappings from data structures to visual displays of their meaning.

One way to augment the semantics of VR may be through combination with concept maps. Such maps typically provide spatial node-link structures that characterize the relations among concepts with varying degrees of labeling. These concept maps use language to identify concepts that are not readily captured in visual form. They are maps insofar as the spatial relations among the concept nodes specify the structure of the underlying conceptual knowledge. They may also serve as a framework within which to link together content knowledge and knowledge resources (Tergan, in this book). At the same time, some of the principles of VR design can be used to enhance the visualization of concept map structure.

The earlier description of NIRVE provides an example of links between the visual (dimensional layout) and the conceptual (grouping of terms into concepts). The system allows a user to modify groupings of keyword search terms that form concept clusters. This results in new groupings of documents with associated changes in the layout of the clusters.

The basic structure in NIRVE could be represented as a text-based concept map. Clusters could be named nodes that were identified by the terms they contained. In turn the concept clusters could be related in a node-link fashion. Our displays provide an example of how such a concept map can be structured in 2-dimensional or 3-dimensional space. Each of the visual aspects in those displays - color, arc-links, bars or varying heights, depth of the cluster nodes - can be thought of as a means to provide a labeled link in a concept map. For example, color-coding could be used to identify a "type of" link, thereby providing an additional form of grouping, minimizing the needs for complex links among different classes of documents. Color could also be used, as in our navigational learning studies, to identify previously visited spaces. Temporal properties of information could be specified by yellowing of documents over time to indicate delay since last visit, age of documents, etc. Exploring the role of concept maps is an especially important way to examine the prospects and limitations on visual semantics.

VR does not solve this problem; rather, it provides a framework for developing enhanced representations and interactions. In this context it makes most sense to think of VR as a bridge between alternative representations rather than as a substitution.

False inference. Unconstrained by "physical" or other "real" properties VEs have the potential to teach the wrong model. In the real world, physics constrains interactions in ways that they are all "meaningful," adhering to the laws of physics and characterizing actual relationships. In VR there are no such constraints; it is possible to make the world behave in an infinite variety of ways. If the underlying model that describes gravitation is wrong, then the resultant learning about gravitational fields will be wrong. And if someone has "experienced" this alternative world, it may be even harder to dislodge an erroneous belief, once established.

Of course, we may not always extract the correct inference from the properties we observe. For example, common sense observation often leads to the conclusion that heavier objects fall faster than lighter ones. VEs provide an opportunity to correct that conclusion by "experiencing" how objects behave in a vacuum. The representational power of VEs is thus both an opportunity and a potential liability.

6.2 From Visualization to Environment

The descriptions here have focused on issues of visual aspects of VR. At the same time, emerging systems will better integrate other sensory channels. The VR model readily suggests how sound (Cohen & Wenzel, 1995) or tactile stimulation (Kaczmarek & Bach-y-Rita, 1995) could be integrated into the broader notion of the way in which information environments might be constructed. In addition, our interaction, which is currently heavily driven by mechanical movements, could be substantially extended by developments in the use of eye-movement as an input device (Jacob, 1995). As progress is made in these other domains, it will be increasingly possible for learning visualizations to become learning environments.

References

Ahlberg, C., & Shneiderman, B. (1994). Visual information-seeking: Tight coupling of dynamic query filters and starfield displays. In B. Adelson, S. Dumais, & J. Olson (Eds.), *Proceedings of the SIGCHI conference on Human factors in computing systems: Celebrating interdependence* (pp. 313-317). New York, NY: ACM Press.

Andrews, K. (1995). Case study: Visualizing cyberspace: Information visualization in the harmony internet browser. In N. Gershon, & S. Eick (Eds.), *Proceedings, Information Visualization* (pp. 90-96). Los Alamitos, CA: IEEE Computer Society

Arnheim, R. (1969). *Visual thinking.* Berkeley, CA: University of California Press.

Baecker, R.M., Grudin, J., Buxton, W.A.S., & Greenberg, S. (1995). A historical and intellectual perspective. In R.M. Baecker, J. Grudin, W. Buxton, & S. Greenberg (Eds.), *Readings in human-computer interaction: Toward the year 2000* (pp. 35-52). San Francisco, CA: Morgan Kaufmann.

Benford, S. Snowdon, D., Greenhalfh, C., Ingram, R., Know, I., & Brown, C. (1995). VR-VIBE: A virtual environment for co-operative information retrieval. *Computer Graphics Forum, 14*(3), C349-C360.

Card, S.K., Moran, T.P., & Newell, A. (1983). *The psychology of human-computer interaction.* Hillsdale, NJ: Lawrence Erlbaum Associates.

Card, S.K., Pirolli, P., & Mackinlay, J.D. (1994). The cost-of-knowledge characteristic function: Display evaluation for direct walk information visualizations. In B. Adelson, S. Dumais, & J. Olson (Eds.), *Proceedings of the SIGCHI conference on Human factors in computing systems: Celebrating interdependence* (pp. 238-244). New York, NY: ACM.

Card, S.K., Robertson, G.G., & York, W. (1996). The WebBook and the Web Forager: An information workspace for the world-wide- web. In M.J.Tauber (Ed.), *Proceedings of the SIGCHI conference on Human factors in computing systems: Common ground* (pp. 111-117). New York, NY: ACM.

Chase, W.G. & Ericsson, K.A. (1982). Skill and working memory. In G.H. Bower (Ed.), *The psychology of learning and motivation* (Vol. 15, pp. 1-58). New York: Academic Press.

Chen, C. (1999). *Information visualization and virtual environments.* London: Springer.

Chen, C., Thomas, L., & Chennawasin, C. (1999). Representing the semantics of virtual spaces. *IEEE Multimedia, 6*(2), 54-63.

Clawson, D.M., Miller, M.S., Knott, B.A., & Sebrechts, M.M. (1998). Navigational training in virtual and real buildings. *Proceedings of the 42nd Annual Meeting of the Human Factors and Ergonomics Society* (pp. 1427-1431). Santa Monica, CA: Human Factors and Ergonomics Society.

Cobb, S., Neale, H., Crosier, J., & Wilson, J.R. (2002). Development and evaluation of virtual environments for education. In K.M. Stanney (Ed.), *Handbook of virtual environments: Design, Implementation, and Applications* (pp. 911-936). Mahwah, NJ: Lawrence Erlbaum Associates.

Cohen, M., & Wenzel, E.M. (1995). The design of multidimensional sound interfaces. In W. Barfield, & T.A. Furness III (Eds.), *Virtual environments and advanced interface design* (pp. 291-346). New York: Oxford University Press.

Dede, C. (1995). The evolution of constructivist learning environments: Immersion in distributed, virtual worlds. *Educational Technology, 35*(5), 46-52.

Dede, C., Salzman, M., Loftin, R.B., & Ash, K. (1999). The Design of Immersive Virtual Environments: Fostering Deep Understanding of Complex Scientific Knowledge. In M.J. Jacobson, & R.B. Kozma (Eds.), *Innovations in Science and Mathematics Education: Advanced Designs for Technologies of Learning.* (pp. 361-413). Mahwah, NJ: Lawrence Erlbaum Associates.

Deerwester, S., Dumais, S.T., Landauer, T.K., Furnas, G.W., & Harshman, R.A. (1990). Indexing by latent semantic analysis. *Journal of the American Society for Information Science, 41*(6), 391-407.

Duffy, T.M., & Jonassen, D.H. (Eds.). (1992). *Constructivism and the technology of instruction.* Hillsdale, NJ: Lawrence Erlbaum Associates.

Fairchild, K. M., Poltrock, S.E., & Furnas, G.W. (1988). SemNet: Three-dimensional representations of large knowledge bases. In R. Guindon (Ed.), *Cognitive Science and its applications for human-computer interaction* (pp. 201-233). Hillsdale, NJ: Lawrence Erlbaum Associates.

Gardner, H. (1998). A multiplicity of intelligences. *Scientific American, 9(4), 18-23.*

Harm, D.L. (2002). Motion sickness neurophysiology, physiological correlates, and treatment. In K.M. Stanney (Ed.), *Handbook of virtual environments: Design, Implementation, and Applications* (pp. 637-661). Mahwah, NJ: Lawrence Erlbaum Associates.

Hetzler, B., Harris, W.M., Havre, S., & Whitney, P. (1998). Visualizing the full spectrum of document relationships. In W. Mustafa El Hadi, J. Maniez, & A.S. Pollitt (Eds.), *Proceedings of the Fifth International* Society for Knowledge Organization *(ISKO) Conference: Structures and Relations in Knowledge Organization* (pp. 168-175). Würzburg: ERGON Verlag.

Hutchins, E.L., Hollan, J.D., & Norman, D.A. (1986). Direct manipulation interfaces. In D.A. Norman, & S.W. Draper (Eds.), *User centered system design: New perspectives on human-computer interaction* (pp. 87-124). Hillsdale, NJ: Lawrence Erlbaum Associates.

Jacob, R.J.K. (1995). Eye tracking in advanced interface design. In W. Barfield, & T.A. Furness III (Eds.), *Virtual environments and advanced interface design* (pp. 258-288). New York: Oxford University Press.

Kaczmarek, K.A., & Bach-y-Rita, P. (1995). Tactile displays. In W. Barfield, & T.A. Furness III (Eds.), *Virtual environments and advanced interface design* (pp. 349-370). New York: Oxford University Press.

Klin, A., Sparrow, S. S., de Bildt, A., Cicchetti, D. V., Cohen, D. J., & Volkmar, F. R. (1999). A normed study of face recognition in autism and related disorders. *Journal of Autism and Developmental Disorders 29*(6), 499 – 508.

Klin, A., Volkmar, F. R., & Sparrow, S. S. (1992). Autistic social dysfunction: some limitations of the theory of mind hypothesis. *Journal of Child Psychology and Psychiatry 33*(5), 861-876.

Knott, B. (1999). *Learning route and survey representations from a virtual reality environment.* Unpublished doctoral dissertation. The Catholic University of America, Washington, DC.

Locke, J. (1964). *An essay concerning human understanding.* New York: New American Library. (Original work published 1690).

Miller, M. S. (2001). *Specificity, transfer, and retention of spatial knowledge from navigation using maps, virtual, and real environments.* Unpublished doctoral dissertation. The Catholic University of America, Washington, DC.

Miller, M.S., Clawson, D.M., & Sebrechts, M.M. (2000) *Spatial knowledge acquired from virtual reality: Transfer and flexibility.* Poster presented at the 41st Annual Meeting of the Psychonomic Society, New Orleans, LA.

Mitchell, W.J.T. (1994). *Picture theory.* Chicago, IL: University of Chicago Press.

Moroney, W.F., Hampton, S., Biers, E.W., & Kirton, T. (1994). The use of personal computer-based training devices in teaching instrument flying: A comparative study. *Proceedings of the Human Factors and Ergonomics Society 38th Annual Meeting* (pp. 95-99). Santa Monica, CA: Human Factors and Ergonomics Society.

Moroney, W.F. & Moroney, B.W. (1998). Simulation. In D.J. Garland, J.A. Wise, & V.D. Hopkin (Eds.), *Human factors in aviation systems* (pp. 358-388). Mahwah, NJ: Lawrence Erlbaum Associates.

Moshell, J.M., & Hughes, C.E. (2002). Virtual environments as a tool for academic learning. In K.M. Stanney (Ed.), *Handbook of virtual environments: Design, Implementation, and Applications* (pp. 893-910). Mahwah, NJ: Lawrence Erlbaum Associates.

Mullin, L.N. (2002). *Virtual environments as a tool for transfer and recall of spatial information.* Unpublished MA thesis. The Catholic University of America, Washington, DC.

Mullin, L.N., & Sebrechts, M.M. (2003). *Enhancing the Utility of a Map for Spatial Learning: A Comparison of Traditional and Interactive Designs.* Poster Presented At The 15th Annual Meeting Of The American Psychological Society, Atlanta, May, 29.

Mullin, L.N., Sebrechts, M.M., & Clawson, D.M. (2000). *Using Virtual Environments to Reinstate Context for Recalling Object Placement.* Poster presented at the 2000 Convention of the American Psychological Association, Washington, DC.

Munzer, T., Hoffman, E., Claffy, K., & Fenner, B. (1996). Visualizing the global topology of the Mbone. In *Proceedings of the IEEE Symposium on Information Visualization* (pp. 85-92). Los Alamitos, CA: IEEE Computer Society.

Norman, D.A. (1994). *Things that make us smart: Defending human attributes in the age of the machine.* New York: Addison Wesley.

Norman, D.A. (1986). Cognitive engineering. In D.A. Norman, & S.W. Draper (Eds.), *User centered system design: New perspectives on human-computer interaction* (pp. 31-61). Hillsdale, NJ: Lawrence Erlbaum Associates.

Papert, S. (1980). *Mindstorms: Children, computers and powerful ideas.* New York: Basic Books.

Parritz, R. H., Mangelsdorf, S., & Gunnar, M. R. (1992). Control, social referencing, and the infant's appraisal of threat. In S. Feinman (Ed.), *Social Referencing and the Social Construction of Reality in Infancy* (pp. 209-228). New York: Plenum Press.

Phillips, W., Baron-Cohen, S. & Rutter, M. (1992). The role of eye contact in goal detection: evidence from normal infants and children with autism or mental handicap. *Development and Psychopathology, 4*(3), 375-383.

Piller, M.J. (2001). *Virtual environments as a tool for transfer and recall of spatial information.* Unpublished MA Thesis. The Catholic University of America, Washington, DC.

Piller, M. J., & Sebrechts, M.M. (2003). *Spatial Learning in Transparent Virtual Environments.* Poster Presented at the 47th Annual Meeting of the Human Factors and Ergonomics Society, Denver, CO.

Piller, M. J., Miller, M.M., & Sebrechts, M.M. (2003). *Restricted Field of View Leads to Specificity of Spatial Learning.* Poster Presented at the 15th Annual Meeting of the American Psychological Society, Atlanta.

Prothero, J.D., & Parker, D.E. (2003). A unified approach to presence and motion sickness. In L.J. Hettinger, & M. Haas (Eds.), *Virtual and Adaptive Environments: Applications, Implications, and Human Performance Issues* (pp. 47-66). Mahwah, NJ: Lawrence Erlbaum Associates.

Salas, E., Oser, R.L., Cannon-Bowers J.A., & Daskarolis-Kring, E. (2002). Team training in virtual environments: An event-based approach. In K.M. Stanney (Ed.), *Handbook of virtual environments: Design, Implementation, and Applications* (pp. 873-892). Mahwah, NJ: Lawrence Erlbaum Associates.

Satava, R.M., & Jones, S.B. (2002). Medical applications of virtual environments. In K.M. Stanney (Ed.), *Handbook of virtual environments: Design, Implementation, and Applications* (pp. 937-957). Mahwah, NJ: Lawrence Erlbaum Associates.

Schank, R.C. (1997). *Virtual Learning: A Revolutionary Approach to Building a Highly Skilled Workforce.* New York, NY: McGraw Hill.

Sebrechts, M.M., Enright, M., Bennett, R.E., & Martin, K. (1996). Using Algebra Word Problems to Assess Quantitative Ability: Attributes, Strategies, and Errors. *Cognition and Instruction, 14*(3), 285-343.

Sebrechts, M.M. & Knott, B.A. (1998). *Learning spatial relations in virtual environments: Route and Euclidean metrics.* Poster presented at the 10th Annual Convention of the American Psychological Society (May), Washington, DC.

Sebrechts, M.M., Knott, B.A., & Clawson, D.M. (1998). *Changes in spatial mental models with alternative virtual reality learning environments.* Poster presented at the 39th Annual Meeting of the Psychonomic Society (Nov.), Dallas, TX

Sebrechts, M.M., Lathan, C., Clawson, D.M., Miller, M.S., & Trepagnier, C. (2003). Transfer of training in virtual environments: Issues for human performance. In L.J. Hettinger, & M. Haas (Eds.), *Virtual and Adaptive Environments: Applications, Implications, and Human Performance Issues* (pp. 67-90). Mahwah, NJ: Lawrence Erlbaum Associates.

Sebrechts, M.M., Mullin, L.N., Clawson, D.M., & Knott, B.A. (1999). *Virtual exploration effects on spatial navigation and recall of location.* Poster presented at the 40th Annual Meeting of the Psychonomic Society, Los Angeles, CA.

Sebrechts, M.M., Vasilakis, J., & Miller, M.S. (2000). *Using task analysis to identify cognitive bases for 3D information visualization design.* Poster presented at the 2000 American Association for the Advancement of Science Annual Meeting, Washington, DC.

Sebrechts, M.M., Vasilakis, J., Miller, M.S., Cugini, J.V., & Laskowski, S.J. (1999). Visualization of Search Results: A Comparative Evaluation of Text, 2D, and 3D Interfaces. In M. Hearst, F. Gey, & R. Tong (Eds.), *Proceedings of SIGIR'99: 22nd International Conference on Research and Development in Information Retrieval* (pp. 3-10). New York: The Association for Computing Machinery.

Singley, K. & Anderson, J.R. (1989). *The transfer of cognitive skill.* Cambridge, MA: Harvard University Press.

Stappers, P.J., Gaver, W., & Overbeeke, K. (2003). Beyond the limits of real-time realism: Moving from stimulation corrspondence to information correspondence. In L.J. Hettinger, & M. Haas (Eds.). *Virtual and Adaptive Environments: Applications, Implications, and Human Performance Issues* (pp. 91-110). Mahwah, NJ: Lawrence Erlbaum Associates.

Stoffregen, T.A., Bardy, B.G., Smart, L.J., & Pagulayan, R. (2003). On the nature and evaluation of fidelity in virtual environments. In L.J. Hettinger, & M. Haas (Eds.), *Virtual and Adaptive Environments: Applications, Implications, and Human Performance Issues* (pp. 111-128). Mahwah, NJ: Lawrence Erlbaum Associates.

Thorndike, E.L. (1906). *Principles of teaching.* New York: A.G. Seiler.

Trepagnier. C. (1996). A Possible Origin for the Social and Communicative Deficits of Autism. *Focus on Autism and Other Developmental Disabilities 11*(3), 170-182.

Trepagnier, C., Gupta, V, Sebrechts, M.M. & Rosen. M, J. (2000). How does he look: Tracking autistic gaze. *Proceedings of the RESNA 2000 Annual Conference*, 28-30.

Trepanier, C., & Sebrechts, M.M. (2002). *Face Processing in Autism.* Paper presented at the International Meeting for Autism Research (IMFAR). Orlando, FL.

Tufte, E.R. (2001). *The visual display of quantitative information* (2nd ed.). Cheshire, CT: Graphics Press.

Tulving, E. (1983). *Elements of episodic memory.* London: Oxford University Press.

Tulving, E. & Thompson, D.M. (1973). Encoding specificity and retrieval processes in episodic memory. *Psychological Review, 80*, 352-373.

Vasilakis, J. (2000). *A CPM-GOMS analysis of information retrieval using text, 2D, and 3D visualization tools.* Unpublished MA Thesis. The Catholic University of America, Washington, DC.

Ware, C. (2000). *Information visualization: Perception for design.* San Francisco, CA: Morgan Kaufmann.

Wickens, C. (1992). Virtual reality and education. *Proceedings of the IEEE International Conference on Systems, Man, and Cybernetics* (pp. 842-847). Chicago, IL: IEEE Press.

Witmer, B. G. Bailey, J.H., Knerr, B.W., & Parsons, K.C. (1996). Virtual spaces and real world places: Transfer of route knowledge. *International Journal of Human-Computer Studies, 45*, 413-428.

Yates, F.A. (1966). *The art of memory.* London: Routledge & Kegan Paul.

The Impact of Dimensionality and Color Coding of Information Visualizations on Knowledge Acquisition

Tanja Keller[1] and Matthias Grimm[2]

[1] Institut für Wissensmedien (IWM), Konrad-Adenauer-Straße 40,
72072 Tuebingen, Germany
t.keller@iwm-kmrc.de
[2] Zentrum für Graphische Datenverarbeitung e.V., Fraunhoferstraße 5,
64283 Darmstadt, Germany
matthias.grimm@zgdv.de

Abstract. Up to now, information visualizations have been mainly used to support information retrieval. In the study presented here, we investigate whether information visualizations can also be used to aid in acquiring knowledge, that is, in memorizing and understanding large abstract data structures. Furthermore, we address the issue of how information visualizations have to be designed in order to support knowledge acquisition of abstract data. To this end, we conducted an experimental study investigating the influence of the factors "dimensionality" and "color coding". The domain was the building industry. The study provided evidence that information visualizations may foster knowledge acquisition and that two-dimensional information visualizations are better suited for supporting knowledge acquisition than three-dimensional ones. In addition, we found a marginal main effect of color coding, that is, the use of color coding slightly increased performance in a knowledge test. To conclude our analysis, we will outline how information visualizations for fostering knowledge acquisition can benefit from the field of knowledge visualization.

1 Introduction and Research Questions

In today's information society, we are constantly confronted with an exponentially increasing amount of information and its ever increasing complexity. Therefore, it is necessary to find methods and technologies to handle large data sets. One solution to this problem can be found in information visualizations, a relatively new technology, which aims at facilitating both the use of data sets and an understanding of the included data structures (Le Grand & Soto, 1999). According to Card, Mackinlay, and Shneiderman (1999), information visualizations can be characterized as "computer-supported, interactive, visual representations of abstract non-physically based data to amplify cognition" (p. 6). Examples of such data are the text-based data of the World Wide Web or elements of large data bases (Däßler & Palm, 1998).

It is a widely held opinion that new technologies have an enormous pedagogic potential. However, past experiences seem to have shown that this is not necessarily true. Some new technologies have not proven to be effective tools for fostering knowledge acquisition. For example, in the 1920's, there was tremendous optimism

S.-O. Tergan and T. Keller (Eds.): Knowledge and Information Visualization, LNCS 3426, pp. 167–182, 2005.

with regard to the pedagogic potential of educational films. However, that potential could not be confirmed (Cuban, 1986). One explanation offered is that the development processes were technology-orientated instead of learner-orientated (Mayer, 2001). This means, new technologies indeed have pedagogic potential, however, this potential has to be made accessible by means of the way the technologies are presented or used. The technology has to be aligned to the user demands. In this contribution, our aim is to discuss the pedagogic potential of information visualizations, which have not previously been used in the context of learning. In addition, the issue is addressed as to how information visualizations have to be designed in order to support knowledge acquisition.

The area of information visualization has made big progress due to the advancement of computer technologies, especially in the field of graphical methods, like VRML (Däßler & Palm, 1998). Currently, there is a trend to develop increasingly technologically complex information visualizations: Viewing the current developments within this field, it has to be remarked that there is an increasing development of three-dimensional and polychromatic information visualizations (see e.g., http://www.cybergeography.org/atlas/info_spaces.html). Research has shown that information visualizations may help users in navigating, using, and exploring large data sets, as well as recognizing the data structures (cf., Däßler & Palm, 1998; Le Grand & Soto, 1999; Wiss, Carr, & Jonsson, 1998). Within the context of information visualizations, the factors "dimensionality" and "color coding" have been studied as factors for facilitating information access: Examples of studies investigating the influence of dimensionality are those of Cockburn and McKenzie (2001, 2002, 2004). Examples of studies focusing on the effect of color coding are those of Carter (1982), as well as Bundesen and Pedersen (1983).

However, up to now, a study has not been conducted as to whether information visualizations, which use two spatial dimensions to represent data, are better suited for fostering knowledge acquisition than those that use three spatial dimensions. In addition, no studies exist investigating the influence of color coding on knowledge acquisition in the context of information visualizations.

This contribution aims at answering these questions. More concretely, the fundamental research questions of this contribution are the following:

- Are information visualizations also suited to foster knowledge acquisition?
- How do information visualizations for fostering knowledge acquisition have to be designed? Particularly, how is knowledge acquisition through information visualizations influenced by dimensionality and color coding?

An experiment (with a 2x2-design plus a baseline group) was conducted with 100 students from the University of Tuebingen. The theoretical background, the method, and the results of the empirical study will be reported in following sections. In a final section, some prospects for fostering knowledge acquisition with information visualizations by means of a knowledge-based approach are outlined.

2 Theoretical Background

2.1 Theories on Information Visualization

The prevailing psychological theories on memory and cognition assume that the information processing systems of the working memory are limited in their cognitive capacity. Therefore, a goal of instructional design is to hinder cognitive overload of one or more information processing systems. In the following paragraphs, we will explain these theories and discuss their implications concerning knowledge acquisition with information visualizations.

Most information visualizations have two components: a visual element complemented with textual clues for enhancing its meaning. Due to the combination of textual and pictorial parts, information visualizations can be considered as multimedia in terms of Mayer (2001). He defined multimedia as the presentation of material that combines verbal (spoken or printed) and pictorial elements. In the context of the project reported herein, information visualizations should be used to foster knowledge acquisition. Therefore, the *Cognitive Theory of Multimedia Learning* of Mayer (2001) seems to be a suitable theoretical foundation. This theory is based on three assumptions: first, there are two information-processing systems (auditory/verbal vs. visual/pictorial), second, the information-processing systems have a limited capacity, and third, active information processing is a necessity.

According to this theory, one has to differentiate between modality and coding. Modality refers to whether the information has to be perceived by the eyes (i.e., visual) or by the ears (i.e., auditory). In the context of information visualizations, all information represented is visual. Therefore, here, modality is irrelevant. However, coding refers to whether information is presented, for example, in a pictorial code or in a verbal code. Due to the fact that information visualizations use different coding systems, the theoretical background has to focus on coding. In compliance with the Cognitive Theory of Multimedia Learning, pictorial coded information is processed in the pictorial/visual channel, whereas verbal coded information that is presented visually as text is processed in both channels, in the visual/pictorial channel and the auditory/verbal one. Both channels are limited in their cognitive capacity. Therefore, to prevent cognitive overload of one channel, which would hinder learning, the information that has to be processed should be coded in a way that the learner has to use both channels for information processing; that is, the information has to present partly in a verbal (e.g., text) and partly in a pictorial manner (cf., the multimedia principle of Mayer, 2001).

Further cognitive theories could be seen as an enhancement of the Cognitive Theory of Multimedia Learning, for example, the *Theory on Visuo-Spatial Working Memory* of Logie (1995). This theory postulates three different specialized systems for information processing. It refers to Baddeley's *Working Memory Model* (Baddeley, 1998) that differentiates a.o. between the *phonological loop* for processing verbal information and the visuospatial sketchpad for processing visual and spatial information. In his approach, Logie (1995) divided Baddeley's visuospatial sketchpad into the autonomous subsystems *visual cache* and *inner scribe*. Whereas the modality independent spatial subsystem (i.e., inner scribe) processes spatial-relational information (like position or spatial interrelations), the modality dependent visual subsystem (i.e., visual cache) processes visually perceived information (like color or shape). This differentiation is according to neuro-scientific results, which show evidence for two separate brain structures, one for spatial and one for visual processes of working memory: the so-called *what-system* processes only visual cues and thus it is modality dependent, whereas the modality independent, so-called *where-system* processes spatial cues (e.g., Ungerleider & Mishkin, 1982; Landau & Jackendoff, 1993).

According to these explications, information representations should be effective learning environments when they make use of several information processing systems to deter cognitive overload in one system. Therefore, they should make use of the verbal system that processes verbal information (e.g., text), the visual system that processes pictorial information (e.g., color), and the spatial system that processes spatial information (e.g., position). Information visualizations are a possibility for such information representations as described. For representing data, they could use text, color coding, as well as spatial coding. Information visualizations should be superior to information representations that activate only one system for information processing, for example, pure text-based information representations (like an Excel spreadsheet) that mainly activate the verbal system for information processing.

Using space for information coding makes it necessary to differentiate between item-specific and relational information (Engelkamp, 1990). According to this differentiation, item-specific information is information relating to one specific item of an item cluster, whereas relational information refers to relations between items of an item cluster. What is viewed as an item is task-dependent. Therefore, an item could be, for example, a picture, a word, or a sentence. It could be assumed that information visualizations especially foster learning of relational information, because information visualizations are developed to facilitate the recognition of data structures. Therefore, in this study, a differentiation between relational and item-specific information was also made.

Another important theory is the *Cognitive Load Theory* (e.g., Sweller, van Merriënboer, & Paas, 1998) that focuses directly on the limited cognitive capacity. Cognitive load is defined as a construct that describes the amount of load on the cognitive system caused by a task. This theory differentiates between three kinds of cognitive load:

- The *intrinsic cognitive load* is the amount of cognitive load caused by the task itself. It describes the cognitive load caused by both the prior knowledge of the user and the intrinsic nature of the material. The latter depends on the number of simultaneously presented elements and their element interactivity.
- The *extraneous cognitive load* is caused by the type of material representation and the subsequent kinds of interaction activities necessary for learning the material.
- The *germane cognitive load* describes the amount of conscious cognitive processes, which are directly relevant for learning.

While using information visualizations, the learner has to handle a large amount of elements that have, in addition, a certain amount of element interactivity. Therefore, knowledge acquisition with information visualizations is a task with a large amount of intrinsic cognitive load. As a consequence, and due to the additivity of the three kinds of cognitive load (Sweller & Chandler, 1994), it is very important to reduce extraneous cognitive load and/or to foster germane cognitive load. Following Cognitive Load Theory, some implications for explaining potential effects of information visualizations can be derived: information visualizations can reduce extraneous cognitive load by visualizing the data structures explicitly, so that the users do not have to develop them on their own. Furthermore, information visualizations use different presentation codes (e.g. verbal, pictorial, spatial) to distribute the cognitive load on different information processing systems. As a result, the user has more free cognitive capacity for managing the learning task.

In addition, the approach of *Computational Efficiency* (Larkin & Simon, 1987) has to be mentioned, which postulates that some information representations (e.g., diagrammatic ones) are computationally more efficient than the informational equivalent of other information representations (e.g., sentential ones). That means, for work on a certain task, some representations are more suitable than others including the same information, because they represent the information in a matter that supports useful and computational processes. In the context of information visualizations, information visualizations could also include computational advantages compared to a pure text-based information representation, as information visualizations group information that belongs together. This results in reduced information search times compared to searching for example in an unordered information list. In addition, information visualizations represent the information structures explicitly, that is, they do not have to be derived by the learners. This also reduces cognitive load. Information visualizations could make use of automatic human information perception processes (for more details, see Ware, in this book). However, to use the computational advantages of a representation, a learner has to be able to make use of them. A necessary prerequisite to make effective use of visualizations is an appropriate level of visual-spatial literacy (Holley & Dansereau, 1984).

The contribution of Ware (in this book) entails further aspects as to why information visualizations may be efficient, albeit from a more perceptual perspective. Keller and Tergan (in this book) discuss a.o. the reasons of why visualizations in general are relevant for supporting processes of learning, comprehension, and information access. They point out some shortcomings of information visualization and suggest that sometimes information visualizations may be augmented in efficiency by making use of knowledge visualization techniques in a synergistic approach.

In summary, according to the aforementioned theoretical derivations, it can be assumed that information visualizations may be efficient tools for fostering the knowledge acquisition of abstract data. In the following section, the influence of dimensionality and color coding on knowledge acquisition with information visualizations will be discussed.

2.2   Design Principles for Information Visualizations for Fostering Knowledge Acquisition

The impact of dimensionality. There is a current trend towards developing three-dimensional information visualizations, however, empirical results concerning the impact of dimensionality in related research fields, especially in the context of information visualization for information retrieval, argue for two-dimensional variants (e.g., Cockburn & McKenzie, 2001, 2002, 2004; Park & Woldstad, 2000). Additionally, according to the theoretical perspective, it has to be assumed that two-dimensional information visualizations are better suited for fostering knowledge acquisition of abstract data than three-dimensional variants. The explanation for this lies in a comparison of both types. Both kinds of information visualizations differ in the possible amount of spatial coding of data. Whereas two-dimensional visualizations could only use two space dimensions for data representation, three-dimensional ones could make use of three space dimensions. Empirical results (e.g., Amorim, Trumbore, & Chogyen, 2000) provide evidence that the "where-system" (cf., Landau & Jackendoff, 1993) that processes spatial information is more effective than the "what-system" that focuses on processing non spatial information. However, one may doubt that this is also the case for three-dimensional information spaces, because using three-dimensional environments comes along with a higher extraneous cognitive load compared to two-dimensional information visualizations. This higher extraneous cognitive load counteracts the advantages of spatial coding. The reason for this has to do with the danger of mutual occlusion of information units in three-dimensional information visualizations; that is, one information unit cannot be seen from a certain perspective, because it is concealed by another unit that is located in front of it. Therefore, to solve this problem, additional interaction possibilities (e.g., the possibility to rotate) are needed in three-dimensional information visualizations. In addition, in three-dimensional environments, there is the danger of "lost in space phenomena" which could also be solved only by higher user interactivity. According to the assumptions just outlined, it is to be expected that using three-dimensional information visualizations results in higher extraneous cognitive load compared to using two-dimensional ones. As a consequence, it has to be assumed that two-dimensional information visualizations are more efficient in fostering knowledge acquisition compared to three-dimensional ones.

The impact of color coding. There are empirical studies in the field of visualizations that have shown that color is an effective graphical device for reducing visual search time (e.g., Bundesen & Pederson, 1983; Carter, 1982; Treisman & Gormican, 1988). That is, color may be helpful to support a fast information access. With regard to supporting knowledge acquisition by means of color coding, the following has to be mentioned: Research on perceptual psychology showed that color is a basic element of visual perception (e.g., Treisman, 1987). Color is a feature that can be processed automatically, i.e., it requires no conscious processes. Studies on memory (e.g., Hanna & Remington, 1996) have shown that color is stored in long-term memory together with other object information. Therefore, color is an additional cue for memory retrieval. As a consequence, it can be assumed that color coding may be helpful with regard to knowledge acquisition with information visualizations.

3 Empirical Study

We conducted an experiment in order to investigate the following research questions:

- Are information visualizations suited to foster knowledge acquisition? To answer this question, information visualizations are compared to a baseline condition, that is, a pure text-based information representation.
- What is the influence of dimensionality and color coding of information visualizations on knowledge acquisition? More concretely, are two-dimensional information visualizations better suited for fostering knowledge acquisition than three-dimensional ones? Is color coding helpful for supporting knowledge acquisition?

3.1 Method

Participants. Participants were 100 students (56 female, 44 male) from the University of Tuebingen, Germany. Average age was 23.2 (SD = 3.7) years.

Materials. This work is associated with the European project "Mummy" of the Computer Graphics Center in Darmstadt (Germany), which focuses on mobile knowledge management using multimedia-rich portals for context-aware information processing in the context of the building industry. Therefore, the study uses an experimental environment, which was designed to provide architects with an overview of the details of their construction projects. Each of these 42 construction projects is described by values for six different project attributes, namely "rate of return", "construction costs per square meter", "number of problems", "construction progress", "size of construction site", and "construction volume".

Design, procedure, and dependent measures. As an experimental baseline condition, the information on the construction projects was represented by means of a spreadsheet, which listed the 42 construction projects (i.e., information units) alphabetically (see Fig. 1). The first column in Fig. 1 represented the name of the construction projects, whereas the other columns contained the values of these projects with regard to the six aforementioned attributes. The last column listed further project information beyond these attributes.

To reduce complexity, the range of possible attribute values was restricted to four (i.e., very small, small, big, and very big). Due to the spreadsheet size, it was impossible to view the data of all projects without scrolling.

In order to implement our experimental manipulation, we represented the same data set by means of information visualizations. These information visualizations differ in the representation of the values of one of the six attributes ("construction progress"). The values on this attribute were visualized either spatially by the third spatial dimension (in three-dimensional information visualizations) or non-spatially (in two-dimensional information visualizations) and either with color coding (in color-coded information visualizations, i.e. polychromatic ones) or without color coding (in non color-coded information visualizations, i.e. monochromatic ones). With regard to the representation of the other five attributes, in all information visualization

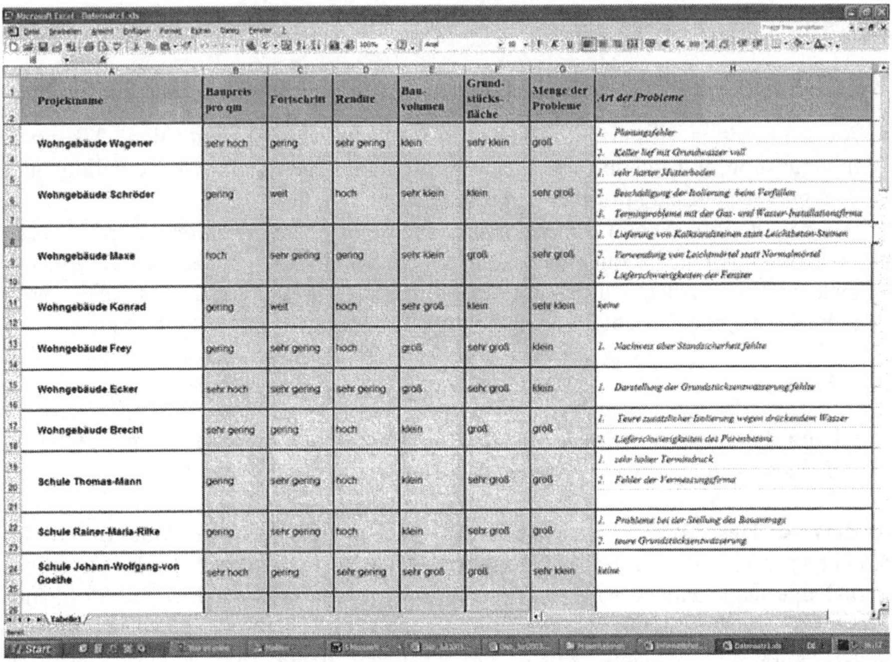

Projektname	Baupreis pro qm	Fortschritt	Rendite	Bauvolumen	Grundstücksfläche	Menge der Probleme	Art der Probleme
Wohngebäude Wagener	sehr hoch	gering	sehr gering	klein	sehr klein	groß	1. Planungsfehler 2. Keller lief mit Grundwasser voll
Wohngebäude Schröder	gering	weit	hoch	sehr klein	klein	sehr groß	1. sehr harter Mutterboden 2. Beschädigung der Isolierung beim Verfüllen 3. Terminprobleme mit der Gas- und Wasser-Installationsfirma
Wohngebäude Maxe	hoch	sehr gering	gering	sehr klein	groß	sehr groß	1. Lieferung von Kalksandsteinen statt Leichtbeton-Steinen 2. Verwendung von Leichtmörtel statt Normalmörtel 3. Lieferschwierigkeiten der Fenster
Wohngebäude Konrad	gering	weit	hoch	sehr groß	klein	sehr klein	keine
Wohngebäude Frey	gering	sehr gering	hoch	groß	sehr groß	klein	1. Nachweis über Standsicherheit fehlte
Wohngebäude Ecker	sehr hoch	sehr gering	sehr gering	groß	sehr groß	klein	1. Darstellung der Grundstücksentwässerung fehlte
Wohngebäude Brecht	sehr gering	gering	hoch	klein	groß	groß	1. Teure zusätzlicher Isolierung wegen drückendem Wasser 2. Lieferschwierigkeiten des Parkettbetons
Schule Thomas-Mann	gering	sehr gering	hoch	klein	sehr groß	groß	1. sehr hoher Termindruck 2. Fehler der Vermessungsfirma
Schule Rainer-Maria-Rilke	gering	sehr gering	hoch	klein	sehr groß	groß	1. Probleme bei der Stellung des Bauantrags 2. teure Grundstücksentwässerung
Schule Johann-Wolfgang-von-Goethe	sehr hoch	gering	sehr gering	sehr groß	groß	sehr klein	keine

Fig. 1. Spreadsheet representation (baseline)

conditions, the values of the two attributes "size of construction site" and "construction volume" were visualized spatially; that is, they were represented by two axes in the information space. The remaining project attributes ("rate of return", "construction costs per square meter", and "number of problems"), as well as the further project information, were represented textually and could be accessed through pop-up windows by clicking on the information units. In addition, the value of the attribute "construction progress" was also represented by a digit attached to the project label.

The 42 information units are represented by squares (labeled by their project name). These information units were arranged in the two- or three-dimensional information space according to their values for these two or three spatially represented attributes. Fig. 2 shows a two-dimensional, color-coded information visualization condition with an open pop-up window.

Learners could move the pop-up windows with their mouse by click, drag, and drop should the window conceal information of interest. To facilitate orientation, the project label of the viewed information unit changed its color from white to red and position lines from the information unit to the axes appeared while contacting the unit with the mouse pointer (position lines, see Fig. 3).

Fig. 3 represents a screenshot of a three-dimensional information visualization condition. To ensure that all information units would be visible in the three-dimensional information visualizations, the users were allowed to rotate the vertical axis by moving the visualization with the mouse button pressed. To avoid "lost in

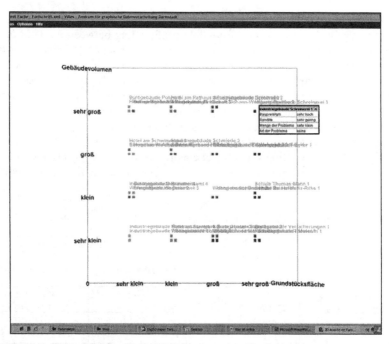

Fig. 2. Two-dimensional, color-coded information visualization with open pop-up window. Note: In the original version the texts and lines were presented in white against a black background; the information units were color-coded

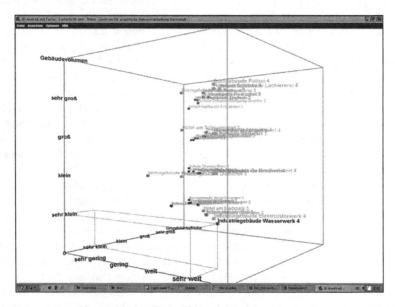

Fig. 3. Rotated three-dimensional, color-coded information visualization with position lines. Note: In the original version the texts and lines were presented in white against a black background; the information units were color-coded

navigation phenomena", users could push a home-button at any time to attain the start perspective again. In order to avoid possible confounding between the kind of attribute and its kind of representation, we developed a further set of information visualizations that only differs from the described one in the style of representation of the attributes. That is, attributes that were visualized spatially in the first set were represented as text in the second set and vice-versa. However, for ease of understanding the experimental design, the study presented in this contribution is only illustrated with examples from one set of experimental materials.

Dimensionality and color coding were both varied between subjects, resulting in a 2x2-design (plus the baseline spreadsheet condition) (Fig. 4). Subjects were randomly assigned to the spreadsheet or to one of the four information visualization conditions.

Baseline condition   **Information visualization conditions**

			Dimensionality	
			two-dimensional	three-dimensional
spreadsheet (presentation set 1 & 2)	**Color coding**	**without**	2D/without (presentation set 1 & 2)	3D/without (presentation set 1 & 2)
		with	2D/with (presentation set 1 & 2)	3D/with (presentation set 1 & 2)

Fig. 4. Design of the empirical study

With regard to the procedure, the participants first received a booklet for measuring different *control variables* like *retentiveness* in a paper-pencil test. Afterwards, they received an *introduction to the experimental environment and its usage.* To ensure that all participants saw the same information, the exploration of the environment during the subsequent practice phase was standardized. In the *learning phase,* subjects were given 50 minutes to accomplish five tasks: According to these tasks, they had to find 14 of the 42 information units and had to learn the data contained in these information units. Consecutively, subjects received another booklet containing 35 *test tasks.* In this test phase, the learning materials were no longer available. There were no time limits during testing. Finally, participants had to fill out a *questionnaire* inquiring as to difficulties regarding the use of the learning materials, the strategies used, as well as assessing the cognitive load experienced during learning.

With regard to the dependent measures, as a first dependent variable, we measured learner performance in different knowledge tasks. We differentiated between different knowledge types: First, *what-knowledge*, that is, knowledge acquired from those attributes that are always represented by text (i.e., the content of a pop-up window); second, *where-knowledge*, that is, knowledge acquired from those attributes that are represented in all information visualization conditions by space; third, *varied-knowledge*, that is, knowledge acquired from the attribute that is varied in its representational format in the different conditions. *Overall performance* was calculated as follows: One point was assigned for each correct answer in those tasks that referred to one knowledge type, whereas two points were assigned for each correct answer in those tasks that referred to two knowledge types. Due to the fact that there were 14 tasks referring to one of the knowledge types and 21 tasks referring to two knowledge types, the maximum overall performance score is 56 points. Due to different task types, this overall performance could be subdivided in sub-performances:

On a first level, due to the different knowledge types, the overall performance resulted from *what-performance* (4 tasks referring to what-knowledge), *where-performance* (4 tasks referring to where-knowledge), *varied-performance* (4 tasks referring to varied-knowledge), and *where/what-performance* (6 tasks referring to where- and what-knowledge) *where/varied-performance* (6 tasks referring to where- and varied-knowledge), *what/varied-performance* (6 tasks referring to what- and varied-knowledge), as well as structure-recognizing performance (5 tasks to recognize correlational structures within the data set; 3 tasks referring to two knowledge types and 2 tasks referring to one knowledge type).

On a second level, due to the fact that with the exception of the structure-recognizing tasks, the different tasks described on level 1 are expressed as either relational or item-specific, the overall performance resulted from 15 relational tasks, 15 item-specific tasks, as well as the 5 structure-recognizing tasks. The *relational performance* referred to relational tasks that asked for comparative judgments with regard to attribute values, whereas *item-specific performance* focused on tasks with regard to specific attribute values.

As a second dependent variable, we measured learners' confidence with regard to the correctness of their answers. Learners rated each answer to a task with regard to whether they felt low, middle, or high confidence that their answer had been correct. In the *overall confidence* measure, these ratings were totalled across all tasks, whereby higher ratings indicated higher confidence. This overall measure was subdivided into *confidence for correct answers,* displaying a participant's belief that a correct answer was correct, and *confidence for wrong answers,* which indicated a participant's conviction that a false answer was correct. Due to the fact that there were 35 items for which every subject had to rate his or her confidence level, and because ratings ranged from one to three, a maximum of 105 points was possible for each of the confidence scores.

As a third dependent variable, we assessed learners' subjective *cognitive load* by asking them how much effort they had to invest into learning and how difficult it had been to remember the contents. The *effort* and the *difficulty* ratings were on a five-point scale, ranging from very low to very high.

3.2 Results and Discussion

The analysis of the data is divided into two parts: First, we compared the baseline spreadsheet condition to the overall means of all information visualization conditions in order to answer the question of whether information visualizations in general are helpful for acquiring knowledge from large data sets compared to a purely text-based representation. In the second analysis, we assessed the effects of dimensionality and color coding by comparing the four information visualization conditions.

Do information visualizations foster learning? In all analyses of variances reported in this chapter, we used retentiveness as a covariate, which was measured by means of a subtest of the LGT-3 (Bäumler, 1974) that focused on verbal-associative learning.

Retentiveness was used as a covariate, because it was an individual difference variable strongly associated with our performance measures. In a first step, we tested whether subjects achieved higher performance with information visualizations than with the spreadsheet condition, without further distinguishing between the different kinds of information visualizations. A univariate ANCOVA showed, in fact, a higher overall performance for information visualizations compared to the spreadsheet condition ($M_{Baseline} = 25.15$; $M_{IVs} = 30.91$; $F(1,97) = 8.02$; $MSE = 85.32$; $p < .01$). However, which kinds of information visualizations produced this effect? To answer this question, each of the four different kinds of information visualizations was compared to the spreadsheet separately.

Whereas the two-dimensional information visualizations were both superior to the baseline condition (without color coding: $M_{2D/without} = 32.65$; $F(1,37) = 6.49$; $MSE = 101.31$; $p < .05$; with color coding: $M_{2D/with} = 35.60$; $F(1,37) = 16.97$; $MSE = 75.19$; $p < .01$), there were no differences between the three-dimensional information visualizations and the spreadsheet condition (without color coding: $M_{3D/without} = 26.50$; $F < 1$; with color coding: $M_{3D/with} = 28.90$; $F(1,37) = 2.62$; $MSE = 62.29$; $p > .10$).

Thus, with regard to the pedagogic potential of information visualizations, these results show, on the one hand, that information visualizations in general (without differentiating between the different information visualization conditions) are better suited to foster knowledge acquisition than a non-spatial representation of the same information (i.e., the baseline condition). On the other hand, the results revealed that not all kinds of information visualizations are more appropriate for supporting learning than a spreadsheet representation: only the two-dimensional information visualizations seem to have a substantial amount of pedagogic potential. The question of how to design information visualizations that are particularly effective was addressed in the subsequent analysis by comparing the different variants of information visualizations.

Which representational format of information visualizations is the most suitable for knowledge acquisition? In a first step, we analyzed the subjects' overall performance by a univariate ANCOVA (dimensionality x color coding with retentiveness as a covariate).

Participants who were presented with a two-dimensional information visualization outperformed participants in the three-dimensional conditions ($M_{2D} = 34.13$; $M_{3D} = 27.70$; $F(1,75) = 15.09$; $MSE = 71.36$; $p < .001$). Additionally, we obtained a marginally significant main effect for color coding in favor of polychromatic information visualizations ($M_{without} = 29.58$; $M_{with} = 32.25$; $F(1,75) = 3.22$; $MSE = 71.36$; $p < .10$). There was no significant interaction between the two factors ($F < 1$). The superiority of the two-dimensional information visualizations was not only confirmed for overall performance, but also for all sub-performance measures - with one exception (see Table 1 and 2 for details). There was no significant difference in performance with regard to what-performance, but this was not surprising, because the information necessary to solve the respective test items was represented the same way across all conditions, namely as text. There were neither significant main effects for color coding nor significant interactions for the sub-performance measures.

Table 1. Means and results of the ANCOVA-analyses for the sub-performance level one

		Dimensionality	Color Coding	Interaction
What-performance	$F(1,75)$	0.34	1.72	1.57
	MSE	1.32	1.32	1.32
	p	.564	.194	.215
	Means	2D: 1.93 3D: 1.83	without: 1.73 with: 2.02	
Where-performance	$F(1,75)$	7.18	0.16	0.45
	MSE	1.25	1.25	1.25
	p	**.009**	.690	.503
	Means	2D: 2.93 3D: 2.15	without: 2.73 with: 2.55	
Varied-performance	$F(1,75)$	16.17	0.87	0.15
	MSE	0.94	0.94	0.94
	p	**<.001**	.355	.701
	Means	2D: 2.45 3D: 1.68	without: 2.00 with: 2.13	
What/where - performance	$F(1,75)$	3.82	3.54	0.00
	MSE	7.35	7.35	7.35
	p	**.054**	**.064**	.986
	Means	2D: 7.45 3D: 6.45	without: 6.45 with: 7.45	
What/varied-performance	$F(1,75)$	3.65	0.00	0.07
	MSE	8.56	8.56	8.56
	p	**.060**	.991	.797
	Means	2D: 7.80 3D: 6.75	without: 7.35 with: 7.20	
Where/varied-performance	$F(1,75)$	14.24	3.08	0.51
	MSE	7.65	7.65	7.65
	p	**<.001**	**.084**	.477
	Means	2D: 8.40 3D: 6.30	without: 6.90 with: 7.80	
Structure-recognizing performance	$F(1,75)$	8.22	2.31	0.28
	MSE	3.54	3.54	3.54
	p	**.005**	.133	.596
	Means	2D: 4.28 3D: 3.15	without: 3.43 with: 4.00	

Concerning the overall confidence learners felt regarding the correctness of their answers, we found that participants learning with two-dimensional information visualizations were more certain that their answers were correct than subjects in the three-dimensional conditions ($M_{2D} = 74.05$; $M_{3D} = 65.93$; $F(1,75) = 8.71$; $MSE = 193.10$; $p < .01$). Further analysis revealed that participants learning with the two-dimensional information visualizations were not only more convinced that the correct answers they had given were correct ($M_{2D} = 50.92$; $M_{3D} = 36.35$; $F(1,75) = 18.07$; $MSE = 287.79$; $p < .001$), they also felt less certain that their false answers might be correct ($M_{2D} = 23.13$; $M_{3D} = 29.30$; $F(1,75) = 8.33$; $MSE = 116.18$; $p < .01$). This pattern of results suggests that participants in the two-dimensional conditions had a more accurate assessment of what they really knew. There were no significant main effects for color coding (all Fs < 1) nor was there a significant interaction (all Fs < 1) with respect to the overall confidence variable and both sub-confidence variables in all three ANCOVA-analyses.

Table 2. Means and results of the ANCOVA-analyses for the sub-performance level two

Level 2		Dimensionality	Color Coding	Interaction
Relational perform-ance	$F(1,75)$	7.51	2.04	0.51
	MSE	17.94	17.94	17.94
	p	**.008**	.158	.478
	Means	2D: 15.75 3D: 13.58	without: 14.15 with: 15.18	
Item-specific performance	$F(1,75)$	13.61	1.59	0.19
	MSE	21.91	21.91	21.91
	p	**<.001**	.211	.663
	Means	2D: 15.20 3D: 11.78	without: 13.00 with: 13.98	
Structure-recognizing performance	$F(1,75)$	8.22	2.31	0.28
	MSE	3.54	3.54	3.54
	p	**.005**	.133	.596
	Means	2D: 4.28 3D: 3.15	without: 3.43 with: 4.00	

With regard to the cognitive load ratings registered after the test phase, we found that participants using three-dimensional information visualizations indicated that they had to invest more effort into learning than participants in the two-dimensional conditions ($M_{2D} = 3.63$; $M_{3D} = 4.05$; $F(1,75) = 4.02$; $MSE = 0.80$; $p < .05$). In addition, they also evaluated learning as being more difficult than subjects in the two-dimensional conditions ($M_{2D} = 3.38$; $M_{3D} = 3.75$; $F(1,75) = 4.87$; $MSE = 0.78$; $p < .05$). There were no significant main effects for color coding (all Fs < 1) nor were there any significant interactions (all Fs < 1).

With regard to the research question of how to design information visualizations to foster knowledge acquisition, the reported results showed that, firstly, two-dimensional information visualizations are better suited to foster learning compared to three-dimensional ones and that, secondly, color-coded information visualizations are slightly better suited for supporting knowledge acquisition than monochromatic ones.

4 Summary and Conclusions

In the experiment, reported evidence for the suitability of information visualizations for knowledge acquisition could be provided. The performance of information visu-alization conditions was higher compared to the baseline condition. This is in accor-dance with the postulated assumption that using different cognitive systems for in-formation processing (cf., information visualizations) results in better learning performances than using only one cognitive system for processing all information (cf., spreadsheet-baseline).

Moreover, we demonstrated that, in general, two-dimensional information visuali-zations are more suitable for fostering knowledge acquisition than three-dimensional ones. As expected, this was caused by the fact that learners had to invest more effort and experienced more difficulties during learning in the latter conditions. The question of whether these demands resulted from the necessity to rotate the three-dimensional information visualization will be addressed in further studies. With regard to the influence of color coding, there were only slight performance increases when information was displayed in color. The fact that this effect was only slight could result from different reasons: the different colors were not distinct enough, the information units that were colored were too small, or color simply does not have a big impact on the particular tasks under investigation. Further studies will focus on answering this question.

Due to the empirical findings regarding the suitability of information visualizations to foster knowledge acquisition, the question of the relation of information visualizations and knowledge visualizations arises. If information visualizations are used in the context of learning, knowledge will be acquired. This acquired knowledge of the information included in the information visualization could in turn be externalized. A visualization of this externalized knowledge, a so-called knowledge visualization, should correspond to the original information visualization from which the knowledge was acquired. Therefore, it can be assumed that an information visualization should be designed in a manner that corresponds to the knowledge the user should acquire. In other words, when designing an information visualization for knowledge acquisition, the designer should be aware of what the learner has to learn and should organize the information included in the information visualization according to the knowledge the learner should acquire. This assumption will be the focus of further research. Coffey (in this book) has already realized this idea in his software LEO, a learning environment organizer.

References

Amorim, M.-A., Trumbore, B., & Chogyen, P. L. (2000). Cognitive repositioning inside a "Desktop" VE: The constraints introduced by first- vs. third-person imagery and mental representation richness. *Presence, 9*, 165-186.

Baddeley, A. D. (1998). *Human memory*. Boston: Allyn & Bacon.

Bäumler, G. (1974). *Lern- und Gedächtnistest LGT-3*. Göttingen: Hogrefe.

Bundesen, C., & Pedersen, L. F. (1983). Color segregation and visual search. *Perception and Psychophysics, 33*, 487-493.

Card, S. K., Mackinlay, J. D., & Shneiderman, B. (1999). Information visualization. In S. K Card, J. D. Mackinlay, & B. Shneiderman (Eds.), *Information visualization. Using vision to think* (pp. 1-34). San Francisco: Morgan Kaufmann.

Carter, R. C. (1982). Visual search with color. *Journal of Experimental Psychology: Human Perception and Performance, 8*, 127-136.

Cockburn, A., & McKenzie, B. (2001). 3D or not 3D? Evaluating the effect of the third dimension in a document management system. In M. Tremaine (Ed.), *Proceedings of CHI'01, ACM Conference on Human Factors in Computing Systems* (pp. 434-441). New York: ACM Press.

Cockburn, A., & McKenzie, B. (2002). Evaluating the effectiveness of spatial memory in 2D and 3D physical and virtual environments. In D. Wixon (Ed.), *Proceedings of CHI'02, ACM Conference on Human Factors in Computing Systems* (pp. 203-210). New York: ACM Press.

Cockburn, A., & McKenzie, B. (2004). Evaluating spatial memory in two and three dimensions. *International Journal of Human-Computer Studies, 61*, 359-373.

Cuban, L. (1986). *Teachers and machines. The classroom use of technology since 1920*. New York: Teachers College Press.

Däßler, R., & Palm, H. (1998). *Virtuelle Informationsräume mit VRML: Informationen recherchieren und präsentieren in 3D*. Heidelberg: dpunkt-Verlag.

Engelkamp, J. (1990). *Das menschliche Gedächtnis. Das Erinnern von Sprache, Bildern und Handlungen*. Göttingen: Hogrefe.

Hanna, A., & Remington, R. (1996). The representation of color and form in long-term memory. *Memory and Cognition, 24*, 322-330.

Holley, C.D., & Dansereau, D.F. (1984). The development of spatial learning strategies. In C.D. Holley & D.F. Dansereau (Eds.), *Spatial learning strategies. Techniques, applications, and related issues* (pp. 3-19). New York: Academic Press.

Landau, B., & Jackendoff, B. (1993). "What" and "where" in spatial language and spatial cognition. *Behavioral and Brain Sciences, 16*, 217-265.

Larkin, J. H., & Simon, H. A. (1987). Why a diagram is (sometimes) worth ten thousand words. *Cognitive Science, 11*, 65-99.

Le Grand, B., & Soto, M. (1999). Navigation in huge information hierarchies. Application to network management. In *Proceedings ACM Workshop on New Paradigms in Information Visualization and Manipulation (NPIVM'99)* (pp. 56-61). Kansas. ACM Press.

Logie, R. H. (1995). *Visuo-spatial working memory*. Hove: Erlbaum.

Mayer, R. E. (2001). *Multimedia learning*. Cambridge: Cambridge University Press.

Park, S. H., & Woldstad, J. C. (2000). Multiple two-dimensional displays as an alternative to three-dimensional displays in telerobotic tasks. *Human Factors, 42*, 592-603.

Sweller, J., & Chandler, P. (1994). Why some material is difficult to learn. *Cognition and Instruction, 12* (3), 185-233.

Sweller, J., van Merriënboer, J.J.G., & Paas, F.W.C. (1998). Cognitive architecture and instructional design. *Educational Psychology Review, 10*, 251-296.

Treisman, A. (1987). Properties, parts, and objects. In K. R. Boff, L. Kaufman, & F. P. Thomas (Eds.), *Handbook of perception and human performance*. Oxford: Clarendon.

Treisman, A., & Gormican, S. (1988). Feature analysis in early vision. Evidence from search asymmetries. *Psychological Review, 95*, 15-48.

Ungerleider, L.G., & Mishkin, M. (1982). Two cortical visual systems. In D. J. Ingle, M. A. Goodale, & R. J. W. Mansfield (Eds.), *Analysis of visual behaviour* (pp. 549-586). Cambridge, MA: MIT Press.

Wiss, U., Carr, D., & Jonsson, H. (1998). Evaluating Three-Dimensional Information Visualization Designs: A Case Study of Three Designs. In E. Banissi (Ed.), *Proceedings IEEE International Conference on Information Visualization* (pp. 137-145). Washington: IEEE.

Synergies

Visualizing Knowledge and Information for Fostering
Learning and Instruction

Digital Concept Maps for Managing Knowledge and Information

Sigmar-Olaf Tergan

Institut für Wissensmedien (IWM), Konrad-Adenauer-Str. 40,
72072 Tübingen, Germany
s.tergan@iwm-kmrc.de

Abstract. Due to the increasing amount and complexity of knowledge and information in many domains, students who self-regulate their study in e-learning
scenarios often suffer from cognitive overload, as well as conceptual and navigational disorientation. Particularly, when studying in resource-based learning
scenarios with complex and ill-structured subject-matter content, there is a need
for both effective learning strategies and the management of knowledge and information. Advanced computer-based concept maps have the potential to foster
spatial learning strategies by visualizing the knowledge and support processes
of individual knowledge management, such as the acquisition, organization,
representation, (self-)evaluation, communication, localization, and utilization of
knowledge. In addition, they have the potential to represent and make accessible the conceptual and content knowledge of a domain, as well as information
associated to it. The aim of this paper is the analysis of the potential of digital
concept maps for supporting processes of individual knowledge management.
Perspectives for research on the use of concept maps for individual knowledge
management are outlined.

1 Introduction

Students who self-regulate their study have to cope with complex arrays of knowledge and information in many domains. With the advent of massive and yet flexible
information resources in learning settings via hypermedia and Internet-based learning
environments, an even stronger demand is made on the students´ own level of responsibility and learning management skills. This is particularly true in resource-based
learning scenarios (Rakes, 1996) when the Internet is used as a tool for providing access to digital information resources. "Resource-based learning can be explained as a
learning mode in which the student learns from his or her own interaction with a wide
range of learning resources rather than from class exposition" (Rakes, 1996, 52).
These scenarios allow students a great amount of freedom for self-evaluating the ap-
propriateness of existing knowledge, searching for additional information, assembling
ideas, (co-)constructing and representing knowledge, sharing and communicating it to
others, as well as for using knowledge and information in a flexible manner for individual problem solutions. Information literacy is needed to make effective use of information resources (Brevik, 1992; Brevik, & Senn, 1994). Many students, however,
have not yet acquired effective strategies for resource-based learning. They suffer

S.-O. Tergan and T. Keller (Eds.): Knowledge and Information Visualization, LNCS 3426, pp. 185–204, 2005.

from cognitive overload and conceptual and navigational disorientation (Bleakley & Carrigan, 1994). Particularly in learning scenarios with a complex and ill-structured subject-matter content, there is a need for fostering learning by means of cognitive tools to overcome limitations of the human mind in thinking, learning, and problem solving (Kommers, Jonassen, & Mayes, 1991). Techniques for the external representation of individual task-relevant knowledge in a visual-spatial format are suggested to help learners coping with complex and ill-structured subject-matter and facilitating "the coherent representation of new information in semantic memory" (Holley & Dansereau, 1984, p. 14; Spiro, Coulson, Feltovich, & Anderson, 1988; Jonassen, Reeves, Hong, Harvey & Peters, 1997).

The term *representation* in cognitive science may refer to knowledge that is either inside or outside the head. *Mental* representations refer to the structures of knowledge and the appertaining cognitive processes, which human intellectual activities are based on (Rumelhart & Ortony, 1977). *External* representations are physical representations that have to be processed cognitively in order to construct meaning and that may be used as cognitive tools for fostering externalized cognition (Cox, 1999). They may be defined in a broad sense as "the knowledge and structure in the environment, as physical symbols, objects, or dimensions and as external rules, constraints, or relations embedded in physical configurations" (Zhang, 1997, p. 180). The view of external representations used in this article is more narrow in scope, consistent with the view outlined by Larkin (1989), Cox and Brna (1995) and Cox (1999). Cox & Brna focus on external representations as "subject constructed representations of domain knowledge" (p. 242) by using cognitive artifacts, for example, "tables, lists, graphs, maps, plans, and set diagrams" (p. 242). Larkin (1989) and Cox (1999) stress the function of external representations as cognitive tools for display-based reasoning and externalized cognition.

Self-constructing and using external representations effectively is part of visual-spatial competency (Holley & Dansereau, 1984). Helping students develop strategies to structure and organize their knowledge is as important as the knowledge itself, since knowledge organization is likely to affect the students' intellectual performance (Bransford, Brown, & Cocking, 1999). Know-how and know-what has to be supplemented with know-where (the understanding of where to find knowledge needed) (Siemens, 2005). Visualization methods may help students to externalize, map, elicit, search for, (co-)construct, structure and restructure, elaborate, evaluate, locate and access, communicate, and use ideas and thoughts (Holley & Dansereau, 1984; Jonassen, Beissner, & Yacci, 1993; Cox & Brna, 1995).

Jonassen et al. (1993) have described a variety of paper and pencil mapping methods for externalizing knowledge in a visual-spatial format. Advanced computer-based mapping tools (e.g. concept mapping and mind mapping tools) have the further potential to represent the content knowledge of a domain in a multi-media format, as well as knowledge about information resources (see Alpert, Coffey in this book). Dansereau (in this book) outlines principles for visualizing knowledge and information with the help of node-link mapping tools.

The idea behind all methods and tools is that cognitive processing of complex subject matter may be enhanced if the task-relevant knowledge is well-organized and the structures behind ideas, knowledge and information, as well as their relevance for comprehension, learning and problem solving, are made explicit by means of visualization. Supporting just-in-time access to task-relevant information resources may help users in coping with task situations when they need additional data and information for cognitive processing.

Computer-based concept mapping tools may contribute to the development of spatial strategies. Representing externally what is known about the subject matter or learning content may help students to organize and represent conceptual and content knowledge about a domain in an integrative manner and to link individual domain knowledge to task-relevant information resources. These features enable concept mapping tools to be used as cognitive tools for managing knowledge and information. They are suggested to support coping effectively with complex knowledge and subject matter in resource-based learning and problem-solving scenarios (Newbern & Dansereau, 1995; Weideman & Kritzinger, 2003). Using maps in this manner may solve – at least partially – problems associated with visualizing information structures to make information more salient to users by providing semantically comprehensible access (see Andrews, in this book; Keller et al., in this book; Sebrechts, in this book). In order to evaluate the suggested potential of digital concept maps in more detail, a brief look at the general characteristics of concept maps and features of concept mapping tools may be helpful.

2 Characteristics of Concept Maps

2.1 Structural Features

Concept mapping is a visualization technique with a long tradition in the educational context. It is an activity derived from psychological research meant to depict one's knowledge, ideas, convictions and beliefs. The technique was invented by Novak and Gowin (1984), based on the ideas of Ausubel (1963), who advocated that an individual's subject-matter knowledge is mentally represented in a hierarchy of concepts. A concept map, according to Novak and Gowin, is a spatial array that represents elements of knowledge by means of nodes and directionally labeled or named links, the nodes representing ideas, concepts and beliefs and the links relations between them. Along with Novak (http://cmap.coginst.uwf.edu/info/), a concept may be defined as "a perceived regularity in events or objects, or records of events or objects, designated by a label. The label for most concepts is a word" (p. 1). Together, nodes and labeled or named links define propositions, assertions about a topic, domain or thing (Alpert, in this book). Sometimes propositions are called semantic units, or units of meaning. For example, the relationships between the concepts *map*, *concept map*, *nodes*, and *links* may be represented by the propositions. "A concept map is a kind of map" and "a concept map has as a characteristic feature nodes and links". These node-link relationships can be represented spatially, as illustrated in Fig. 1.

Different geometric shapes of nodes like rectangles, ovals, circles and other shapes, as well as different spatial configurations, icons, colors and sizes, may be used for symbolizing different semantic aspects of knowledge elements and for conveying meaning (see Alpert, in this book). Multiple linkages between concepts may depict how each concept is related to other concepts belonging to different sections of a concept map. Concept maps are particularly useful for representing networks of concepts, where links do not only connect adjacent concepts, but are often linked to concepts in different sections of the concept map. This type of structural flexibility makes concept mapping highly suitable for hypermedia environments, since the type of linking employed in concept maps is an excellent representation of hypermedia's nonlinear paradigm. The links may be directional (lines with arrowheads) or non-directional (lines without arrowheads) and may be highlighted by means of line strength and color. Wiegman, Dansereau, McCagg, Rewey, and Pitre (1992) have shown that different organizational principles and the use of varied highlighting of links in interaction with different learner prerequisites may lead to different effects in processing concept maps (see also Dansereau, in this book).

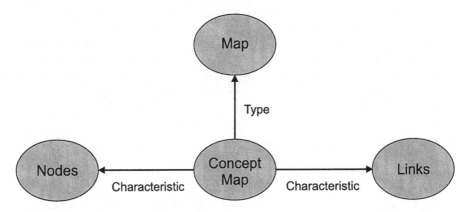

Fig. 1. Node-link structure of elements in a concept map

Dansereau (in this book) distinguishes different types of concept mapping: Freestyle mapping (if a map is self-produced), guided mapping (if students use a template for mapping), and information mapping (if an expert map is presented to students by an instructor). Research has shown that all types of concept mapping can be useful in improving outcomes in different domains, e.g. education and counseling, depending on variables like task requirement, structure of content and individual prerequisites of the user (e.g. Bruillard & Baron, 2000; O`Donnell, Dansereau, & Hall, 2002; Dansereau, in this book).

Due to variations in mapping conceptual knowledge structures, authors of mapping tools use different labels, e.g. cognitive maps, knowledge maps, network maps, concept maps, or mind maps. For example, concept mapping is sometimes called cognitive mapping, because of the network structure of represented concepts. The labels "knowledge mapping" and "semantic networking" are used with a quite similar meaning as "concept mapping" (see Holley & Dansereau, 1984). Concept mapping combines features of "networking" and "mapping", because it is intended to represent both the network structure of concepts in semantic memory and its visualization in a map by means of the spatial configuration and special representational features to represent and emphasize meaning. The only difference is that the resulting map is based on a set of links with predefined labels (Holley & Dansereau, 1984; Wiegman et al., 1992; O`Donnell, Dansereau, & Hall, 2002) instead of links that may be labeled arbitrarily by using names and attributes as in concept mapping. A kind of neutral label "node-link map" covering all kinds of node-link-based mapping diagrams has been suggested by Dansereau and collegues (see e.g. Dansereau, in this book).

Varieties of concept mapping approaches have recently been outlined by Åhlberg (2004). According to Åhlberg, the only mapping techniques that deserve the label concept mapping are those that are both clearly based on the seminal writings of Novak and his research group from 1981 to 2002 and that fulfill the basic requirement that meaningful propositions may be produced out of linked concepts. He points out that in following Novak´s standards, there are some unnecessarily complex rules, which may be overcome in the future. For example, he suggests that improved concept maps may also include whole phrases to signify the meaning of a concept instead of short labels, that multimedia resources may be connected to maps, and that, in some cases, numbers may be included showing the order in which the propositions should be read.

Concept mapping is different from mind mapping and concept maps from mind maps, although both types of maps have some features in common (see Jonassen et al., 1993). The main difference is that in mind maps, concepts and ideas are represented, without signifying the particular meaning imposed on the relationships (Buzan, 1995). Other differences relate to the kind of organization of ideas. Whereas concept maps allow for representing concepts both in a hierarchical and web manner the typical organization format of mind maps is a tree structure with one central node in the center and many branches originating from the center. Another difference between concept maps and mind maps is the lack of representation of cross-relationships between mapped elements. Whereas this is a typical feature of concept maps, mind maps typically make sparse use of representing interrelationships between ideas.

The term "concept mapping" in the domain of learning and instruction for knowledge representation is used quite differently as compared to the term "knowledge mapping" in the domain of knowledge management in business. In business, the term "knowledge maps" is used for tools aiming at mapping meta-information. Knowledge maps generally consist of two elements: a ground layer representing the context (e.g. a project, a network of experts) and individual elements representing details (e.g. experts, milestones). The maps do not represent knowledge per se, but rather pointers to information resources and examples of expert knowledge in use (Burkhard & Meier, in this book).

2.2 Representational Features of Concept Maps

Recently, the representational facilities of traditional paper and pencil-based concept maps with the focus on conceptual knowledge have been criticized as too abstract and narrow and not appropriate for capturing an individual´s knowledge about a subject-matter domain in a comprehensive manner (Alpert & Gruenenberg, 2000; Alpert, in this book). Because traditional concept maps represent *concept knowledge* only, i.e., the conceptual macrostructure of a knowledge domain, idiosyncratic individual content knowledge about a domain, as well as knowledge about relevant information resources, are left unrepresented. *Content knowledge* represents the microstructure of an individual´s declarative domain knowledge, which is relevant for coping with a particular task. It is strongly related to the more abstract conceptual knowledge. It may be externalized, for example, by means of personal notes, sketches, personal verbal explanations (abstracts, summaries), and examples illustrating the meaning of a concept (Cañas, Leake, & Wilson, 1999). Content knowledge also refers to individual images and mental models about objects, episodes and events, actions, processes, and procedures and may be externally represented by using different semiotic codes and perceptual modes (Alpert, in this book). *Resource knowledge* means knowing where to find task-relevant information (Siemens, 2005), what the information is about, and how the information is related to the abstracted conceptual knowledge represented in the map. In concept maps it is represented by means of hyperlinks indicating the connection between a concept and a particular information resource and vice versa. *Information resources* in a strict sense are storage devices containing and making accessible all kinds of data and information represented in different formats. The data and information may be stored in repositories and media – e.g. PC files, hypermedia data bases, web sites, web logs, virtual realities – either online or offline, using different codes and modes, e.g. text, image, graphic, audio, video.

The externalized structure of an individual´s conceptual, content, and resource knowledge defines her or his personal knowledge perspective on a particular subject matter. Accessing and locating information from a knowledge basis tailored for coping with a particular cognitive task may be more effective and useful than any kind of information visualization using a visual semantic. The request for an "improved visual semantic" (Sebrechts, in this book) may be satisfied in some way if abstract data and information are made accessible on a knowledge basis by using concept maps as a knowledge repository and cognitive management tool (Weideman & Kritzinger, 2003; Tergan, 2003).

In order to get access to information resources as potential sources for knowledge acquisition and problem solving, different kinds of scenarios may be considered. One kind of scenario is a problem-solving scenario (see Jonassen, in this book). If a problem representation has been constructed by means of a concept-mapping tool, information resources that contain data relevant for elucidating elements of the problem space might be hyperlinked with the problem elements. In order to be linked to a concept in the map, the information resource must have been pre-selected from a variety of information resources and checked for the conceptual relevance of its contents. A link between a concept and an information resource signifies that there is additional information available, which is strongly related to the respective concept and the task for which the concept map has been constructed. On the other hand, the concept itself represents an abstraction of the meaning, which can be constructed on the basis of the data inherent in the information resource. The data may be used for defining, comprehending, elaborating, exemplifying, supplementing, and amplifying a particular concept and may contribute to enrich, adapt, and restructure the conceptual knowledge structure represented in the map. Data in information resources may be accessed for confirming an idea, for generating new knowledge, thus, serving as knowledge resources for outlining concept-related subject matter contents. They may also be easily accessed when looking for appropriate background material for presenting the results of a knowledge acquisition process or a problem-solving task. The other kind of scenario is an information presentation scenario. For example, structures of information resources in an educational course may be visualized by means of a concept map by making the underlying central concepts and their interrelations explicit (see Coffey, in this book; Dansereau, in this book). The map may help learners in the orientation and navigation of the course materials.

Advanced computer-based concept mapping tools provide facilities for representing and accessing different kinds of knowledge: conceptual knowledge, content knowledge, as well as information resource knowledge. Content knowledge and information resources may be directly accessed from a concept node by just clicking on an icon associated with the node or on a hyperlink connecting the abstract concept with the related resource (see Alpert, in this book; Cañas, in this book). Some examples of digital mapping tools are: IHMC CmapTools, http://cmap.ihmc.us/; Knowledge Manager, http://www.knowledgemanager.us/; Mind Manager, http://www. mindjet. com/; Inspiration, http://inspiration.com/productinfo/inspiration/features/ index.cfm; SemNet, htttp://trumpet.sdsu.edu/semnett.html); Axon Idea Processor, http://web.singnet.com.sg/~axon2000/; Webster (Alpert, in this book); SMART Ideas, http://www.smarttech.com/products/smartideas/index.asp.

Alpert (in this book) has described and visualized the concept mapping tool "Webster", which is an example of existing computer-based mapping tools with special features for the representation of knowledge. Webster permits broad flexibility in terms of the kind of knowledge and information to be represented and the structuring of the visual representation. The tool exemplifies facilities, which are necessary to use concept maps as tools for managing knowledge.

The features in Webster correspond to the features of IHMC CmapTools, a web-based "knowledge modeling kit" developed at the Institute for Human and Machine Cognition at the Texas Christian University for empowering users to construct, navigate, share, and criticize knowledge models represented as Concept Maps (Cañas, Hill, Carff, Suri, Lott, Eskridge et al., 2004; Cañas, Carff, Hill, Carvalho, Arguedas, Eskridge, Lott & Carvajal, in this book). The browser supports the representation of numerous forms of resources like images, text, movies, web pages, PDF files, and sound resources. As in Webster, the IHMC Toolkit shows the type of the resource by an icon that appears below the concept. One can view these resources by clicking on the icons and selecting a name from the list. The CmapTools software may be downloaded for free for individual users (http://cmap.ihmc.us/downloadv2Clients/ SSDownload.html). In a recent approach, Safayeni, Derbentseva & Cañas (in press) have even amplified the representational facilities of the CmapTools to also represent knowledge of functional or dynamic relationships between concepts. Burkhard and Meier (in this book), aiming at yielding synergies between information visualization and knowledge visualization, go even further. They suggest a framework that allows researchers to apply and invent new visualization methods for the domain of concept mapping.

Concept Maps may be used to coherently represent in virtual space abstract conceptual knowledge, content knowledge, and related information . They may particularly be useful to supplement visualizations of information which are based on visual semantics only (Sebrechts, in this book), and may help to make sense of the semantic relations between knowledge and information (Coffey, in this book). They serve as a vehicle for the implementation of an individual´s, a group of individuals, or a company´s knowledge repository, and as a navigational tool for digital environments (e.g. hypermedia environments, virtual realities, digital libraries, World Wide Web), and for providing knowledge-based access to information (Weideman & Kritzinger, 2003; Cañas, Ford & Coffey, 1994; Cañas, Leake & Wilson, 1999; Coffey, Hoffmann, Cañas & Ford, 2002; Shen, Richardson & Fox, http://vw.indiana.edu/ivira03/shen-et-al.pdf; Carnot, Dunn, Cañas, Gram & Muldoon, http://www.ihmc.us/users/acanas/Publications/CMapsVSWebPagesExp1/CMapsVSWebPagesExp1.htm). Further, digital concept maps may be used for knowledge management purposes (Newbern & Dansereau, 1995; Cañas, Leake & Wilson, 1999; Tergan, 2003).

A model of concept map-based representation and access of conceptual knowledge, content knowledge and information is depicted in Fig. 2. On the one hand, the model visualizes the relation of conceptual knowledge, content knowledge and information resources. On the other hand, it shows how advanced digital concept mapping tools can simultaneously enable a knowledge-based visual organization, search and access of conceptual knowledge, content knowledge, and related information.

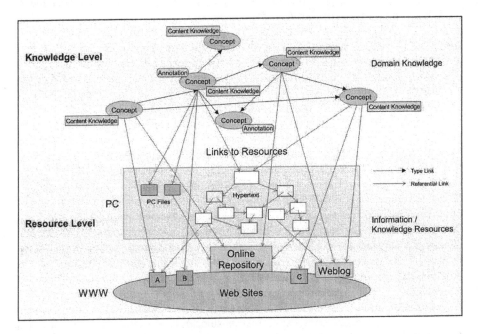

Fig. 2. Model of concept map-based representation and access of domain knowledge and related information

2.3 Processing Features

A major processing feature characterizing concept mapping is that humans self-explain, make explicit, externalize, and organize knowledge, which is only implicit to learning and problem solving and may not be retrieved and reconstructed easily. Concept maps are suggested "to take advantage of the remarkable capabilities of the human visual perception system and the benefits of visual information representation. These benefits include (a) ease of recognition, (b) the possibility to quickly scan a picture and find differences or keywords, (c) compactness of representation, and (d) the observation that it seems to be easier to keep an overview" (Kommers & Lanzing, 1997, p. 423). Concept maps can enhance our processing ability by visualizing abstract relationships of human knowledge and may serve as a basis for externalized cognition (Cox, 1999). Cox and Brna (1995) and Jonassen et al. (1997) list several cognitive properties of graphical external representations which also apply to concept maps: For example, concept maps may reduce cognitive load in terms of searching, maintaining, and retrieving knowledge elements by organizing information by location. During the process of learning and problem solving, a concept map may help the learner overcome problems that are due to the limitations of working memory in both capacity and duration of stored information. They expand the capability of an individual´s memory for coping with complex cognitive task requirements (Larkin & Simon, 1987; Cox & Brna, 1995). During learning and problem solving they may be used for depicting the changing status of knowledge.

Concept maps as graphic displays seem to permit problem solving by facilitating perceptual judgements of a kind that are almost effortless for humans, and can act as aids to retrieval (Larkin & Simon, 1987; Larkin, 1989). They help to exploit the "rapid processing capabilities of the human visual system" and "very easy perceptual judgements are substituted for more difficult logical ones" (Page & Simon, 1966). An additional cognitive advantage of concept maps results from combining visual and verbal modes in externally representing knowledge. By using verbal labels for indicating the kind of relationship between nodes, the semantics of a spatial configuration of nodes may be comprehended and communicated more easily due to advantages resulting from dual coding of visual and verbal stimuli (Paivio, 1986).

Concept mapping is considered to be essential for a constructivist approach to learning and problem solving. "Constructing concept maps stimulates us to externalize, articulate, and pull together information we already know about a subject and understand new information as we learn". ... "It stimulates a learner to find contours of his/her knowledge" (Kommers & Lanzing, 1997, p. 424). Comparing different concept maps may stimulate users to think about commonalities, and differences, as well as personal views and contextual embeddings of the represented knowledge and to elaborate and tune their own knowledge (Novak, Wurst, Schneider, Fleischmann & Strauss, 2003; Novak & Wurst, in this book). In addition to the potential of concept maps for reducing cognitive load (Sweller, 1988, 1994) and extending the capacity of the human working memory, they may serve functions which go far beyond the function of a simple memory extension.

There is a great deal of evidence indicating that the use of concept maps is a valuable strategy for supporting cognitive processing in a variety of learning and instructional settings, a.o. idea and knowledge generation, self-assessment of understanding and knowledge, collaborative work in distributed cognitive tasks (a.o. Novak, 1990; Jonassen, 1987; Zhang & Norman, 1994; Gaines & Shaw, 1995; Bruillard & Baron, 2000; Canas, Ford, Novak, Hayes, Reichherzer & Suri, 2001; O'Donnell, Dansereau & Hall, 2002). It has also been shown, however, that the advantages of concept maps for fostering cognitive processing may be mediated by the user´s cognitive prerequisites, as well as the requirements of the tasks (a.o. Cox, 1999; Cox & Brna, 1995; Dansereau, in this book). In particular, self-constructed concept maps pose high cognitive demands on analyzing and externalizing knowledge and associated knowledge resources. "Private representations tend to be less labeled, sparser and may only be partially externalized - whereas those intended for sharing with others will tend to be more richly labeled, better formed and more conventional" (Cox, 1999, p. 347).

2.4 Usability Features

In addition to the processing features and enhanced representational facilities, computerized concept-mapping tools provide typical office-software usability facilities, e.g. free editing to be used for (re)constructing, (re)organizing, and (re)representing mapped knowledge. Storing, printing, representation in different formats (outline, graphic), e-mailing and web-implementation of concept maps in html format are possible. Functions for interactive access to linked knowledge elements on the basis of the conceptual structure of a domain may be used to enhance the localization and use of individual conceptual elaborations, as well as information resources. Some of these tools also provide functions for reviewing the creation process of a map, e.g. by means of backtracking, and provide functions for web-conferencing (e.g. SMART Ideas). Most of the tools also support functions for a collaborative construction of concept maps, enabling distributed teams to collectively develop and access maps (see Cañas, Leake & Wilson, 1999; Novak & Wurst, in this book).

In the past, concept maps have been used for the representation of conceptual knowledge and the presentation of information only. The usability of digital concept maps in different education contexts has been documented extensively (Bruillard & Baron, 2000; O`Donnell, Dansereau & Hall, 2002). Curriculum designers and instructors may use concept maps for course design. The conceptual structure in curricular approaches reflects the macrostructure of the learning content to be presented in a course. An example of a learning environment organizer approach (LEO) based on a computer-based mapping tool is outlined by Coffey (in this book). In LEO the same concept maps may be used by instructors for organizing course contents and by students as advanced organizers for fostering orientation and learning. In some instructional approaches, the concepts represented in a map are equivalent to the knowledge to be acquired by a student (Wiegman et al., 1992). Teachers use concept maps as tools to assess knowledge and learning progress (see e.g. Kommers & Lanzing, 1997; Bruillard & Baron, 2000). Dansereau (in this book) distinguishes three types of node-link mapping approaches with different practical use: *Information maps* are expert generated maps used for the presentation of information, as well as for orientation and navigation, *guided maps* are maps constructed by novice users with the help of a construction template, and *freestyle maps* are maps generated by users in a self-regulated manner. Concept maps generated in a free style mode by different persons on the same topic are necessarily different, as each represent´s its creator´s personal knowledge (Cañas et al., in this book).

Due to the processing features of concept maps, as well as the enhanced representational and usability functions provided by computer-based mapping tools, digital concept maps may be particularly helpful as cognitive tools for self-regulated students in open resource-based e-learning scenarios designed according to a constructivist design rationale (Rakes, 1996). These learning scenarios call for visualization tools for managing both knowledge and information resources (Neumann, Gräber & Tergan, in this book).

3 Concept Mapping for Fostering Processes of Knowledge Management

The concept of using concept-mapping technology for fostering resource-based learning and problem solving is very much concordant with a concept of individual knowledge management as part of advanced self-regulated resource-based learning, which is gradually fading into the field of e-learning (Maurer & Sapper, 2001). Digital concept mapping may be used as a multipurpose method for fostering processes of individual and cooperative knowledge management (Newbern & Dansereau, 1995; Cañas et al., 1999; Tergan, 2003). In the following diagram, a framework for analyzing the potentials of computerized concept mapping for different process categories of individual knowledge management is suggested (Fig. 3). The framework is oriented towards a model of basic knowledge management processes as described by Probst, Raub and Romhardt (1999, p. 58). The processes focused on are cognitive as well as meta-cognitive processes framed into categories, which are relevant for knowledge management processes in advanced e-learning, problem solving, and resource-based learning. It is suggested that the framework may be used for analyzing and tailoring research on concept mapping used for supporting processes of knowledge and information visualization in individual knowledge management.

According to Malhotra (2000), the focus of knowledge management is on an interaction of technology-based tools and the people using these tools in a task-appropriate manner for coping with the cognitive requirements of managing both mental and external representations of knowledge. Based on the model of Probst et al. (1999) (see also Reinmann-Rothmeier & Mandl, 2000, for a revised version of the model), several highly interdependent process categories of knowledge management may be identified. The categories are: knowledge representation / organization, knowledge identification / diagnosis, information search, knowledge generation, knowledge communication, and knowledge use.

Knowledge representation / organization. The process of knowledge representation is at the center of all knowledge management processes. It is closely related to all other processes. The term "knowledge representation" in individual learning, problem solving, and knowledge management refers to the dynamic cognitive structure of knowledge elements that has to be constructed by a person in order to cope effectively with a particular cognitive task situation. In order to make knowledge accessible for future use, it must be mentally organized according to a semantic or pragmatic rationale, and represented in a format mirroring the cognitive affordances for coping effectively with a particular task situation. It must also be adaptable according to changes in task affordances, personal goals, and newly generated knowledge in the course of learning, problem solving, and cooperative work. In complex and knowledge-rich cognitive processing tasks, it is necessary not only to represent the conceptual knowledge of a domain, but also the content knowledge (generally stored in local files) and resource knowledge (often represented on the Internet) and indicate relations by means of linking the respective knowledge elements.

Concept maps allow for the representation of concept knowledge, content knowledge, and resource knowledge in a coherent representational format. If concept maps are used for externalizing individual knowledge, they serve as cognitive tools for

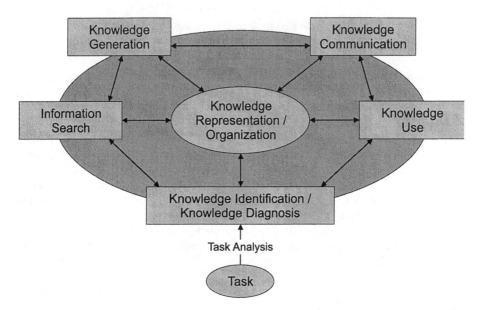

Fig. 3. Process categories of knowledge management (adapted from Probst et al., 1999, p. 58)

augmenting capacities of human memory and allowing for externalized cognition (Jonassen, Carr & Yueh, 1998; Cox, 1999). Digital maps can provide easy access to the represented knowledge elements and make them more manageable during learning and problem solving. Computer-based mapping tools provide functions for externalizing knowledge structures in arbitrary formats. Computer-based maps are no longer two-dimensional spatial arrays that represent concept knowledge in the form of a node-link-node diagram. Computer-based tools also allow for mappings in a hypertext-like format by using sub-maps and links (e.g. Alpert & Gruenenberg, 2000; Alpert, in this book).

Knowledge identification / knowledge diagnosis. Knowledge identification and diagnosis are closely related meta-cognitive processes performed by an individual. After an initial process of task analysis, goal setting, and knowledge representation, a student coping with a complex cognitive task has to first identify task-relevant knowledge and then evaluate it with respect to its adequacy for coping effectively with a particular task situation. Self-evaluation of individual knowledge may be done with the help of a map-based representation of knowledge. For example, if the task is to acquire expert knowledge, the structure of knowledge as represented in an individual knowledge map may be compared with the knowledge structure of an expert as represented in an expert map. The potential of knowledge maps as means for diagnosing individual structures of knowledge has been shown in a variety of empirical studies (a.o. Jonassen et al., 1997). In self-regulated learning scenarios, the particular contribution of computer-based concept maps is that of supporting self-assessment (Shavelson, Lang & Lewin, 1994; Kommers & Lanzing, 1997).

Information search. When individual knowledge has been evaluated as inappropriate for effectively coping with a cognitive task situation and knowledge gaps have been identified, it is necessary to look for task-relevant content and resource knowledge to fill the gaps and acquire appropriate knowledge. Learners in virtual learning scenarios may, for example, get access to subject matter content knowledge as represented in texts or multimedia documents, which are stored in repositories provided by the learning environment on CD-ROM, or they may access knowledge resources available on the World Wide Web. Concept maps have been used as a navigation device for students who need orientation while they explore expansive information domains like hypermedia documents available on CD-ROM or on the World Wide Web (Kommers & Lanzing, 1997; Potelle & Rouet, 2003; see also Lee, in this book). They "serve to provide learners with navigational clues, in order to facilitate navigation through the materials and ... the construction of new knowledge" (Bruillard & Baron, 2000). For example, McDonald and Stevenson (1998) and Carnot, Dunn, Cañas, Gram & Muldoon   (http://www.ihmc.us/users/acanas/Publications/CMapsVSWebPagesExp1/ CMapsVSWebPagesExp1.html) found that concept maps provide an efficient access to web-based information resources. This effect is more pronounced with low knowledge-level students than with high knowledge-level students and when students are meaningful learners compared to rote learners. An innovative use of concept maps for enhancing web searches was recently presented by Carvalho, Hewett, and Cañas (2001). Concept maps combined with filtering and ranking algorithms of the results of search engines (Google, Altavista, Yahoo, Excite) were found to enhance identifying pages that the subjects considered relevant to the context of the map.

Until now, concept maps have only been used as a device for navigating large data structures, e.g. available in hypermedia, digital libraries, resource repositories, and on the World Wide Web (Bruillard & Baron, 2000; Shen, Richardson & Fox, 2003; Weideman & Kritzinger, n.d.). It has been suggested that concept maps may also be used as personal repositories. An approach that illustrates how a mapping tool may be used as an interface for representing and accessing individual knowledge, ideas, and information resources in resource-based learning is presented by Neumann, Gräber & Tergan (in this book).

Knowledge generation. New knowledge is generated by constructive cognitive processes like integrating, elaborating, reorganizing, and reformatting existing knowledge structures and linking knowledge elements (concept knowledge, content knowledge, resource knowledge) with contexts and situations. Concept mapping has been used effectively in instructional settings to foster processes of knowledge generation (e.g. Wallace, West, Ware & Dansereau, 1998; O'Donnell et al., 2002; Bruillard & Baron, 2000). For example, Gaines and Shaw (1995) describe the rationale of a prototype Learning Web implementation, as well as tools, such as concept maps and repertory grids, used within the Web for knowledge generation. Advanced mapping tools also provide functions to annotate nodes as a means for the elaboration of knowledge. Knowledge generation is supported by providing functions for adding, renaming, and deleting nodes and links, as well as reorganizing and reformatting existing knowledge maps, thus, reflecting processes of accretion, tuning and restructuring as described by Rumelhart and Norman (1978).

Knowledge communication. Knowledge communication, as a knowledge management process, may serve different purposes, for example, to disseminate knowledge from a tutor to students, between students, and from a student to a tutor. Students working together in a collaborative instructional scenario communicate and share knowledge in order to contribute to the construction of shared knowledge or to the design and development of a common cognitive artifact. Computer-based mapping tools may contribute to fostering processes of knowledge communication in several ways. They may, for example, be used to communicate the concept structure of a subject matter and enhance knowledge acquisition and shared understanding of a subject-matter domain (McAleese, Grabinger & Fisher, 1999; Fischer & Mandl, 2001). They may also be used as a basis for fostering cooperative work (Jacobson & Levin, 1995). Mapping tools may be particularly useful in fostering coping skills in a task situation that requires knowledge, which is too comprehensive, and conceptual views, which are too diverse, for a single person to manage successfully. During the construction phase, concept maps may contribute to foster grounding processes and acquiring shared knowledge by visualizing the domain knowledge of the group members (a.o., Coffey, Hoffmann, Cañas & Ford, 2002; McAleese et al., 1999; Fischer & Mandl, 2001; Novak et al., 2003). Novak and Wurst (in this book) present "Knowledge Explorer", which is an interactive tool for the collaborative elicitation and visualization of community knowledge perspectives. These knowledge perspectives are based on the construction of personalized knowledge maps and shared concept networks that incorporate implicit knowledge and personal views of individual users. It is shown how this model supports explicit and implicit exchange of knowledge and knowledge resources in cross-community learning. Concept mapping may foster cooperative work by visualizing both the shared knowledge and knowledge discrepancies between participants. Concept maps may be used by participants to provide access to the information elements for elaborating their domain knowledge, restructuring it in case of observed misconceptions, and for reaching a common understanding. Concept maps may also be used in counseling and consulting scenarios (Dansereau, in this book), as well as for the visualization of arguments (Bruggen, Kirschner, & Jochems, 2002). However, the potential for mapping the structure of arguments and ideas has yet to be explored.

Knowledge use. In order to facilitate knowledge use, representations of knowledge have to be structured task-appropriately. Knowledge representations must be easily restructured and adaptable to different situations, tasks, individual interests and contexts of use (Spiro, Feltovich, Jacobson & Coulson, 1991). It has been suggested that concept mapping may enhance the processing capacities of the human brain. A necessary precondition for this theory is that the knowledge must be represented explicitly in an external representation and knowledge elements must be freely accessible and easily trackable. Map-based visualizations of ideas and individual knowledge representations match these conditions. Concept mapping has proved to be a valuable cognitive tool for supporting cognitive functions in a variety of learning and instructional settings, among them scaffolding cognitive processing in knowledge acquisition and problem solving (Jonassen, 1992; Fischer & Mandl, 2001; O'Donnell et al., 2002), and designing hypermedia products (see Kommers & Lanzing, 1997). Concept maps used to manage individual resource knowledge may be particularly useful in resource-based learning scenarios like WebQuest (http://webquest.sdsu.edu/). Concept maps in WebQuest scenarios may help the learners maximize the use of information obtained from online resources when the resources are made accessible by a concept map (Carvalho et al., 2001).

4 Perspectives for Application and Research

It is important to develop concepts of how to use strategies and tools for knowledge management for the purpose of coping with knowledge-rich task situations more effectively (Malhotra, 2000). Up to now, there have only been isolated approaches aimed at using concept mapping tools for e-learning and knowledge management (e.g. Gaines & Shaw, 2002; Neumann, Graeber & Tergan, in this book). Concept mapping has proven to be a valuable technique for visualizing conceptual knowledge. Advanced digital concept mapping tools also allow for the representation of multi media domain knowledge and knowledge resources in one coherent visual representation. It may be suggested that future representations of knowledge with concept maps will be further augmented by using information visualization strategies for highlighting contexts, structures, knowledge types and individual perspectives (e.g. Burkhard & Meier, in this book). The synergies inherent in a combination of knowledge visualization and information visualization techniques for managing knowledge and knowledge resources are just being discovered. With their additional computational facilities, digital concept maps have a high potential to support resource-based learning with learners studying both individually and collaboratively. The task of instruction is to develop learner-centered instructional scenarios and to integrate the use of mapping tools for managing individual and shared knowledge and knowledge resources. This is particularly true for e-learning environments. In order to provide users convenient access to concept mapping tools, the tools should be an integral part of the environments.

Research on the effective use of digital concept maps for supporting the management of domain knowledge and knowledge resources in e-learning scenarios has to be initiated. Past research has shown that concept mapping is rarely used spontaneously by students, because it is a cognitively demanding activity, and that the process of map modification may sometimes be messy and cumbersome. Concept mapping used for knowledge management requires skills in generating appropriate maps and using them efficiently (Newbern & Dansereau, 1995). As Zhang (1997) points out, externalization is beneficial if the cost associated with the externalization process is outweighed by the benefits of using the external representation. The kind of task, map characteristics, the amount of training and subject-matter knowledge, the tendency for rote or meaningful learning, or for learning with verbal or visualized contents are variables that may affect the effective use of concept maps in learning scenarios (Lambiotte & Dansereau, 1992; Wiegman et al., 1992; O'Donnell, Dansereau & Hall, 2002; Bruillard & Baron, 2000; Dansereau, in this book). In order to evaluate the potential of computer-based concept mapping for knowledge management in resource-based learning, research has to focus on the individual, group, and situational conditions for effective use of digital mapping tools for knowledge management. Additionally they have to focus on how managing processes may be fostered by technical features and instructional measures.

A rationale for a research program on studying the conditions of effective management of knowledge and knowledge resources with computerized concept mapping tools was presented by Tergan, Gräber & Reinmann-Rothmeier (2003) at the 10th Biennial Conference of the European Association for Research on Learning and Instruction (EARLI) in Padova (Italy). A further impetus for research on the potential of concept maps for organizing and visualizing large bodies of individual knowledge and knowledge resources was given by the International Workshop on Visual Artifacts for the Organization of Information and Knowledge held at the Knowledge Media Research Center (Tübingen, Germany) in May 2004 (http://www.kmrc.de/workshops/visual_artifacts/). The workshop was intended to bring together researchers from both fields, knowledge visualization and information visualization, to think about potential synergies by integrating ideas and approaches, and to initiate a discussion on synergistic approaches.

This book reflects the rationale, concepts, and approaches, which were of central relevance for the Workshop. Several papers in this book focus on the potential of digital concept maps for bridging the gap between information visualization and knowledge visualization (a.o. Alpert, Cañas, Coffey). A variety of features and functions are outlined, which are necessary for concept mapping tools when they are used for fostering processes of knowledge management. Neumann et al. (in this book) show how a mapping tool (Mind Manager) may be used successfully for managing knowledge and knowledge resources in classroom settings. These results are encouraging. However, externalizing and mapping ideas, in particular self-constructing concept maps, is a highly demanding cognitive activity, which has to be trained thoroughly (see http://www.udel.edu/chem/white/teaching/ConceptMap.html for a construction guide). In instructional settings, it is suggested that concept mapping is best used in a guided mode (Dansereau, in this book). Until now, empirical research has focused on traditional concept mapping and the use of concept maps for learning and instruction. Analysis of the potential of digital concept maps as tools for managing knowledge and information, as well as suggestions for their effective use in resource-based learning and problem-solving scenarios, are long overdue.

References

Åhlberg, M. (2004). Varieties of concept mapping. In A.J. Cañas, J.D. Novak & F.M. González (Eds.), *Concept maps: Theory, methodology, technology. Proceedings of the 1st international conference on concept mapping*. Pamplona, Spain: Universidad Públia de Navarra. Available online: March 30, 2005: http://cmc.ihmc.us/papers/cmc2004-206.pdf.

Alpert, S.R., & Gruenenberg, K. (2000). Concept mapping with multimedia on the web. *Journal of Educational Multimedia and Hypermedia, 9*(4), 313-330.

Ausubel, D.P. (1963). *The psychology of meaningful verbal learning*. New York: Grune & Stratton.

Bleakley, A., & Carrigan, J.L. (1994). *Resource-based learning activities: Information literacy for high school students*. Chicago: American Library Association.

Bransford, J.D., Brown, A.L., & Cocking, R.R. (Eds.). (1999). *How people learn: Brain, mind, experience, and school*. Washington, D.C.: National Academy Press.

Brevik, P.S. (1992). Education in the information age. In D.W. Farmer, & T.F. Mech (Eds.), *Information literacy: Developing students as independent learners* (pp. 5-13). San Francisco: Jossey-Bass Publishers.

Brevik, P.S., & Senn, J.A. (1994). *Information literacy: Educating children for the 21st century*. New York: Scholastic Inc.

Bruggen, J.M., Kirschner, P.A., & Jochems, W. (2002). External representation of argumentation in CSCL and the management of cognitive load. *Learning and Instruction 12*(1), 121-138.

Bruillard, E., & Baron, G.-L. (2000). Computer-Based Concept Mapping: a Review of a Cognitive Tool for Students. In D. Benzie, & D. Passey (Eds.), *Proceedings of Conference on Educational Uses of Information and Communication Technologies (ICEUT 2000)* (pp. 331-338). Beijing: Publishing House of Electronics Industry (PHEI).

Buzan, T. (1995). *The Mind Map book.* 2 ed. London: BBC Books.

Cañas, A.J., Ford, K., & Coffey, J. (1994). *Concept Maps as a hypermedia navigational tool.* Paper presented at the seventh Florida Artificial Intelligence Research Symposium, Pensacola, Fl.

Cañas, A. J., Ford, K. M., Novak, J. D., Hayes, P., Reichherzer, T. R., & Suri, N. (2001). Online Concept Maps: Enhancing collaborative learning by using technology with concept maps. *The Science Teacher, 68*(2), 49-51.

Cañas, A.J., Leake, D.B., & Wilson, D.C. (1999). Managing, mapping and manipulating conceptual knowledge. *AAAI Workshop Technical Report WS-99-10: Exploring the synergies of knowledge management & case-based reasoning.* Menlo Park, CA: AAAI Press

Cañas, A.J., Hill, G., Carff, R., Suri, N., Lott, J., Eskridge, T., et al. (2004). CmapTools: A knowledge modeling and sharing environment. In A.J. Cañas, J.D. Novak, & F.M. González (Eds.), *Concept maps: Theory, methodology, technology. Proceedings of the 1ˢᵗ international conference on concept mapping* (pp. 125-133). Pamplona, Spain: Universidad Públia de Navarra.

Carnot, M.J., Dunn, B., Cañas, A.J., Gram, P., & Muldoon, J. (n.d.). *Concept Maps and Web pages for information searching and browsing.* Institute for Human and Machine Cognition / University of West Florida. Available online: November 10ᵗʰ, 2004: http://www.ihmc.us/users/acanas/Publications/CMapsVSWebPagesExp1/CMapsVSWebPagesExp1.htm

Carvalho, M., Hewett, R., & Cañas, A.J. (2001). Enhancing web searches from concept-map based knowledge models. In *Proceedings of the SCI. Fifth Multi-Conference on Systems, Cybernetics and Informatics.* Orlando, FL.

Coffey, J.W., Hoffmann, R.R., Cañas, A.J., & Ford, K.M. (2002). *A Concept Map-Based Knowledge Modeling Approach to Expert Knowledge Sharing.* Available online: February 2004: http://www.coginst.uwf.edu/users/acanas/Publications/IKS2002/IKS.htm.

Cox, R. (1999). Representation, construction, externalised cognition and individual differences. *Learning and Instruction, 9*, 343-363.

Cox, R., & Brna, P. (1995). Supporting the use of external representations in problem solving: The need for flexible learning environments. *Journal of Artificial Intelligence in Education, 6*(2/3), 239-302.

Derbentseva, N., Safayeni, F., & Cañas, A. (2004). *The effects of map structure and concept quantification during concept map construction.* In A.J. Cañas, J.D. Novak, & F.M. González (Eds.), *Concept maps: Theory, methodology, technology. Proceedings of the 1ˢᵗ international conference on concept mapping* (pp. 209-216). Pamplona, Spain: Universidad Públia de Navarra.

Fischer, F., & Mandl, H. (2001). Facilitating the construction of shared knowledge with graphical representation tools in face-to-face and computer-mediated scenarios. In P. Dillenbourg, A. Eurelings, & K. Hakkarainen (Eds.), *Proceedings of euro-CSCL 2001* (pp. 230-236). Maastricht: McLuhan Institute.

Gaines, B.-R., & Shaw, M.L.G. (1995). Concept maps as hypermedia components. *International Journal of Human Computer Studies, 43*(3), 323-361.

Gaines, B.-R., & Shaw, M.L.G. (2002). *WebMap: Concept Mapping on the Web*. Available online: February 2004: http://ksi.cpsc.ucalgary.ca/articles/WWW/WWW4WM/

Holley, C.D., & Dansereau, D.F. (1984). The development of spatial learning strategies. In C.D. Holley, & D.F. Dansereaau (Eds.), *Spatial learning strategies. Techniques, applications, and related issues* (pp. 3-19). New York: Academic Press.

Jacobson, M.J., & Levin, J.A. (1995). Conceptual frameworks for network learning environments: Constructing personal and shared knowledge spaces. *Journal of Educational Telecommunications, 1*(4), 367-388.

Jonassen, D., Carr, C., & Yueh, H.P. (1998). Computers as mindtools for engaging learners in critical thinking. *Teachtrends*, March, 24-32.

Jonassen, D.H. (1987). Assessing cognitive structure: Verifying a method using pattern notes. *Journal of Research and Development in Education, 20* (3), 1-14.

Jonassen, D.H. (1992). Semantic networking as cognitive tool. In P.A.M. Kommers, D.H. Jonassen, & J.M. Mayer (Eds.), *Cognitive tools for learning* (pp. 12-22). Berlin: Springer.

Jonassen, D.H., Beissner, K., & Yacci, M. (1993). (Eds.). *Structural knowledge. Techniques for representing, conveying, and acquiring structural knowledge*. Hillsdale, NJ: Lawrence Erlbaum Associates.

Jonassen, D.H., Reeves, T.C., Hong, N., Harvey, D., & Peters, K. (1997). Concept mapping as cognitive learning and assessment tools. *Journal of Interactive Learning Research, 8*(3/4), 289-308.

Kommers, P., & Lanzing, J. (1997). Student´s concept mapping for hypermedia design. Navigation through the world wide web (WWW) space and self-assessment. *Journal of Interactive Learning Research 8*(3/4), 421-455.

Kommers, P.A.M., Jonassen, D.H., & Mayes, J.T. (Eds.). (1991). *Cognitive tools for learning*. NATO ASI Series, Series F: Computer and Systems Sciences, Vol. 81. Berlin: Springer.

Lambiotte, J.G., & Dansereau, D.F. (1992). Effects of knowledge maps and prior knowledge on recall of science lecture content. *Journal of Experimental Education, 60*, 189-201.

Larkin, J.H. (1989). Display-based problem solving. In D. Klahr, & K. Kotovsky (Eds.), *Complex information processing. The impact of Heribert Simon* (pp. 319-342). Hillsdale, NJ: Lawrence Erlbaum Associates.

Larkin, J.H., & Simon, H.A. (1987). Why a diagram is (sometimes) worth 10,000 words. *Cognitive Science, 11*, 65-100.

Malhotra, Y. (2000). From information management to knowledge management: Beyond the 'Hi-Tech Hidebound' systems. In K. Srikantaiah, & M.E.D. Koenig (Eds.), *Knowledge management for the information professional* (pp. 37-61). Medford, NJ: Information Today Inc.

Maurer, H., & Sapper, M. (2001). E-Learning has to be seen as part of general knowledge management. In C. Montgomerie, & J. Viteli, (Eds.), *Association for the Advancement of Computing in Education (AACE). Proceedings of the ED-MEDIA 2001* (pp. 1249-1253). Charlottesville, VA: AACE.

McAleese, R., Grabinger, S., & Fisher, K. (1999). *The Knowledge Arena: a learning environment that underpins concept mapping*. Paper presented at the AERA ´99 conference. (Available online: February 2004: http://www.cst.hw.ac.uk/~ray/3_01.PDF).

McDonald, S., & Stevenson, R.J. (1998). Navigation in hyperspace: An evaluation of the effects of navigational tools and subject matter expertise on browsing and information retrieval in hypertext. *Interacting with Computers, 10*, 129-142.

Newbern, D., & Dansereau, D.F. (1995). Knowledge Maps for knowledge management. In K.M. Wiig (Ed.), *Knowledge management methods: Practical approaches to managing knowledge* (Volume 3 of Knowledge Management Series). Arlington TX: Schema Press.

Novak, J.D. (1990). Concept mapping: a useful tool for science education. *Journal of Research in Science Teaching, 27*, 937-949.

Novak, J.D. (n.d.). *The theory underlying concept maps.* Available online: November 10th, 2004, from the Institute for Human and Machine Cognition. The University of West Florida Web site: http://cmap.coginst.uwf.edu/info/

Novak, J.D., & Gowin, D.B. (1984). *Learning how to learn.* Cambridge: Cambridge University Press.

Novak, J., Wurst, M., Schneider, M., Fleischmann, M., & Strauss, W. (2003). Discovering, visualizing and sharing knowledge through personalized learning knowledge maps - an agent-based approach. In L. von Elst, V. Dignum, & A. Abecker (Eds.), *Proceedings of the AAAI Spring Symposium on Agent-mediated Knowledge Management (AMKM03)* (pp. 213-228). Heidelberg / New York: Springer.

O`Donnell, A.M., Dansereau, D.F., & Hall, R.H. (2002). Knowledge maps as scaffolds for cognitive processing. *Educational Psychology Review, 14*(1), 71-86.

Paige, J.M., & Simon, H.A. (1966). Cognitive processes in solving algebra and word problems. In B. Kleinmuntz (Ed.), *Problem solving: Research, method and theory* (Chap. 3). New York, NY: Wiley.

Paivio, A. (1986). *Mental representations. A dual coding approach.* New York: Oxford University.

Potelle, H., & Rouet, J.-F. (2003). Effects of content representation and reader´s prior knowledge on the comprehension of hypertext. *International Journal of Human-Computer Studies 58*, 327-345.

Probst, G., Raub, S., & Romhardt, K. (1999). *Wissen managen. Wie Unternehmen ihre wertvollste Ressource optimal nutzen.* Frankfurt am Main, Wiesbaden: FAZ/Gabler.

Rakes, G.C. (1996). Using the internet as a tool in a resource-based learning environment. *Educational Technology*, September-October, 52-56.

Reinmann-Rothmeier, G., & Mandl, H. (2000). *Individuelles Wissensmanagement. Strategien für den persönlichen Umgang mit Information und Wissen am Arbeitsplatz.* Bern: Huber.

Rumelhart, D.E., & Ortony, A. (1977). The representation of knowledge in memory. In R.C. Anderson, R.J. Spiro, & W.E. Montague (Eds.), *Schooling and the acquisition of knowledge* (pp. 99-133). Hillsdale, NJ: Lawrence Erlbaum Associates.

Rumelhart, D.E., & Norman, D.A. (1978). Accretion, tuning and restructuring: Three modes of learning. In J.W. Cotton, & R.L. Klatzky (Eds.), *Semantic factors in cognition* (pp. 37-53). Hillsdale, NJ: Lawrence Erlbaum Associates.

Safayeni, F.N., Derbentseva, A.J., & Cañas, A (in press). A theoretical note on concepts and the need for cyclic concept maps. *Journal of Research in Science Teaching*.

Shavelson, R.J., Lang, H., & Lewin, B. (1994). *On concept maps as potential "authentic" assessments in science.* (Technical Report 388). Los Angeles: UCLA, Center for the Study of Evaluation (CSE/CRESST).

Shen, R., Richardson, R., & Fox, E. (n.d.). *Concept maps as visual interfaces to digital libraries: summarization, collaboration, and automatic generation.* (Available online:January 20, 2004: http://vw.indiana.edu/ivira03/shen-et-al.pdf)

Siemens, G. (2005). Connectivism. A learning theory for the digital age. *Int. J. of Instructional Technology & Distance Learning*, 2(1). (Available online: January 20, 2005: http://www.itdl.org/Journal/Jan_05/article01.htm).

Spiro, R.J., Feltovich, P.J., Jacobson, M.J., & Coulson, R.L. (1991). Cognitive flexibility, constructivism and hypertext: Random access instruction for advanced knowledge acquisition in ill-structured domains. *Educational Technology*, 31, 24-33.

Sweller, J. (1988). Cognitive load during problem solving: Effects on learning. *Cognitive Science, 12*, 257-285.

Sweller, J. (1994). Cognitive load theory, learning difficulty and instructional design. *Learning and Instruction, 4*, 295-312.

Tergan, S.-O. (2003). Managing knowledge with computer-based mapping tools. In D. Lassner, & C. Mc Naught (Eds.), *Proceedings of the ED-Media 2003 World Conference on Educational Multimedia, Hypermedia & Telecommunication* , Honolulu, Hawaii (pp. 2514-2517). Norfolk, VA: AACE.

Tergan, S.-O., Gräber, W., & Reinmann-Rothmeier, G. (2003*). A framework for research on mapping tools as means for managing individual knowledge.* Paper presented at the EARLI '03 Symposium "Managing knowledge with computerized mapping tools", Padova, Italy (August 26-30, 2003).

Wallace, D.S., West, S.W.C., Ware, A., & Dansereau, D.F. (1998). The effect of knowledge maps that incorporate gestalt principles on learning. *Journal of Experimental Education, 67*, 5-16.

Weideman, M., & Kritzinger, W. (2003). *Concept Mapping - a proposed theoretical model for implementation as a knowledge repository.* Working paper from the "ICT in Higher Education" research project. University of Western Cape - South Africa. Available online: January 20, 2005: http://www.uwc.ac.za/ems/is/hicte.

Wiegmann, D.A., Dansereau, D.F., McCagg, E.C., Rewey, K.L., & Pitre, U. (1992). Effects of knowledge map characteristics on information processing. *Contemporary Educational Psychology, 17*, 136-155.

Williams, D. (1997). *Concept Mapping: foundations, research, and implications for hypermedia/multimedia design.* Paper presented at ED-MEDIA 97--World Conference on Educational Multimedia and Hypermedia, Calgary, Canada, 1997.

Zhang, J. (1997). The nature of external representations in problem solving. *Cognitive Science, 21*(2), 179-217.

Zhang, J., & Norman, D.A. (1994). Representations in distributed cognitive tasks. *Cognitive Science, 18*, 87-122.

Concept Maps: Integrating Knowledge and Information Visualization

Alberto J. Cañas, Roger Carff, Greg Hill, Marco Carvalho, Marco Arguedas,
Thomas C. Eskridge, James Lott, and Rodrigo Carvajal

Institute for Human and Machine Cognition,
Pensacola, FL 3202, USA
{acanas, rcarff, ghill, mcarvalho, marguedas, teskridge,
jlott, rcarvajal}@ihmc.us

Abstract. Information visualization has been a research topic for many years,
leading to a mature field where guidelines and practices are well established.
Knowledge visualization, in contrast, is a relatively new area of research that
has received more attention recently due to the interest from the business community in Knowledge Management. In this paper we present the CmapTools
software as an example of how concept maps, a knowledge visualization tool,
can be combined with recent technology to provide integration between knowledge and information visualizations. We show how concept map-based knowledge models can be used to organize repositories of information in a way that
makes them easily browsable, and how concept maps can improve searching
algorithms for the Web. We also report on how information can be used to
complement knowledge models and, based on the searching algorithms, improve the process of constructing concept maps.

1 Introduction: Information and Knowledge Visualization

Information visualization is a well-studied, broad topic. Since the earliest cave paintings, man has consistently pursued more effective and elegant ways of conveying information. More recently, advances in technology and in our understanding of cognition and perception have lead to new techniques and methods for visualizing
information. Card, Mackinlay and Shneiderman (1999) provided a comprehensive
overview of research that has been done on the topic. Tufte (1997, 2001) wrote extensively on information design and demonstrated the maturity of the field. Workshops,
symposiums, and conferences are frequently held on information visualization, for
example, IEEE has an annual conference on the subject (e.g. IEEE, 2003).

Knowledge visualization, on the other hand, is a new field that is only recently receiving attention from the research and business communities. Burkhard and Meier
(2004) defined knowledge visualization as the use of visual representations to transfer
knowledge between at least two persons. From an Artificial Intelligence perspective,
the knowledge engineering and knowledge representation communities for years have
been primarily concerned with knowledge elicitation methodologies and the formal
notation used to represent knowledge, and have dedicated little effort to visualization.

S.-O. Tergan and T. Keller (Eds.): Knowledge and Information Visualization, LNCS 3426, pp. 205–219, 2005.
© Springer-Verlag Berlin Heidelberg 2005

The recent interest in Knowledge Management on the part of the business community (Becerra-Fernandez, Gonzalez & Sabherwal, 2003; Takeuchi & Nonaka, 2004; Tiwana, 2000) has brought attention to the effective portrayal and sharing of knowledge, and awareness to the issue of knowledge visualization.

To distinguish between information and knowledge visualization, we first need to distinguish between information and knowledge, a differentiation that is not always straightforward. Typical distinctions between them in the Knowledge Management literature are not of much use. They are either inadequate for our purposes as in "Knowledge is bigger than information" and "Knowledge is information in action", or just plain wrong: "Our organizations are awash in information, but until people use it, it isn't knowledge" (Grayson & O'Dell, 1998), I may be knowledgeable about a subject and never use that knowledge – is it then *not* knowledge?). Tiwana (2000) referred to knowledge as "... a fluid mix of framed experience, values, contextual information, expert insight and grounded intuition that provides an environment and framework for evaluating and incorporating new experiences and information. It originates and is applied in the mind of knowers." Encyclopedia definitions are not of much help either: "Knowledge is distinct from simple information. Both knowledge and information consist of true statements, but knowledge is information that has a purpose or use." (Knowledge, 2004, November 21). These definitions don't really tell us what knowledge *is*. For the purpose of this paper, we will provide a pragmatic distinction between knowledge visualization and information visualization. But first we must present our understanding of what "knowledge" is, and introduce the concept map as a knowledge visualization tool.

Our interpretation of "knowledge" is based on the theories of knowledge and learning from Ausubel, Novak and Hanesian (1978) and Novak (1977) on which our research is supported. Novak proposed that the primary elements of knowledge are *concepts* and relationships between *concepts* called *propositions*. Concepts are defined as "perceived regularities in events or objects, or records of events or objects, designated by a label" (Novak, 1998). Propositions consist of two or more concept labels connected by a linking relationship that forms a semantic unit (Novak & Gowin, 1984). Most researchers agree that knowledge is a human creation. Using these propositions, we construct new knowledge by linking new concepts to knowledge we already have. Knowledge is constructed through meaningful learning (in contrast to rote learning or memorization), which takes place when the learner deliberately seeks to relate and incorporate new information to relevant knowledge he/she already possesses (Ausubel et al., 1978).

2 Concept Map: A Knowledge Visualization Tool

Novak and Gowin's (1984) research into human learning and knowledge construction led to the development of Concept Maps: a graphical tool that enables anybody to express their knowledge in a form that is easily understood by others. Concept Maps are a graphical two-dimensional display of knowledge that is comprised of concepts (usually represented within boxes or circles), connected by directed arcs encoding brief relationships (linking phrases) between pairs of concepts. These relationships usually consist of verbs, forming propositions or phrases for each pair of concepts. The simplest concept map would consist of two nodes connected by an arc representing a simple sentence such as 'grass is green,' but they can also become quite intricate. Fig. 1 shows a concept map about concept maps by Novak (2003). 'Concept Maps represent Organized Knowledge' is one of the propositions of this map. 'Organized Knowledge is comprised of Concepts' and 'Organized Knowledge is comprised of Propositions' are two other propositions. By convention, links run top-down unless annotated with an arrowhead. The vertical axis expresses a hierarchical framework for the concepts. More general, inclusive concepts are found at the highest levels, with progressively more specific, less inclusive concepts arranged below them.

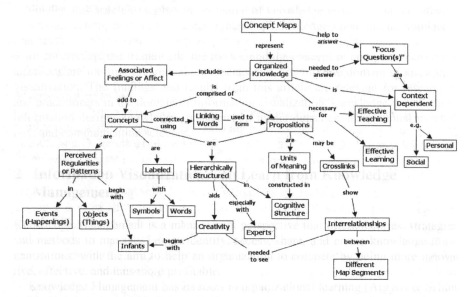

Fig. 1. Concept map about concept maps (Novak, 2003)

The structure of a concept map is dependent on its context. Consequently, maps having similar concepts can vary from one context to another and are highly idiosyncratic. The strength of concept maps lies in their ability to measure a particular person's knowledge about a given topic in a specific context. Therefore, concept maps constructed by different persons on the same topic are necessarily different, as each represents its creator's personal knowledge. Similarly, we cannot refer to *the* correct concept map about a particular topic, as there can be many different representations of the topic that are correct.

Concept mapping techniques have helped people of all ages examine many fields of knowledge. When concepts and linking words are carefully chosen, these maps are powerful tools for observing nuances of meaning. Their rich, expressive power derives from each map's ability to allow its creator to use a *virtually unlimited* set of linking words to show how meanings have been developed. There are no restrictions on what words can be used to form concepts or linking phrases. Concepts tend to be nouns and linking phrases are usually verbs, and it is recommended that both consist of as few words as possible. Linking phrases can express any type of relationship, and are not limited to a defined set (e.g., is-a, part-of, etc.) as in other diagramming techniques such as semantic networks. However, it is this freedom in the construction of linking phrases in particular that prevents concept maps from being automatically translatable to any formal representation.

In a "well constructed" concept map,

1. Each pair of concepts, together with their joining linking phrase, can be read as an individual statement or proposition that makes sense. Hoffman, Coffey, Novak and Cañas (2005) referred to a concept map where all the triples (concept, linking phrase, concept) are well-formed propositions, as being propositional coherent. In addition, in well constructed concept maps:
2. Concepts and linking phrases are as short as possible, possibly single words.
3. The structure is hierarchical and the root node of the map is a good representative of the topic of the map.

Concept maps have been demonstrated to be an effective means of representing, visualizing, and communicating knowledge. From an education perspective, there is a growing body of research that indicates that the use of concept maps can facilitate meaningful learning (Coffey, Carnot, Feltovich, Feltovich, Hoffman, Cañas, 2003a). During concept map construction, meaning making occurs as the learner makes an effort to link the concepts to form propositions. The structure of these propositions into a map is a reflection of his/her understanding of the domain. Mapping techniques are employed to help students "learn how to learn" by bringing to the surface cognitive structures and self-constructed knowledge (Novak & Gowin, 1984).

Concept maps have also proven to be valuable as a knowledge acquisition tool during the construction of both expert systems (Ford, Coffey, Cañas, Andrews & Turner, 1996) and performance support systems (Coffey, Cañas, Reichherzer, Hill, Suri, Carrff, Mitrovich & Eberle, 2003b), and as a means for capturing and sharing experts' knowledge (Coffey, Hoffman, Cañas & Ford, 2002). The results of these elicitation and modeling efforts are browsable knowledge models that visually represent the knowledge of the experts. Fig. 2 shows a screen capture of the STORM-LK[1] system (Hoffman, Coffey & Ford, 2000). It illustrates a collection of concept maps and associated media (video, satellite image, and a text Web page) that visually represent the knowledge needed for weather forecasting in the Gulf of Mexico, as elicited from experts from the U.S. Navy's Meteorology and Oceanography Command (METOC) in Pensacola, FL.

The sample concept maps and associated media shown in Fig. 2 lead us to our distinction between knowledge and information visualization. For the context of this paper, we regard the concept maps to be the visualization of knowledge, and all other media (images, videos, text, sound, charts, etc.) to be the visualization of information. We understand that some of the associated media (e.g., text) may depict knowledge, but this distinction will simplify the discussion of how concept maps can be used to integrate knowledge and information visualization.

---

[1] The STORM-LK model can be browsed at http://www.ihmc.us/research/projects/StormLK/

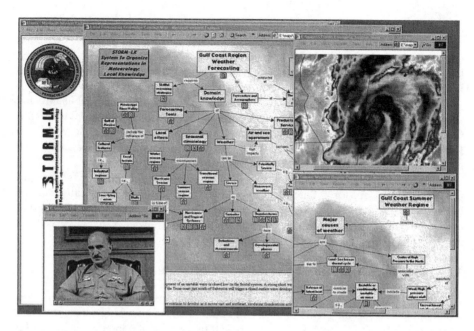

Fig. 2. A screen shot from STORM-LK, a browsable visual model of weather forecasting expertise (Hoffman et al., 2000)

3   Integration of Knowledge and Information Visualization

Traditionally, concept maps have been used primarily as a tool for students to demonstrate their understanding of a topic so that teachers could evaluate them. Early software programs for concept mapping mimicked this behavior, allowing students to construct a map, save it, and print it. In some cases, the possibility of including colors, shapes, and links to resources located on the student's computer, were added. However, it is the integration of concept mapping with information resources (Cañas, Ford & Coffey, 1994; Ford, Cañas & Coffey, 1993) and the later development of the Web that has generated a new role for concept maps as a knowledge visualization tool, thus creating the possibility of integrating knowledge visualization and information visualization. In the rest of this paper we provide examples of such integration.

3.1   CmapTools: A Knowledge Modeling and Sharing Environment

Concept maps are an effective way to visually represent a person's understanding of a domain of knowledge. Technology can further help by making it easy to construct and modify these representations, to manage large representations for complex domains, to integrate knowledge and information to create knowledge models, and to allow groups of people to share in the construction of the concept maps. CmapTools[2]

---

[2] The CmapTools software is available free for educational and non-profit use from http://cmap.ihmc.us

(Cañas, Hill, Carff, Suri, Lott, Eskridge, Goméz, Arroyo & Caravajal, 2004b) is a software environment developed at the Institute for Human and Machine Cognition that empowers users, individually or collaboratively, to represent their knowledge using concept maps; to link media resources to them, to share them with peers and colleagues, and to publish them.

Public servers have been established to encourage and support the publishing and sharing of knowledge by users of all ages from anywhere on the Internet (Cañas, Hill, Granados, Pérez & Pérez, 2003a; Cañas et al., 2004b). On these CmapServers (e.g., IHMC Public Cmaps), using the CmapTools client program, any user can create his/her own folder and publish a concept map and associated resources.

The user interface and functionality of CmapTools have been designed to be simple enough to be apt for children and naïve users without much technical expertise, but powerful enough to support the advanced needs of expert knowledge engineering users. As a result, thousands of users are constructing knowledge models based on concept maps and sharing them through the public CmapServers.

3.2   CmapTools: Integrating Knowledge and Information Visualization

In CmapTools, we have extended the use of concept maps beyond knowledge representation, to serve as the browsing interface to a domain of knowledge and associated resources (Cañas et al., 1994; Ford et al., 1993). In the case of a large domain, or of a detailed representation of a domain, a single concept map can become unmanageable for the user to comprehend, display, and manipulate. To facilitate the construction of large representations, CmapTools allows the user to split them into collections of concept maps. To show the relationships between the concept maps in the set, the software facilitates the linking of concept maps, enabling the navigation from one concept map to another. Additionally, the user can establish links to other types of resources (e.g., images, videos, sound clips, text, Web pages, documents, presentations, and other concept maps) that help explain and complement the information in the map.

In CmapTools, a set of concept maps and associated resources about a particular domain of knowledge is referred to as a "knowledge model" (Cañas, Hill & Lott, 2003b). Fig. 3 shows several opened windows, the result of navigating through the CMEX (NASA's Center for Mars Exploration) knowledge model about Mars (Briggs, Shamma, Cañas, Carff, Scargle & Novak, 2004)[3]. The "Mars" concept map in the figure is the top-level map, the entry point to this knowledge model. Some concepts in the "Mars" concept map have small icons underneath them. These icons indicate that there are other resources (e.g., images, text, videos, Web pages, other concept maps) that contain additional information, refer to, or further explain that particular concept. By clicking on the "concept map" icon underneath a concept, a list of available concept maps is displayed, which the user can select and open. For example, by clicking on the "concept map" icon underneath the "Exploration Strategy" concept, from the list of concept maps displayed, the user can select and open a "Mars Exploration Strategy" concept map (not displayed in Fig. 3). In this concept map, a concept labeled "Robotic Exploration" has a "concept map" icon that leads to a "Space

---

[3] The CMEX Mars model can be browsed at http://www.cmex.arc.nasa

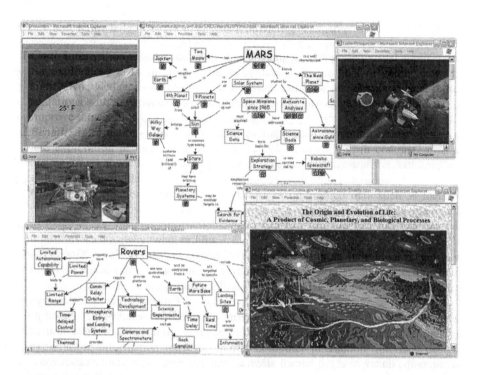

Fig. 3. The CMEX knowledge model on the Mars domain consists of over 100 linked concept maps and over 600 MBs of resources

Missions to Mars" concept map (not displayed in Fig. 3); The "Space Missions to Mars" concept map has a "concept map" icon that leads to the "Rovers" concept map shown in Fig. 3. The other images shown are opened by a similar navigation through the icons in the concept maps.

The CMEX Mars knowledge model consists of over 100 concept maps that are used as a means to browse and search through over 600 MBs of resources of all types. The concept maps become the navigational tool with which the user navigates through this particular domain of knowledge, thereby integrating the "knowledge" and "information" representations. These concept maps are mainly used as a means to help the user to locate the information of interest. The concepts act as a set of "categories" from which the user selects during his/her navigation effort, whereas the linking phrases help by explaining how these "categories" are related: They reduce the "variability" between these categories (Cañas, 1985). Geoffrey Briggs, Director of CMEX and an expert on Mars, constructed the CMEX Mars maps, and his deep understanding of the domain led to an easy to navigate set of maps. They were constructed with the purpose of being a navigational aid, not as a means for the expert to convey his complete understanding of the topics in the maps. The in-depth descriptions of the topics are found in the associated resources. Using concept maps as a means to organize large repositories of media and as a browser for navigation through a large domain is particularly effective, as discussed by Carnot, Dunn, Cañas, Graham and Muldoon (2001).

The STORM-LK maps, in contrast, are much more "dense" in terms of the number of propositions they contain. The maps are meant to represent the experts' knowledge, whereas the associated media are intended to complement the knowledge in the maps.

The two knowledge models demonstrate different types of integration between knowledge and information. In the CMEX Mars model, the concept maps are the organizing and browsing mechanism to a large collection of information represented in a variety of media. In STORM-LK, the media complements the expert's knowledge represented in the concept maps. The type of integration is determined by the purpose of the knowledge model.

4   Searching and Mining the Web from Concept Maps

Search engines have become a hot topic as the Web grows into what a few years ago was an unimaginable size. The act of Web browsing has been replaced lately with large-scale search engines. Nobody "surfs" the Web any more: Users "Google" into the topic they are interested in and then leave. That is, many Web users rely on the large-scale server farm to index billions of Web pages for them.

To retrieve relevant Web pages, search engines rely on the query specified by the user, but users rarely provide a "good" query: The average search query, from a recent study, is 2.2 words (Spink, Wolfram, Jansen & Saravevic, 2001). As a result, the list of retrieved documents is often too large or contains information that has no relevance to the query. We propose to alleviate this problem by taking advantage of the context provided by concept maps to both (a) provide more complete queries to the search engines, and (b) enhance the ranking of the results provided by the engines. Additionally, we leverage on this concept map-based search to aid users in the construction of their concept maps. These tools provide another level of integration between knowledge representations and large repositories of information.

To achieve these goals, we take advantage of the semantic and topological characteristics of concept maps. We have found that following Novak and Gowin's (1984) guidelines in terms of making concepts single words and linking phrases as short as possible leads to concept maps that, although not readily translatable to a more formal notation, provide an abundance of information that can be taken advantage of by *smart* tools (Cañas & Carvalho, 2004) that can search and mine the Web. In addition, these tools take advantage of the particular characteristics of concept maps.

1. Concept maps have structure: By definition, concept maps tend to have a hierarchical structure where more general concepts are presented at the top and more specific concepts at the bottom. Additionally, other structural information, for example, the number of ingoing and outgoing links of a concept, may provide additional information regarding a concept's role in the map. (Leake, Maguitman, & Reichherzer, 2004a, presented experimental support for the cognitive importance of such factors.)
2. Concept maps are based on propositions: Every two concepts along with their linking phrase form a "unit of meaning." This propositional structure distinguishes concept maps from other tools such as Mind Mapping and The Brain, and provides semantics to the relationships between concepts.

3. Concept maps have a context: A concept map is a representation of a person's understanding of a particular domain of knowledge. As such, all concepts and linking phrases are to be interpreted within that context.

4.1 Searching the Web from a Concept Map

By allowing users to search the Web from a concept map, CmapTools provides another type of integration between knowledge and information representations. The user constructs a visual knowledge representation as a concept map and CmapTools takes this as the basis for the search, retrieving information that is relevant to the map.

The user can easily and concisely specify the context of the search in a concept map, which will be used for the automatic construction of queries. The Web-search algorithm implemented in CmapTools allows the user to select a concept and ask the system to search for Web information that is relevant to the concept within the context of the concept map. The process consists of (a) analyzing the concept map to prepare a relevant query to use in searching the Web, (b) retrieving relevant documents from the Web, (c) ranking the retrieved Web pages according to relevance, and (d) presenting the results to the user. Each of these steps is described briefly below, though a more detailed explanation can be found in Carvalho et al. (2001). To generate the query, key concepts are selected from the map. These include the words in the selected concept itself, the root of the concept map, and the authority nodes: those with the highest number of outgoing links to other nodes. We assume that the number of outgoing links is indicative of further elaboration of these concepts, and therefore, a gauge of their relevance in the context of the map. We use the query constructed from the key concepts in the previous step to retrieve Web pages and build our collection of documents. We have developed a metasearch engine, based primarily on Google (Brin & Lawrence, 1998), in order to retrieve an initial set of documents from the public Web. Once retrieved, these documents are added to a local cache for ranking, which is based on comparing distance matrices calculated from the concept map and from each of the candidate documents. The distance matrices are symmetric, and provide a weighted list of the concept terms in the map and the documents. Weights between terms in the concept map are proportional to the number of linking phrases between each concept. For the documents, the weights are estimated as a function of the number of words between each concept map term found in the text. Lower distances between terms represent a higher weight, as terms are more likely to form a proposition.

Experimental results reported in Carvalho et al. (2001) showed that the algorithm scored similarly or better than the best of four publicly available search engines in ranking retrieved documents for relevance to the concept map according to the subjects' criteria, and clearly performed better than the other three. The combination of leveraging on the structure of the concept map in generating the query, and utilizing the propositional nature and hierarchical topology of concept maps to provide contextual information to identify and rank retrieved documents that are more relevant, seems to provide an improvement over the ranking provided by publicly available search engines. Fig. 4 shows the result of performing a search on the concept "Propositions" within the context of the concept map from Fig. 1. The retrieved list of Web pages shows how relevant results are obtained by leveraging on the concept map to perform the search.

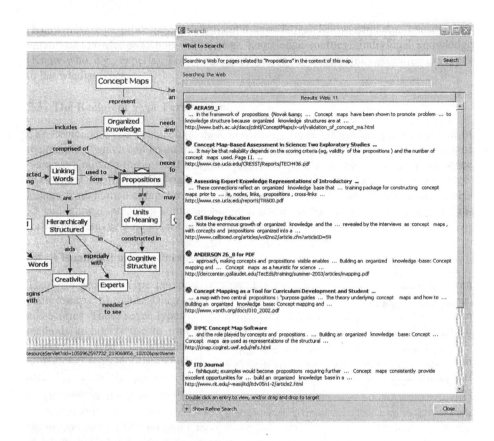

Fig. 4. Result of performing a Web search from the map in Fig. 1 on the concept "proposition" shows a retrieved list of Web pages that are relevant to the term in the context of the concept map

4.2 Mining the Web to Aid Concept Map Construction

CmapTools' Web search capabilities can also aid the user in the process of building a concept map. The CmapTools application proactively monitors the context of an open concept map to autonomously search for Web information that could be relevant to the user. At the user's discretion, this information can be utilized to verify, correct, or extend his/her concept maps during browsing or authoring. From the point of view of knowledge and information integration, the information from the Web aids the user in the construction of knowledge representations.

This capability is integrated with the editor, and Web-based suggestions can be provided in two forms, namely a) a list of relevant Web-pages that can be used as references by the user, or b) a list of relevant concepts that the user can, at his/her discretion, add to the concept map to broaden or clarify the content. This information is proactively offered by the application as the map context changes, but it can also be requested on-demand by the user.

The suggestion of Web pages is based on an enhanced version of the search algorithm used to obtain relevant pages from the Web, based on the current stage of the concept map (Leake, Maguitman, Reichherzer, Cañas, Carvalho, Arguedas & Eskridge, 2004b). A key difference in the proactive suggestion of Web pages is that the whole map is taken into account. This is in contrast to the on-demand search, where the user is allowed to specify a concept within the map that is used to focus the search.

CmapTools can also suggest "concepts" during the construction of a map. Concept map construction is a meaning-making process in which listing the concepts that will be included in the map is a less central task than selecting the appropriate linking phrase to form propositions. Often, however, we have found that users struggle to "remember" new concepts to add to their maps, and we believe that they should be able to concentrate their efforts on determining the linking phrases between concepts in the map. We have implemented in the CmapTools software a proactive *concept suggester* (Cañas, Carvalho, Arguedas, Leake, Maguitman & Reichherzer, 2004a) module which, during map construction, analyzes the concept map, creates a relevant query to search the Web for documents related to the map, extracts relevant concepts from the retrieved Web pages, and presents the results as suggestions to the user. This module searches for new suggestions whenever it determines that the map has suffered significant changes.

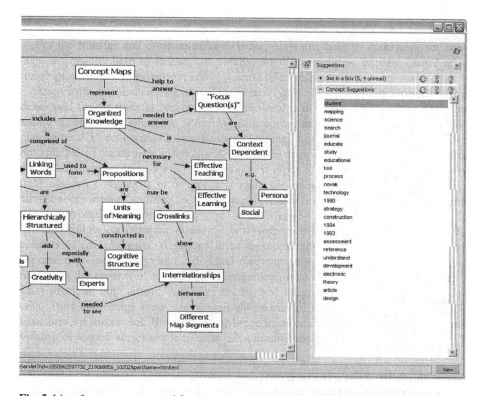

Fig. 5. List of concepts suggested for the concept map in Fig. 1. Observe that "Novak" is one of the concepts suggested

Cañas et al. (2004a) described tests of this module with a group of users, and reported that their results indicate that the module is effective in presenting relevant concepts to the users. This effectiveness, however, diminishes as the map grows, which implies that the algorithm should be revised to take into account that in larger maps, users are most likely working on a piece of the map, and suggested concepts should be determined by the context of that piece. Fig. 5 shows the list of concepts suggested by CmapTools for the concept map about concept maps in Fig. 1. Observe that "Novak" is one of the suggested concepts – the inventor of concept mapping should be part of the concept map about concept maps.

The search and mining mechanisms show how we can take advantage of the particularities of "knowledge" and "information." The characteristics of the visual representation of knowledge in the form of a concept map provides the possibility of generating "smart" queries that lead to improved retrieval from large information repositories, for example, the Web. Taking this feature one step further, mining the Web from these queries allows CmapTools to take advantage of the abundance of information on the Web to suggest to the user "concepts" and "Web pages" that can be used to improve the map under construction.

5 Prospects and Perspectives

Knowledge visualization techniques bring new approaches to an already mature field of information visualization. Leveraging on modern computer-based mapping tools and the Internet, an integration of knowledge and information visualization has the potential of impacting the management of knowledge, information, and education in a variety of contexts, among them self-regulated resource-base learning (Coffey & Cañas, 2003), sense-making information visualization, and cross-community knowledge and information exchange (Novak, Fleishman, Strauss, Schneider, Wurst, Morik & Kunz, 2002). The attention that knowledge visualization is receiving from the business community in the context of knowledge management brings both commercial and research opportunities. Commercial, since corporations are carefully analyzing how a better elicitation, representation and administration of their knowledge can give them a competitive advantage. Research, because there is still a long research path to follow before we fully comprehend how to "manage knowledge."

Concept mapping, a technique that has been around in the education arena for close to thirty years, has shown to be an effective technique for representing knowledge. A rationale for using concept maps for managing knowledge and knowledge resources has been presented by Tergan (2003) and is outlined by Tergan in more detail In this book. In this paper we have shown that with CmapTools –a concept map-based knowledge modeling and sharing software environment– knowledge models can be used to organize large repositories of information and to provide an effective navigational tool. Moreover, information in the form of diverse media types can be used to complement the knowledge in the concept maps. We have also described how, by taking advantage of the particular topological and semantic characteristics of concept maps, knowledge models can be used to construct a search environment that improves on the results of commercial search engines, and takes advantage of the large amounts of information contained by these search engines to aid users during the construction of concept maps. We believe, and propose that, as better tools are developed that take advantage of the characteristics of concept maps, further integration and synergies between knowledge and visualization tools will emerge.

References

Ausubel, D. P., Novak, J. D., & Hanesian, H. (1978). *Educational psychology: A cognitive view (2nd ed.)*. New York: Holt, Rinehart and Winston.

Becerra-Fernandez, I., Gonzalez, A., & Sabherwal, R. (2003). *Knowledge management challenges, solutions, and technologies*. Upper Saddle River, NJ: Prentice Hall.

Briggs, G., Shamma, D. A., Cañas, A. J., Carff, R., Scargle, J., & Novak, J. D. (2004). Concept maps applied to Mars exploration public outreach. In A. J. Cañas, J. D. Novak, & F. González (Eds.), *Concept maps: Theory, methodology, technology. Proceedings of the first international conference on concept mapping* (Vol. I, pp. 109-116). Pamplona, Spain: Universidad Pública de Navarra.

Brin, S., & Lawrence, P. (1998). The anatomy of a large-scale hypertextual web search engine. *Computer Networks, 30*(1-7), 107-117.

Burkhard, R., & Meier, M. (2004). Tube map: Evaluation of a visual metaphor for interfunctional communication of complex projects. In K. Tochtermann, & H. Maurer (Eds.), *Proceedings of I-KNOW '04* (pp. 449-456). Graz, Austria: Know-Center Austria.

Card, S. K., Mackinlay, J. D., & Shneiderman, B. (1999). *Readings in information visualization: Using vision to think*. San Francisco, CA: Morgan Kaufmann Publishers.

Carnot, M. J., Dunn, B., Cañas, A. J., Graham, P., & Muldoon, J. (2001). *Concept maps vs. Web pages for information searching and browsing*. From http://www.ihmc.us/users/acanas/Publications/CMapsVSWebPagesExp1/CMapsVSWebPagesExp1.htm

Carvalho, M. R., Hewett, R., & Cañas, A. J. (2001). Enhancing web searches from concept map-based knowledge models. In N. Callaos, F. G. Tinetti, J. M. Champarnaud, & J. K. Lee (Eds.), *Proceedings of SCI 2001: Fifth multiconference on systems, cybernetics and informatics* (pp. 69-73). Orlando, FL: International Institute of Informatics and Systemics.

Cañas, A. J. (1985). *Variability as a measure of semantic structure in document storage and retrieval*. Waterloo, Ontario: University of Waterloo.

Cañas, A. J., & Carvalho, M. (2004). Concept maps and AI: An unlikely marriage? In *Proceedings of SBIE 2004: Simpósio brasileiro de informática educativa*. Manaus, Brasil: SBC.

Cañas, A. J., Carvalho, M., Arguedas, M., Leake, D. B., Maguitman, A., & Reichherzer, T. (2004a). Mining the web to suggest concepts during concept map construction. In A. J. Cañas, J. D. Novak, & F. M. González (Eds.), *Concept maps: Theory, methodology, technology. Proceedings of the 1st international conference on concept mapping* (Vol. I, pp. 135-142). Pamplona, Spain: Universidad Pública de Navarra.

Cañas, A. J., Ford, K. M., & Coffey, J. W. (1994). *Concept maps as a hypermedia navigational tool*. Paper presented at the Seventh Florida Artificial Intelligence Research Symposium (FLAIRS), Pensacola, FL.

Cañas, A. J., Hill, G., Carff, R., Suri, N., Lott, J., Eskridge, T., Gómez, G., Arroyo, M., & Carvajal, R. (2004b). CmapTools: A knowledge modeling and sharing environment. In A. J. Cañas, J. D. Novak, & F. M. González (Eds.), *Concept maps: Theory, methodology, technology. Proceedings of the first international conference on concept mapping* (Vol. I, pp. 125-133). Pamplona, Spain: Universidad Pública de Navarra.

Cañas, A. J., Hill, G., Granados, A., Pérez, C., & Pérez, J. D. (2003a). *The network architecture of CmapTools* (Technical Report No. IHMC CmapTools 2003-01). Pensacola, FL: Institute for Human and Machine Cognition.

Cañas, A. J., Hill, G., & Lott, J. (2003b). *Support for constructing knowledge models in Cmap-Tools* (Technical Report No. IHMC CmapTools 2003-02). Pensacola, FL: Institute for Human and Machine Cognition.

Coffey, J. W., Carnot, M. J., Feltovich, P. J., Feltovich, J., Hoffman, R. R., Cañas, A. J., & Novak, J. D. (2003a). *A summary of literature pertaining to the use of concept mapping techniques and technologies for education and performance support* (No. Technical Report submitted to the US Navy Chief of Naval Education and Training). Pensacola, FL: Institute for Human and Machine Cognition.

Coffey, J. W., & Cañas, A. J. (2003). Leo: A learning environment organizer to support computer-mediated instruction. *Journal for Educational Technology, 31*(3).

Coffey, J. W., Cañas, A. J., Reichherzer, T., Hill, G., Suri, N., Carff, R., Mitrovich, T., & Eberle, D. (2003b). Knowledge modeling and the creation of el-tech: A performance support system for electronic technicians. *Expert Systems with Applications, 25*(4), 483-492.

Coffey, J. W., Hoffman, R. R., Cañas, A. J., & Ford, K. M. (2002). A concept-map based knowledge modeling approach to expert knowledge sharing. In M. Boumedine (Ed.), *Proceedings of IKS 2002 - the IASTED international conference on information and knowledge sharing* (pp. 212-217). Calgary, Canada: Acta Press.

Ford, K. M., Cañas, A. J., & Coffey, J. W. (1993). Participatory explanation. In D. D. Dankel, & J. Stewman (Eds.), *Proceedings of the sixth Florida artificial intelligence research symposium* (pp. 111-115). Ft. Lauderadale, FL: FLAIRS.

Ford, K. M., Coffey, J. W., Cañas, A. J., Andrews, E. J., & Turner, C. W. (1996). Diagnosis and explanation by a nuclear cardiology expert system. *International Journal of Expert Systems, 9*, 499-506.

Grayson, C. J., & O'Dell, C. (1998). *If we only knew what we know: The transfer of internal knowledge and best practice.* New York, NY: The Free Press.

Hoffman, R. R., Coffey, J. W., & Ford, K. M. (2000). *A case study in the research paradigm of human-centered computing: Local expertise in weather forecasting.* Report on the contract "human-centered system prototype". Washington, DC: National Technology Alliance.

Hoffman, R. R., Coffey, J. W., Novak, J. D., & Cañas, A. J. (2005). Application of concept maps to web design and web work. In R. W. Proctor, & K.-P. L. Vu (Eds.), *Handbook of human factors in web design* (pp. 156-175). Mawah, NJ: Lawrence Erlbaum Associates.

IEEE (2003). *Proceedings of the seventh international conference on information visualization.* Los Alamitos, CA: IEEE Computer Society Press.

Knowledge (2004, November 21). *Wikipedia: The free encyclopedia.* Retrieved Nov. 21, 2004, from http://en.wikipedia.org/wiki/Knowledge.

Leake, D. B., Maguitman, A., & Reichherzer, T. (2004a). Understanding knowledge models: Modeling assessment of concept importance in concept maps. In R. Alterman, & D. Kirsch (Eds.), *Proceedings of the twenty-sixth annual conference of the cognitive science society* (pp. 795-800). Mahwah, NJ: Lawrence Erlbaum.

Leake, D. B., Maguitman, A., Reichherzer, T., Cañas, A. J., Carvalho, M., Arguedas, M., & Eskridge, T. (2004b). Googling from a concept map: Towards automatic concept-map-based query formation. In A. J. Cañas, J. D. Novak, & F. M. González (Eds.), *Concept maps: Theory, methodology, technology. Proceedings of the first international conference on concept mapping* (Vol. I, pp. 409-416). Pamplona, Spain: Universidad Pública de Navarra.

Novak, J., Fleishmann, M., Strauss, W., Schneider, M., Wurst, M., Morik, K., & Kunz, C. (2002). Augmenting the knowledge bandwidth and connecting heterogeneous expert communities through uncovering tacit knowledge. In *Proceedings of the IEEE workshop on knowledge media networking* (pp. 87): IEEE Computer Society.

Novak, J. D. (1977). *A theory of education.* Ithaca, NY: Cornell University Press.

Novak, J. D. (1998). *Learning, creating, and using knowledge: Concept maps as facilitative tools in schools and corporations.* Mahwah, NJ: Lawrence Erlbaum Associates.

Novak, J. D. (2003). *Concept map about concept maps.* Retrieved April 12, 2004, from http://pavo.coginst.uwf.edu/servlet/SBReadResourceServlet?rid=1064009710027_14832703 40_27090&partName=htmltext

Novak, J. D., & Gowin, D. B. (1984). *Learning how to learn.* New York, NY: Cambridge University Press.

Spink, A., Wolfram, D., Jansen, B., & Saracevic, T. (2001). The public and their queries. *Journal of the American Society for Information Science and Technology, 52*(3), 226-234.

Takeuchi, H., & Nonaka, I. (2004). *Hitotsubashi on knowledge management.* Singapore, Asia: John Wiley & Sons.

Tergan, S.-O. (2003). Managing knowledge with computer-based mapping tools. In D. Lassner, & C. M. Naught (Eds.), *Proceedings of the ed-media 2003 world conference on educational multimedia, hypermedia & telecommunication* (pp. 2514-2517). Honolulu, HI: University of Honolulu.

Tiwana, A. (2000). *The knowledge management toolkit.* Upper Saddle River, NJ: Prentice Hall.

Tufte, E. R. (1997). *Visual explanations: Images and quantities, evidence and narrative.* Cheshire, CN: Graphics Press.

Tufte, E. R. (2001). *Visual display of quantitative information.* Cheshire, CN: Graphics Press.

Comprehensive Mapping of Knowledge and Information Resources: The Case of Webster

Sherman R. Alpert

IBM T.J. Watson Research Center, PO Box 218,
Yorktown Heights, NY 10598, USA
salpert@us.ibm.com

Abstract. To maximize the representational and pedagogical effectiveness of computer-based concept maps, such maps should be able to incorporate any sort of media that can be represented in the computational environment. This chapter proposes cognitive and educational rationale for this thesis, and discusses an instantiation of these ideas in the form of a Web-based concept mapping tool named Webster. Webster permits broad flexibility in terms of the kinds of knowledge and information that may be represented and the structuring of their visual presentation. One result of this approach is the integration of knowledge visualization and information visualization in a single representational medium. These facilities also make Webster a convenient tool for personal knowledge management, facilitating individual organization of knowledge and external knowledge and information resources for reference and learning purposes.

1 Introduction

Many tools have been created to allow learners to visualize the content and structure of knowledge of a domain (Jonassen, Beissner & Yacci, 1993). Among the most useful and widely used of these are concept map tools (Novak, 1999). A concept map consists of nodes representing concepts, objects, events, or actions, connected by directional links defining the relationships between and among nodes. Graphically, a node is typically represented by a shape (such as a rectangle or oval) containing a textual name, and relationship links are textually labeled lines with an arrowhead at one or both ends (note that in some concept map representations, textual labels are disallowed for links, resulting in an arguably semantically inferior representation). Together, nodes and *labeled* or named links define propositions, assertions about a topic, domain, or thing. For example, a directed line labeled "can" beginning at a node labeled "birds" and pointing to a "fly" node represents the proposition "birds can fly" and might be a portion of a concept map concerning *birds* (see Fig. 1).

Concept maps have evolved from paper-and-pencil to computer-based tools. Extant software tools have been adapted for creating concept maps (e.g., HyperCard adapted by Reader & Hammond, 1994; NoteCards adapted by McAleese, 1992). Many research-based computer-based concept mapping tools have also been reported (for example, Fisher, 1992; Flores-Méndez, 1997; Kommers & DeVries, 1992; Kozma, 1992; Novak 1999). And there now exist commercial products for this endeavor (e.g., Inspiration®, Axon Idea Processor, Decision Explorer®, Semantica®). Many concept

S.-O. Tergan and T. Keller (Eds.): Knowledge and Information Visualization, LNCS 3426, pp. 220–237, 2005.

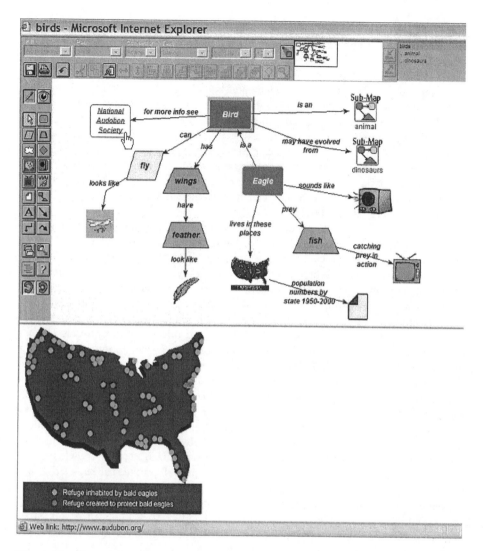

Fig. 1. Webster in a Web browser. The upper pane contains the main concept map tool; the lower pane contains a full-size information visualization that appears as result of the user clicking the corresponding image node near the bottom of the concept map (the node that looks like a map of the US). "Television" nodes represent videos or animations. "Radio" nodes represent audios. On the left side of the map is an animated image: the bird flaps its wings in-place in the map. Submap nodes (here, *animal* and *dinosaurs*) represent other layers of the overall map, which can be brought into view by clicking on the corresponding submap node. A document node at the bottom of the map references a spreadsheet with eagle population data

mapping tools focus exclusively on conceptual and (in most but not all cases) propositional knowledge, accommodating only a linguistic, text-based representational format. However, not only should concept map tools allow for the representation of other types of knowledge but they also ought to permit the inclusion, in an integrative manner, of information resources associated with the knowledge. Knowledge visualization and information visualization are, individually, powerful tools for learning and the integration of the two should synergistically contribute to enhanced learning.

This chapter is based on the simple premise that concept maps are ideal vehicles for organizing and integrating both elemental knowledge of a domain and associated information and information visualizations; this premise, however, relies on the equally simple assumption that computer-based concept maps should be able to incorporate any knowledge or informational artifacts in any medium that can be digitally represented. This includes static, passive, and interactive graphics and animations, written and spoken text, video, audio, and so on. Such media of course thereby include static, passive, and interactive information visualizations. This chapter describes a concept map tool with such capabilities, named Webster (Alpert, 2003; Alpert & Grueneberg, 2000, 2001).

Webster is a Web-based concept map application that permits broad flexibility in terms of the kinds of knowledge and information that may be represented as well as the structuring of that knowledge and information. With regard to structure, Webster simplifies the construction and navigation of multi-layer maps representing multiple abstract levels, permitting maps to possess representational, visual, and cognitive perspicuity which should support understanding and therefore learning. With respect to representation, Webster offers expressive power for the representation of *core knowledge* of a domain as well as external knowledge and information *resources*. The essential mechanism supporting representational breadth is the notion of permitting digital media of any sort to be incorporated directly into concept maps. Thus, maps may include semantically labeled links to and among audio, video, animations, as well as information resources such as external Web sites and spreadsheet, text, and slide presentation files; the ability to incorporate any form of digital media allows information visualizations, in the form of static graphics, animations, audio, or video, to become integral parts of a concept map. Thus Webster maps can represent the core, fundamental, essential knowledge of a domain - externalized implicit knowledge and visual and auditory imagery integral to a domain - as well as external knowledge and information resources that support a deeper understanding of the domain. These facilities also make Webster a convenient tool for personal knowledge management, facilitating individual organization of knowledge and external knowledge and information sources for reference purposes, as well as supporting sharing of these elements for learning.

The bulk of this chapter describes the facilities in Webster for representing and structuring knowledge and information resources, including the ability to integrate a broad range of types of knowledge and information. The cognitive and pedagogical rationale and implications of these facilities is discussed. The chapter also briefly discusses the use of concept maps for knowledge management purposes.

2 What Representations Should Concept Maps Provide?

A concept map consists of nodes representing concepts, objects, or actions, connected by directional links defining the relationships between and among nodes. Assuming relationship links may be textually labeled to describe the semantic relationship between the connected nodes, together nodes and links define propositions, assertions about a topic, domain, or thing. For example, a directed link labeled "produces" pointing from a node labeled "green plants" to another node labeled "oxygen" represents the proposition "green plants produce oxygen" and might be a portion of a concept map about photosynthesis.

Representing knowledge in this fashion is similar to semantic network knowledge representations (e.g., Quillian, 1968) and one view of concept maps is strictly as a knowledge representation mechanism, a means to make internal, tacit knowledge of a domain explicit and scrutable (e.g., McAleese, 1992). Others support the notion that concept maps are (or can be) accurate reflections of their authors' cognitive structures (e.g., Jonassen, 1992). On the other side of the argument, the notion of concept map as direct mirror of cognitive knowledge representation has been challenged (Fisher, 1992). Nonetheless, whether concept maps provide a representational scheme that is identical or isomorphic to cognitive representations, a concept map *is* an external and visual representation of knowledge of a domain.

Jonassen (1992) poses what is therefore a crucial question: "What constraints does the software impose on the product?" (p. 20). In other words, what limitations do concept map tools impose on the knowledge that may be expressed using those tools? For example, if one can express only textual propositions using a particular tool (as indeed is the case with some concept map tools), then clearly only a subset of knowledge about a domain may be expressed. Because people possess a broader range of cognitive knowledge representations than simply language-based propositions, concept maps ought to offer a concomitantly broad range of representational facilities. By capitalizing on the capabilities of modern personal computers and the Internet, we can provide for much richer knowledge representation and greater flexibility of expressiveness in computer-based concept map tools. And such enhanced flexibility of expressiveness may extend to enhanced learning (Heeren & Kommers, 1992).

2.1 Imagery and Dynamic Media

At the least, concept maps ought to incorporate static visual imagery because unmistakably people possess this sort of knowledge about the world in addition to verbal or language-based propositional encodings (Kosslyn, 1980; Paivio, 1986; Johnson-Laird, 1983; Baddeley, 1982). From a pedagogical perspective, intuitively, being able to see something of visual importance or interest offers a learning experience qualitatively distinct and superior to simply reading a textual description - no matter how well organized into nodes and links (for example, see the incredible photographs of cranes dancing on the water's surface, flying silhouetted against a sunset sky, and others at http://magma.nationalgeographic.com/ngm/cranecam/gallery01.html, or the staggering images of distant space phenomena created by the Hubble Space Telescope at http://heritage.stsci.edu/gallery/gallery.html; words cannot do justice to such imagery). Imagery can reify concepts described by textual means. Experiments have demonstrated that abstract textual information is better understood and learned when accompanied by illustrations, which serve to reify the concepts for learners (Moore & Skinner, 1985). There is evidence that memory for visual imagery is more robust than that for purely textual information (Shephard, 1967) and that information encoded both visually and verbally is more memorable than when encoded in either format alone (Paivio, 1986). Mayer asserts on the basis of numerous studies (summarized in Mayer, 2001 and Clark & Mayer, 2003) that students that learn from text and static illustrations perform better in subsequent tasks and tests than students who study text alone. Chandler and Sweller (1991) have further shown that procedural instructions are better understood when text is explicitly linked to images; when concept maps are capable of incorporating images, they can link specific textual nodes to particular images with meaningfully named links.

Going a step further, in order to more effectively portray knowledge, concept maps ought to include not only static images but temporally dynamic content as well, such as animated images, video, and audio. Again, humans cognitively represent memories for dynamic visual imagery (e.g., Johnson-Laird, 1983) and auditory information (e.g., Dowling & Harwood, 1986). For example, one's knowledge of horses might include not only what a horse looks like in a static sense, but what a race horse looks like when galloping full speed around a track amidst a field of thoroughbreds, how galloping and trotting differ in appearance - how they involve different coordinated movements of a horse's legs, what a herd of stampeding wild horses looks and sounds like, what a horse's neigh sounds like. An automobile mechanic diagnosing an engine problem relies not only on visual inspection of the engine but also on the sounds made by the engine - differing sounds, mapped onto specific engine problems, are part of his domain-specific memories. Dynamic media can also demonstrate how elements of a domain interact with one another, such as how lions in the wild behave cooperatively when attacking other wild animals, or how specific chemicals react with other chemicals producing visual and aural effects. Certainly such elements can be part of long-term memories for these respective domains: from a knowledge representation perspective some aspects of one's mental model of a domain may be expressible only via dynamic visual or auditory media. We ought to be able, then, to represent such elements in concept maps to demonstrate our own knowledge of those domains or to use concept maps as instructional resources.

From a pedagogical perspective, if, as a popular expression goes, a (static) picture is worth a thousand words (see Mayer & Gallini, 1990; Mayer & Sims, 1994; Larkin & Simon, 1987 for critical discussions of this notion), then a scene of multiple pictures in motion may be worth 10,000 words. One can explain with words how to perform a physical skill but a video *showing how to*, say, swing a golf club can be an invaluable tool for learning to perform the skill. One can explain in text how an eagle catches food, but a video portraying an eagle swooping down over a lake with talons flared, grabbing a fish just below the surface, and flapping off with a meal in its talons makes for a much higher impact and memorable learning experience. Returning to Mayer's work, studies of his have demonstrated a robust learning effect for instructional animations (Mayer, 2001; Clark & Mayer, 2003). Faraday and Sutcliffe (1999) have also demonstrated that multimedia documents with explicit co-references between text and dynamic imagery can result in better comprehension; concept maps' nodes-and-links format offers an extremely simple mechanism for clearly linking text and multimedia information.

With regard to audio, Faraday and Sutcliffe (1997) found better recall for propositions expressed by a combination of speech and imagery than those expressed by images alone. Lee and Bowers (1997) found superior learning effects when students listened to spoken text while viewing graphical images, far greater learning effects than for students reading text or hearing spoken text alone, and in fact better learning than students reading text while viewing the graphics. If studying the domain of blues music, a teacher can explain in words that the blues scale is a modified minor pentatonic scale and watch her students' eyes glaze over, or might explain that the scale is derived by flatting the 3rd, 5th, and 7th notes of a major scale, but also demonstrating the different scales by playing them on a piano will make the lesson more meaningful and memorable, and, further, without the student actually hearing and experiencing a performer playing the blues, he would really *understand* nothing about that musical form.

With regard to combining dynamic visual and auditory information, Mayer (2001; Mayer & Gallini, 1990) has repeatedly demonstrated in behavioral studies that students viewing an instructional animation while simultaneously listening to an explanatory narration are capable of generating many more useful solutions to subsequent problem-solving transfer questions than students who listened to the same narration but without viewing the animation.

Imagery (visual and/or aural) capabilities may also help to accommodate individual differences among students using concept maps to demonstrate their own knowledge or acquire new knowledge, thereby better supporting students with differential abilities, learning styles, and learning preferences or needs. For example, hearing impaired learners tend to prefer or require visually oriented learning materials. As a Teacher of the Hearing Impaired has told me, to explain textually-represented concepts "I spend half my time drawing pictures for my students" (Bomus, 2001). Concept maps that incorporate image-based nodes linked to text-only nodes should better suit the learning needs of such students.

In Webster, an individual node can *be* an image or may *reference* a media file containing dynamic imagery or audio. Static image and in-place animated image nodes may appear directly in the map, that is, the map node itself appears as an image (animated GIF89a images (CompuServe, 1990) or motionless graphics). For example, in Fig. 1 the bird image is flapping its wings (we must of course be judicious in the use of such *in situ* animations so as to not distract learners, especially from other knowledge elements (Faraday & Sutcliffe, 1999)). "TV" and "radio" nodes reference files with multimedia content: audio nodes appear as radio icons in the map, and dynamic imagery nodes look like televisions. In addition to traditional video, "TV" nodes may have associated with them any computational media that the user's Web browser is capable of playing - that is, any media type for which the browser has a plug-in. Concept maps may therefore incorporate VRML virtual reality scenes such as three-dimensional virtual walkthroughs, interactive Flash and Shockwave animations and games, and so on.

Dynamic media resources are thus integrated into the concept map as "first-class" elements of the map. Note that these media nodes are *visually typed*: imagery nodes appear as TV icons and audio nodes as radios, rather than having a uniform appearance for all nodes. This typing cues the user as to a node's medium; the user using a map as learning material can visually search the nodes of a concept map when specifically looking for video or audio related to the represented domain, and users know what type of medium to expect when "playing" such a node.

As mentioned earlier, incorporating such capabilities in a concept map tool enhances the tool's and its users' flexibility of expressiveness (Heeren & Kommers,

1992). Concept map authors can express, and learners can perceive from maps, a much richer set of knowledge and information, with concomitant pedagogical benefits. Concept maps can portray what the entities of a domain look like when in motion, what particular things sound like, how domain elements behave, react, move, and sound in specific contexts or situations, dynamic interactions between people and objects of a domain.

With static and dynamic imagery as first-class elements, concept maps can portray *essentially visual* elements of a domain per se (for example, in a map about wild animals, an image of a (difficult to discern) lynx in the wild against a natural backdrop, demonstrating how the lynx's spotted fur acts as camouflage in its natural environment) as well as *information visualizations* related to a domain (for example, a map of the United States annotated to indicate bald eagle refuges, see Fig. 1). In addition to static visualizations, *any* sort of information visualization can become part of a concept map. Our *birds* concept map could link to, say, an MPEG-encoded video showing the evolution of human population growth and concomitant eagle population decrease associated with urban expansion in a particular locale, or an animated-GIF image demonstrating population effects on wading birds of wet and dry seasons (e.g., see the animated visualizations at http://www.sfwmd.gov/org/wrp/wrp_evg/projects/birds/animations.html). An interactive programmatic visualization (encoded in, e.g., Flash, ShockWave, VRML) might demonstrate weather conditions, temperature variations, and bird migration patterns over time, in an area clicked on by the user, illustrating how and why birds navigate to widely distant locations at different seasons. Thus concept maps can naturally integrate both knowledge visualization - in the content and structure of the concept map per se - and information visualization - in the form of static, dynamic, and interactive imagery within or linked from the concept map.

2.2 Document Nodes

Concept maps ought to be able to reference external materials, including information and data associated with specific application programs or application categories (such as spreadsheets, graphs, slide presentations, databases, text documents). Thus textual and graphical information and data "stored" in, for example, Microsoft® Excel or Lotus® 1-2-3 spreadsheets, PowerPoint or FreeLance presentations, Word or Word-Pro documents, Access or Approach databases can become part of the knowledge and information integrated into any concept map. For example, Webster has been used by Chemistry students in an Ivy League university. Students used Webster to map their evolving knowledge of photosynthesis, incorporating newly learned information based on laboratory experimentation with their previously learned "book knowledge." In their concept maps, students linked scientific facts and experimental observations to lab-based data expressed in spreadsheets and graphs. Thus students were able to integrate external documents naturally into their maps, and later use those maps in laboratory reports and for studying for course examinations. Presentation-based applications that can, for example, visually portray data in tabular and graph formats, naturally support the notion of information visualization in concept maps as well.

To include documents associated with external applications in a concept map, Webster users create document nodes (see Fig. 1) and associate an application-specific file with such a node. When a user clicks on a node of this type, the document is displayed in a separate browser window. Webster provides this functionality in a Web-based application.[1] And, as above, in Webster document nodes are visually typed by their unique appearance within the map, providing users with an advanced notion of the node's content type. Thus, document nodes look like documents, rather than all nodes having a similar appearance.

2.3 Web Nodes

A more recent enhancement to the capabilities of personal computers is accessibility to the information and content available on the Internet. Firstly, the Web offers an unprecedented opportunity to educational technologists with regard to deploying instructional tools. No longer are we required to deal with the logistics of getting software applications onto individual computers so they can be used by students. Web-based concept map tools (or any educational application) offer the ability to reach greater numbers of students. Students are no longer constrained with respect to where or when they can access the tools. The Internet allows us to easily have a single centralized database so that all student maps reside in a single location on a server so that students can interrupt their work and continue to work on the same map later from a different location. Further, having applications - in Webster's case a downloadable client applet and a server-side servlet to access the centralized database - reside in a single location results in students always using the current version of the software. Bug fixes and tutor enhancements are immediately available to everyone, rather than again having to deal with the logistics of distributing and installing software updates. A centralized database of maps also opens the door for formal collaboration in map creation. For example, in Webster, students can import external maps created by others into their own maps.

Additionally, and more to the focus of this chapter, Webster concept maps also incorporate Web-hyperlink nodes that allow maps to "reach out" to the vast store of knowledge and information available on the Web. Webster provides Web-hyperlink nodes, in which a Web address (URL) can be specified. The node's associated URL may be hidden in the viewable concept map and its visible text may be something more meaningful than the URL itself (for example, see the hyperlink node labeled "National Audubon Society" in Fig. 1). Clicking on a Web-hyperlink node opens a secondary browser window to the associated site. This provides access to static and dynamic information incorporated into external Web pages, including live Web cams, and programmed facilities such as Java applets and other applications embedded in Web pages, which can offer rich and interactive information visualizations, and (see, for example, the live video of cranes in a wetland area at

---

[1] Because Webster runs in a Web browser, an application-specific document may be viewed if the browser can display the document, which sometimes means the browser must have incorporated a plug-in for the particular document type. Many applications provide such Web-browser plug-ins - for example, Microsoft Excel Viewer for spreadsheets, Microsoft Word Viewer and Adobe Acrobat Reader for text documents, Microsoft PowerPoint Viewer and Lotus Freelance Graphics Plug-In for slide presentations. There also exist third party plug-ins (e.g., Quick View Plus) that allow browser-based viewing of files associated with a broad range of applications.

http://magma.nationalgeographic.com/ngm/cranecam/cam.html, and the interactive climatology and atmospheric visualizations at http://ingrid.ldgo.columbia.edu/SOURCES/.LEVITUS94/.ANNUAL/html+viewer? and elsewhere on the ingrid. ldgo.columbia.edu site). Allowing concept maps to incorporate access to the Web can enhance further the expressiveness and learning potential of concept maps and Web-based knowledge and information resources can become "part of" concept maps. Secondarily, this sort of tool can foster a new type of student research involving mining relevant information sources from the Web.

2.4 Other Node Types?

While there are commercial and research applications of haptic and tactile computer interfaces, these are typically of the form of providing force feedback to a user's hand when some distinguished event occurs, such as the cursor is over a button or a virtual object has been "grabbed" by the user (e.g., Oakley et al., 2000). The state of the art is not yet at the point where a computer can "output," and a user experience, the feel of an object such as an animal's fur. Other researchers are working on olfactory computer interfaces (e.g. Kaye, 2004). When sensory information of these types becomes widely available on personal computers, nodes representing such information should also be incorporated in concept maps. For example, the overriding distinguishing feature of the Rafflesia plant is its odor (it smells like decaying meat, thereby attracting insects which then become participants in the pollination process). A concept map about the Rafflesia should be able to "portray" this feature if we are to fully learn or "know" about them - a user should be able to experience the smell the plant to truly learn about the plant in a very real sense. A concept map about sharks should allow us to feel the texture of sharks' skin to fully understand sharks more fully (sharks' skin serves survival purposes and is made up of dental material that is very abrasive to the touch).

The point is, in order to fully represent and transmit knowledge, concept maps should be able to incorporate any information that can be represented in digital form and accessible via a computer. In fact, digital representations of sensory information allows users to learn by experiencing that which is dangerous or otherwise cannot be experienced in real life, such as the close-up sight and sound of a volcanic eruption or the tactile feel of a sting ray's barb-tipped tail, which is not only extremely sharp but toxic when encountered in real life. This of course also includes "invisible" phenomena, such as the structure of atoms and temporally dynamic data such as weather-related temperature fluctuations, which can be made visible and observable through information visualizations.

3 Multiple Abstraction Levels

The ability to represent many types of knowledge and information enhances the expressive and educational power of concept maps; however if learners find particular concept maps confusing and difficult to use as learning materials due to visual characteristics of the maps, that power is deeply diminished. Concept maps that contain a large amount of nodes and links - geometric figures and lines - can become visually confusing and the knowledge and information within them opaque. One solution to this problem is to apply the same sort of clarifying mechanisms that people employ cognitively, that is the notions of chunking and abstraction as described below; in the case of Webster concept maps, this results in multiple layer maps that are easy to create and navigate.

Another fundamental characteristic of human cognition is the ability, and in fact necessity, to exploit knowledge abstraction. Abstraction implies the ability to represent a concept, action, or object by a single node at one level of detail while possessing the knowledge to expand that single node into an elaborated definition of its own. That is, a single knowledge element (or *chunk*) at one level of abstraction may subsume a number of lower level elements at a more detailed knowledge level (Anderson, 2000; Rich, 1983). This is to be differentiated from atomic nodes that have no underlying elaboration. This abstraction mechanism may be applied iteratively and recursively; that is any number of elements at a particular abstraction level may represent chunked knowledge and at a more detailed abstraction level, further chunks may appear as well. The resulting representation involves multiple abstraction levels that in a concept map are represented by multiple layers, each containing its own set of knowledge and information elements (nodes and links). Multiple-layer concept maps permit users to apply heuristics of visual and informational perspicuity and visual aesthetics.

Absent abstraction mechanisms, concept maps appear as a single diagram, that is, nodes and links representing all of the knowledge of a domain are drawn in a single network or layer. In such networks, a weak notion of abstraction can be represented only by generality-specificity relationships between nodes: a node representing a specific concept (say, *bird*) may have a link, labeled *is a* or *a kind of*, to a more general or abstract concept (say, *animal*). But the more abstract node might have additional links connected to other concept nodes (for example, portraying attributes of *animals*, such as *animals breathe oxygen*). There might also be relationship links and associated concepts connected to the *bird* node (e.g., a *bird has wings* and a *bird can fly*). This format can extend several levels of abstraction in either direction (e.g., a *goose is a bird*, a *lizard is an animal*, an *animal is a living thing*). Such a map does not reasonably mirror the cognitive representation of this knowledge that would exploit abstraction mechanisms to represent categories or concepts at differing levels of detail. More importantly for educational purposes, very quickly such a map can become visually crowded and confusing, and learning from such a map might be difficult.

Many concept map tools lack adequate visual or structural abstraction mechanisms altogether. While some tools do provide for the notion of submaps or child maps within concept maps, few do so in both an easy-to-perceive, easy-to-understand, and easy-to-use fashion. In Webster concept maps, a conceptual abstraction is visually represented by a single node in one layer of the map, and this single concept can be expanded into another (sub)map of knowledge elements representing the fuller, more detailed meaning and constituent parts at a more specific layer of the overall map. So for example, a concept such as *lizard* can be represented at one level of abstraction or detail by a single node, without cluttering that map level with all the detailed information about lizards, and yet those details are available in another layer of the overall concept map by "opening" the *lizard* submap node to view its "insides." We thereby gain the ability to portray the knowledge in a manner isomorphic to the way a person might cognitively represent it, and we further gain the benefit of making the knowledge representation more graphically parsimonious, thus easier to decipher, understand, and learn from.

For example, the concept map in Fig. 1 portrays knowledge and information about birds and, more specifically, about eagles. Without a great deal of knowledge elements, already this map is becoming visually noisy. And one might ask further, do the details specific to eagles really belong at the same knowledge level as those specific to (the more general concept) birds? In Webster, one may solve the visual and knowledge comprehension problems by simply selecting the eagle-specific elements and "pushing" them down (by a single button click) to a more detailed map layer. The result is shown in Fig. 2: a submap node - a visual abstraction - takes the place of the eagle-specific elements that had been in the original map layer, and a new "eagle" submap is created which may be opened to view those more detailed knowledge elements specific to eagles. Visual abstractions - submap nodes and their associated submaps - can be created in a variety of other intuitive and flexible ways, including importing an existing external concept map as a submap (see Alpert, 2003, for details).

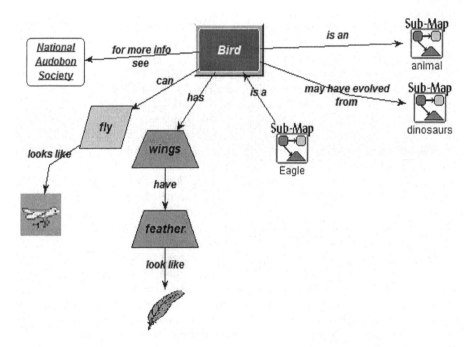

Fig. 2. The main level of the concept map shown in Fig. 1, now with an "Eagle" abstraction represented by a submap node. The corresponding submap layer can be opened to view the eagle-related elements that were formerly visible in this map layer. The abstraction/submap facility provides for visual perspicuity in the concept map

4   Outline Translations

Alternative representations support developing deeper understanding of a domain, and this may be particularly true when multiple representations of the same information are linked to one another in a learning environment (Kaput, 1989). A rational alternative representation for the information contained in a concept map is a traditional outline. Many students are comfortable with seeing their thoughts arranged in outline form. This may be especially true for students organizing ideas in preparation for prose composition. Outlines present concepts in a line-by-line numbered format

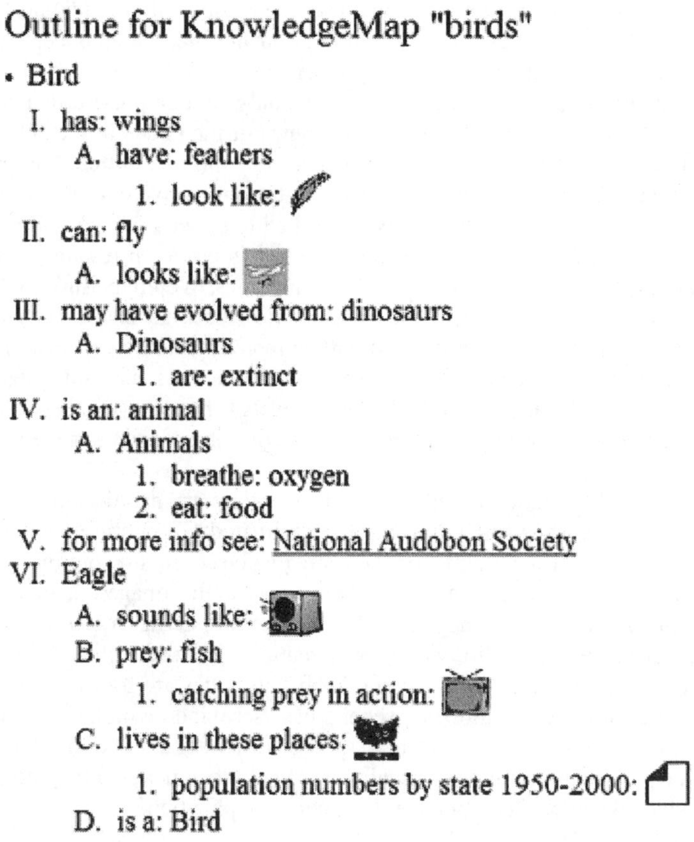

Outline for KnowledgeMap "birds"

- Bird
    I. has: wings
        A. have: feathers
            1. look like:
    II. can: fly
        A. looks like:
    III. may have evolved from: dinosaurs
        A. Dinosaurs
            1. are: extinct
    IV. is an: animal
        A. Animals
            1. breathe: oxygen
            2. eat: food
    V. for more info see: National Audobon Society
    VI. Eagle
        A. sounds like:
        B. prey: fish
            1. catching prey in action:
        C. lives in these places:
            1. population numbers by state 1950-2000:
        D. is a: Bird

Fig. 3. The *birds* concept map partially shown in previous figures translated to a multimedia outline. The outline includes the information contained in all submap abstractions (Eagle, Dinosaurs, Animals) at the appropriate indentation levels. Webster presents the outline as a Web page; all nodes are translated to appropriate HTML objects. Radio and TV images are hyperlinks to playback audio and video files. The document image hyperlinks to a spreadsheet application. Thumbnails of the image nodes that had been in the concept map may be clicked here to view as full size images. The Web-link node in the map for the National Audubon Society appears as a normal hyperlink

with subordinate or associated terms in physically subordinate locations in the outline - subordinate terms appear indented below their immediately higher level concept - and this physical superconcept-subconcept scheme may repeat itself.

Webster, like several other concept map tools, offers automatic translation of concept maps into outlines. Based on Kaput's (1989) assertion regarding the pedagogical effectiveness of multiple representations, as well as common sense regarding a user's needs and expectations, outline representations should contain the equivalent semantic content as the corresponding concept map. As a counter-example, while other concept map tools, such as Inspiration®, may incorporate static and animated-in-place images in addition to textual nodes, the image nodes are absent in its outline translation of a map. Similarly, though Inspiration nodes may link to a video or audio file, its outline translation of a map with such nodes includes only the textual labels of those nodes. Further, the textual labels of all relationship links in a concept map are elided in Inspiration outlines. The knowledge elements in child maps are absent as well in the outline translation of a concept map. The only content present in a concept map to appear in the outline "translation" is the names of the nodes in the single level of the overall concept map that was visible when the "outline" button was pressed. These deficiencies may defeat users' goals in using the alternative outline representation.

In Webster, concept maps may be translated (also via a single button click) to outlines containing all of the map's knowledge and information resources. Static and animated images, videos, audios, interactive animations, Web hyperlinks, links to external data and information visualizations, relationship labels, all elements that are part of a concept map appear in the associated outline representation, as shown in Fig. 3. All of the information contained in all concept map abstractions (i.e., submaps) appears in a single outline at the appropriate indentation levels - thus, as we expect the user desires, the outline presents the organization of all thoughts and concepts in the overall map in a single place.

With regard to static and animated images, they are handled much as they are in concept maps: images (including in-place animated-GIFs) are embedded and visible directly within outline items. Images are displayed in the outline with a default thumbnail size and users may click them to view the images in their original size. Radio and TV nodes also appear in the outline and act as hyperlinks that reference and playback specific audio, video, or animation files: users click on embedded radio and television images to "play" them. Web-link nodes are translated into normal hyperlinks that when clicked open a second browser window on the associated site. External information resources, such as spreadsheets, textual and graphical documents, and slide presentations, appear visually as a small document (as they do in the concept map) which when clicked open the document's application.

5 Discussion

"Students studying self-regulated in e-learning scenarios are often overwhelmed by complex and ill-structured subject matters. In order to study effectively they often need to organize and represent information and knowledge in a manner that may help them to get quick and flexible access to relevant information and knowledge." Thus reads a portion of the rationale for this book and its associated Workshop. In response to this, another perspective on the use of concept maps is as tools for knowledge management.

For example, there is a vast amount of content available on the Web, and the Web has increasingly become a primary source for information. But for learning, users need that content organized in some fashion, focused on a particular topic or domain. Rather than a generic search engine to (hopefully) find relevant content and a resulting flat view of information, a concept map provides a centralized "place" to access knowledge and information, and one that visually organizes relevant content in lucidly structured ways while providing semantic links between knowledge and information elements. Concept maps can be the silver bullet to help the students described above by imposing order on the perhaps overwhelming amounts and complexity of knowledge of, and information germane to, a domain (especially when that knowledge and information is distributed across disparate locations on the Web). Concept maps can serve as "personal knowledge management" tools for students. To fully succeed in this arena, concept map tools must naturally incorporate and integrate external information such as Web sites and Web content, and act to filter vast amounts of knowledge and information resources to only those relevant to a specific domain.

As we've seen above, Webster provides for the representation of varied forms and sources of knowledge and information. Capitalizing on these facilities permits a Webster map to include *fundamental knowledge* about a domain as well as knowledge and information *resources*. That is, concept maps thus become tools for organizing core factual, conceptual, and sensory knowledge about a domain - facts and assertions about the central objects and concepts of a domain, fundamental visual and aural knowledge related to a domain, and the semantic relationships between them - along with nodes that reference external learning resources relevant to that domain - video files, audio files, any information and content available on the World Wide Web, text documents, spreadsheet data, slide presentations, databases, and so on, including the relationship links between one another and relations to fundamental knowledge elements. (Note that dynamic imagery can be a fundamental piece of knowledge, such as what a bald eagle looks like (which defines its being labeled "bald"), as well as an external information resource, such as a dynamic information visualization of the bald eagle population in a particular location, which deepens understanding of a domain but might not be considered a *core* knowledge element of the domain[2].)

We must also remember that the benefits of a representation are meaningless if we disregard the ease of *using* the representation. One aspect of a representation's usability and effectiveness is the ease of finding information therein (Larkin & Simon, 1987). Abstraction mechanisms enable the economical and visually lucid expression of knowledge in a concept map. Abstraction in concept maps is not important only because of it is analogous to cognitive knowledge representations, but it's also simply a *good idea* for organizing knowledge and information for any use, including learning or reference. Abstraction allows for visual and informational perspicuity in knowl-

---

[2] The differentiation between *knowledge* and *information* may be quite subtle and difficult to adequately define. Certainly there is, however, a qualitative difference between tacit *knowledge* and various types of external knowledge and information *resources* (including information and scientific visualizations). The differences between knowledge and information are at the center of some debate as well in the knowledge management community (see, e.g., Tuomi 1999). At any rate, whatever the definitional differences may be, concept maps can serve as explicit, visual, organizational vehicles for both knowledge elements and knowledge and information resources.

edge renderings. Thus a student can learn from a map in a layered manner, studying the information at a single level without being overwhelmed by, and before tackling, too much or more complex information.

We thereby have a superlative knowledge management tool that, in a single place, visually portrays and provides access to the knowledge and resources about any particular domain. It appears that this brand of knowledge management is just the sort that ought to be useful in educational contexts.

6   Conclusion

The essential idea expressed here is quite simple, namely, for knowledge representation purposes, for pedagogical reasons, and for using concept maps as knowledge management tools, computer-based concept maps should permit the integration of *any* type

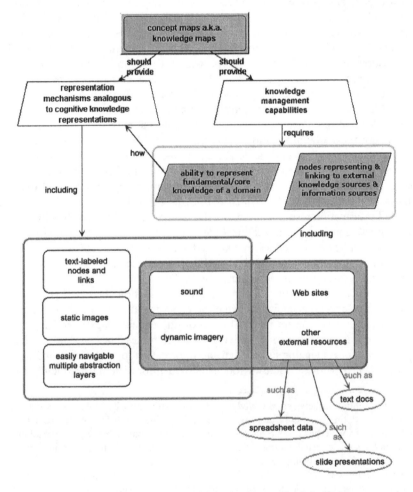

Fig. 4. Types of representations and functionality available in Webster

of information resource available in digital format. Such capabilities allow full integration into concept maps of external information and information visualizations, thereby coupling them with the knowledge visualization provided by the concept map itself.

Throughout this chapter I have deliberately used the term *concept map*; in previous work I have stated a preference for the term *knowledge map*, but now I believe this may be equally inadequate: maps visually and explicitly portray core knowledge of a domain, but also may incorporate external information sources that, while adding to a fuller understanding of a domain, might not be considered fundamental *knowledge* with regard to the domain - it is the combination of the two, knowledge and information, that maps can provide when appropriately designed and implemented. What then, however, should such maps be called? Knowledge and information maps? Wisdom maps? Comprehension maps? Learning maps? I leave this as an exercise for readers.

At any rate, integrating the capabilities presented here into concept mapping software provides the opportunity to:

- allow students to represent their knowledge more comprehensively;
- provide richer expressive power and representational choices, that is, enhanced flexibility of expressiveness;
- offer the illustrative and pedagogical advantages of dynamic visual imagery, audio, and (eventually) other sense-based information for students learning new concepts and domains;
- integrate knowledge visualization with information visualization;
- better accommodate individuals with differential learning needs or preferences;
- allow concept map authors to apply heuristics of visual clarity and perspicuity via multiple map layers and abstractions;
- perhaps provide for a more engaging student experience;
- offer engagement of the learner's senses for perhaps deeper and more intuitive understanding of a domain;
- perhaps, allow students to represent their knowledge in ways analogous to their own cognitive representations;
- support the use of concept maps for personal knowledge management.

Overall, enhancing concept maps by allowing them to access and incorporate any type of digitized information offers learners the opportunity to obtain a full and deep understanding of the domain of interest. It seems appropriate to sum up this chapter visually: Fig. 4 portrays the capabilities discussed in this chapter and their high-level rationale. This figure graphically portrays the types of knowledge and information concept maps should, and Webster does, make available to learners to capitalize on both knowledge and information visualization as educational tools.

Acknowledgments. Lotus® is a registered trademark of Lotus Software. Microsoft® is a registered trademark of the Microsoft Corporation. Shockwave™ and Flash™ are trademarks of Macromedia, Inc. Java® is a registered trademark of Sun Microsystems, Inc. Inspiration® is a registered trademark of Inspiration Software, Inc. Decision Explorer® is a registered trademark of Banxia Software Ltd. Semantica® is a registered trademark of Semantic Research, Inc.

References

Alpert, S.R. (2003). Abstraction in Concept Map and Coupled Outline Knowledge Representations. Journal of Interactive Learning Research, 14(1), 31-49.

Alpert, S.R., & Grueneberg, K. (2001). Multimedia in Concept Maps: A Design Rationale and Web-Based Application. In C. Montgomerie & J. Viteli (Eds.), *Proceedings of Ed-Media 2001: World Conference on Educational Multimedia, Hypermedia and Telecommunications* (pp. 31-36). Charlottesville (VA): Association for the Advancement of Computing in Education.

Alpert, S.R., & Grueneberg, K. (2000). Concept Mapping with Multimedia on the Web. *Journal of Educational Multimedia and Hypermedia, 9*(4), 313-330.

Anderson, J. R. (2000). *Cognitive Psychology and Its Implications (5th Edition)*. New York, NY: Worth.

Baddeley, A. (1982). Domains of recollection. *Psychological Review, 89*, 708-729.

Bomus, A. (2001). Personal communication.

Chandler, P., & Sweller, J. (1991). Cognitive load theory and the format of instruction. *Cognition and Instruction, 8*, 293-332.

Clark, R.C., & Mayer, R.E. (2003). *e-Learning and the Science of Instruction: Proven Guidelines for Consumers and Designers of Multimedia Learning*. San Francisco: Pfeiffer.

CompuServe (1990). CompuServe Corporation GIF89a specification, http://www.w3.org/Graphics/GIF/spec-gif89a.txt.

Dowling, W.L., & Harwood, D.L. (1986). *Music Cognition*. Orlando, FL: Academic Press.

Faraday, P., & Sutcliffe, A. (1999). Authoring animated Web pages using "contact points." In *Proceedings of CHI'99* (pp. 458-465). New York, NY: ACM.

Faraday, P., & Sutcliffe, A. (1997). Designing effective multimedia presentations. In *Proceedings of CHI'97* (pp. 272-278). New York, NY: ACM.

Fisher, K.M. (1992). SemNet: A tool for personal knowledge construction. In P.A.M. Kommers, D.H. Jonassen, & J.T. Mayes (Eds.), *Cognitive Technologies for Learning* (pp. 63-75). Berlin: Springer-Verlag.

Flores-Méndez, R.A. (1997). Java concept maps for the learning web. In B. Collis, & R. Oliver (Eds.), *Proceedings of ED-MEDIA'97*. Charlottesville, VA: AACE. Also http://www.cpsc.ucalgary.ca/~robertof/publications/edmedia97.

Heeren, E., & Kommers, P.A.M. (1992). Flexibility of expressiveness: A critical factor in the design of concept mapping tools for learning. In P.A.M. Kommers, D.H. Jonassen, & J.T. Mayes (Eds.), *Cognitive Technologies for Learning* (pp. 85-101). Berlin: Springer-Verlag.

Johnson-Laird, P.N. (1983). *Mental Models*. Cambridge, UK: Cambridge University Press.

Jonassen, D.H. (1992). Semantic networking as cognitive tools. In P.A.M. Kommers, D.H. Jonassen, & J.T. Mayes (Eds.), *Cognitive Technologies for Learning* (pp. 19-21). Berlin: Springer-Verlag.

Jonassen, D.H., Beissner, K., & Yacci, M.A. (1993). *Structural knowledge: Techniques for representing, conveying, and acquiring structural knowledge*. Hillsdale, NJ: Erlbaum.

Kaput, J.J. (1989). Linking Representations in the Symbol Systems of Algebra. In S. Wagner, & C. Kieran (Eds.), *Research agenda for mathematics education: Research Issues in the Learning and Teaching of Algebra* (pp. 167-194). Reston, VA: National Council of Teachers of Mathematics.

Kaye, J. (2004). Making scents: Aromatic output for HCI. *ACM interactions, 11*(1), 48-61.

Kommers, P.A.M., & DeVries, S.A. (1992). TextVision and the visualization of knowledge: School-based evaluation of its acceptance at two levels of schooling. In P.A.M. Kommers, D.H. Jonassen, & J.T. Mayes (Eds.), *Cognitive Technologies for Learning* (pp. 33-62). Berlin: Springer-Verlag.

Kosslyn, S.M. (1980). *Image and Mind*. Cambridge, MA: Harvard University Press.

Kozma, R.B. (1992). Constructing knowledge with Learning Tool. In P.A.M. Kommers, D.H. Jonassen, & J.T. Mayes (Eds.), *Cognitive Technologies for Learning* (pp. 23-32). Berlin: Springer-Verlag.

Larkin, J.H., & Simon, H.A. (1987). Why a diagram is (sometimes) worth ten thousand words. *Cognitive Science, 11*, 65-100.

Lee, A.Y., & Bowers, A.N. (1997). The effect of multimedia components on learning. In *Proceedings of the Human Factors and Ergonomics Society 41st Annual Meeting (Vol. 1.)* (pp. 340-344). Santa Monica, CA: Human Factors and Ergonomics Society.

Mayer, R.E. (2001). *Multimedia Learning*. New York, NY: Cambridge University Press.

Mayer, R. E., & Gallini, J. K. (1990). When is an illustration worth ten thousand words? *Journal of Educational Psychology, 82*, 715-726.

Mayer, R. E., & Sims, V. K. (1994). For whom is a picture worth a thousand words? Extensions of a dual-coding theory of multimedia learning. *Journal of Educational Psychology, 86*, 389-401.

McAleese, R. (1992). Cognitive tools: The experience of CASP, NoteCards, SemNet. In P.A.M. Kommers, D.H. Jonassen, & J.T. Mayes (Eds.), *Cognitive Technologies for Learning* (pp. 77-83). Berlin: Springer-Verlag.

Moore, P.J., & Skinner, M.J. (1985). The effects of illustrations on children's comprehension of abstract and concrete passages. *Journal of Research in Reading, 8*, 45-56.

Novak, J.D. (1999). *Learning, Creating, and Using Knowledge: Concept Maps as Facilitative Tools in Schools and Corporations*. Mahwah, NJ: Lawrence Erlbaum Associates.

Oakley, I., McGee, M.R., Brewster, S., & Gray, P. (2000). Putting the feel in 'Look and Feel'. In *Proceedings of ACM CHI 2000* (pp. 415-422). The Hague: ACM Press.

Paivio, A. (1986). *Mental Representations: A Dual Coding Approach*. New York: Oxford University Press.

Quillian, M.R. (1968). Semantic memory. In M. Minsky (Ed.), *Semantic Information Processing* (pp. 227-270). Cambridge, MA: MIT Press.

Reader, W., & Hammond, N. (1994). Computer-based tools to support learning. *Computers and Education, 22*(1/2), 99-106.

Rich, E. (1983). *Artificial Intelligence*. New York, NY: McGraw-Hill.

Shephard, R.N. (1967). Recognition memory for words, sentences, and pictures. *Journal of Verbal Learning and Verbal Behaviour, 6*, 156-163.

Tuomi, I. (1999). Data is more than knowledge: Implications of the reversed knowledge hierarchy for knowledge management and organizational memory. *Journal of Management Information, 16*(3), 107-121. Also http://www.jrc.es/~tuomiil/articles/DataIsMore.pdf.

Towards a Framework and a Model for Knowledge Visualization: Synergies Between Information and Knowledge Visualization

Remo Aslak Burkhard

University of St. Gallen, Blumenbergplatz 9,
CH-9000 St. Gallen, Switzerland
Remo.Burkhard@unisg.ch

Abstract. This article presents synergies between the research areas information visualization and knowledge visualization from a knowledge management and a communication science perspective. It presents a first theoretical framework and a model for the new field of knowledge visualization. It describes guidelines and principles derived from our professional practice and previous research on how architects successfully use complementary visualizations to transfer and create knowledge among individuals from different social, cultural, and educational backgrounds. The findings and insights are important for researchers and practitioners in the fields of information visualization, knowledge visualization, knowledge management, information design, media didactics, instructional psychology, and communication sciences.

1 Introduction: Knowledge Visualization in Organizations

This article illustrates the difference between the research areas information visualization (Card, Mackinlay & Shneiderman, 1999; Chen, 1999; Spence, 2000; Ware, 2000) and knowledge visualization (Burkhard, 2004a; Eppler & Burkhard, 2004) from a knowledge management (Alavi & Leidner, 2001) and a communication science (Fiske, 1982) perspective, and aims to illustrate synergies for both fields. To do so, it introduces a *Knowledge Visualization Framework*, a *Knowledge Visualization Model*, and the concept of *complementary visualizations*.

First, this article illustrates related insights from the field of business knowledge management. This section extends the previous contributions in this book with an additional perspective: The organizational perspective.

Second, it presents insights from the field of cognitive neuroscience of vision (Farah, 2000) and visual perception (Goldstein, 2001; Ware, 2000). This section aims to get a deeper understanding of our powerful innate abilities to process visual representations.

Third, it discusses the differences between the research areas information visualization and knowledge visualization from an organizational perspective and introduces an effective concept of architects to create and transfer knowledge: *complementary visualizations* (Burkhard, 2004a, b).

S.-O. Tergan and T. Keller (Eds.): Knowledge and Information Visualization, LNCS 3426, pp. 238–255, 2005.
© Springer-Verlag Berlin Heidelberg 2005

Fourth, based on the analysis how architects use complementary visualizations to create and share knowledge, the key features for knowledge visualization are derived which allows to propose a first conceptual framework for the field knowledge visualization. The framework consists of four perspectives, and aims to mediate among different research areas and to illustrate how information visualization and knowledge visualization complement one another.

Fifth, this article introduces a first *Knowledge Visualization Model*. The model identifies and relates the salient features in knowledge visualization and complements established models in communication sciences. Further, guidelines for practitioners are discussed.

Finally, this article describes the potential of knowledge visualization for information visualization, both in the larger context of knowledge creation and knowledge transfer.

In concluding, the framework, the model, and the concept of complementary visualizations are the first theoretical approaches that structure the domain of knowledge visualization. The findings and results from this article are relevant for researchers and practitioners in the domain of information visualization, knowledge visualization, information design, knowledge management, media didactics, instructional psychology, and communication sciences.

2   Information Visualization Can Learn from Knowledge Management

Knowledge Management is a management perspective that offers theories, strategies, and methods to manage, i.e., to identify, access, share, and create knowledge in organizations, with the aim to help an organization to compete by being more innovative, effective, and thus more profitable.

Knowledge Management has its roots in organizational learning (Argyris & Schön, 1978; Fiol & Lyles, 1985; Senge, 1990), strategic management, and information science. The *knowledge-based theory* sees knowledge as a key productive and strategic resource, which is embedded in an organizational culture, in systems, documents, and individuals. The knowledge-based theory is described by various researchers (Grant, 1996; Nonaka, 1991; Nonaka & Takeuchi, 1995; Spender, 1996).

As a result of the knowledge-based perspective, research and management practice has become more knowledge-focused, e.g., through establishing knowledge cultures, implementing knowledge strategies, introducing knowledge audits, communities of practice, and knowledge management systems, or sharing lessons learned from project debriefings.

In the past, different knowledge management strategies have been introduced and established. But these strategies and perceptions differ depending on the understanding of knowledge. If knowledge is viewed as an *object*, knowledge management aims to build information repositories. If knowledge is understood as a *process*, the focus is on optimizing the knowledge-intense processes, e.g., identifying, creating, and sharing knowledge. Knowledge seen as a *capability* focuses on the strategic advantage of knowledge, to build core competencies, and to create intellectual capital. If knowledge is seen as a condition of *access* to information, then knowledge management focuses on methods to identify, retrieve, and gain access to information. Finally, if knowledge is seen as a *state* of knowing and understanding, knowledge management supports individuals to expand their knowledge.

In spite of these diverging understandings of knowledge, all perspectives have in common, that knowledge management is seen as a dynamic and continuous task, with three main objectives: (1) to optimize business processes from a knowledge perspective, (2) to introduce systems for storing, identifying, retrieving, and gaining access to information, and supporting individuals to collaborate, (3) to develop a corporate knowledge culture that motivates employees to envision, create, and share knowledge, alone, in teams, or across units and regions.

The main processes in knowledge management can be divided into four processes (Alavi & Leidner, 2001): (1) the creation, (2) the storage and retrieval, (3) the transfer, and (4) the application of knowledge. However, this article concentrates on the process of transferring knowledge, because this process is an important process and a process that has been neglected by information visualization researchers. Thus, they can learn from knowledge management by expanding their focus from the creation of knowledge to the creation and transfer of knowledge.

The transfer of knowledge is a core process in knowledge management and difficult to manage (Probst, Raub & Romhardt, 1997). The transfer of knowledge occurs at various levels: Among individuals, from individuals to groups, among groups, among individuals/groups and an organization. Based on Gupta and Govindarajan (2000) five elements for a successful knowledge transfer can be distinguished: (1) the perceived value of the sender's knowledge, (2) the motivation and willingness of the sender to share his knowledge, (3) the existence and richness of transmission channels, (4) the motivation of the recipient to acquire knowledge from the sender, and (5) the absorptive capacity of the recipient, i.e., the ability not only to acquire but also to use knowledge. To do so, knowledge must be recreated by the receiver, which brings us to the challenge: Individuals who need to transfer knowledge to one or more individuals, from the same or different backgrounds, not only need to convey the relevant knowledge, but also need to convey it in the right context, so it can be used and applied.

Concluding, the process of knowledge transfer is a key process for knowledge-intense organizations and faces various problems. But luckily, for exactly this challenging process we have a very powerful and yet rarely used skill that can be exploited: Our innate ability to effectively process visual representations.

3 Our Innate Abilities to Process Visual Representations

A majority of our brain's activity deals with processing and analyzing visual images. To understand perception, it is important to remember that our brain does not differ greatly from our ancestors, the troglodytes. At that time, perception helped for basic functions, for example for hunting (motion detection), seeking food (color detection), or applying tools (object-shape perception).

To comprehend visual perception, the Gestalt Principles (Ellis, 1938; Koffka, 1935) are helpful to understand how we perceive groups of objects or parts of objects, by identifying various perceptual phenomena. The Gestalt Principles provide descriptive insights into form and pattern perception. But unfortunately they do not offer explanations of these phenomena. To understand how or why we perceive forms and patterns, we need to consider explanatory theories of perception. But before we come to these theories it is introduced how visual information is being processed (Farah, 2000; Goldstein, 2001; Gregory, 1998; Ware, 2000).

Visual information processing can be divided into two stages: In the first stage, information is parallel processed in the eye and the primary visual cortex, where individual neurons in specific areas (called V1, V2, V3, V4, MT) are specialized to identify particular features (e.g., orientation, color, texture, contour, or motion). At this early stage information processing proceeds pre-attentively and very rapidly. In the second stage, information processing is divided into two functionally independent complementary subsystems, "*two cortical visual systems*" in the terminology of Ungerleider and Mishkin (1982): One visual subsystem is more important for object identification (~what) and the other for spatial localization (~where).

But these findings from visual information processing do not explain yet how we visually perceive form. This subject is being investigated by visual perception research (Goldstein, 2001; Ware, 2000), where two complementary theoretical approaches exist: bottom-up (*direct perception*) and top-down (*constructive perception*) theories:

Direct perception (bottom-up) believes that all the information we need to perceive is in the sensory input we receive. Three main bottom-up approaches can be differentiated: (1) The *template-matching theory* states that we have highly detailed templates of patterns stored in our mind, (2) the *prototype-matching theory* believes in classes of prototypes with the most typical features of a pattern, (3) and the *feature-matching theories* suggest that we match features (i.e., line orientation) of a pattern to features stored in memory.

Constructive perception (top-down) (Bruner, 1957; Gregory, 1980; Rock, 1983) in contrast believes that an individual's perception is based on the combination of sensory information with prior knowledge and previous experience.

Above I introduced the theoretical background of visual image processing and visual perception. This background can be important to understand when we want to exploit our innate abilities to process visual representations. Next, several functions of visual representations are discussed. Visual representations help for instance (1) to address emotions, (2) illustrate relations, (3) discover trends, patterns, outliers, (4) to get and keep the attention of recipients, (5) to support remembrance and recall, (6) to present both an overview and details, (7) to facilitate learning, (8) to coordinate individuals, (9) to motivate people and establish a mutual story, or (10) to energize people and initiate actions by illustrating options to act.

Several studies prove the power of visualizations with regard to these functions. Some examples: (1) Miller (1956) reports that a human's input channel capacity is greater when visual abilities are used. (2) Our brain has a strong ability to identify patterns, which is examined in Gestalt psychology (Ellis, 1938; Koffka, 1935). (3) Visual imagery (Kosslyn, 1980; Shepard & Cooper, 1982) suggest that visual recall seems to be better than verbal recall. Yet, it is not clear how images are stored and recalled, but it is clear that humans have a natural ability to use images. (4) Several empirical studies show that visual representations are superior to verbal-sequential representations in different tasks (Bauer & Johnson-Laird, 1993; Glenberg & Langston,

1992; Larkin & Simon, 1987; Novick, 2001). (5) Instructional psychology and media didactics investigate the learning outcomes in knowledge acquisition from text and pictures (Mandl & Levin, 1989), or Weidenmann (1989) who explores aspects of illustrations in the learning process.

This section introduced the theoretical background to help understand, how our innate abilities to process visual representations can be exploited to create and share insights. Understanding these abilities further, allows to distinguish the concept of information visualization versus knowledge visualization, which both exploit this potential, but in different ways.

4 The Difference Between Information Visualization and Knowledge Visualization

In Burkhard (2004a) the first definition of knowledge visualization was introduced, which allowed to discuss the difference between knowledge visualization and information visualization. This first definition also helped to differentiate knowledge visualization and knowledge domain visualization (Börner & Chen, 2002; Chen, 2003). Today the following definition of knowledge visualization is being accepted by information visualization, knowledge visualization, and knowledge domain visualization experts: "*Knowledge Visualization examines the use of visual representations to improve the transfer and creation of knowledge between at least two persons*". (Burkhard, 2004a; Burkhard & Meier, 2004; Eppler & Burkhard, 2004).

Information visualization is a rapidly advancing field of study both in terms of academic research and practical applications. Early information visualization proponents created static paper based visualizations (i.e., a map or a drawing) (Bertin, 1967; Tufte, 1983, 1990, 1997), but recently the research area information visualization is being claimed by a more computer-based community (Card et al., 1999; Chen, 1999; Spence, 2000; Ware, 2000), which define information visualization, as "*... the use of computer-supported, interactive, visual representations of abstract data to amplify cognition*" (Card et al., 1999). This definition is well established and represents a consensus among computer scientists active in this field.

However, four limitations can be identified: First, non-computer based visualizations disappeared from the research field information visualization. Second, knowledge types (e.g., insights, experiences, tacit knowledge) that cannot be put into a digital carrier (i.e., a database) were ignored. Third, the role of the recipient was not studied enough. Fourth, applying the new methods to knowledge and business processes, and real problems, was not investigated systematically.

These issues were the starting point for a new research direction: Knowledge visualization. Researchers in this field therefore often have a background in knowledge management, psychology, didactics, architecture, or communication studies.

In general, researchers in the fields of information visualization and knowledge visualization are both exploiting our innate abilities to effectively process visual representations; but the way of using these abilities differs in both domains. Next, I try to differentiate the fields by discussing ten differences concerning the goals, origin, and techniques of both fields.

4.1 Goal: Knowledge Creation Versus Knowledge Transfer

1.*Goal.* Information visualization aims to use computer-supported visual applications for exploratory tasks in large amounts of data, with the goal of getting new insights. Knowledge visualization, in contrast, aims to use one or more visual representations with the goal to improve the transfer of knowledge among people and to improve the creation of knowledge in groups.

2.*Benefit.* Information visualization aims to improve information access, retrieval and exploration of large data sets. Knowledge visualization, in contrast, aims at augmenting knowledge-intensive processes (e.g., knowledge transfer, communication) among individuals by using one ore more visual representations.

3.*Content.* Information visualization concentrates on explicit data such as facts or numbers, while knowledge visualization also cares for other knowledge types, such as experiences, insights, instructions, assumptions - knowledge types that answer questions such as why, who, or how.

4.*Recipients.* Information visualization typically supports an individual to get new insights. Knowledge visualization, in contrast, concentrates on supporting individuals or a group of individuals to transfer knowledge and to create new knowledge in collaborative settings.

5.*Influence.* Information visualization provides new insights for the fields of information science, data mining, data analysis, and for problems such as information exploration, information retrieval, human-computer interaction, interface design. Knowledge visualization provides new insights for the fields of visual communication science, knowledge management, and for problems such as knowledge exploration, -transfer, -creation, -application, learning, information quality, information overload, design, interface design, visual communication. However, some of these points also apply to information visualization.

4.2 Origin: Computer Science Versus Architecture

6.*Proponents.* Information visualization researchers typically have a background in computer science. Knowledge visualization researchers, in contrast, mainly have a background in knowledge management, psychology, design, or architecture.

7.*Contribution.* Information visualization is more innovation-oriented; researchers in this field mainly create new technical methods. Knowledge visualization is more solution-oriented and tries to apply such novel, but also traditional visualization methods, to solve predominant problems. Only if no method exists or works, they invent a new method. Knowledge visualization is integrative and offers urgently needed theoretical structures for the whole field of visualization research, with the aim to improve collaboration among these isolated fields.

8.*Roots*: Information visualization is a young field of research that became only possible with the introduction of computers. Knowledge visualization is an even newer term, but grounded in cultural and intellectual achievements, e.g., of architects and philosophers, which use complementary visual representations to transfer and create knowledge, e.g., Aristotle on the power of metaphors in (Eco, 1984). Namely the practice of architects to use complementary visualization is a source for further investigations with relevance for knowledge management, communication science, and information visualization researchers. Because of three reasons: (1) Architects combine, structure, and integrate different concepts. (2) Architects intuitively use complementary visualizations for knowledge-intense tasks. (3) Architects are experts in interfunctional communication (e.g., among decision makers, site constructors, local authorities). (4) Architects constantly think in and switch among different conceptual levels (e.g., urban scale or detail of a house).

4.3 Technique: Interactive Applications Versus All Visual Representations

9.*Means.* Information visualization uses computer-supported methods. Knowledge visualization, in contrast, uses computer-support, but also non-computer supported visualization methods, like early information visualization proponents, architects, artists, or designers use them.

10.*Complementary Visualizations.* Information visualization combines different visualization methods using the same medium in one interface, by tightly coupling them; this concept is called *multiple coordinated views*. Knowledge visualization combines different visualization methods using one and/or different media (e.g., a software, a poster, or a physical object) with the aim to illustrate knowledge from different perspectives and to exploit different functions of visual representations. In knowledge visualization this concept is called *complementary visualizations.* Complementary visualizations are defined as the use of at least two visual representations that complement each other to augment knowledge-intense processes. This concept is derived from the professional practice of architects and urban planners, who use complementary visualizations to envision, think, innovate, communicate, disseminate and document complex knowledge (Burkhard, 2004a, b).

This juxtaposition of ten points is not exclusive, and should rather be seen as a starting point for others to extend the arguments. It is a first attempt to find synergies for both fields by describing the individual strengths and weaknesses. The juxtaposition makes clear that information visualization and knowledge visualization can benefit from one another and together improve learning, or the creation and transfer of knowledge.

The next section discusses four perspectives that need to be considered when transfer and creation of knowledge are intended and should be optimized.

5 Structuring the Field: The Knowledge Visualization Framework

For an effective transfer and creation of knowledge through visualizations, four perspectives (Fig. 1) should be considered, based on four relevant questions:

- Why should knowledge be visualized? (aim)
- What type of knowledge needs to be visualized? (content)
- Who is being addressed? (recipient)
- Which is the best method to visualize this knowledge? (medium)

These key questions lead to the Knowledge Visualization Framework, which is grounded in previous frameworks (Burkhard, 2004a; Eppler & Burkhard, 2004) as seen in Fig. 1.

FUNCTION	KNOWLEDGE TYPE	RECIPIENT	VISUALIZATION TYPE
Coordination	Know-what	Individual	Sketch
Attention	Know-how	Group	Diagram
Recall	Know-why	Organization	Image
Motivation	Know-where	Network	Map
Elaboration	Know-who		Object
New Insight			Interactive Visualization
			Story

Fig. 1. The Knowledge Visualization Framework consists of four perspectives that need to be considered when creating visual representations that aim to transfer and create knowledge: A *function perspective* answers why a visualization should be used, a *knowledge type perspective* clarifies the nature of the content, a *recipient type perspective* points to the different backgrounds of the recipient/audience, and finally the *visualization type perspective* structures the main visualization types according to their individual characteristics

5.1 The Function Perspective

The Function Perspective distinguishes six functions of visual representations that can be exploited. The social, emotional, and cognitive functions of visualizations can be summarized in the CARMEN-Acronym (Eppler & Burkhard, 2004):

- *Coordination.* Visual representations help to coordinate individuals in the communication process (e.g., Knowledge maps, visual tools for collaboration, heuristic sketches).
- *Attention.* Visual representations allow to get the attention by addressing emotions (e.g., advertising), to keep the attention (e.g., sketching on a flipchart) by identifying patterns, outliers and trends (e.g., information visualization).
- *Recall.* Visual representations improve memorability, remembrance and recall, because we think in images, (e.g., visual metaphor, stories, conceptual diagrams).
- *Motivation.* Visual representations inspire, motivate, energize, and activate viewers (e.g., knowledge maps, mutual stories, instructive diagrams).
- *Elaboration.* Visual representations foster the elaboration of knowledge in teams (e.g., discussing scenarios of a new product by the use of heuristic sketches or a physical model).
- *New Insights.* Visual representations support the creation of new insights by embedding details in context and showing relationships between objects (e.g., information visualization) or lead to a-ha effects (e.g., visual metaphors).

5.2 The Knowledge Type Perspective

The Knowledge Type Perspective aims to identify the type of knowledge that needs to be transferred. Such different types of knowledge are investigated in the field of knowledge management. For our framework, five types of knowledge are distinguished: Declarative knowledge (Know-what, e.g., facts), procedural knowledge

(Know-how, e.g., processes), experimental knowledge (Know-why, e.g., causes), orientational knowledge (Know-where, e.g., knowledge sources), individual knowledge (Know-who, e.g., experts). Today no classification exists that links visualization types to knowledge types.

5.3 The Recipient Type Perspective

The Recipient Type Perspective aims to identify the target group and the context of the recipient which can be an individual, a team, a whole organization or a network of persons. Knowing the context and the cognitive background of the recipient/audience is essential for finding the right visualization method for the transfer of knowledge. Except from human computer interaction researchers (HCI) who focus on task analysis and ethnographic user studies, academic researchers in information design and information visualization do not focus on the Recipient Type perspective.

5.4 Visualization Type Perspective

The Visualization Type Perspective structures the visualization methods into seven main groups: Sketches, Diagrams, Images, Maps, Objects, Interactive visualizations, and Stories. These seven types are grounded and derived from the seven visualization methods architects use to transfer and create knowledge (Burkhard, 2004a). Each visualization type has particular strengths and weaknesses that are discussed next:

Sketches represent the main idea, are atmospheric, and help to quickly visualize an idea (Fig. 2 and 3). Sketches are used to assist the group reflection and communication process by making knowledge explicit and debatable.

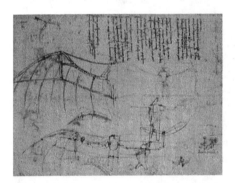

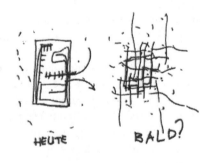

Fig. 2. A sketch from Leonardo da Vinci represents the main idea of a new concept [1]

Fig. 3. Various sketches helped to assist the group reflection processes in a workshop for new ideas [2]

For the transfer and creation of knowledge, sketches have five strengths: (1) sketches represent the main idea and key features of a preliminary study and support reasoning and arguing. (2) They are atmospheric, versatile, and universally accessible.

[1] Retrieved on the 20th of August 2004 from http://www.visi.com/~reuteler/vinci/fly3.jpg
[2] ETH Science City: http://www.sciencecity.ethz.ch

(3) They are fast to create, and help to quickly visualize an idea. (4) They keep the attention (e.g., the use of a pen on a flipchart attracts the attention towards the communicator). (5) Sketches allow room for own interpretations and foster the creativity in groups.

Diagrams by contrast are abstract, schematic representations used to explore structural relationships among parts (Fig. 4). Garland (1979) defines a diagram as a "*visual language sign having the primary purpose of denoting function and/or relationship*". The type of knowledge that is conveyed by diagrams is analytic; diagrams are therefore structured and systematic.

Fig. 4. Diagrams are schematic depictions of abstract ideas that use standardized shapes to structure information and illustrate relations

For the transfer and creation of knowledge, diagrams help to make abstract concepts accessible, help to reduce complexity, amplify cognition, explain causal relationships, structure information, and to discuss relationships.

Apart from established diagrams (Fig. 4) new types of diagrams are currently being developed for the transfer and creation of knowledge in teams. This is done again by architects and urban planners. Why? When it comes to complex factors, such as social, cultural, or economic factors in urban planning, the diagrams discussed above are not suitable to create new insights and to transfer such insights. Therefore architects and urban planners were forced to develop new types of diagrams that allow to illustrate a higher complexity or to represent more variables in a single diagram. Today, almost every leading architecture or urban planning office[3] in the world has developed their own visual diagramming language for knowledge-intense processes.

Maps follow cartographic conventions to reference knowledge. A map generally consists of two elements: A ground layer represents the context (e.g., a network of experts, a project, a city) and individual elements (e.g., experts, project milestones, roads). In the context of knowledge management, maps are called knowledge maps. They illustrate both an overview and details, and interrelationships among these details. Thus knowledge maps are graphic directories of knowledge-sources, -assets, -structures, or -processes. However, knowledge maps can also be fictitious and address visions, or stories, for example to establish a mutual context in an organization. Fig. 5

---

[3] Examples: Asymptote Architecture (www.asymptote-architecture.com), Morphosis (www.morphosis.net), MVRDV (http://www.mvrdv.archined.nl), The Office for Metropolitan Architecture OMA with its research department AMO (www.oma.nl), Eisenman Architects, (www.eisenmanarchitects.com) or the UN Studio (www.unstudio.com).

presents a fictitious map that improved interfunctional communication of a complex project in an organization, based on the power of visual metaphors.

For the transfer and creation of knowledge, maps help to present the overview and the details, to structure information, to motivate and activate employees, to establish a common story, and to ease access to information.

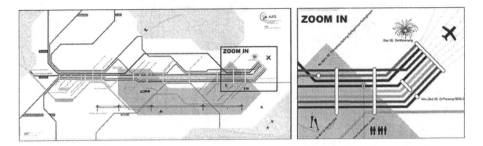

Fig. 5. The *tube map visualization*[4] is an example where a fictitious map was transferred into a business context to improve interfunctional communication in a complex project. The ground layer used the metaphor of a subway system, shown as a tubemap. The individual elements are subway lines (=target groups) and project milestones (=stations)

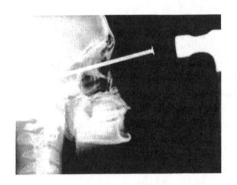

Fig. 6. Images address emotions and are widely used in advertising[5]

Fig. 7. Images can clarify complex projects and motivate different stakeholders[6]

Images are impressive, expressive, or represent reality. Images address emotions and they are inspiring, appealing, motivating, and energizing. Thus, they are widely used as a key instrument in advertising (Fig. 6). Images can be grasped and recalled in less than a second and sometimes be remembered for decades (i.e., key-images of the war in Vietnam or Iraq). The same effects can be used for the transfer of business related knowledge, e.g., by using visual metaphors (Fig. 7). *"To convert tacit knowledge into explicit knowledge means finding a way to express the inexpressible. Unfor-*

---

[4] Copyright of the tube map visualization: http://www.vasp.ch
[5] Image for a seminar on the effective use of visualizations: http://www.2sekmanager.ch
[6] ETH Science City: http://www.sciencecity.ethz.ch

tunately, one of the most powerful management tools for doing so is also among the most frequently overlooked: the store of figurative language and symbolism that managers can draw from to articulate their intuitions and insights" (Nonaka, 1991). Visual metaphors support remembrance, lead to a-ha effects, support reasoning, and communication. They are instant and rapid, highly instructive, and facilitate learning. The potential of visual metaphors is discussed in (Eppler, 2003).

For the transfer of knowledge, images help to get the attention (e.g., advertising), inspire recipients (e.g., art), address emotions (e.g., advertising), improve recall (i.e., signs, visual metaphors), or initiate discussions (e.g., satirical comic).

Fig. 8. Objects in this Info-Structure attract people[7]

Fig. 9. Objects and images complement each other, e.g., in an exhibition

Objects in Space exploit the third dimension and allow experiencing materials. Objects in space are helpful for example for information points (Fig. 8), knowledge fairs, or exhibitions (Fig. 9) to complement physical and digital visualizations and to show the content from different points of view.

For the transfer of knowledge, objects help to attract recipients, support learning through constant presence, or allow to integrate digital interfaces.

Interactive Visualizations allow to access, explore, and make sense of different types of information. An example of a visualization application[8] (Fig. 10) allows to explore the data of a survey on the project ETH Science City. This application allows to filter the result sets by using different sliders and is based on previous work, e.g., described in (Brodbeck & Girardin, 2003). Another application, the Infoticle application (Vande Moere, Mieusset & Gross, 2004) uses data-driven particles (*Infoticles*) to explore large time-varying datasets with reoccurring data objects that alter in time in an immersive environment (Fig. 11). Animating these Infoticles leads to an animation that allows to see the behavior of individual data entries or the global context of the whole dataset.

---

[7] Fig. 8 and 9: ETH Science City: http://www.sciencecity.ethz.ch
[8] http://www.macrofocus.com

To transfer knowledge, interactive visualizations help to fascinate people, enable interactive collaborations across time and space, allow to represent and explore complex data, or to create new insights.

Stories, the last visualization type, are imaginary (not physical) visualizations that are efficient in transferring and disseminating knowledge across time and space. The use of stories, called storytelling, allows to transport an illustrative mental image by the use of spoken or written language and can be used in organizational practice (Loebbert, 2003).

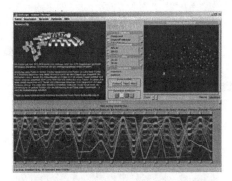

Fig. 10. An interactive visualization allows to get new insights by visually exploring data of a survey based on the method described in (Brodbeck & Girardin, 2003)[9]

Fig. 11. The Infoticle application allows to explore large time-varying datasets in an immersive environment (Vande Moere et al., 2004)[10]

To transfer knowledge, imaginary visualizations complement the other six visual formats and are valuable to establish a shared vision, a mutual story, to motivate and activate individuals.

6 Synthesis: The Knowledge Visualization Model

The analysis of the previous examples and the argumentation has shown that the use of visual representations can serve for different functions, and is an effective strategy for the transfer and creation of knowledge. However, choosing the right format demands skills and experience. To assist practitioners and to mediate among different fields, a first conceptual model is introduced next. The model identifies and relates the features that contribute most to a successful behavior when complementary visualizations are used to transfer and create knowledge.

Such a *Knowledge Visualization Model* is needed for three reasons: First, communication science models (Gerbner, 1956; Jakobson, 1960; Lasswell, 1948; Newcomb, 1953; Shannon & Weaver, 1949) are too general with regard to the use of visual representations. Second, visualization scientists do not offer a holistic model for the

---

[9] http://www.macrofocus.com
[10] http://blue-c.ethz.ch

transfer and creation of knowledge with visual representations. Third, it complements the Knowledge Visualization Framework and together can achieve the goals of knowledge visualization discussed above.

6.1 The Knowledge Visualization Model

The *Knowledge Visualization Model* (Fig. 12) is divided into three parts: a sender, a medium, and a recipient. These three parts are all interlinked in an interaction and communication loop.

The model describes inter- and intrapersonal iterative processes: The process starts with a *sender* who wants to transfer some of his knowledge (*knowledge*) to a *recipient*. His mental model of this knowledge (*mental model sender*) is being externalized into various explicit and *complementary visual representations*, which can be divided into three sub processes (*1, 2, 3*) following a temporal sequence: First, the sender needs to get the *attention* (*1*) of the recipient, for instance by using a provocative image. Second, the sender needs to illustrate the *context* (*2*), provide an *overview* (*2*), and present *options to act* (*2*). Only then the sender can point to selected *details* (*3*), which ideally happens in a dynamic dialog with the recipient (*D*), who re-constructs (*C*) similar knowledge (*Knowledge'*) with these complementary visualizations and an own mental image (*mental model recipient*). But due to different assumptions, believes, or backgrounds, inferences and misinterpretations can occur (*E*), which can lead to a failure of the knowledge re-construction. In this process, the sender iteratively refines or adds further visual representations (*F*), until the knowledge transfer process was successful.

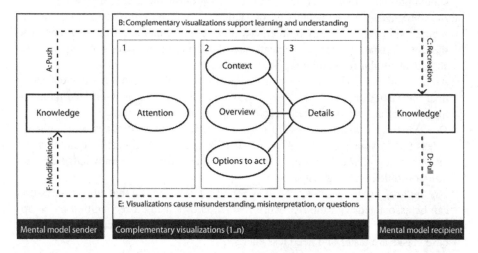

Fig. 12. The Knowledge Visualization Model with a sender, a recipient and complementary visualizations as a medium

The model introduces the salient features that need to be considered when complementary visual representations are used to transfer or create knowledge. Next, I discuss ten principles that should be considered when applying this model.

6.2 Guidelines for Applying the Knowledge Visualization Model

To design effective visualizations, different principles should be considered. These principles are derived from our practical work[11]:

1. *Know your data.* A designer must first understand and evaluate the information that is the basis for a visualization, and decide whether the data is complete, reliable, and relevant.
2. *Know your audience.* A designer should be aware of the diversity of the audience, their different needs and various social, cultural and educational backgrounds. People think, understand, and solve problems in different ways. It is further important to know whether an individual, a group, an organization, or a network is being addressed.
3. *Prevent misinterpretation.* The visualization should prevent misuse, misinterpretation, or misunderstanding. It is important to address the context, to present an overview, and to present options for how the knowledge can be applied. Visualizations should further be combined with text to prevent misuse.
4. *Compress your knowledge.* To increase the information quality and prevent information overload, a designer should concentrate on the quality, rather than the quantity, and concentrate on the essence. Tufte suggests compressing as much information into an as small space as possible.
5. *Present an overview and details.* Shneiderman's Mantra *"overview first, zoom in and filter, then show details on demand"* (Shneiderman, 1996) for information visualization interfaces is also valid for knowledge visualization. A designer should present both an overview of the data, and allow the user to access details.
6. *Be consistent.* Complementary visualizations should be consistent. Consistent in regard to the logic, the way to interact with it (e.g., in interactive applications), and the use of visual elements. Elements such as color, shape, size, symbols, or fonts should be similar for similar types of data in all visualizations.
7. *Avoid decoration.* The visualization should cause thinking about the content rather than the visualization itself. Therefore one should be careful with decorations or the unnecessary use of elements such as clip-arts or strong colors.
8. *Don't distract your audience.* Do not use visualizations to distract your audience unless this is your intention. A lot of visualizations (i.e., clip arts) do nothing but divert the attention of the user, and distract the user from their knowledge acquisition or problem-solving tasks.
9. *Use natural representations.* Natural representations mean that the visualization can be associated with the real-world, which allows using a recognition-based approach instead of one that requires recall. This is important because recognition-based tasks are faster and need less energy.
10. *Motivate your audience.* Visual representations should be designed to envision, to cause thinking, and to encourage users to elaborate knowledge. Use imaginary visual representations to establish a shared vision.

---

[11] The author is a partner in a knowledge visualization company: vasp datatecture GmbH, www.vasp.ch

7   Conclusion: Architects Are Knowledge Visualization Experts

Knowledge visualization offers opportunities for synergies with the field of information visualization. Because (1) it extends the field with regard to other knowledge types, (2) knowledge processes other than information exploration (namely knowledge transfer and knowledge creation in groups), and (3) additional computer based and non-computer based visualization methods, (4) because it points to psychological, social, and cognitive factors of different recipients, and (5) integrates findings from other research fields such as knowledge management, communication science, architecture, or psychology.

Knowledge visualization is defined as *the use of complementary visual representations to transfer and create knowledge between at least two persons* and differs from the field of information visualization with regard to - among other points - the goals, means, and background of the proponents, as well as its roots.

This article presented both a theoretical framework and a theoretical model for the domain of knowledge visualization, and guidelines for practitioners to overcome the current intolerable situation, where individuals learn for years how to write and calculate, but not how to visually communicate. Further, this article explained how information visualization and knowledge visualization can learn from the expertise of architects, in regard to interfunctional communication, the use of complementary visualizations in collaborative innovation and design processes (collaborative knowledge creation), or new conceptual diagrams to map complexity.

In conclusion, the *Knowledge Visualization Framework*, the *Knowledge Visualization Model*, and the concept of *Complementary Visualizations* presented in this article are important to researchers and practitioners in the fields of information visualization, knowledge visualization, knowledge management, information design, media didactics, instructional psychology, and communication sciences.

References

Alavi, M., & Leidner, D. (2001). Knowledge Management and Knowledge Management Systems: Conceptual Foundations and Research Issues. *MIS Quarterly, 25*(1), 107-136.

Argyris, C., & Schön, D.A. (1978). *Organizational Learning: A Theory of Action Perspective.* Reading, MA: Addison-Wesley.

Bauer, M., & Johnson-Laird, P. (1993). How diagrams can improve reasoning. *Psychological Science, 4*(6), 372-378.

Bertin, J. (1967). *Sémiologie Graphique.* Paris: Gauthier-Villars.

Börner, K., & Chen, C. (Eds.). (2002). *Visual Interfaces to Digital Libraries.* LNCS 2539. Heidelberg: Springer-Verlag.

Brodbeck, D., & Girardin, L. (2003). Design Study: Using Multiple Coordinated Views to Analyze Geo-referenced High-dimensional Datasets. In *Proceedings of 2003 International Conference on Coordinated and Multiple Views in Exploratory Visualization* (pp. 104-111). London: IEEE.

Bruner, J.S. (1957). On perceptual readiness. *Psychological Review, 64*, 123-152.

Burkhard, R. (2004a). Learning from Architects: The Difference between Knowledge Visualization and Information Visualization. In Proceedings of *Eighth International Conference on Information Visualization (IV04)* (pp. 519-524). London: IEEE.

Burkhard, R. (2004b). Visual Knowledge Transfer between Planners and Business Decision Makers. In J.P. Van Leeuwen, & H.J.P. Timmermans (Eds.), *Developments in Design & Decision Support Systems in Architecture and Urban Planning* (pp. 193-208). Eindhoven: Eindhoven University of Technology.

Burkhard, R., & Meier, M. (2004). Tube Map: Evaluation of a Visual Metaphor for Interfunctional Communication of Complex Projects. In K. Tochtermann, & H. Maurer (Eds.), *Proceedings of I-KNOW '04* (pp. 449-456). Graz, Austria: Know-Center Austria.

Card, S.K., Mackinlay, J.D., & Shneiderman, B. (1999). *Readings in Information Visualization; Using Vision to think.* Los Altos, CA: Morgan Kaufmann.

Chen, C. (1999). *Information Visualisation and Virtual Environments.* London, UK: Springer.

Chen, C. (2003). *Mapping Scientific Frontiers: The Quest for Knowledge Visualization.* London, UK: Springer.

Ellis, W.D. (1938). *A Source Book of Gestalt Psychology.* New York: Harcourt, Brace & World.

Eppler, M., & Burkhard, R. (2004). *Knowledge Visualization. Towards a New Discipline and its Fields of Application.* Retrieved September, 5th, 2004, from http://www.netacademy.com

Eppler, M.J. (2003). The Image of Insight: The Use of Visual Metaphors in the Communication of Knowledge. In K. Tochtermann, & H. Maurer (Eds.), *Proceedings of I-KNOW '03* (pp. 81-88). Graz, Austria: Know Center.

Farah, M.J. (2000). *The cognitive neuroscience of vision.* Malden, MA: Blackwell Publishers.

Fiol, C.M., & Lyles, M. (1985). Organizational Learning. *Academy of Management Review, 10*(4), 803-813.

Fiske, J. (1982). Communication theory. In J. Fiske (Ed.), *Introduction to Communication Studies* (pp. 6-24). London/New York: Methuen.

Garland, K. (1979). Some General Characteristics Present in Diagrams Denoting Activity, Event and Relationship. *Information Design Journal, 1*(1), 15-22.

Gerbner, G. (1956). Toward a General Model of Communication. *Audio Visual Communication Review, 3*, 171-199.

Glenberg, A., & Langston, M. (1992). Comprehension of Illustrated Text: Pictures Help to Build Mental Models. *Journal of Memory and Language, 31*(2), 129-151.

Goldstein, B.E. (2001). *Sensation and Perception* (6th edition). Pacific Grove: Cole Publishing.

Grant, R.M. (1996). Toward a Knowledge-based Theory of the Firm. *Strategic Management Journal, 17*, 109-122.

Gregory, R.L. (1980). Perceptions as hypotheses. *Philosophical Transactions of the Royal Society of London, Series B, 290*, 181-197.

Gregory, R.L. (1998). *Eye and Brain. The Psychology of Seeing (5th edition).* Princeton, NJ: Princeton University Press.

Gupta, A., & Govindarajan, V. (2000). Knowledge Flows within Multinational Corporations. *Strategic Management Journal, 21*(4), 473-496.

Jakobson, R. (1960). Closing Statement: Linguistics and Poetics. In T.A. Sebeok (Ed.), *Style in language* (pp. 350-377). Cambridge, MA: The MIT Press.

Koffka, K. (1935). *The Principles of Gestalt Psychology.* New York: Harcourt, Brace & World.

Kosslyn, S.M. (1980). *Images and Mind.* Cambridge, MA: Harvard University Press.

Larkin, J., & Simon, H. (1987). Why a Diagram is (Sometimes) Worth Ten Thousand Words, *Cognitive Science, 11*, 65-99.

Lasswell, H. (1948). The structure and function of communication in society. In L. Bryson (Ed.), *The Communication of Ideas* (pp. 37-51). New York: Institute for Religious and Social Studies.

Loebbert, M. (2003). *Storymanagement - Der narrative Ansatz für Management und Beratung*, Stuttgart: Klett-Cotta.

Mandl, H., & Levin, J.R. (1989). *Knowledge Acquisition from Text and Pictures*. Amsterdam: North-Holland.

Miller, G.A. (1956). The magical number seven, plus or minus two: Some limits on our capacity for processing information. *Psychological Review, 63*, 81-97.

Newcomb, T. (1953). An approach to the study of communication acts. *Psychological Review, 60*, 393-40.

Nonaka, I. (1991). The Knowledge-Creating Company. *Harvard Business Review, 69*(6), 96-104.

Nonaka, I., & Takeuchi, H. (1995). *The Knowledge-Creating Company. How Japanese Companies Create the Dynamics of Innovation*. Oxford, UK: Oxford University Press.

Novick, L.R. (2001). Spatial diagrams: Key instruments in the toolbox for thought. In D.L. Medin (Ed.), *The psychology of learning and motivation*, Vol. 40 (pp. 279-325). San Diego, CA: Academic Press.

Probst, G., Raub, S., & Romhardt, K. (1997). *Wissen managen, Wie Unternehmen ihre wertvollste Ressource optimal nutzen*. Wiesbaden: Gabler/FAZ.

Rock, I.. (1983). *The logic of perception*. Cambridge, MA: MIT Press.

Senge, P. (1990). The Leader´s New Work: Building Learning Organizations. *Sloan Management Review*, Fall, 7-23.

Shannon, C., & Weaver, W. (1949). *The Mathematical Theory of Communication*. Urbana, IL: University of Illinois Press.

Shepard, R.N., & Cooper, L.A. (1982). *Mental Images and Their Transformations*. Cambridge, MA: MIT Press.

Shneiderman, B. (1996). The eyes have it: A task by data type taxonomy for information visualizations. In W. Citrin, & M. Burnett (Eds.), *Proceedings of 1996 IEEE Visual Languages* (pp. 336-343). Los Alamitos, CA: IEEE Society Press.

Spence, B. (2000). *Information Visualization*. New York, NY: ACM Press.

Spender, J.C. (1996). Making Knowledge the Basis of a Dynamic Theory of the Firm. *Strategic Management Journal, 17* (Special Issues), 45-62.

Tufte, E. (1983). *The Visual Display of Quantitative Information*. Cheshire, CT: Graphics Press.

Tufte, E. (1990). *Envisioning Information*. Cheshire, CT: Graphics Press.

Tufte, E. (1997). *Visual Explanations*. Cheshire, CT: Graphics Press.

Ungerleider, L.G., & Mishkin, M. (1982). Two Cortical Visual Systems. In J. Ingle, M.A. Goodale, & R.J.W. Mansfield (Eds.), *Analysis of visual behavior (*pp. 549-586). Cambridge, MA: MIT Press.

Vande Moere, A., Mieusset, K.H., & Gross, M. (2004). Visualizing Abstract Information using Motion Properties of Data-Driven Particles. In *Proceedings of Conference on Visualization and Data Analysis 2004, IS&T/SPIE Symposium on Electronic Imaging 2004, San Jose, CA* Seitenangabe.

Ware, C. (2000). *Information Visualization: Perception for Design*. San Francisco, CA: Morgan Kaufmann.

Weidenmann, B. (1989). When Good Pictures Fail: An Information-Processing Approach to the Effect of Illustrations. In H. Mandl, & J.R. Levin (Eds.), *Knowledge Acquisition from Text and Pictures* (pp. 157-170). Amsterdam, NL: North-Holland.

ParIS – Visualizing Ideas and Information in a Resource-Based Learning Scenario

Anja Neumann[1], Wolfgang Gräber[1], and Sigmar-Olaf Tergan[2]

[1] Leibniz-Institute for Science Education (IPN), Olshausenstraße 62,
24098 Kiel, Germany
{neumann, wgraeber}@ipn.uni-kiel.de
[2] Institut für Wissensmedien (IWM), Konrad-Adenauer Str. 40,
72072 Tübingen, Germany
s.tergan@iwm-kmrc.de

Abstract. The project ParIS (Partnership Industry and School) emphasizes the teaching of scientific literacy in problem-based learning scenarios in German science classes. In order to foster self-regulated learning and scientific literacy, a resource-based learning approach has been used for enhancing teaching and learning. Conventional lessons are supplemented by phases of project-based work, engaging students in self-regulated coping with everyday questions concerning science phenomena, using the Internet as a central learning resource. A spatial learning strategy (Mind Mapping) has been implemented for fostering both the management of knowledge and knowledge resources, as well as promoting the development of cognitive and meta-cognitive competencies. In order to support effective teaching and learning, the resource-based learning scenario has been embedded in a 'cognitive apprenticeship' approach. This paper describes the rationale for the design and implementation of ParIS in a 10th grade chemistry class at a German Waldorf school. Preliminary results of a pilot study focusing on the acceptance and usability of the instructional approach are outlined.

1 Introduction

Traditional teaching is often accused of being not very effective, leaving the students with no lasting understanding of issues and not promoting the acquisition of knowledge relevant in practice. There is a lack of strategies for teaching interdisciplinary knowledge transfer to foster the development of competencies that enable students to master complex and interdisciplinary problems. An additional problem with conventional teaching is that it does not match affordances resulting from the complexity of knowledge and knowledge resources very well. "With the coming of massive and yet flexible information resources in learning settings as hypermedia and Internet-based connections, a stronger appeal is made on tthe students' own responsibility and learning management skills" (Kommers, 2003). Learners have to acquire competencies to cope with the complexity of knowledge and knowledge resources in many domains. There is a need for fostering the development of scientific literacy and visual-spatial strategies (Holley & Dansereau, 1984) to support cognitive processing. There is also a

S.-O. Tergan and T. Keller (Eds.): Knowledge and Information Visualization, LNCS 3426, pp. 256–281, 2005.

need for teaching self-regulated, resource-based learning. The results of PISA (Deutsches Pisa-Konsortium, 2001) have shown that this is particularly true for science education.

The effective interaction with learning resources, information and knowledge, as well as the increasing use of the Internet in school as a learning resource in science education, require the development of special competencies for self-regulated, resource-based learning and information literacy as components of scientific literacy (Gräber & Bolte, 1997) in addition to the development of traditional learning and thinking strategies (Friedrich, 1999).

The project ParIS (Partnership Industry and School) has been designed to tackle current problems in the field of science education. The project emphasizes the teaching of scientific literacy in problem-based learning scenarios in science classes at German schools. In order to foster self-regulated learning and scientific literacy, a resource-based learning approach outlined by Rakes (1996) and Dodge (n.d.) has been adapted for enhancing teaching and learning. Conventional lessons are supplemented by phases of project-based work, engaging students in self-regulated coping with everyday questions concerning science phenomena, using the Internet as a central learning resource. A spatial learning strategy (Mind Mapping) has been implemented for fostering the management of knowledge and knowledge resources (Kommers, 2003) and promoting the development of cognitive and meta-cognitive competencies. In order to support effective teaching and learning, the resource-based learning scenario has been embedded in a 'cognitive apprenticeship' approach (Collins, Brown & Newman, 1989). The ParIS students work in groups or alone on self-generated questions drawn from everyday life, using the computer and the Internet to solve the problems. The issues are mainly concerned with the manufacture, composition or properties of products that are of interest to the students, but that are often very complex and poorly defined.

We are going to report the rationale for the design and implementation of ParIS and preliminary results of a pilot study focusing on the acceptance and usability of the instructional approach. The focus is on Mind Mapping as a visual-spatial strategy for generating, organizing, and visualizing structures of ideas, thoughts, and concepts, as well as a managing tool for storing and accessing information that is related to the conceptual knowledge. The study is intended (1) to assess evaluative data on the success of implementing the ParIS approach in classes and on the degree of acceptance of Mind Mapping as a spatial learning strategy in resource-based learning, and (2) to test the content validity and the usefulness of a questionnaire for assessing data concerning the usability and acceptability of the instructional measures used to support self-regulated, resource-based learning.

2 Theoretical Background

In order to outline the theoretical background of the approach, some basic concepts have to be outlined: Self-regulated learning, resource-based learning, Mind Mapping and 'cognitive apprenticeship' teaching.

2.1 Self-regulated Learning

The development of self-regulated learning strategies is one of the most important educational goals. It has become even more important in the context of learning scenarios, which allow the learners themselves much freedom in coping with complex learning tasks (PBL, RBL, Web Quest). Self-regulation in learning is based on cognitive, meta-cognitive, motivational and enactive strategies that can be applied flexibly in order to acquire and process knowledge and knowledge resources. Self-regulated students must be able to motivate themselves, to set learning goals, to recognize their learning needs, to determine learning goals, to plan their learning, to apply optimal learning strategies to realize the goals and to evaluate the results (Konrad, 2000; Simons, 1993). Meta-cognitive control strategies and learning and management strategies are central for self-regulation in learning. Students know how to plan, allocate resources, seek help, evaluate their own performance, and revise and correct their own work using standards of excellence. Strategies like planning, supervising and regulation direct students' cognitions (Wild & Schiefele, 1994). With the help of meta-cognitive activity, students try to use their knowledge of strategies and optimize their decisions about further procedures and the use of the strategies (Pintrich & De Groot, 1990). Learning and management strategies enable students to use cognitive, temporal and learning resources efficiently and to solve learning problems systematically. They also support positive motivational convictions like belief in one's own effectiveness (Pintrich, Roeser & De Groot, 1994). In a self-regulated learning process, the learners have to control the use of cognitive strategies that relate to understanding, encoding, retrieving and transferring through meta-cognitive strategies, such as monitoring, evaluating and regulating (Steiner, 1993).

In order to develop self-regulated learning strategies in school, expert modeling, training and support is necessary. A teaching strategy, which has proven to be effective and appropriate in managing the interplay between coaching and fading, is the 'cognitive apprenticeship' approach (Collins et al., 1989).

2.2 Resource-Based Learning

Resource-based learning (RBL) is a special kind of self-regulated learning. It takes place in contexts when learners have to cope (self-regulated) with the complexity of knowledge and knowledge resources. Particularly in learning scenarios where information is stored electronically on servers all over the world, learners have to search, localize, represent and make efficient use of the information, as well as relate the information to their personal knowledge in a self-regulated manner. Whereas conventional instructional approaches address known learning goals using well-organized sequences, resources, and activities, individuals in resource-based learning settings must recognize and clarify learning needs, plan a strategy to address these needs, locate and access resources, evaluate their veracity and utility, modify approaches based on an assessment of learning progress, and otherwise manage their learning. Methods for supporting context-specific, user-centered learning are slow to develop. Principles and problems of resource-based learning are outlined by Dodge (1995) and Rakes (1996). "Resource-based learning can be explained as a learning mode in which students learn self-regulated from interaction with a wide range of learning resources rather than from class exposition. Resource-based learning involves examining a topic and locating the information necessary to answer questions or to solve problems related to the topic. Learning resources could include print and non-print media, ranging from books and articles to sound and video recordings, to electronic databases and other computer-based resources" (Rakes, 1996).

In resource-based learning scenarios, students often suffer from cognitive overload (Sweller, 1994) and need scaffolding and cognitive tools to cope with complex task situations. In order to foster learning, to convince students that a particular task is "doable", and to give them a sense of security as they go about the task, Rakes (1996) introduces several guidelines for developing an appropriate lesson plan. Central is the introduction of a set of self-regulated strategies that the students are expected to apply in order to reach a task-appropriate problem solution, a.o. documenting the origin of resources and collecting, evaluating the adequacy of, and organizing ideas and data according to some logical pattern. Up to now, strategies for the organization and visualization of ideas, concepts and information resources have not been used very often. In resource-based learning approaches, it is suggested that using visual-spatial strategies may reduce cognitive load and help learners in managing their ideas and related information resources. It is also suggested that novice students have to be coached and scaffolded to use resource-based learning strategies effectively and may need performance support for effective learning and for managing knowledge and information resources (Hannafin, Hill & McCarthy, in press).

2.3 Visual-Spatial Strategies

The use of visual-spatial strategies has been suggested as a means to support cognitive processes in complex learning tasks (Holley & Dansereau, 1984; Jonassen, Beissner & Yacci, 1993). There are a variety of visualization techniques aimed at helping students in representing, conveying, and acquiring structural knowledge. These techniques allow for the representation and externalization of structures of conceptual knowledge. Content knowledge about a knowledge domain, as well as knowledge of information resources relevant for coping with a particular task, are not the focus. Advanced digital concept mapping tools provide functions for visualizing - in a coherent manner - different aspects of knowledge in a node-link structure and allowing for a knowledge-based access to information resources. Due to the computational features of the mapping tools, visual-spatial strategies may be enhanced. These strategies may particularly apply to some of the sub-competencies of self-regulated learning, such as the generation and structuring of ideas and concepts, the construction of meaning, the meta-cognitive control of learning and goal achievement, and the storage and retrieval of information that is related to the ideas and concepts in mind.

Mapping tools have been shown to foster meta-cognitive processes in learning and problem solving (Holley & Dansereau, 1984). Advanced computer-based mapping tools may be used to visualize not only concept knowledge like traditional concept mapping tools, but may also represent content knowledge (annotations, text and multimedia cognitive artifacts), as well as knowledge about knowledge resources (e.g. web sites, WBT programs, tools), by means of linking knowledge elements to information and knowledge resources that may be stored in digital repositories like files on the learner's own computer, in digital libraries, as well as on Internet servers. Because of these functions, computer-based mapping tools may be used as cognitive tools for the visualization of knowledge and knowledge resources and for enhancing cognitive processing (Jonassen et al., 1993). They may provide free interactive access to mapped knowledge elements and, thus, may enhance knowledge use. It is suggested that computer-based mapping tools may augment the capacity of the human brain in managing knowledge when students cope in a self-regulated manner with complex cognitive processing tasks, e.g. problem-based learning and web-based studying. The potential of mapping tools for the management of knowledge and information has recently been outlined by several researchers (Alpert & Grueneberg, 2000; Coffey, Hoffmann, Canas & Ford, 2002; Kommers, 2003; Tergan, in this book).

Concept mapping is a well-known visual-spatial strategy invented by Novak (Novak & Gowin, 1984). It has proven to be a powerful visualization strategy for representing the structure of concepts underlying individual declarative knowledge about a subject-matter domain. It may also be used effectively for visualizing the organization of an individual's knowledge structure and the information as potential knowledge resources, which is associated with the individual concepts of the structure (see Alpert, Cañas, Coffey, Dansereau, in this book). Reviews of research have revealed positive effects of using concept maps for fostering, a.o. knowledge acquisition, knowledge diagnosis, instructional design, as well as orientation and navigation (Kommers & Lanzing, 1997; Bruillard & Baron, 2000; O'Donnell, Dansereau & Hall, 2002). However, concept mapping is a sophisticated strategy for knowledge structuring requiring a lot of training and a high level of visual-spatial competency. For generating ideas in initial learning and problem solving with students in elementary classes, it may not be the first choice in visualization strategies. Mind Mapping may be more appropriate. Mind Mapping is a visual-spatial strategy, which was first outlined by Buzan (1974) and then elaborated on in more detail by Buzan (1995). Starting from a central idea mapped in a central node, associated ideas, thoughts, and concepts are mapped in a tree-like structure with several branches (Fig. 1). The technique is suggested to be useful for brainstorming, planning, structuring ideas, thoughts, and concepts, knowledge generation, and fostering self-regulated learning and problem solving (Jonassen, Beissner & Yacci, 1993; Buzan & Buzan, 1996). Mind Mapping is sometimes regarded as a fairly simple technique that has been around since cave painting when humans graphically depicted what they were thinking. The potential of Mind Mapping for fostering knowledge acquisition may be estimated to be relatively insignificant, because Mind Mapping allows for representing knowledge elements, but does not support the active construction of knowledge structures due to a lack of facilities for constructing networks of knowledge and representing and labeling semantic relations between elements. However, this thinking neglects the potential of advanced digital mapping technologies that not only allow for painting, but also for planning, sensemaking, easy structuring and restructuring of ideas and concepts, as well as for communication. They also allow for annotating ideas and concepts and for hyperlinking them with associated information resources stored in external data bases, digital libraries, the Internet, in hypermedia learning environments and in personal repositories. Thus, they may be used successfully for supporting the visualization and management of knowledge elements and knowledge resources in resource-based learning.

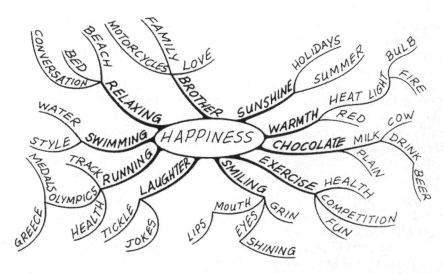

Fig. 1. Example mind map visualizing the structure of ideas, thoughts, and concepts in a tree-like structure (Buzan, 1995)

At German schools, the Mind Mapping tool "Mind Manager Smart" (http://www.schule.comunetix.de/mindjet/) is often used as the standard mapping technology for students to visualize their ideas and thoughts. The Mind Manager Smart is a simplified version of the Mind Manager (www.mindjet.com), which has been adapted for use at schools and in vocational training. The tool offers facilities to quickly represent knowledge and information elements in a visual-spatial display using a hierarchical branch-like structure (Fig.1). Users may get help by the tool itself in the procedure of mapping ideas, knowledge, and information resources by adding nodes and links, and emphasizing individual elements with color, symbols or graphs. The "notes" or "links" function makes it possible to annotate a node by adding a short text, e.g. a sentence describing a water molecule. Longer texts, such as descriptions of experiments, minutes or summaries, as well as multimedia documents, may be stored on the hard disc and connected to the mind map by a link. Task-relevant information like multimedia documents and Web sites can be hyperlinked with the mapped conceptual knowledge and may be quickly retrieved by visual search. The mapped ideas, concepts and integrated notes and documents may be altered, supplemented and re-organized when needed. The maps may be exported in different formats to be used in other documents, e.g. web sites and Word documents. Until now the Mind Manager has mostly been used for structuring ideas, concepts and thoughts. It has not been used at schools in the context of learning and instruction to facilitate the representation of information and the access to information resources, which have been selected as relevant for coping with a particular task situation.

2.4 Cognitive Apprenticeship

Neither resource-based learning as a cognitively demanding self-regulated activity nor techniques for the visualization of ideas, thoughts, concepts and the information resources associated with them can be acquired effectively by novices without being scaffolded by instructional measures. The 'cognitive apprenticeship' approach developed by Collins, Brown and Newman (1989) is a teaching approach designed for fostering self-regulated learning and the transfer of knowledge into practice. It aims primarily at teaching the processes that experts use to handle complex tasks. The focus of this learning-through-guided-experience is on cognitive and meta-cognitive skills. Applying 'cognitive apprenticeship' requires the externalization of processes that are usually carried out internally. Observing the processes by which an expert listener or reader thinks and practices these skills can teach students to learn on their own more skillfully (Collins, Brown & Newman, 1989). The 'cognitive apprenticeship' approach includes the following teaching methods:

1. Modeling - involves an expert's carrying out a task so that students can observe and build a conceptual model of the processes that are required to accomplish the task. For example, a teacher might model the reading process by reading aloud in one voice, while verbalizing her thought processes (summarize what she just read, what she thinks might happen next) in another voice.
2. Coaching - consists of observing students while they carry out a task and offering hints, feedback, modeling, reminders, etc.
3. Scaffolding - includes instructional measures to support students in coping with a particular task.
4. Articulation - includes any method of getting students to articulate their knowledge, reasoning, or problem-solving processes.
5. Reflection - enables students to compare their own problem-solving processes with those of an expert or another student.
6. Exploration - involves pushing students into a mode of problem solving on their own. Forcing them to do exploration is critical, if they are to learn how to frame questions or problems that are interesting and that they can solve (Collins, Brown & Newman, 1989).

Characteristic features of the 'cognitive apprenticeship' approach are its focus on fostering active and constructive cognitive processes and the focus on the social embeddedness of learning. The approach suggests authentic learning situations as a starting point for effective learning, the development of intrinsic motivation, and the exploiting of cooperation in cooperative learning scenarios. Results of empirical studies point out that students' knowledge and learning strategies can profit to a high degree from modeling strategies (Mandl & Fischer, 2000). It has been shown that students use effective strategies more often when they first have a model of an expert's strategy at their disposal (Gräsel, 1997).

3 The Resource-Based Learning Environment ParIS

3.1 Rationale of the Approach

ParIS has been designed to put ideas of fostering scientific literacy and self-regulated resource-based learning into practice in order to prepare students for lifelong learning in a modern knowledge society. The focus is on self-regulated problem solving in the domain of chemistry. Authentic problems leading to experiences situated in the learner's own social environment, connecting new ideas and concepts with prior knowledge, drawing conclusions, evaluating them and presenting an individual problem solution are fundamental for the ParIS approach. The 'cognitive apprenticeship' approach is applied as a teaching method to coach and scaffold learners in developing self-regulated learning strategies and scientific literacy and to provide performance support. This form of teaching was as new to the students as it was for the teacher. The Mind Mapping strategy is implemented to supplement the teacher's efforts to support students in resource-based learning by means of gathering and structuring ideas and knowledge and managing knowledge and knowledge resources. We assume that this procedure helps the students to cope with answering a question or solving a problem on their own. Part of the preparation involves precisely formulating the goal, activating previous knowledge and being conscious of missing information. Performing a task includes searching for necessary information, relating it to previously acquired knowledge, and managing knowledge and information resources. An important, often underrated phase in learning and problem solving is that of monitoring and reflecting. The learning results are reflected on, as are the ways to attain them, and are compared to and revised according to the goals or peer results. Finally, newly acquired knowledge is communicated to others and applied to new task situations.

The teaching/learning process in ParIS, according to the underlying 'cognitive apprenticeship' approach, starts with a modeling phase. The teacher introduces the students to the relevant concepts and processes of a new field and gives an example of how to use models and strategies to solve a problem. For example, based on the question, "How to clean oily hands?", the teacher - as an expert - introduces the students to the field of "soaps and detergents" and shows them how to work on such a topic, which questions to ask, how to plan the project, how to generate and map ideas and thoughts, how to find, handle, map, and evaluate information and how to present and discuss the results. Although the teacher controls the procedure, the students are not simply passive consumers, but rather actively join in by asking questions, experimenting or thinking.

In the second phase, the students work in small groups without help from the teacher unless requested and, by imitating the teacher, they elaborate upon a self-chosen issue from the same field. The teacher's role has moved from an information provider to a learning-process moderator; the teacher's support of students through coaching and scaffolding is gradually fading. The students acquire the learning content actively, articulate and reflect upon their results, discuss them in groups and explore new information. At the end, they prepare presentations for the whole class, viz. with posters, PowerPoint presentations or websites.

In the following section, the procedure of a typical teaching / learning sequence with modeling and group work phases in ParIS is described. The sequence is about soaps and detergents. The superordinate goal is the acquisition of knowledge about the concepts of soaps and detergents, surface tension, the behavior of hydrophilic and lipophilic solutions and their chemical structure, as well as successfully mastering the accompanying experiments. Working on a question independently requires competencies in self-regulated learning and scientific reasoning. Students have to define their own goals, plan how to proceed, and to locate and manage task-relevant information.

They have to reflect on their own actions in order to assess goal attainment and to present the results.

3.2 Visualizing Knowledge and Information in ParIS

The basic processes for effective problem solving are modeled during a modeling phase: The teacher enters the classroom with oily hands looking for a suitable way to clean them. Neither cold nor hot water were enough; soap and detergent had to come to the rescue. But, how do they work? A mind map helps to represent the problem, to retrieve and reconstruct previous knowledge and to generate questions (Fig. 2). Questions are generated, but not formulated explicitly; rather they are reduced to meaningful concepts. "Why does fat not dissolve in water?" is coded in the main branch "fats/oils" under "characteristics". The teacher drafts a map representing the labels for the four materials in the main branches. Since the interest is focused on the characteristics of the materials, concepts and ideas concerning their composition and creation procedure are mapped.

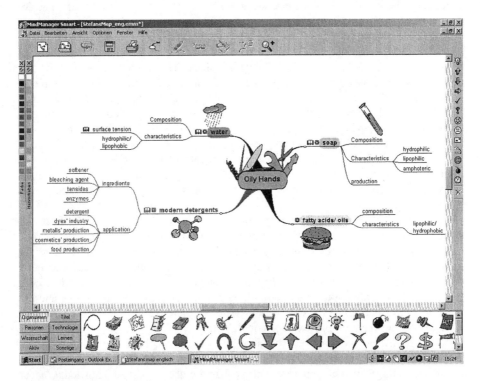

Fig. 2. Mind Map generated by the teacher. The figure visualizes different mapping features, as ell as the computer interface of the Mind Manager Smart

The instructional sequence starts with a twenty-minute-long general introduction to the Mind Manager Smart. Students are first shown and then have to practice the mapping techniques with an example map. The maps are introduced as tools for helping with elaborating upon and fixing the goals, planning how to proceed, and reflecting on progress in problem solving. Students were advised to also use the Mind Mapping tool as a managing device for integrating personal annotations to ideas and storing and accessing knowledge concerning subject-matter domain elements (e.g. multimedia documents), as well as Web-based information resources hyperlinked with elements of the map.

After the teacher has cleaned his oily hands using detergent, the way the solution interacts with the materials involved is studied systematically in a demonstration experiment. During this modeling phase, the students were instructed to each produce their own mind map. The use of the Mind Manager was obligatory. At the end of the sequence, the students presented the results in two formats using a mind map and a verbal outline of the problem-solving process.

In principle, they imitate the teacher's map with variations in colors, drawings, and their own notes. For the most part, the students formulate their observations and interpretations of the experiments self-regulated. The map serves as a cognitive tool for fostering joint reflection, communication, and grounding in small groups. In order to externalize the individual problem space, the students create a personal map reflecting the group's project work and problem solution. The result is a complete map that summarizes the student's work and considerations during the modeling phase (see chapter 5).

4 The Pilot Study

A pilot study has been performed for evaluating the impact and usability of the instructional methods used in ParIS. The focus is on assessing data concerning general acceptance, as well as advantages and problems, of using the Mind Mapping strategy for fostering self-regulated, resource-based learning and the acquisition of scientific literacy. It is intended as a study to yield evaluative data to build upon in a follow-up field-based experimental approach on the effects of the Mind Mapping strategy on learning and the management of ideas, concepts, as well as content background knowledge and associated information resources, under more constrained experimental and environmental conditions. The following general questions are in the foreground:

- Can Mind Mapping be successfully implemented as a visual-spatial strategy in the resource-based learning approach of ParIS?
- Is Mind Mapping accepted by learners and teachers?
- How is the Mind Mapping strategy used by the students?
- Is the instructional approach of ParIS accepted by students and teachers?
- How does it contribute to fostering self-regulated, resource-based learning?

4.1 Design

The instructional approach of ParIS as outlined in chapter 3 was used to implement a resource-based learning approach into school practice. Students from two 10th grade classes of the Waldorf school in Kiel (Germany) participated in the study. Student questionnaires and student and teacher interviews were used for data assessment.

4.2 Materials

Questionnaire. Evaluative questions used in instruments presented by Konrad (2000), Weinstein (1988) and Weinstein & Palmer (1992) have been adapted for the ParIS study. The questionnaire consists of a total of 113 questions. It is divided into two parts: part one has a total of 44 items. They focus on project lessons and refer to five dimensions of self-regulated learning as suggested by Konrad (2000): experienced self-regulation, learning motivation, self-monitoring, self-concept, and information processing. The items referring to the dimension "experienced self-regulation" ascertain the subjective experience with self-regulation and individual responsibility for learning. Examples: "I play an active role in forming the learning processes in the lessons"; "When learning, I have the feeling I am doing what I want to do myself". Items referring to the "learning motivation" dimension address the personal incentives for learning and for overcoming learning barriers. Examples: "In class, I tried to do my best to acquire knowledge and skills"; "I made an effort in class even when I did not like it". The dimension "self-monitoring" focuses on the meta-cognitive activities of testing and monitoring the completion of the learning. Examples: "When learning, I paid attention to where the gaps were in my knowledge: "When repeating the material, I asked myself questions and/or set myself tasks". The items referring to the dimension self-concept concentrate on evaluating learning competencies: Examples: "I made important contributions in class"; "I am usually successful in class". The information-processing dimension refers to the more intensive elaboration of the object of learning and cognitive processing strategies. Examples: "When I learn, I try to connect the content in my mind"; "I learn concepts and formulas by heart without really understanding them".

Part two of the questionnaire consists of 66, 4-point Likert-scale items (scales ranging from 1 to 4) explicitly directed at Mind Mapping with the 'Mind Manager Smart'. The first 32 items of part two are Likert statements also referring to the five dimensions mentioned about self-regulated learning according to Konrad (2000). The remaining 34 questions are tailored to assessing acceptance of the mapping tool, the mapping strategy and annotation strategies for fostering learning. With 4 questions, the students could freely express their opinions about the program. An additional 3 questions focused on learning prerequisites (achievements in chemistry, skills in using the mind manager, knowledge about using the Internet) of the students.

Student and teacher interviews. Student and teacher interviews were used to assess evaluative data concerning the adequacy, acceptance, and success of using ParIS under different treatment conditions. Student interviews were based on a half-structured questionnaire with 15 questions altogether, 6 questions focusing on self-evaluating the acceptability and effectiveness of the self-regulated learning strategy in project-based learning, 5 questions focusing on the acceptability and effectiveness of the 'Mind Manager Smart' and the book-marking strategy, and 4 questions focusing on the effectiveness of the strategies used for fostering knowledge acquisition.

Teacher interviews were based on a half-structured questionnaire with 12 questions altogether, 2 questions focused on the teacher's evaluation of the instructional effectiveness of the Mind Manager mapping tool and the 'cognitive apprenticeship' strategy for fostering self-regulated learning, 3 questions on the quality of implementing both strategies in the curriculum, 3 questions focusing on evaluating the acceptability the Mind Mapping strategy as an effective strategy for fostering learning, 2 questions referring to general learning prerequisites, and 2 other questions focusing on the evaluation of the performance level of the students.

4.3 Participants

Between October 2003 and July 2004, 19 students from one 10th grade class of the Waldorf school in Kiel (Germany) participated in the study. The students (12 girls, 7 boys), aged 15 to 17, were instructed for 6 weeks in two weekly afternoon sessions by the same teacher on the same subject (cosmetics in chemistry project lessons). None of them had ever taken part in a research study before. None of the students had known or had ever used the Mind Manager for learning before. Participation in the study was voluntary.

4.4 Procedure

The study was conducted by one and the same teacher (a PhD) candidate from the IPN) within the classrooms of a Waldorf school in Kiel. The study took place during regular lessons and lasted through six weeks of lesson units. The lessons took place twice a week on Wednesdays from 9:00 to 10:30 a.m. and Thursdays from 1:30 to 3:00 p.m. Before the beginning of the study, the students in each group were briefly introduced to the procedure. Questions that arose were discussed. The anonymity of the data was declared.

Students received an introduction into the Mind Mapping technique with the 'Mind Manager Smart' and had a 20-minute training phase to become acquainted with the program. During the training session, the students were also introduced to the bookmarking facilities of the 'Mind Manager Smart' by means of hyperlinking ideas to information resources. Every student visualized their individual ideas, concepts and associated information sources by completing their own mind map on their own laptop with permanent Internet access. The teacher casually reminded the students of the instructions on how to proceed during the lesson.

A questionnaire for assessing the acceptance of the learning scenario by the students and for assessing the level of self-reported competency in self-regulated, resource-based learning was administered at the end of the lesson unit. To ensure full attention was given, the teacher read the questions aloud to the students. 45 minutes were allowed for answering the questions.

4.5 Results

The reported results concern the general research questions outlined earlier. They focus on evaluative data of students concerning the implementation of the instructional approach, in particular the acceptance and usefulness of the Mind Mapping strategy for supporting self-regulated, resource-based learning.

1. Can Mind Mapping be successfully implemented as a visual-spatial strategy in the resource-based learning approach of ParIS?
2. Is Mind Mapping accepted by learners and teachers?

3. How is the Mind Mapping strategy used by the students?
4. How does the ParIS approach contribute to fostering self-regulated, resource-based learning?

(1) Can Mind Mapping be successfully implemented as a visual-spatial strategy in the resource-based learning approach of ParIS? Questionnaire data and supplementary data from the interviews form the basis for evaluating the process of implementing the Mind Manager. The data reveal that both the Mind Mapping method and the mapping tool were easy to use for both the teacher and the students. All of the students – without exception – were able to use the program without difficulties. As can be seen in Table 1, most students disagreed with the statement that "You need intensive training to use the Mind Manager" (M = 1.37; SD = .76). It can also be seen in Table 1 that most students also disagreed that using other procedures would be more helpful (M = 1.67, SD = .69).

The analysis of the interview data revealed that the teacher and the students described the method and the program as "well-suited for the classroom" and stated that "the program is easy to learn and offers many helpful functions". Digital mapping was clearly preferred over mapping with "paper and pencil". The teacher and the students particularly liked the possibility of entering links, attaching notes and making clean, quick changes according to one's own wishes. The distinct preference for computer-supported mapping as opposed to paper and pencil mapping shows that there is a clear motivational preference for using a computer tool for Mind Mapping. The motivational preference of digital Mind Mapping over paper and pencil mapping is taken as an indication that Mind Mapping was successfully implemented as a visual-spatial strategy in the resource-based learning approach of ParIS.

(2) How is the Mind Mapping accepted by learners and teachers? In order to evaluate the general implementation (see question 1) and acceptance of the Mind Manager as a visualization technique, 4 items were used (see Table 1).

The results of the analysis of the questionnaire data confirm the assumption that the mapping tool is a meaningful supplement for learning and teaching in the classroom. Most of the students agreed with the statement "I like to work with the Mind Manager", reflecting a high acceptance of the tool by the students (M = 3.53; SD = .51). Most students disagreed that using other procedures would be more helpful (M = 1.67; SD = .69). Most students also disagreed that intensive training is necessary to use the Mind Manager (M = 1.37; SD = .76). There was a moderate tendency in the questionnaire data to indicate that students would use the Mind Manager outside the school (M = 2.47; SD = 1.07). However, as interview data revealed, two thirds of the students continued to use the program at school after the end of the study. No significant gender differences were found with reference to the acceptance of the mapping tool.

Both the teacher and the students evaluated the mapping tool positively. According to the interview data, the teacher also likes to work with the mapping tool and would continue using it in lessons, as well as in extracurricular pursuits.

In the final part of the questionnaire, the students could freely express their opinions about working with the Mind Manager Smart. There were no negative statements about the tool. The following answers are examples of the students' statements:

Table 1. Average ratings (Means) on questionnaire items concerning acceptance of Mind Mapping with 'Mind Manager Smart' (scale: 1 = does not apply, 2 = does not really apply, 3 = applies more than not, 4 = applies)

	N	Mean	Standard Deviation
I like to work with the Mind Manager	19	3.53	0.51
I would also use Mind Manager outside the school	19	2.47	1.07
You need intensive training to use the Mind Manager	19	1.37	0.76
I find using other procedures more helpful	18	1.67	0.69

- "I like the fact that the program is so easy to operate and that I can understand it without a lot of effort. Although I usually never work at the computer, the program made things easier for me."
- "You can clearly organize your thoughts and since you have your ideas in front of you, it is easier to develop new ideas."

Student interview data also revealed that the students liked to work with the 'Mind Manager Smart', and several even planned to use it in other contexts, i.e. outside of school. The data further revealed that some students suggested the fields of planning, structuring, and organizing as possible areas of use for the Mind Mapping technique. The facilities provided by the Mind Manager make this tool especially suitable for working with the Internet. Content knowledge, as well as links to knowledge resources, can easily be represented in a Mind Map and subsequently retrieved again by means of a simple mouse click. This makes managing information that has been retrieved from the Internet much easier. According to the interview data, the students also used the tool in other curricular and task contexts, e.g. in order to plan and present a paper.

Two statements by the students concerned the technical facilities of the Mind Manager. Some students answered that they missed having a feature to attach more than one link to an idea in order to also refer to other information resources stored outside the program on the Internet. On the whole, the teacher's and students' acceptance of the mapping tool was predominantly positive.

(3) How is the Mind Mapping strategy used by the students? We assume that the Mind Mapping method can help students in coping with everyday chemistry problems. Two areas of support can be differentiated. On the one hand, the Mind Manager is suggested to support managing processes concerning planning, visualization of knowledge, storing and presenting results (Tergan, 2003). On the other hand, mapping can be the basis for higher-level cognitive and meta-cognitive learning processes, as, for example, understanding problems, recognizing relationships and thinking systematically (Holley & Dansereau, 1984; Jonassen et al., 1993).

A factor analysis (Main Component Analysis / Varimax rotation) performed on the questionnaire items related to processing information confirmed this assumption. Based on their factor loads, the items can be categorized into 2 factors with highly reliable internal consistencies of items:

Factor A: Items on knowledge and information managing processes
Factor B: Items on higher-level cognitive and meta-cognitive processes (Table 2)

Table 2. Alpha-reliability coefficients and number of items loading on factors A and B

Factors	Number of items	Alpha
A (knowledge and information managing processes)	8	.86
B (higher-level meta-cognitive processes)	11	.94

The results of the analysis of the questionnaire data suggest that the students confirm the support (see Table 3) through the Mind Manager in both areas (A and B). As to its support for knowledge and information managing (A), there is an average rating of M = 3.12 (SD = .78); concerning higher-level meta-cognitive processing, the average rating is M = 2.77 (SD = .80). A two-fold analysis of significance revealed a difference, which is significant at a 2% level (p = .017; df = 17). The mapping tool was evaluated as especially suitable for managing processes, such as storing, finding and presenting information, for illustrating ideas and for visualizing knowledge (factor A). In general, the students felt more supported in managing processes than in higher-level cognitive processing.

Table 3. Comparison of means of scales A and B. The table shows average data of students' opinions (scale: 1 = does not apply, 2 = does not really apply, 3 = applies more than not, 4 = applies)

Factors	Mean	Sample	Standard Deviation
A	3.12	18	.784
B	2.77	18	.801

This finding is analyzed in more detail with respect to the following processing categories:

Planning: preparation for problem solving and learning (e.g. setting goals, analyzing the question, activating and organizing existing knowledge, becoming conscious of missing information).

Performing: Executing processes of problem solving and learning (e.g. researching information, administrating information, representing results, connecting and understanding contents).

Knowledge transfer: Applying the acquired knowledge (e.g. presenting results, relating contents to new facts, transfer).

Reflecting / Monitoring helps in coordinating learning actions, evaluating results, and in reflecting about and thinking over the question-answering / problem-solving procedure.

The questionnaire items pertaining to factors A and B conform well with these processing categories (see Tables 4 and 5). In accordance with the rationale of ParIS, the Mind Mapping strategy is used by all students as a tool for solving everyday chemistry problems in a self-regulated manner. The results of the questionnaire show that Mind Mapping was evaluated to be useful for supporting many processes in self-regulated, resource-based learning. The different maps presented below are showing (a) different problem solutions and (b) different kinds of use for the Mind Manager for representing and managing ideas, concepts, personal notes, documents and links to information resources, which are evaluated as relevant for the problem solution.

Table 4. Average ratings (Means) on questionnaire items about working with the 'Mind Manager Smart' (scale: 1 = does not apply, 2 = does not really apply, 3 = applies more than not, 4 = applies)

Category	Items factor A	N	Mean	Standard Deviation
I	Mind Mapping helped collate the ideas of all the students	19	2.84	1.07
I	Mind Mapping helped me plan the work steps	19	2.95	0.97
II	Mind Mapping helped me remember information and its sources	19	3.37	0.90
II	Mind Mapping helped me find information and its sources	19	2.84	1.21
II	Mind Mapping helped me organize information and its sources	19	3.37	0.90
II	Mind Mapping helped me record the results of my work	19	3.53	0.96
III	Mind Mapping helped me present my ideas and thoughts clearly	19	3.37	0.96
III	Mind Mapping helped me prepare the presentation of the results	19	2.79	1.03

Planning. The results of the analysis of the questionnaire data (see Tables 4 and 5) show that Mind Mapping is evaluated to foster planning processes. Ideas can be collected with the help of the map and pre-knowledge can be activated. Mind Mapping was assessed to help to "organize what I knew and make it conscious" (M = 3.16; SD = 1.07), "to help me plan the work steps" (M = 2.95; SD = .97), and to help "collate the ideas for all students" (M = 2.84; SD= 1.07). As the student map II (see Fig. 3) shows, planning learning steps is a practical application of Mind Mapping.

Table 5. Average ratings (Means) on questionnaire items about working with the 'Mind Manager Smart' (scale: 1 = does not apply, 2 = does not really apply, 3 = applies more than not, 4 = applies)

Category	Items factor B	N	Mean	Standard Deviation
I	Mind Mapping helped me organize what I knew and make it conscious	19	3.16	1.07
II	Mind Mapping helped me think more systematically	19	2.79	0.92
II	Mind Mapping helped me make connections between previous knowledge and new knowledge	19	2.79	1.08
II	Mind Mapping helped me acquire new knowledge	19	3.00	1.05
II	Mind Mapping helped me solve the tasks more easily	18	2.83	0.92
II	Mind Mapping helped me better remember newly acquired knowledge	19	2.79	1.08
II	Mind Mapping helped me better understand the contents	19	2.74	0.81
II	Mind Mapping helped me understand connections	19	2.47	0.70
III	Mind Mapping helped me recognize when the acquired information could be useful in real life	19	2.37	0.90
III	Mind Mapping helped me inform others about the project results and explain them	19	2.95	1.08
III	Mind Mapping helped me relate what I learned in class with my world outside of class	18	2.22	1.06

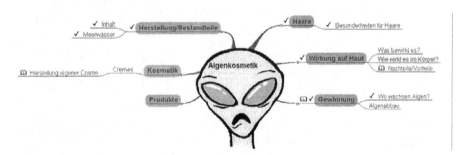

Fig. 3. Mind Map II showing mapping activities related to the planning phase

Map II (see Fig. 3) shows a student's (sub)map about "algae cosmetics". After brain storming about "algae cosmetics", the collected ideas are sorted according to the individual subtopics and the field as structured by the student using the map. Beyond the contextual structuring, the map has planning elements; here, it is especially lucid in the form of formulated questions. These questions are answered one after the other by the student and the completed branches are marked with a symbol (a check mark).

Performing. As can be seen in Tables 4 and 5, the results suggest that the mapping method especially helps the students in performing the task. Some particularly prominent and enlightening results referring to management processes (Factor A) include the following: Mind Mapping was assessed to "find information and its sources" (M = 2.84; SD = 1.21), to help "remember information and its sources" (M = 3.37; SD = .90), to "record the results of my work " (M = 3.53; SD = .96), and to "organize information and its sources "(M = 3.37; SD = .90). Examples of results related to higher-level meta-cognitive processes (Factor B) are: "Mind Mapping helped me acquire new knowledge" (M = 3.00; SD = 1.05), "Mind Mapping helped me solve the tasks more easily" (M = 2.83; SD = .92), "Mind Mapping helped me think more systematically" (M = 2.79; SD = .92), and "Mind Mapping helped me to make connections between previous knowledge and new knowledge" (M = 2.79; SD = 1.08).

According to the questionnaire data, digital Mind Mapping seems to be best-suited for managing knowledge and information, but is also assessed as a strategy that may help in higher-level cognitive processing. According to the interview data, the managing function is predominant when evaluating the potential of digital Mind Mapping for learning and problem solving. The statement of one student that information stored in the map could be quickly searched and easily accessed is characteristic of this evaluation.

A detailed analysis of the student maps shows that students do not adhere to the teacher map presented in the modeling phase, but prefer to use their own maps to structure and store information (see Maps II and III, Fig. 3 and 4). This result is in accordance with results recently published by Yin, Vanides, Ruiz-Primo, Ayala and Shavelson (2005), who found similar results with concept mapping. The analysis of interview and questionnaire data further revealed that the students would like to be able to use the storage function more comprehensively for notes and links. Since the Mind Manager Smart only allows for storing one link per branch, and since the text field for notes is not clearly laid out and is small, a fully comprehensive management of knowledge and of information with the Mind Mapping tool is not possible.

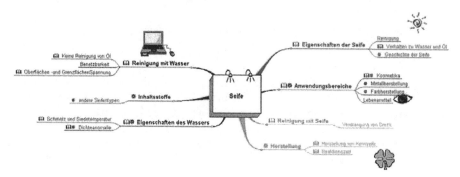

Fig. 4. Mind Map III showing mapping activities related to the performance phase

The student map III (Fig. 4) shows one student's comprehensive work with the Mind Mapping method. The student first structured the topic into central areas and then worked out one area after the other. She not only mapped ideas and concepts, but also task-relevant information she had found on the Internet and in other repositories. The branches were used extensively to represent notes and links. The map was used by the student as a medium for both a comprehensive problem representation (see Jonassen, in this book), and for the presentation of the results of her problem-solving process.

Knowledge transfer. Can Mind Mapping support knowledge transfer? As Tables 4 and 5 show, Mind Mapping with the Mind Manager Smart is evaluated as suitable for both the presentation of results and as a means for communicating them to others. Some results referring to the managing function of digital Mind Maps (Factor A) include the following: "Mind Mapping helped me to present my ideas and thoughts clearly" (M = 3.37; SD = 1.03), "Mind Mapping helped me prepare the presentation of the results" (M = 3.13; SD = 1.11). The following statement casts some light on higher-level cognitive processing functions concerning knowledge transfer: "Mind Mapping helped me recognize when the acquired information could be useful in real life" (M = 2.37; SD = .90).

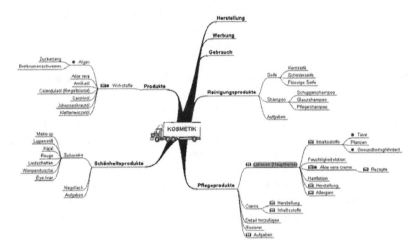

Fig. 5. Mind Map IV used for representing a problem and communicating results of a problem-solving process (Topic: Cosmetics)

The student interview data revealed further insights. Some students stated that the map served as a kind of "guideline for discussion" of the status of the problem-solving process and how to proceed in coping with the task. Knowledge transfer also refers to the transfer of skills. As mentioned earlier, the interview data show that the majority of the students continued to use Mind Mapping for preparing and making presentations in different school contexts. Fig. 5 shows an example of a Mind Map demonstrating the complexity and elaborated nature of a problem representation and how results of a problem solution may be communicated to others.

Reflecting/Monitoring. Processes of reflecting and monitoring are given special importance in ParIS lessons. In the modeling phase, the teacher repeatedly points out that the students should control their own learning actions during the individual phases of coaching and scaffolding. Based on the Mind Mapping tool, reflection should be made easier by visualizing the status of a problem-solving process, as well as the information resources relevant for the problem solution. It may be suggested that students are encouraged to check the status of their work with the help of a map, to re-orient themselves and to note where information is still missing (Tergan, in this book). Maps II and III (see Fig. 3 and 4) are examples where a Mind Map is used for getting an overview of the degree of task completion. The branches are worked on one after the other and codes mark the development status.

As the questionnaire results in Tables 4 and 5 show, mapping helps the students clearly present their ideas and thoughts. Based on their map, students are able to readily inform classmates and their teacher about their own level of knowledge and to explain the contents. The contents of the maps and one's own method of problem solving are reflected on and compared with other data through the discussions within groups.

Although there are no "hard" data available, an intuitive qualitative analysis of the resulting Mind Maps suggests that maps constructed by males and females differed in appearance. The following map is an example of a map constructed by a male student (Fig. 6). In general, male students focus on structure to use maps as a structuring device. In contrast to female students, they seldom use colors, symbols or pictures.

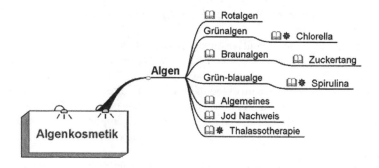

Fig. 6. Mind Map V of a male student focusing on structure without using colors, symbols, and pictures

Mind Map VI (see Fig. 7) is an example of a map constructed by a female student. Preliminary analysis of the maps constructed by the students suggests that female students use more functions of the Mind Manager more often. They seem to use the "Note" function more often, to use more links, and to focus not only on structure, but also on the "outer appearance" of the map.

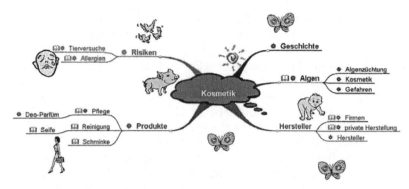

Fig. 7. Mind Map of a female student focusing on structure and using colors, symbols, and pictures

5 How Does the ParIS Approach Contribute to Fostering Self-regulated, Resource-Based Learning?

Data concerning the acceptance of the instructional approach of ParIS relate to both the 'cognitive apprenticeship' approach as a dominant instructional strategy and the use of Mind Mapping as a visual-spatial strategy for fostering self-regulated, resource-based learning.

According to the teacher's statements, the implementation of the 'cognitive apprenticeship' in ParIS was very successful in class. The design approach could be integrated into the lesson well and could be executed within the time frame. The approach seems to have a good chance of being effectively used in science classes for fostering the development of science learning competencies and promoting self-regulated, resource-based learning.

The students rated the 'cognitive apprenticeship'-type of lesson as interesting and indicated that independent work would be more possible than in traditional lessons with a more teacher-centered style. One student stated: "I found the lesson interesting and I would like to experience this kind of lesson more often". Their own work within the frame of 'cognitive apprenticeship' was not seen as being too demanding; rather, the students felt they received just the right amount of support from the teacher. The vast majority of students stated their desire to complement normal lessons with the new teaching method.

Data concerning the acceptance of the overall instructional approach refer to student questionnaires, as well as to student and teacher interviews. The students rated the ParIS approach very positively (see Table 6). In particular, it helps students to recognize relationships. The ParIS lesson was evaluated as helpful in imagining situations where the new concepts are important (M = 2.89; SD = .66). It helped to integrate new knowledge contents into a logical network (M = 2.78; SD = .88) and helped to relate new knowledge to one's own experiences (M = 2.94; SD = .60). The ParIS lesson was also evaluated as helpful in imagining how the learned information itself could be helpful in everyday life (M = 3.16; SD = .90) and in making connections between previous and new knowledge (M = 3.26; SD = .45).

Table 6. Average ratings (Means) on questionnaire items concerning acceptance of the overall instructional approach (scale: 1 = does not apply, 2 = does not really apply, 3 = applies more than not, 4 = applies)

Item	N	Mean	Standard Deviation
The ParIS lesson helped me to imagine situations where the new concepts are important	19	2.89	0.66
The ParIS lesson helped me to integrate the contents in a logical network	18	2.78	0.88
The ParIS lesson helped me relate contents to my own experiences	18	2.94	0.60
The ParIS lesson helped me to imagine how the learned information could be helpful in everyday life	19	3.16	0.90
The ParIS lesson helped me to make connections between previous and new knowledge	19	3.26	0.45

To sum up, it may be ascertained that the students readily accepted the ParIS approach and got a good idea of how to use the acquired knowledge in everyday life.

6   Is the Instructional Approach of ParIS Accepted by Students and Teachers?

In addition to supporting resource-based learning and knowledge management, the focal point of the ParIS hypothesis is that of promoting skills for self-regulated learning. The results of the questionnaire that indicate how the students experience self-

Table 7. Average ratings (Means) on questionnaire items concerning acceptance of the overall instructional approach (scale: 1 = does not apply, 2 = does not really apply, 3 = applies more than not, 4 = applies)

Item	N	Mean	Standard Deviation
The lesson form allowed me more freedom in learning	19	3.53	0.77
I felt I was responsible for what I learned in class	19	3.53	0.61
In class, I had the feeling I could do what I wanted to do	19	3.47	0.70
The lessons supported my self-accountable learning	19	3.21	0.92

regulated learning in ParIS are presented in Table 7. The results clearly show that the students feel supported in independent learning. The students perceived more freedom in learning (M = 3.53; SD = .77), and they had the feeling they "could do what they themselves wanted to do" (M = 3.47; SD = .70), and were responsible for what they learned in class (M = 3.53; SD = .61). In addition, our analysis has shown that the students felt strongly supported in their self-accountable learning (M = 3.21; SD = .92) through the instructional approach.

Interview statements make this positive evaluation of the new teaching procedure even more clear. The students stated that they have considerably more possibilities for self-directed learning with the 'cognitive apprenticeship' procedure than in traditional lessons. This new teaching procedure was, however, evaluated as not being too demanding and the students indicated that they had received just the right amount of support from the teacher in difficult situations. An often expressed request of the students was to experience this kind of lesson more often. The lessons were evaluated as being a welcome change from traditional ones.

7   General Discussion

Both the efficiency and the acceptance of mapping techniques as teaching/learning strategies heavily depend on how well the students can handle the technique (McCagg & Dansereau, 1991). Although neither the teacher nor the students in ParIS lessons knew the mapping methods beforehand, the integration of the tool into the classroom can be viewed as successful. The program was used by all of the students on the first try and there were no problems in applying it. The students' evaluative statements, as well as the teacher's observations, give rise to the hope that many students will use the Mind Mapping strategy - in different courses, as well as outside of class and in everyday life.

One general problem of accepting systematic learning techniques like Mind Mapping is that they are only transmitted very late in the students' cognitive development. The re-learning that is then necessary and the interference with learning strategies and techniques already acquired often leads to a temporary loss of efficiency (large amount of time required, decreased performance) (Friedrich & Mandl, 1992), which in turn can make the student dismiss the new learning techniques too quickly as not being suitable. This observation could not be made in the study, which could have been due to the very simple Mind Mapping technique implemented o. utilized when using the 'Mind Manager Smart'.

In summary, it may be concluded that the implementation of Mind Mapping as a visual-spatial strategy for organizing and managing ideas and information in the resource-based learning environment ParIS and its instructional support through the 'cognitive apprenticeship' procedure was successful.

8   Conclusion and Perspectives

When studying in resource-based learning scenarios with complex and ill-structured subject-matter contents, there is a need for effective visual-spatial strategies for learning and the management of knowledge and information resources. The presented approach ParIS is based on the premise that advanced computer-based Mind Mapping - if introduced in a learner-centered manner - may be used to foster spatial learning strategies, self-regulated learning, and processes of individual knowledge management, particularly in elementary classes. A pilot study was performed to assess data concerning the success in implementation and the degree of acceptance of using the Mind Manager as a strategy for visualizing structures of ideas concepts and representing associated content information. The questionnaire and interview data of the students and the teacher participating in the pilot study yielded a lot of evidence proving that this premise is valid. This result is of importance because Mind Mapping has been appraised to be a fairly simple technique as compared to Concept Mapping. Although this thinking may be right, it neglects to include the potential of advanced digital mapping technologies that allow for more than just painting, but also for the easy structuring and restructuring of ideas and knowledge elements, and for hyperlinking information resources stored in external data bases, digital libraries, the Internet, in hypermedia learning environments, and in personal repositories. They also allow for Web-based communication, as well as the interactive access to the information when needed during learning, working, and problem solving. The functionalities provided by advanced digital Mind Mapping tools like the Mind Manager Smart, which is used in the ParIS approach, seem to be helpful for supporting visual-spatial processing strategies, self-regulated learning, as well as several processes of knowledge management. In order to maximize the potential of Mind Mapping, the use of the mapping technique, as well as the technology, should be trained in order to avoid increasing the cognitive load of learners in coping with complex tasks.

In conclusion, digital Mind Mapping seems to be a fruitful strategy to introduce into elementary classes for enhancing self-regulated, resource-based learning. It opens up new possibilities for the visualization and managing of ideas and information that exceeds the potential of traditional paper and pencil applications. Digital Mind Mapping is suggested as an alternative to the more complex and ambitious digital Concept Mapping techniques. The potential of Mind Mapping for fostering knowledge acquisition may be estimated as relatively small/insignificant due to a lack of facilities for constructing networks and labeling semantic relations between the represented elements. However, it has the advantage of being an easy-to-learn technology, which opens up new possibilities for fostering self-regulated, resource-based learning and idea and information management that should be examined in more detail in future research.

References

Alpert, S.R. & Grueneberg, K. (2000). Concept Mapping with Multimedia on the Web. *Journal of Educational Multimedia and Hypermedia, 9*(4), 313-330.

Bruillard, E., & Baron, G.-L. (2000). Computer-Based Concept Mapping: a Review of a Cognitive Tool for Students. In D. Benzie, & D. Passey (Eds.), *Proceedings of Conference on Educational Uses of Information and Communication Technologies (ICEUT)* (pp. 331-338). Bejing: Publishing House of Electronics Industry (PHEI).

Buzan, T. (1974). Use both sides of your brain. New York: E.P. Dutton.

Buzan, T. (1995). *The Mind Map book* (2 ed). London: BBC Books 81.

Buzan, T., & Buzan, B. (1996). *Das Mind Mapping Buch: Die beste Methode zur Steigerung ihres geistigen Potentials.* München: Mod. Verlagsgesellschaft.

Coffey, J.W., Hoffmann, R.R., Cañas, A.J., & Ford, K.M. (2002). A Concept Map-Based Knowledge Modeling Approach to Expert Knowledge Sharing (Available online: http://www.coginst.uwf.edu/users/acanas/Publications/IKS2002/IKS.htm

Collins, A., Brown, J.S., & Newman, S.E. (1989). 'Cognitive Apprenticeship': Teaching the crafts of reading, writing, and mathematics. In L.B. Resnick (Ed.), *Knowing, Learning, and Instruction: Essays in honor of Robert Glaser* (pp. 453-494). Hillsdale, NJ.: Erlbaum & Associates.

Deutsches Pisa-Konsortium (Hrsg.). (2001). *Pisa 2000. Basiskompetenzen von Schülerinnen und Schüler im internationalen Vergleich.* Opladen: Leske + Budrich.

Dodge, B. (1995). Web Ouests A technique for Internet-based learning. *Airstance Educator, 1*(2), (1995) 10-13.

Dodge, B. (n.d.). *Some Thoughts about WebQuests* [WWW document]. San Diego State University URL: http://edweb.sdsu.edu/courses/edtec596/about_webquests.html (May 5, 1997)

Friedrich, H.F., & Mandl, H. (1992). *Lern- und Denkstrategien. Analyse und Intervention.* Göttingen: Hogrefe.

Friedrich, H.F. (1999). Unterrichtsmethoden und Lernstrategien. In J. Wiechmann (Ed.), *Unterrichtsmethoden* (pp. 163-172). Weinheim: Beltz.

Gräber, W., & Bolte, C. (Eds.). (1997).: *Scientific Literacy – An International Symposium.* Kiel: IPN.

Gräsel, C. (1997). *Problemorientiertes Lernen.* Göttingen: Hogrefe.

Hannafin, M.J., Hill, J.R., & McCarthy, J.E. (in press). Designing resource-based learning performance support systems. In D. Wiley (Ed.), *The instructional use of learning objects.* Bloomington, IN: Association for Educational Communications & Technology.

Holley, C.D., & Dansereau, D.F. (1984). Networking: technique and the empirical evidence. In C.D. Holley, & D.F. Dansereau (Eds.), *Spatial learning strategies: Techniques, applications, and related issues* (pp. 81-108). Orlando: Academic Press.

Jonassen, D.H., Beissner, K., & Yacci, M. (Eds.). (1993). *Structural knowledge. Techniques for representing, conveying, and acquiring structural knowledge.* Hillsdale, NJ: Lawrence Erlbaum Ass.

Kommers, P. (1997). Conceptual Awareness for Students Navigation in the Information Ocean, Available online March 15, 2005: http://hpk.felk.cvut.cz/iso2/poskole/historie/kommers97.htm

Kommers, P., & Lanzing, J. (1997). Student's concept mapping for hypermedia design. Navigation through the world wide web (WWW) space and self-assessment. *Journal of Interactive Learning Research, 8*(3/4), 421-455.

Konrad, K. (2000). Selbstgesteuertes Lernen: Differentielle Effekte unterschiedlicher Handlungsfelder und demographischer Variablen. *Unterrichtswissenschaft, 28,* 75-91.

Mandl, H., & Fischer, F. (2000). *Wissen sichtbar machen. Wissensmanagement mit Mapping-Techniken.* Göttingen: Hogrefe.

McCagg, E.C., & Dansereau, D.F. (1991). A convergent paradigm for examining knowledge mapping as a learning strategy. *Journal of Educational Research, 84* (6), 317-324.

Novak, J.D., & Gowin, D.B. (1984). *Learning how to learn.* New York: Cambridge University Press.

O'Donnell, A.M., Dansereau, D.F., & Hall, R.H. (2002). Knowledge maps as scaffolds for cognitive processing. *Educational Psychology Review, 14*(1), 71-86.

Pintrich, P.R., & De Groot, E.V. (1990). Motivational and self-regulated learning components of classroom academic performance. *Journal of Educational Psychology 82,* 33-40.

Pintrich, P.R., Roeser, R.W., & De Groot, E.V. (1994). Classroom and individual differences in early adolescents' motivation and self-regulated learning. *Journal of Early Adolescence, 14*,139-161.

Rakes, G.C. (1996). Using the Internet as a tool in a resource-based learning environment. *Educational Technology 36*, 52-56.

Simons, P.R.-J. (1993). Constructive learning: The role of the learner. In: Th. M. Duffy, J. Lowyck, & D.H. Jonassen (Eds.), *Designing environments for constructive learning* (pp. 291-313). Berlin: Springer.

Steiner, G. (1993). Übung macht den Meister. *Computer und Unterricht, 9* (3), 4-9.

Sweller, J. (1994). Cognitive Load theory, learning difficulty and instructional design. *Learning and Instruction, 4*, 295-312.

Tergan, S.-O. (2003). Managing knowledge with computer-based mapping tools. In D. Lassner, & C. Mc Naught (Eds.), *Proceedings of the ED-Media 2003 World Conference on Educational Multimedia, Hypermedia & Telecommunication* (pp. 2514-2517), June 23-28, 2003. Honolulu, Hawaii (USA). Norfolk, VA, USA: AACE.

Weinstein, C. E. (1988). Assessment and training of student learning strategies. In R.R. Schmeck (Ed.), *Learning strategies and learning styles* (pp. 291-316). New York: Plenum Press.

Weinstein, C.E., & Palmer, D.R. (1992). LASSI-T, Potential Item Set. September 9.

Wild, K.-P., & Schiefele, U. (1994). Lernstrategien im Studium: Ergebnisse zur Faktorenstruktur und Reliabilität eines neuen Fragebogens. *Zeitschrift für Differenzielle und Diagnostische Psychologie, 15*, 185-200.

Yin, Y., Vanides, J., Ruiz-Primo, M.A., Ayala, C.C., & Shavelson, R.J. (2005). Comparison of two concept-mapping techniques: Implications for scoring, interpretation, and use. *Journal of Research in Science Teaching, 42*(2), 166-184.

Knowledge-Oriented Organization of Information for Fostering Information Use

LEO: A Concept Map Based Course Visualization Tool for Instructors and Students

John W. Coffey

The Institute for Human and Machine Cognition and
Department of Computer Science, The University of West Florida
Pensacola, FL 32514, USA
jcoffey@uwf.edu

Abstract. This work describes a software program named LEO, a Learning Environment Organizer that provides information and knowledge visualization capabilities to students and instructors. LEO provides a Concept Map-like interface that in enhanced with extra features for course design and delivery. As such, it serves as a meta-cognitive tool for course designers and an advance organizer for students. This article contains a description of how LEO supports information and knowledge visualization for students and instructors, in the context of courseware development and course delivery.

1 Introduction

The volume of information and knowledge that is available to students and instructors in a modern course of study has never been greater than it is today. Additionally, the increasingly student-centered nature of modern e-learning courses means that students have arguably never before had greater *opportunity* or greater *responsibility* to determine what is relevant to a learning activity. Tools that can help students comprehend large quantities of information and that can organize knowledge pertaining to a course can play a valuable role in educational system efficacy.

Instructors can benefit from software tools that foster conceptualization of courses and the organization of content as well. Well-conceived software tools that help instructors organize and present courses either face-to-face, in hybrid fashion with both a face-to-face and a distance component, or at a distance, are clearly of value.

A goal of the work reported in this article is to find what is believed to be a natural overlap between those visual representations and methods that help students and teachers understand information and others that help them visualize and understand knowledge. Information visualizations can involve schemes to visualize large data sets, different aggregations of data or changing data over time, typically represented in a graphical representation. To the degree that information visualizations afford the user the ability to look at information in different ways, information visualizations are knowledge-based visualizations. Additionally, knowledge visualizations may be viewed as well-structured information visualizations with additional semantic content.

This article contains a description of a Learning Environment organizer named LEO that helps both students and instructors to visualize and organize large quantities of information and knowledge. LEO is comprised of elements that implement in a

S.-O. Tergan and T. Keller (Eds.): Knowledge and Information Visualization, LNCS 3426, pp. 285–301, 2005.
© Springer-Verlag Berlin Heidelberg 2005

highly integrated way, several human-computer interface features that have been suggested by the information visualization and knowledge visualization literature.

The rest of this article contains a brief summary description of information and knowledge visualization literature that pertains to educational technology for course presentations. The information visualization discussion describes formative work in areas such as focus and context visualizations, fisheye lens, and the like. The knowledge visualization component describes graphical representations of knowledge such as advance organizers and meta-cognitive tools, and closes with a discussion of Concept Map-based knowledge modeling of the sort that was originated at the Institute for Human and Machine Cognition (IHMC). LEO is described in the context of this review. Several examples of interface features that support information and knowledge visualization are presented and described. The article closes with a case study and a summary and discussion of issues raised and addressed by this work.

2 Information and Knowledge Visualizations and Educational Software

This section contains a review of literature pertaining to the visualization of information and knowledge. The literature addresses approaches that allow users to visualize large amounts of information and to retrieve information efficiently. It also describes visual representations of knowledge, mostly in the form of graphical representations for humans to utilize. A method of knowledge modeling and visualization that was originated at IHMC is briefly discussed. For more information on methods and software that support this form of knowledge modeling, see the paper by Alberto Cañas in this volume.

2.1 Information Visualization Approaches

A large body of literature exists on various types of information visualizations. This brief review will address a few of the major approaches that have been identified. Visual representations of data encompassing a range from simple bar charts and histograms through complex, dynamical, 3-dimensional visualizations have been described. Information visualization techniques clearly have applicability to information related to instruction.

The obvious course components that might be visualized include the overall organization of the course, instructional resources associated with topics, evaluation elements such as assignments and tests, communications among students and teacher, etc. Capabilities that facilitate access to individual course components such as these are of value in understanding the scope and organization of the course. The following describes a few representative approaches from information visualization literature that might be brought to bear on the organization, presentation and manipulation of these elements.

Furnas (1981) did ground-breaking work in information visualization. An early idea was to show at close distance, things near the center of the display, while the rest of the structure may be seen in less detail as one scans further away from the center. Such an approach allows the user to start with a low-detail global view, and to zoom in on selected parts of a specific region, while maintaining a visualization of the remainder of the global view.

Card, Mackinlay & Schneiderman (1999) contains descriptions of other context and focus schemes. These include Bifocal Lens (Spense & Apperley, 1999) and 2D and 3D distortion viewing (Carpendale, Cowperthwaite & Fracchia, 1999). These techniques involve creating distorted views of the information space to enable the area upon which the user is focusing to be large enough to read, while maintaining a view of the entire space. Schneiderman (1998) presents several heuristics for context/focus ratios, the need to maintain aspect ratio between the context and focus, etc.

Chuah, Roth, Mattis, and Kolojejchick (1995) describe selective dynamic manipulations of data. They describe deficiencies in static representations of data and illustrate several 3D representations that allow selection of an area of interest, and highly interactive manipulations of the data of interest. They discuss several foundational issues pertaining to dynamic manipulations of the visualization including the method of selecting an area of interest, the sorts of interactive operations that are permitted, and the sorts of display and feedback that is provided to the user.

Andrews (1999) presents a taxonomy of information visualization techniques including two-dimensional link maps which indicate connections among nodes in potentially large graphs, three-dimensional views, tree maps which can represent large quantities of hierarchically organized data, hyperbolic visualizations of large trees, etc. In this work, Andrews discusses his "Harmony Information Landscape," a composite, three-dimensional structure map that presents a two-dimensional overview of the information space, and a three-dimensional focus on a subset of the space.

This review briefly surveys the wide range of information visualizations that have been identified and described, from simple, static representations to highly interactive complex representations of multi-dimensional data. Several means through which the user can manipulate the interface to widen or narrow the information bandwidth have been incorporated into LEO. These elements will be described after the next section on knowledge visualization literature.

2.2 Knowledge Visualization

Knowledge visualizations require some representation scheme for the externalization of knowledge, and some sort of organizing factor for the externalized knowledge. As an example, the overall organization of the knowledge in a linear text such as this article is difficult to glean without a summarization such as an outline. As with information visualization schemes, the problem of representation is made more difficult by having large volumes of knowledge to visualize. A variety of representations and tools have been made to address this problem. The following sections review and summarize literature pertaining to advance organizers and meta-cognitive tools for knowledge representation and visualization.

Advance Organizers. Advance Organizers are devices that are used to present global summarizations of content to be learned to the student. Advance Organizers have been used and described in a wide range of courses from elementary school (Kang, 1996) to graduate research methodology courses (DaRos & Onwuegbuzie, 1999).

They have also been used in a wide variety of knowledge domains such as biology (Shapiro, 1999), foreign language (Herron, 1994), and economics (Peterson & Bean, 1998).

Ausubel (1968) was one of the early advocates of the use of advance organizers to foster meaningful learning, and he describes their role in the progressive differentiation of learned concepts. Advance organizers support the notion of subsumptive learning by making explicit the general, superordinate concepts to be learned, and how they interrelate. Ausubel states that by presenting a global representation of the knowledge to be learned, advance organizers foster "integrative reconciliation" of the subdomains of knowledge, and the ability to understand in a meaningful way, the interconnections among the subdomains. Integrative reconciliation occurs because organizers make explicit either the ways in which previously learned concepts are related, or the fact that they are not related.

The advent of the Internet and hypermedia/multimedia, have given rise to a broad range of possible representations that may be utilized as advance organizers. Modern advance organizers take the form of text passages /Kang; 1996; Herron, 1994), graphical representations and maps (Jones, Farquhar & Surry, 1995), and description + pictures (Herron, 1994; Herron, Hanley & Cole, 1995). When created for hypermedia systems, advance organizers have been used to represent global concepts, indicate paths through the content, or provide access to individual components. Krawchuk (1996) presents a taxonomy of advance organizers that includes traditional textual summaries and basic themes that are presented before instruction, graphical organizers that provide organizations rendered in lines and arrows (like flowcharts), and pictorial graphic organizers. The latter category includes Concept Maps.

Concept Maps can be utilized as advance organizers (Willerman & Mac Harg, 1991). Concept maps are comprised of concepts, which are "perceived regularities in events or objects, or records of events or objects designated by a label" (Novak & Gowin, 1984; Novak, 1998). Concept maps structure a set of concepts into a semi-hierarchical framework. More general, inclusive, superordinate concepts are found at the highest levels, with progressively more specific, less inclusive, subordinate concepts arranged below them.

The concepts in concept maps are linked together by linking phrases that make explicit their relationships and form propositions. Propositions form semantic units by linking together two or more concepts. Novak states that propositions are the principle units that form meaning. Concept Maps used as advance organizers help the student visualize and understand how the map creator, presumably an expert on the subject, structures knowledge of a domain. The interface in LEO is a Concept Map that is augmented with many elements that tailor it to use for course creation and presentation.

Meta-cognitive tools. In the broadest sense, meta-cognition is thinking about one's thought processes. Most of the literature on meta-cognitive tools addresses general-purpose tools for students and others. However, a well-conceived meta-cognitive tool could play a valuable role in helping instructors to reflect on the important elements of a course, topics, and any necessary sequencing issues relative to mastery of the content. The remainder of this section describes tools that might potentially be of use to instructors who are developing courses.

Several graphical representations that are meant to foster reflection and meta-cognition, such as Concept Maps (Novak & Gowin, 1984), Semantic Networks (Fisher, 1990), Mind Maps (Buzan & Buzan, 1996), and Knowledge Maps (Lambiotte, Skaggs & Dansereau, 1993), have been described in the literature. These representations and their accompanying tools help users to externalize and understand what they know about a knowledge domain. Although all these are graphical depictions used to represent conceptual knowledge, they differ in a variety of ways. For instance, in some cases the linking lines drawn between concepts are labeled, in others they are not. If linking phrases are labeled, the set of labels may be pre-specified or unconstrained. Concepts may be comprised of single words, short phrases, sentences, or entire paragraphs. Some of the tools available for these representations allow association of other resources with the concepts that are represented. *SemNet* (Fisher, 2000) permits creation of Fisher's Semantic Networks. Several tools such as *Mind Manager* (2003) and *Visual Mind* (2003) facilitate creation of Mind Maps.

Novak and Gowin (1984) describe Concept Maps and Vee diagrams as meta-cognitive tools. The Concept Map is the least constrained of the various meta-cognitive tools enumerated above, and provides excellent capabilities for both students and teachers to represent and reflect upon what they know about a knowledge domain. Novak and Iuli (1991) discuss the use of Concept Maps as meta-cognitive tools that help people to think about thinking.

In the broader context, Kasowitz (2000) describes a wide range of tools that she states foster reflection on instructional designs including advisory systems, information management systems, and authoring tools for computer-based instruction. Her article provides a general taxonomy that illustrates the range of tools that support development of instructional materials. Nkambou, Frasson, Gauthier, & Rouane (2001), describe their Curriculum Representation and Acquisition Model (CREAM) which supports creation and organization of the curriculum by domain, pedagogical approach, and didactic aspects of the teaching. Ritter & Blessing (1998) describe their *Visual Translator*, a tool designed to support development of large-scale educational systems.

Other sorts of meta-cognitive tools have been described in the literature as well. Hedberg (1997) discusses meta-cognitive tools that he describes as being embedded in an "information landscape." These tools are designed to assist students in their investigation of scientific topics and with the writing process. In his book, Hyerle (2000) examines the use of visual tools such as task-specific organizers, and thinking-process maps that are similar to Concept Maps and Mind Maps. He describes ways that various categories of users use these tools, and the beneficial effects such tools have on reading and writing.

CmapTools **and knowledge models.** *CmapTools* (Cañas, Coffey, Reichherzer, Hill, Suri, Carff, Mitrovich & Eberle, 1998; Cmap Tools, 2003; Ford, Coffey, Cañas, Turner & Andrews, 1996), which are described in the chapter by Alberto Cañas in this volume, provide substantial support for the creation and representation of knowledge models pertaining to a knowledge domain. Knowledge models created with *CmapTools* are based upon Concept Maps. These tools allow for the development and perusal of hierarchically structured, Concept Map-based, knowledge models, and the attachment of accompanying resources to concepts within the maps.

As such, *Cmaptools* may be characterized as a knowledge visualization tool. Knowledge models created with *CmapTools* may be developed and accessed over a network. Knowledge models created with *CmapTools* can serve as instructional content for courses organized with LEO, the topic of the next section.

3 LEO: A Learning Environment Organizer

The ideas behind LEO, a Learning Environment Organizer (Coffey, 2000; Coffey & Cañas, 2003), extend Ausubel's notion of an advance organizer (Ausubel, 1968), and Novak's characterization of Concept Maps as meta-cognitive tools. LEO augments the capabilities of *CmapTools* by adding features that support courseware design and delivery.

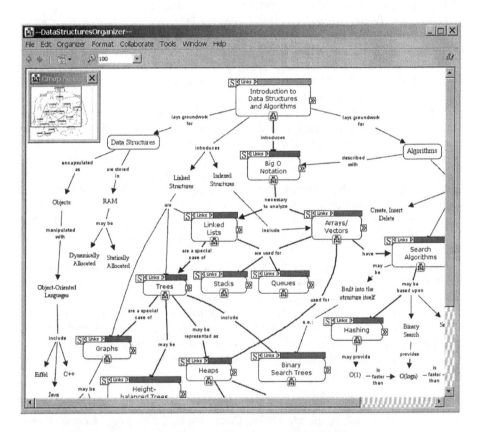

Fig. 1. A Learning Environment Organizer as the student would see it

The idea of instructors creating representations in a meta-cognitive tool that fosters reflection on the topics that they teach and the organization of their course, and then having the representation created in the tool become the interface to the course that the student uses when the course is deployed, is compelling. LEO was designed to serve as a tool for courseware designers by providing a visual representation of the course being developed, and when the course is completed and deployed, the visual representation is the course interface for the student. In the following sections, we describe the basic features of LEO and a strategy for the creation of a course Organizer using this tool.

3.1 Basic Features of LEO

An Organizer provides a framework to organize all information associated with a course. An Organizer is a graph-like structure comprised of two different types of nodes: instructional topic nodes and explanation nodes that explain about the topics. The topic nodes have a variety of adornments that distinguish them from the corollary explanatory nodes. Fig. 1 presents a view of an Organizer as a student would see it. In Fig. 1, topic nodes are depicted as those surrounded with rounded rectangles, and populated with a variety of icons. For example, "Introduction to Data Structures," "Big O Notation," "Linked Lists," "Arrays/Vectors," etc., are topic nodes. The topic nodes are linked together by heavy lines that convey prerequisite relationships among topics. For instance, the topic " Big O Notation " is a prerequisite for " Linked Lists," and "Arrays/Vectors." In turn, "Linked Lists" is a prerequisite for "Stacks," "Queues," "Trees," etc.

A variety of information is accessible through the topic nodes. Icons beneath the topics indicate links to the instructional content that can be used to learn about the topic under consideration and to descriptions of the tasks or activities associated with the topic. Additionally, other icons provide access to collaboration tools and a progress indicator. A clickable region above the topic label (currently displaying "links" in the topic nodes in Fig. 1) allows the user to toggle through displays of these items. The student or instructor can click on the selector to move through a sequence of displays that includes: <links> (links to instructional content), <criteria> (the completion criteria for the topic), <tools> (collaboration tools associated with each topic - instant messaging and threaded discussions) and <progress> (an indication of progress the student is making with the various completion criteria associated with the topic). When the user selects any of these choices, the set of icons associated with that element of that topic display.

When the user clicks an icon associated with one of these elements, a pull-down menu appears to indicate the links to electronic resources that are available in that context. Separate icons exist for the various electronic media types to which a link might be made such as text, graphics, other Concept Maps, Web pages and other application programs. The icon to the left of a topic node indicates whether the student can indicate completion of a topic's requirements or if deliverables (projects, papers, tests, etc) are required and the instructor is the one to indicate when the topic has been completed. Explanation nodes, which are also visible in Fig. 1, elaborate the relationships among the topic nodes and have no adornments.

3.2 LEO as an Information and Knowledge Visualization Tool for Students

The Organizer is created by the course instructor or instructional designer, and deployed when a course is offered. When students are added to the database associated with an instance of a course, a profile is created on the server for each one. When the student logs on to the system, the profile and all accompanying information is retrieved. As the student works through the course completing topics, the profile is updated to reflect the progress. At any given time, the status of each of the topics in a course is one of the following: {completed, ready, current, not-ready}. The topic nodes have colored bars at the top that change color to reflect the changing status of the topics as the student works through the course. Information pertaining to student progress is loaded from the student profile each time the student logs on and is used to update the student's display.

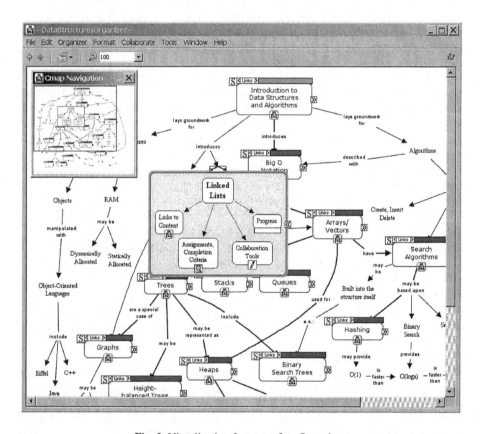

Fig. 2. Visualization features of an Organizer

Fig. 2 contains a display of an Organizer illustrating two of the visualization features. The first feature is the floating window in the upper left of the large window. It is a context view of the Organizer that presents a reduced view of the entire organizer. It contains a rectangle that represents the focus area in the large view and it enables the user to navigate around the organizer easily. This presentation was motivated by the work on focus and context visualizations, and it adheres to principles from the literature such as the preservation of aspect ratio between focus and context.

The second feature is the expanded node labeled "Linked Lists" near the center of the focus view. This capability affords the user a simultaneous view of all the information associated with the topic – the links to instructional content, the various assignments and completion criteria for the assignments, the collaboration tools, and the progress indicator. Clicking the small button on the right side of the containing rectangle of the expanded node closes the node so that it looks like the other topic nodes. Clicking the same button on a closed node such as "Arrays/Vectors" causes the node to open like the node containing the elements pertaining to Linked Lists.

Interface features like these allow the user to broaden or narrow the information bandwidth associated with an organizer. They allow the instructor to view the instructional resources that have been associated with a topic at a glance, and they allow the student to access any of the resources easily. Closing the expanded node allows the user to read the organizer itself in order to glean the conceptual relationships among the topics and explanatory nodes. These features allow tailoring of the organizer to serve purposes that range from highly conceptual (the Organizer as a global view of the conceptual relationships among topics in a course) to utilitarian (the Organizer as a highly sophisticated electronic filing system, affording access to course resources).

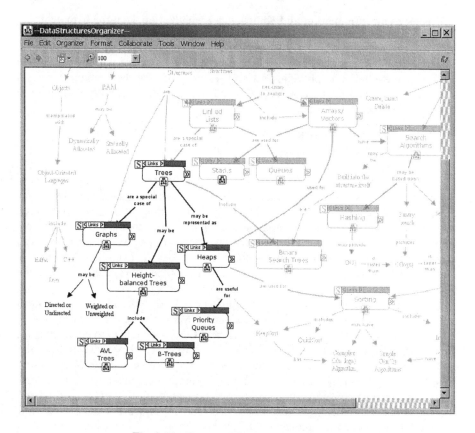

Fig. 3. The Focus and Regional Context view

Another feature that helps users tailor the display to their own needs is the show/hide feature. The student or instructor can configure the display in terms of elements that can be viewed or grayed out. Fig. 3 illustrates a case in which the user has selected the part of the organizer pertaining to trees and graphs as the focus of attention. The relevant nodes and links are displayed normally, but the surrounding context is grayed to minimize distractions. This approach is called a *"focus and regional context"* representation. It enables the user to define a specific focus while still being able to see, read and comprehend the neighborhood around the focus. This capability enables the user to address the elements of interest while still seeing the neighboring context.

Students can also utilize a capability to show or hide specific categories of organizer elements. For instance, the student can show or gray out all the explanatory information, leaving the topics, their sequences, and the labeled links among them. The student can also show or gray the topics that they have completed, the items for which they are not yet ready because of not having completed a prerequisite, etc. These customizations allow the student to set up the organizer in a wide range of configurations.

3.3 LEO as an Information and Knowledge Visualization Tool for Instructors

LEO affords two broad categories of capabilities for information and knowledge visualization for the instructor. First, LEO serves as a meta-cognitive tool for courseware creation and evolution by providing a visual representation of the evolving course. It also provides an information organization and management capability pertaining to two critical elements of a course:

- The organization of instructional materials associated with the course.
- The progress of the students in a currently-offered course.

Creating and maintaining courses. The use of an editor to create Concept maps fosters reflection on the organization of the course, and an organizing factor for instructional resources pertaining to the course. LEO's editing environment provides a modeless drawing capability that greatly simplifies the creation of a graphical representation of the course. The editing environment inherits the drag-and-drop capabilities for the association of resources with nodes in maps that *CmapTools* provides. Additionally, the editing environment affords the course designer the same that the student can use.

A close relationship exists between Organizers and Concept Maps. A method has been presented for the conversion of a Concept Map into an Organizer (Coffey, 2000). The basic approach is to analyze and modify a concept map to ensure that all the important information is in the map and then to create the organizer from the modified map. The approach starts by ensuring that all potential topics are in the map, followed by a "leveling" of the map to an appropriate granularity. Once all the important concepts are in the map, and an appropriate level of granularity has been attained, topics are identified and sequenced, and resources are associated with them. Table 1 presents a summary of the method. Working from a visual representation of the course Organizer greatly facilitates the performance of the steps enumerated in Table 1.

The use of LEO plays two helpful roles in fostering the reuse of existing course specifications and instructional content (Coffey & Cañas, 2001). It fosters the creation of course templates that can be modified for specific audiences. The environment also provides a semi-automated means of cataloguing content that has been used with xml-based, IMS compliant metadata tags. This cataloguing facilitates identification of content in order to foster its reuse.

Table 1. A process to convert a Concept Map into a course Organizer

Analysis of the Concept Map
1. Identify and delete noise nodes, remove any redundancies, remove any overly detailed nodes.
2. Determine if any important concepts (that might become topics) do not appear in the Concept Map and add them if any are identified.
3. Reconstruct the Concept Map.
Transformation of the map into a course description
4. Select and mark topic nodes.
5. Map dependency or prerequisite relationships among topic nodes, including alternative organizations of the dependencies.
6. Rearrange the maps to accommodate the dependency links.

A Concept Map created with *CmapTools* can be opened in the LEO editor and can be made into an Organizer by designating a node in the map as a topic. From there it can be augmented with the accoutrements of course topics such as links to instructional content, assignments, completion criteria for topics, tests, etc. Likewise, an organizer created with LEO may be saved as a Concept map by removing all topic nodes and saving. Such an operation places items associated with assignments in the appropriate resource group of the Concept Map representation.

Information management in a deployed course. Once a course has been constructed and is being offered, LEO provides capabilities to track student progress. The instructor can access an organizer from the "Views" window in *CmapTools* by double clicking the organizer of interest. Fig. 4 presents the instructor's view of a course from within LEO. The instructor's view of the organizer is similar to the student's, but with some extra functionality. The instructor can see all the instructional resources through the same views that the student has. Additionally, the panel on the right in Fig. 4 can be opened or closed. When it is opened, the instructor can see all his or her currently active course sections. Clicking on the [+] symbol next to a course opens the course and displays all the students in the course.

This display provides information about the entire class and about individual students. Next to the course name is an overall indication of the percentage of topics completed by the entire class. Next to each student name is an indication of the progress that student has made. When the instructor clicks on a student name in the list, the student's profile is retrieved and the color codings on the organizer's topics are updated to reflect the current status of the student. The instructor can also access the threaded discussions associated with each topic in the course from this display. The instructor can update topic status in individual student profiles through this interface, typically by changing the status to completed. Additional functionality on the server allows the instructor to update student records from a different view as well.

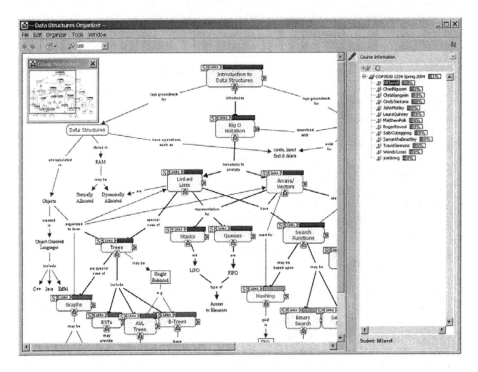

Fig. 4. The Instructor's view of an Organizer with a student profile selected

3.4   Issues Pertaining to Uses by Students and Instructors

The LEO environment allows significant visual tailoring or personalization of the environment both for instructors and students. However, these tailorings pertain to the display they see, not to the content that is linked into a course. *CmapTools* provides password protection of knowledge models, and within authorized users, read-only and read-update levels of access. The instructor has the option of allowing students to add items into a knowledge model pertaining to a course. Students could potentially enhance the richness of the instructional materials by adding resource links into a knowledge model, but empirical work needs to be done to determine if this approach is feasible and desirable. For instance, with update-level access, a student also would be able to delete items as well.

In future versions, students will be able to customize their organizer environments by adding additional resource links. For instance, they will be able to attach notes to topics in the Organizer, to create links to Web sites and other instructional resources that pertain to the course, etc. Since these changes will be persisted in the individual student's profile, they will not clutter up other students' workspaces with items other students may not be interested in viewing. Furthermore, the capability will be limited to "add."

However, it should be noted that students will not be allowed to change topics or sequences that have been established by the instructor. Such mid-stream changes impose significant difficulties in sequence tracking for prerequisites, and are deemed undesirable. Accordingly, it is incumbent upon the instructor to ensure that the set of topics and their organization or sequence is conceptually sound and complete for the course s/he wishes to present, and then to freeze that part of the Organizer before the course is published. The visual representation of topics and sequences enables the instructor to get to a good course layout before deploying the course.

3.5 An Example Organizer and Knowledge Model

Fig. 5 is a graphic of a course that has content rendered in a knowledge model built with *CmapTools*, and an Organizer created with LEO. The scenario depicted in Fig. 4 has the student opening an Organizer from the "Views" window in the back-left. The student is working on the "Linked List" topic in the Organizer. It can be seen in the

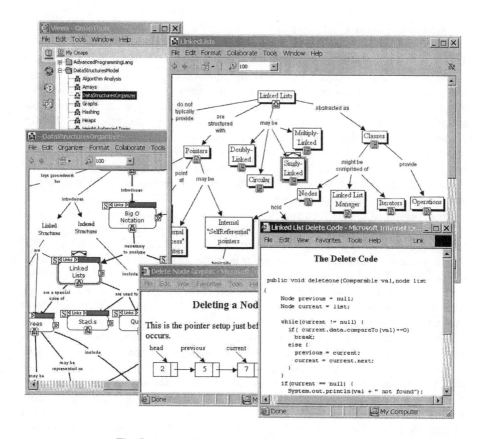

Fig. 5. An example organizer with a knowledge model

Organizer that the student has completed prerequisites for the Linked Lists topic. The student selected the link to content and navigated into a Concept Map pertaining to linked lists. That window is visible in the top right. From there, the student selected a piece of program code pertaining to insertion of a node into a linked list, and is also viewing an accompanying graphic of the operation.

The student has substantial capability at this point. Search capabilities in *Cmap-Tools* allow the student to search for content having descriptors of interest both within *CmapTools* and on the World Wide Web. The student can view the completion criteria for the topic and work through the instructional materials the instructor has provided. The student can access questions or other learning activities associated with the topic, directly from the topic itself. The student can make postings to threaded discussions pertaining to the topic, or can chat with others who are having instant messaging sessions. Additionally, the student will shortly be able to take on-line testing via a capability that is near completion called *xTEST*. All of this capability is tied together by a visual representation of the course and its associated components that has been constituted in accordance with principles of information and knowledge visualization and sound pedagogical theory.

4 Summary and Conclusions

This paper contains a description LEO, a network-enabled software tool based upon extensions to Concept Maps. LEO can be used to help course designers or instructors to visualize and plan course organizations, and is then used to present the visualization of the course to the student. A learning environment organizer is a graph-like structure in which some of the nodes are designated as topics and others provide supplementary information that elucidates the relationships among the topics. Topic nodes have a variety of relevant information attached including links to content pertinent to the topic, completion criteria or assignments pertaining to the topic, a variety of collaboration capabilities including instant messaging and threaded discussions, and an indication of student progress.

Ideas behind LEO take their impetus from Ausubel's Assimilation Theory (1968). Assimilation theory holds that a representation such as an advance organizer, that fosters progressive differentiations of subsumable concepts and the integration of superordinate concepts, can play a salutary role in the meaningful learning of a domain of knowledge. LEO is based upon a graphical representation of concepts and their interrelationships that explicitly presents a global conceptual organization of a knowledge domain to the learner. Visual representations of advance organizers have been shown to be effective in fostering meaningful learning.

LEO incorporates several elements that foster information and knowledge visualization. Information visualization literature identifies representations including focus and context, the ability to show or hide or to emphasize or de-emphasize elements in a display. Information visualization is also fostered by allowing for customizable information presentation spaces. LEO provides the user with a focus and context scheme that facilitates navigation around a potentially large course organizer. LEO presents the capability to tailor a display to the needs of the individual user by emphasizing or de-emphasizing sub-graphs within the organizer. The user can emphasize or gray out the explanatory elements in an organizer, any category of topics such as those that are completed or for which the user is not ready, or user selected subgraphs.

These basic features are all realized in the context of a knowledge visualization scheme. Graphical Advance organizers are graphical representations of the global structural knowledge in a course. LEO is a graphical advance organizer based upon Concept Maps with the added capabilities to mark individual concepts as the topics in the course, and to indicate the conceptual relationships among all the concepts including the topics. Additionally, since Concept Maps and organizers are directed graphs, LEO provides a capability to indicate prerequisite relationships among the topics in the course. It is also possible to indicate a relationship between topics that does not indicate a prerequisite relationship.

Just as LEO provides an advance organizer for the student, it provides a metacognitive tool for course designers or instructors to foster reflection on course organizations. The visual representation of the course layout facilitates exploration of different course organizations for the designer.

Acknowledgements. The author would like to acknowledge the significant contributions of his dissertation advisor, Dr. Alberto Cañas in the formulation of ideas contained in this work. The author would also like to thank Chad Carff, Michael Webb, John Wernicke, and Michael Wooten for the many insights they gleaned and provided in the process of developing LEO. This work was partially funded by the Office of the Chief of Naval Education and Training, USA.

References

Andrews, K. (1999). Visualizing cyberspace: Information visualization in the Harmony Internet Browser. In S. Card, J. Mackinlay, & B. Shneidermann (Eds.), *Readings in information visualization: Using vision to think* (pp. 493-502). San Francisco, CA: Morgan Kaufmann Publications.

Ausubel, D.P. (1968). *Educational psychology: A cognitive view.* New York: Rinehart and Winston.

Buzan, T., & Buzan, B. (19969). *The Mind Map book: How to use radiant thinking to maximize your brain's untapped potential.* New York: Plume.

Cañas A.J., Coffey, J.W., Reichherzer, T., Hill, G., Suri, N., Carff, R., Mitrovich, T., & Eberle, D. (1998). El-Tech: A performance support system with embedded training for electronics technicians. In D.J. Cook (Ed.), *Proceedings of the Eleventh Florida AI Research Symposium (FLAIRS '98)* (pp. 79-83). Menlo Park, CA: AAAI Press.

Card, S.K., Mackinlay, J.D., & Shneiderman, B. (1999). Focus and context. In S. Card, J. Mackinlay, & B. Shneidermann (Eds.), *Readings in information visualization: Using vision to think* (pp. 307-309). San Francisco, CA: Morgan Kaufmann Publications.

Carpendale, M.S.T., Cowperthwaite, D.J., & Fracchia, F.D. (1999). Extending distortion viewing from 2D to 3D. In S. Card, J. Mackinlay, & B. Shneidermann (Eds.), *Readings in information visualization: Using vision to think* (pp. 368-380). San Francisco, CA: Morgan Kaufmann Publications.

Chuah, M.C., Roth, S.F. Mattis, J., & Kolojejchick, J. (1995). SDM: Selective Dynamic Manipulation of Visualizations. In G. Robertson (Ed.), *Proceedings of UIST ' 95, the Eighth Annual Symposium on User Interface Software and Technology* (pp. 61-70). New York, NY: ACM Press.

CmapTools (2003). *IHMC Concept Map Software, a knowledge construction toolkit.* Online available: http://cmap.coginst.uwf.edu/.

Coffey, J.W., & Cañas, A.J. (2003). LEO: A Learning Environment Organizer to support computer mediated instruction. *Journal of Educational Technology Systems, 31*(3), 275-290.

Coffey, J.W., & Cañas, A.J. (2001). Tools to foster course and content reuse in online instructional systems. In W.A. Lawrence-Fowler, & J. Hasebrook (Eds.), *Proceedings of WebNet 2001: World Conference on the WWW and Internet* (pp. 207-213). Norfolk, VA: AACE.

Coffey, J.W. (2000). LEO: *A Learning Environment Organizer to accompany constructivist knowledge models.* Unpublished Doctoral Dissertation. The University of West Florida, Pensacola, FL.

DaRos, D., & Onwuegbuzie, A.J. (1999). The Effect of Advance Organizers on Achievement in Graduate-Level Research Methodology Courses. *National Forum of Applied Educational Research Journal-Electronic, 12*(3), 83-91.

Fisher, K.M. (1990). Semantic networking: The new kid on the block. *Journal of Research in Science Teaching, 27*(10), 1001-1018.

Fisher, K.M. (2000). SemNet Software as an Assessment Tool. In J.J. Mintzes, J.H. Wandersee, & J.D. Novak (Eds.), *Assessing Science Understanding* (pp. 179-221). San Diego, CA: Academic Press.

Ford, K.M., Coffey, J.W., Cañas, A.J., Turner, C.W., & Andrews, E.J. (1996). Diagnosis and explanation by a Nuclear Cardiology Expert System. *International Journal of Expert Systems, 9*(4), 499-506.

Furnas, G.W. (1981). *The fisheye view: A new look at structured files.* Murray Hill, NJ: Bell Laboratories Technical Memorandum #81-11221-9.

Hedberg, J., Harper, B., & Wright, R. (1997). Employing cognitive tools within interactive multimedia applications. In M. Simonsen (Ed.), *Proceedings of Selected Research and Development Presentations at the 1997 National Convention of the Association for Educational Communications and Technology* (pp. 67-75). Bloomington, IN: AECT.

Herron, C.A., Hanley, J., & Cole, S. (1995). A comparison study of two advance organizers for introducing beginning foreign language students to video. *The Modern Language Journal, 79*(3), 387-395.

Herron, C.A. (1994). An investigation of the effectiveness of using an advance organizer to introduce video in a foreign language classroom. *The Modern Language Journal, 78*(2), 190-198.

Hyerle, D. (2000). *A field guide to using visual tools.* FOUND IN ERIC microfiche ED443784.

Jones, M.G., Farquhar, J.D., & Surry, D.D. (1995). Using metacognitive theories to design user interfaces for computer-based learning. *Educational Technology, 35*(4), 12-22.

Kang, S. (1996). The effects of using an advance organizer on students' learning in a computer simulation environment. *Journal of Educational Technology Systems, 25*(1), 57-65.

Kasowitz, A. (2000). Tools for Automating Instructional Design. *Educational Media and Technology Yearbook, 25*, 49-52.

Krawchuk, C.A. (1996). *Pictorial graphic organizers, navigation, and hypermedia: Converging constructivist and cognitive views.* Doctoral Dissertation. West Virginia University.

Lambiotte, J., Skaggs, L., & Dansereau, D. (1993). Learning from lectures: Effects of knowledge maps and cooperative review strategies. *Applied Cognitive Psychology, 7*, 483-497.

Mind Manager: Mind Manager (2003). *The visual tool for brainstorming and planning.* [Online] available: http://www.mindjet.com/index.shtml.

Nkambou, R., Frasson, C., Gauthier, G., & Rouane, K. (2001). An Authoring Model and Tools for Knowledge Engineering in Intelligent Tutoring. *Journal of Interactive Learning Research, 12*(4), 323-357.

Novak J.D., & Iuli, R.J. (1991). *The use of meta-cognitive tools to facilitate knowledge production.* A paper presented at the Fourth Florida AI Research Symposium (FLAIRS '91), Pensacola Beach, FL.

Novak, J.D., & Gowin, D.B. (1984). *Learning how to learn.* Cambridge, UK: Cambridge University Press.

Novak, J.D. (1998). *Learning, creating, and using knowledge: Concept maps as facilitative tools in schools and corporations.* Mahweh, NJ: Lawrence Erlbaum Associates.

Peterson, D., & Bean, J.C. (1998). Using a Conceptual Matrix to Organize a Course in the History of Economic Thought. *Journal of Economic Education, 29*(3), 262-273.

Ritter, S., & Blessing, S.B. (1998). Authoring Tools for Component-Based Learning Environments. *Journal of the Learning Sciences, 7*(1), 107-132.

Shneiderman, B. (1998). *Designing the user interface: Strategies for effective human-computer interaction* (3rd Ed.). Menlo Park, CA: Addison Wesley.

Shapiro, A.M. (1999). The Relationship between Prior Knowledge and Interactive Overviews During Hypermedia-Aided Learning. *Journal of Educational Computing Research, 20*(2), 143-167.

Spense, R., & Apperley, M. (1999). Database navigation: An office environment for the professional. In S. Card, J. Mackinlay, & B. Shneidermann (Eds.), *Readings in information visualization: Using vision to think* (pp. 333-340). San Francisco, CA: Morgan Kaufmann Publications.

Visual Mind (2003). *Visual Mind: The software that helps you think.* [Online] available: http://www.visual-mind.com/.

Willerman, M., & Mac Harg, R.A. (1991). The concept map as an advance organizer. *Journal or Research in Science Teaching, 28*(8), 705-711.

Navigating Personal Information Repositories with Weblog Authoring and Concept Mapping

Sebastian Fiedler[1] and Priya Sharma[2]

[1] University of Augsburg, Universitätsstr. 10,
86135 Augsburg, Germany
sebastianfiedler@cognitivearchitects.de
[2] The Pennsylvania State University, Instructional Systems Program,
314C Keller Building, University Park, PA 16802, USA
psharma@psu.edu

Abstract. The advent of the Web and the information economy has changed the requirements for learning in the workplace and higher education. To deal with ill-structured, amorphous information, learners need to become self-organized learners capable of identifying both content and process of own learning. Engagement in the learning conversations of self-organized learning requires methods for representing information spontaneously as well as organizing information within a meaningful structure. In this chapter, we identify the role of the emerging practices of Weblog authoring and concept mapping in supporting knowledge construction and meaning-making in amorphous domains. We indicate how the structure and practices of Weblog authoring support construction of a personal repository of information as well as ability to engage in shared dialogue about artifacts. We then identify the facilitatory role of concept mapping in organizing knowledge, and conclude with suggestions for visual mapping tools to support seamless integration of information archival and mapping.

1 Introduction

The advent of the information age has changed the demands for learning in the workplace and in higher education. Organizations demand individuals who can learn and adapt on the job. In the globalized information economy, successful learning is less concerned with mastering discrete bodies of content; instead it is more related to mastering and refining one's learning and information search strategies (Sculley, 1991). It is within this context that we explore the role of two specific forms of information representation in furthering individual learning. In this chapter, we present and describe the role of two discrete technologies - Weblogs and concept mapping - in supporting development of personally meaningful repositories of knowledge.

The Web has become a dominant source for information in the past decade, allowing for the capture, sharing, and refinement of knowledge assets (Brown, 2000). Making sense of the rapidly expanding information base that is accessible at our fingertips requires individuals to engage in conscientious, reflective evaluation of their learning and information retrieval strategies. Brown (2000) identifies two new forms of

S.-O. Tergan and T. Keller (Eds.): Knowledge and Information Visualization, LNCS 3426, pp. 302–325, 2005.
© Springer-Verlag Berlin Heidelberg 2005

learning needed in the information age: one, navigational literacy, wherein individuals navigate complex information spaces with confidence, and two, the ability to build personally relevant tools to support discovery learning. We suggest that this type of learning requires a fundamentally different approach from the type of learning implicit in a designed learning environment. In most instructionally designed environments, content tends to be relatively well structured, sequenced, and appropriately delimited. The structured nature is consistent with the goals of instructional design - that is to create effective learning sequences for learners (Smith & Ragan, 1993). Apart from offering pre-designed content, designed environments also tend to present learners with effective learning strategies to support specific types of learning.

The structure and external management implicit in this type of learning is inapplicable in the general Web informational space. On the Web, content is generated daily, in a variety of forms, and for a variety of purposes. Although the Web is only one example, we use it to illustrate many of the characteristics that are inherent in any non-designed or informal learning environment. Here learning must be individually driven, which means that individuals must take responsibility for both content and process of learning as opposed to being presented with an a priori structure and procedure. The difference from a formal learning environment is the active transfer of responsibility of learning to the learner rather than to an external authority.

This attribute is vitally important in the emerging contexts of the Web and the information age. Tergan and Keller (in this book) in their general analysis of the new demands and challenges in a world of information abundance, suggest that from an educational perspective "learning contents are often complex, ill-structured, represented in different information repositories, not pre-selected and pre-designed and sometimes have to be searched for by the learners themselves." Thus, learners will need to negotiate unknown content and simultaneously create new strategies to deal with the unknown domain. We would like to suggest that in many circumstances, a learner's search for content and strategies will become the norm rather than the exception. In fact, there is a wide agreement that the Web in its entirety could be described as a complex, ill-structured information repository, requiring active searching, filtering, selecting, organizing and structuring for most purposes that would qualify as educational in the broadest sense. One could suggest then that the outcome of learning, although purposive, is not completely known until it is achieved (Harri-Augstein & Thomas, 1991).

We are most concerned with the representation of knowledge structures in this type of organic, individually defined learning, as opposed to the more delineated, structured learning that is common to formal educational settings. Thus, instead of focusing on how individuals represent structures for discrete content knowledge, we are concerned with strategies and artifacts that individuals construct and use to navigate within amorphous, unfamiliar information. In some sense, neither the path nor the scope of needed information is initially defined. Within this process, individuals must take responsibility for all aspects of learning including dynamic goal identification, process selection, and strategy and outcome evaluation. While one portion of this activity is akin to general problem solving processes, another is related to individual control and evaluation of own learning - in other words, becoming an independent and self-organized learner.

2   Constructing Meaningful Artifacts

Self-organized learning is a theory that focuses on how individuals can take control of their own learning and how they can develop their learning skills (Harri-Augstein & Thomas, 1991, p. 88). A self-organized learner accepts responsibility for own learning and in doing so, the individual actively reflects on the functional components of personal learning processes. These components include the ability to (1) recognize needs and establish a purpose, (2) identify and use appropriate strategies and resources to meet the identified purposes, (3) evaluate the quality of outcomes, and (4) identify and employ better learning processes based on a review of the existing processes. In this context, learning consists of a series of inner and outer conversational activities - that is, learning conversations that allow individuals to learn by systematically reflecting on their processes of meaning construction through an examination of personally created artifacts as well as artifacts created by others. Learning conversations become the medium for individuals to become self-organized learners through "conversational construction, reconstruction and exchange of personally significant, relevant and viable meanings with awareness and controlled purposiveness" (Harri-Augstein & Thomas, 1991, p. 27).

The inner conversation is a dialogue with self that raises the learner's awareness of learning and processes of learning. The outer conversation is a dialogue with others and the artifacts of others to identify standards that contribute to the individual's self-evaluation about quality of learning processes and strategies. Specifically, artifacts are considered to be extant texts or conversational triggers created by others - thus, engagement with artifacts is akin to engagement with another. Engagement in the inner and outer conversations of self-organized learning requires the individual to employ appropriate representational forms that make tacit understanding and meaning more explicit (Harri-Augstein & Thomas, 1991). Ideally, the form of representation should allow construction of a structure of meaning that allows the individual to elicit items of meaning, sort relationships between items, and display a final pattern. Harri-Augstein and Thomas (1991, pp. 270-71) also suggest that the format used for representing meaning should be: (1) naturally occurring and open to multi-faceted forms of expressing and experiencing personal meaning, (2) capable of displaying hierarchy and relationship of elements within a system of meaning, (3) able to express thought and feeling as a pattern in time, and, (4) capable of allowing the individual to become aware of the intentionality underlying thoughts, feelings, and action.

In the context of the Web and new information learning ecologies (Brown, 2000), navigating information spaces requires the learner to interpret social artifacts for personal learning. Thus, individuals must be skilled in representing their learning process and learning in the form of personally relevant artifacts that guide further learning and action. To achieve a reflexive understanding of his or her own learning process, the learner must engage in internal and external dialogue using appropriate and meaningful representational forms. In this context, the next section introduces the use of Weblog technologies and concepts maps as meaningful forms of individual representation for self-organized learning.

3 Weblog Authoring

It is becoming increasingly apparent that the Web is evolving into a major platform of convergence for all kinds of digital (or digitized) artifacts. In our networked societies, considerable portions of the population have already begun to treat the Web as the primary information source. Needless to say, this perception is altering our information gathering and manipulating habits in fundamental ways, thus influencing how people work, play, communicate and learn. While the commercial boom of the late 1990's focused on the Web's advantages for distribution by bridging of time and space, recent years have seen a trend going back to the original vision of a Two-Way-Web (Berners-Lee, 2000), which allows not only for the consumption of information and services but also for personally meaningful expression, creation, and production.

One instantiation of this overall trend is the recent rise of personal and collaborative Web publishing tools and practices that radically simplify the information gathering, filtering and publishing cycle on the Web. Web publishing tools and practices support individuals in taking active roles as content collectors, editors, and authors of Web-based content, and have quickly gathered a user base which grew exponentially in the past three years. Particularly, the authoring of Weblogs developed into a major movement that now influences diverse fields including journalism, political campaigning, public relations, knowledge management, and social networking. By being a truly Web-native format and practice for gathering and publishing content (Blood, 2002), Weblog authoring supports on the development and maintenance of personal content repositories, as well as the emergence of social networks providing various types of conversational exchanges. In addition, Weblogs support collective information filtering and routing. Before we explore these characteristics in more detail, a rough description of the technical and conceptual anatomy of Weblogs might be useful to illustrate specific characteristics that support the technical requirements for self-organized learning.

3.1 Content Management Plus Publishing

Most Weblogs are currently maintained via a combined content management and publication system. The underlying technical architecture of these systems can vary, but most Weblog authors either interface with a server-based application through a standard Web browser, or run a desktop-based application on a personal computer that supports publishing on the Web. In either case these personal Weblog authoring solutions distinguish between content and presentation. Thus it is possible to gather and organize content (text, images, sound files, etc.) in a database, assemble and publish it selectively to the world or restricted groups, and tweak the style of visual presentation independently. Templates are generally coded in HTML and open for redesign by anyone who is able to read and write in this "lingua franca" of the Web. All current personal Weblog authoring solutions offer a set of default templates that allow instant Web publishing. Content is processed through the available style templates and is finally rendered as standard HTML. Rendering is either done in a dynamic fashion at the time when a page is requested by a remote client, or the rendered content is stored on a Web server that simply serves static HTML. In addition to the automatic HTML rendering of published content, most current Weblog authoring solutions can also encode selected content in XML (Extensible Markup Language) or any of its derivative formats (such as RSS, which is described later) to offer a "Webfeed" for syndication and aggregation. We will address this feature in more detail shortly.

Fig. 1 provides an illustration of a general Weblog format. The title of the Weblog is sometimes accompanied by a tagline, which can extend the Weblog's description or add detail about the Weblog's purpose. Visible immediately below the title are a series of time-stamped posts, which are probably the most standard element in any Weblog. Other components visible in this graphic are a list of the author's favorite links (sometimes referred to as a blogroll, if the links are primarily to other personal Weblogs) and a search box for finding archived posts. Additional structural elements can be present in a Weblog and can be customized by the author: We will identify some of these components in more detail in the next few sections.

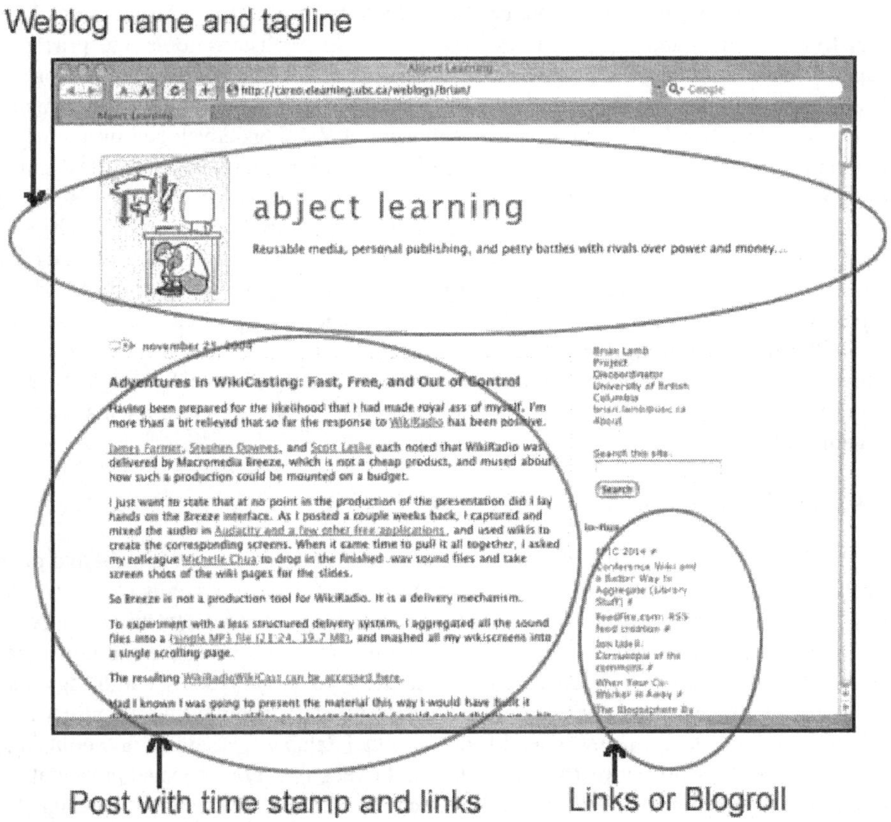

Fig. 1. Sample Weblog and basic elements

3.2 Fundamental Building Blocks

The fundamental building block of the Weblog publication format is the post. A post is a self-contained piece of content that can stand on its own in a meaningful way.

Though the current Weblog authoring praxis is dominated by text, posts can also contain images or other embedded media formats. Considerable variety exists in the presentation of Weblog posts, but recurrent elements are easy to identify. Posts usually have a title and a body of content, which is sometimes split into a summary or abstract and the main body, especially if longer pieces are published. Each post is identified by a permanent link - its own URL - that is used to address or reference this particular piece of published content on the Web. Therefore some people also speak of microcontent publishing.

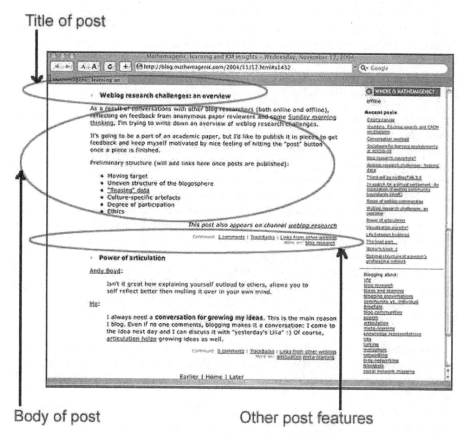

Fig. 2. Sample of a post with identified components

Fig. 2 presents a general illustration of the format of a post. For example, the post has a meaningful title, accompanied by a body, which can be of varying lengths. As illustrated in the graphic, the body of the top-most post is longer and has a different format from the body of the next post. The body also consists of hyperlinks (which are underlined and blue in color). Below the post, the author has chosen to include a variety of options that refine a visitor's ability to interpret and gather more relevant information about the post content; for example, the author has chosen to include a comment feature to allow visitor comments, a set of links to other related content, and a mechanism for visitors to cite the specific post (also called *trackback*, this feature is explained in more detail later). The features included by this specific author may be very different from those included by another Weblog author. It is important to note the availability of a set of pre-configured options, which authors can use to customize and personalize the presentation and interpretation of their content.

Weblog authoring solutions also assign a variety of metadata to each published post. The most common metadata elements are title, body of post, author of post, time stamp of publication, and a content category label of some type.

In addition posts can also carry a comment feature, allowing for direct feedback or comment by specific readers or the general public. Another popular addition is a rudimentary reference tracking solution called *trackback*, which tracks and displays instances of referencing of a particular post by other Weblog authors.

3.3 Organizational Principles

A common organizational principle of Weblogs is the reverse chronological presentation of posts. A Weblog homepage usually displays a serial collection of recently published posts. The most recent item is published at the top of this collection while older items fall off the homepage. The Weblog homepage thus functions as a window on a specified number of most recent content items. Of course, older items do not disappear. They are usually accessible through some type of chronological archive - in most cases, a hyperlinked calendar tool or an author-defined arrangement. Each published item retains its permanent URL and thus its general accessibility on the Web. Apart from the chronological organization of content, most Weblog authoring tools offer features to develop and assign a simple content category scheme. In its simplest and currently most common format, Weblog authors define a list of categories and assign each post manually to only one specific category. More elaborated tools would allow for the creation of customized metadata elements to each post for additional keywords, topics, and so forth, and for the assignment of multiple category labels to a single post.

Beyond the reverse chronological flow of posts on the homepage, Weblogs usually contain a number of more static content elements. These elements are either integrated into the overall template of the homepage, or published on dedicated Web pages.

One of these elements that are found on most Weblog homepages is a collection of hyperlinks to other Weblogs. Weblog authors select and organize these *blogrolls* according to various criteria, such as shared interests, geographical or community relations, or recurrent themes. Most Weblog authors publish a *blogroll* to define and indicate a conversational space of some sort. They make transparent whose posts they read and refer to on a regular basis, thus providing a view on their personal selection of trusted sources.

Fig. 3 illustrates three sample blogrolls from different Weblogs. The left-most blogroll indicates only topics, the centered blogroll indicates names of people as well as blog names, and the third blogroll indicates only names of bloggers. In each of these cases, the representation as well as types of links indicates a personal preference

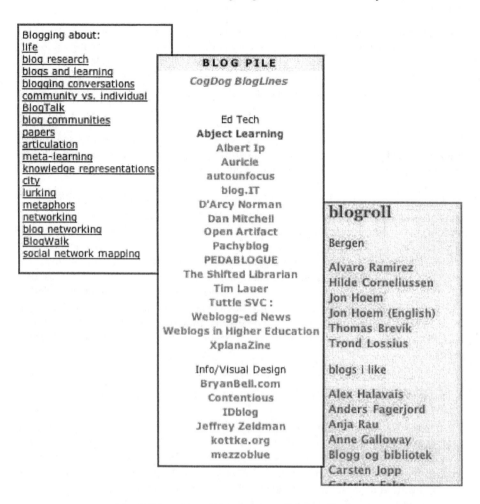

Fig. 3. Blogrolls and links on three different Weblogs

on the part of the author. A cursory glance at these links indicates that one author's interests are mostly related to the practice of blogging, learning through blogging, and social networking with blogs. The second author provides a topical list of links related to educational technology and information design. The last author, on the other hand, includes only the names of various bloggers, indicating preference for a certain type of writing, blogging, and content, which one can only discover by actually visiting each of the links. By establishing a blogroll, the authors refine the intent of their blog and at the same time invite a specific type of audience to participate in a conversation. For example, a blogger who is interested in social networking and meta-learning is likely to visit the first author's Weblog and engage in a conversation either by linking to this external Weblog or providing a comment directly on a post of interest. Similarly, a reader interested in an overview of educational technology or information design is likely to engage in conversation with the author of the second Weblog. Thus, blogrolls and link lists immediately provide site visitors with tangible information about the author's focus, interests, and community. On a more intangible level, a detailed exploration of the blogrolls can identify practices within a community - that is, how do individuals within the group participate in conversations? What rules, forms of etiquette, and conversational styles are encouraged? Over time, the content of the Weblog tends to become refined and it is likely to represent a vivid snapshot of the author's interests, philosophy, and style.

Some Weblog authors even encode their blogrolls in OPML (an XML outline format) to be able to syndicate their content, or create and manage these link collections via specialized Web services (such as blogrolling.com), thus freeing their users from manipulating the static HTML of their Weblog templates anytime they want to edit their blogroll.

It also is very common to provide information about the Weblog author, including contact data and the purpose of the publishing project (Herring, Scheidt, Bonus, & Wright, 2004; Nardi, Schiano, & Gumbrecht, 2004). In fact, most Weblog authoring solutions provide means to create and publish an unlimited amount of content pages that are independent of the stream of posts that make up the main content flow of a Weblog. Many Weblog authors build additional, static content pages to display lists of favorite resources, longer texts or essays, or personal hyperlink directories. This is where the Weblog format merges with elements of normal Website building. The more powerful content management and personal publishing solutions are quite capable of comprehensive Website development beyond the mere maintenance of Weblog projects.

4 Conversation with Self – Building a Personal Repository

We agree with Alpert (in this book) who suggests that "... there is a vast amount of content available on the Web, and the Web has increasingly become a primary source for information. But for learning, users need that content organized in some fashion, focused on a particular topic or domain." Weblog authoring can be seen as an expression of this need to structure and organize the personal history of engagement with the vast amount of available content on the Web.

Though meaning in Weblog authoring is mostly encoded in writing, Downes (2004, p. 52) expresses this perspective:

... blogging isn't really about writing at all; that's just the end point of the process, the outcome that occurs more or less naturally if everything else has been done right. Blogging is about, first, reading. But more important, it is about reading what is of interest to you: your culture, your community, your ideas. And it is about engaging with the content and with the authors of what you have read - reflecting, criticizing, questioning, reacting.

4.1 Publication and Customization

From the previous perspective it becomes apparent that over time Weblog authoring can result in the construction of a personal repository of content. What is remarkable here is the process of content creation. Weblog authoring is rarely limited to the selection and mere re-publication of material authored by someone else. As Downes

(2004) describes, Weblog authoring is about engagement with content and their authors, about contextualization, elaboration, interpretation, personal meaning making, and the recording and representation of items of experience. Much of this engagement is achieved through the application of hyperlinks, the Web's native format, to express relations and to enrich representations of patterns of meaning. Hyperlinks point to material that is quoted, referred to, critiqued, praised, or that somehow elaborates, illustrates, and enriches the content of a particular Weblog post. Thus, hyperlinks allow authors to embed their externalized thoughts, feelings, and actions in a wider web of relations that contains numerous contextual cues. Oravec (2003) suggests that hyperlinks have personal, social, and technological purposes and thereby allow bloggers to situate themselves in the context of contemporary artifacts. Herring et. al. (2004) suggest that although blog authors and scholars emphasize the external, interactive, and linked nature of blogs, they tend to ignore the potential of blogs as an individual and intimate form of expression.

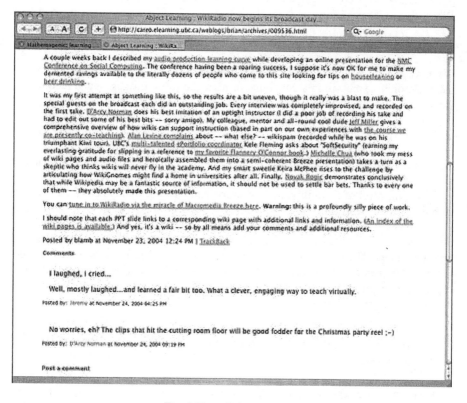

Fig. 4. Hyperlinked blog post

For example, in Fig. 4, a sample post by an author on the topic of audio production indicates numerous links to contextualize the writing. For example, the author is describing production of an audio broadcast and the learning curve involved. In the length of the post, he manages to integrate links to a conference, to actual produced audio material, to the Weblogs of four colleagues, and to external commentary on a Web page among others. The point of this illustration is to indicate the level of personalization by the author and the ability of hyperlinks to provide a context that frames this writing. Thus, hyperlinks become a vital component of the conversational context and illustrate a chain of conversation on the part of the author. What links are used to support the author's position? Conversely, what links are used to indicate disagreement with specific material? What links indicate the author's likes and dislikes? And how do they all contribute to the author's reasoning and writing within the post?

Regardless of the level of individual self-expression that Weblog authors integrate into their initial publishing, the resulting repositories of digital artifacts "can then function as the basic material for reflective conversational practices resulting in further elaboration, organization, and integration of patterns of meaning and action over time" (Fiedler, 2003, p. 204). They can support reflection and the inner conversation with oneself, a crucial component of most significant personal change and growth processes (Boud, Keogh, & Walker, 1985; Harri-Augstein & Thomas, 1991; Schön, 1987).

4.2 Toolkits for Individual Expression

We have noted above that Weblog posts usually consist of self-contained items of meaning, often expressed in a colloquial or narrative form. Images, sound recordings, video-clips and other digital formats that can be served on the Web are slowly trickling into the praxis of Weblog authoring, but these elements mostly serve an auxiliary or illustrative function. Nevertheless, text-based representations of meaning or records of action can be enriched or even substituted by other types of digital media. Depending on the availability of tools, broadband connections, and the necessary production skills it is likely that Weblog authors will broaden their expressive toolkit.

Given this level of flexibility, it is unsurprising that some authors consider Weblog authoring as a "hybrid of existing genres" (Herring et al., 2004, p. 10), integrating elements of personal journal writing, editorials, letters to the editor of a newspaper, project journals, field research records, paper notes to oneself, email exchanges and personal letters. The tremendous diversity that can be found in Weblog content (Halavais, 2002) can also be interpreted as an indicator of their widespread purpose "to express the author's subjective, often intimate perspective on matters of interest to him or her" (Herring et al., 2004, p. 6).

5   Conversation with Artifacts and Others – Refining Personal Repositories

So far we have focused on the description of Weblog authoring mainly from the perspective of building and maintaining a personal repository of digital artifacts on the Web by (self-) publishing items of micro content. However, we have already identified a number of common features such as item level comments from readers, cross-referencing via trackback, blogroll lists of other Weblog authors who function as primary resources of information, and RSS encoded Webfeeds, that add to Weblog authoring capabilities to support conversational exchanges of various kinds.

5.1 The Nature of Commentary and Conversation

Efimova & de Moor (2005) identify Weblog conversations as those where a specific Weblog post triggers a reaction from others - either through comments on the original post or references in other linked Weblogs. These two main mechanisms of reacting to published posts deserve a closer look. Comment features in Weblogs allow the direct attachment of comments to a particular post. They basically function like discussion threads in asynchronous discussion forums on the Web. Comments provide a quick and easy way for readers to add their perspectives and hyperlink resources that might be of interest to the author and other interested readers. However, regardless of the purpose of a particular comment, one major disadvantage for the commentator is that the message essentially enters the content management system of the original post's author.

Thus, while the personal repository of the Weblog author might be enriched by the comment, the commentators cannot build their own repository. They are simply annotating somebody else's content. Managing one's own comments that have been distributed over a large number of Weblogs becomes almost impossible over time. The lack of reliable tracking mechanisms adds to this problem. Some systems offer email notification features to the Weblog author whenever a new comment is published and to the author of a particular comment whenever somebody replies to it. For readers of a particular Weblog, it is still difficult to track the development of a comment thread over time. Readers will normally need to access a specific post via the HTML rendered homepage or archive pages of the Weblog. Given the Weblog format's focus on current content and the lack of elaborated tracking features, the findings of Herring et al. (2004) are hardly surprising: "It appears that entries do not continue to collect comments over time, but rather are only commented on while they are new" (p. 8).

A recent development is the publication of specific comment threads as RSS encoded Webfeeds in some Weblog authoring solutions. Once subscribed to a Webfeed via a Webfeed reader, it is relatively easy to monitor a thread even over longer periods of time. Unfortunately, this practice has not spread widely, so it is too early to evaluate if Weblog authors, readers, and software developers will embrace the practice of monitoring comment threads via RSS.

5.2 Tracking Comments

Apart from leaving comments on a specific Weblog post, interaction between Weblog authors is expressed by citing and linking to content published in another Weblog. Since every Weblog post is associated with a permanent URL, it is easy to cite a portion of the content and to reference its original location on the Web. This practice has various advantages. First of all, it allows readers to travel back to the original item and its context, thus allowing for an evaluation of the original source as well as the contextualization inherent in the secondary citation. Second, most Weblog authoring solutions track and record citations to a specific Weblog. These "referrer" links help the author of a Weblog (and its readers) to identify other Weblogs that reference a specific post. Fig. 5 presents a snapshot of screens to show how one can use referrer logs to identify cited posts. The first screen is a referrer list from a personal Weblog and clicking on the first link takes one out to another Weblog. In the referrer Weblog (that is, the Weblog that we link out to), we see evidence of a citation to the original author and clicking on the link brings us back to the original post cited by the referrer. Thus, the author of the first Weblog could click on the individual referrer links, identify the external Weblogs that cite his posts, and then by clicking on the links in the external Weblogs, he can identify the specific post of interest in each case.

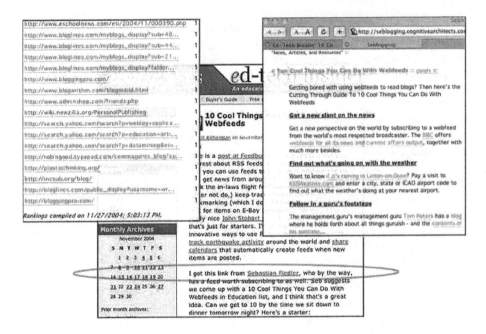

Fig. 5. Referrer lists

Recently, we have seen the emergence of a number of specialized tracking and monitoring Web services that attempt to harvest these continuously fluctuating link ecologies. The popular Service Technorati (http://www.technorati.com), for example, claims to currently track almost five million Weblogs with about 700 million links. Given the URL of a Weblog's homepage, Technorati displays the most recent links that other authors have made to any post that is part of this particular Weblog.

The introduction of the *trackback* feature in some Weblog authoring systems, as we have mentioned it earlier in this chapter, tried to establish a mechanism for notifying other Weblog systems of a new entry referring to a particular post. Though one-to-one linking between individual Weblog posts is presently the predominant application of *trackback*, the mechanism can also be used to notify shared content repositories. Thus, Weblog authors can create and feed shared repositories by using simple Web services like the Internet Topic Exchange together with the trackback mechanism. So far trackback features have not been included in the majority of Weblog authoring systems, and the ability of trackbacks to play a major role in managing Weblog conversations in the near future is still debatable. However, we believe it is important to identify this feature as one more supportive tool in building networks of shared conversations within the Weblog ecology.

5.3 Identifying Conversational Flows

We briefly mentioned earlier that most Weblog authoring systems can encode published content in XML/RSS and publish it as a Webfeed. RSS is a lightweight XML vocabulary that is used to describe metadata about Websites and single items of content that are published on a particular site. It was originally crafted for the description, syndication, and aggregation of news feeds that focused on "what is new" and that were chronologically updated and organized. There is still some lack of consensus about whether RSS means Rich Site Summary or RDF Site Summary; furthermore, different groups have developed different versions of RSS or proposed derivatives of various kinds.

However, Webfeeds, even though based on different RSS versions, have probably become the most successful XML format and implementation on the Web. The simplicity of RSS and its general readability has fostered its rapid dissemination and adoption. What makes RSS so powerful is its ability to glue data from diverse sources such as content management and knowledge management systems, information portals, and Webpublishing systems. Once all this data is available in a simple standardized format such as RSS, value-added services and special tools can be built on top of this new layer of information flows. This is precisely what occurred in the area of Weblog authoring where various tools and services were built on top of RSS to support conversational exchanges.

Personal and shared Webfeed readers or aggregators (also called news readers, or simply RSS readers) mark the most prominent category of software clients and services that co-evolved with the dissemination of RSS encoded Webfeeds. Web-based aggregators harvest large numbers of Webfeeds and offer different views on aggregated content. These views could be topic based, simply chronological, or personalized in various ways.

Fig. 6 illustrates an example of a free aggregator site that compiles various Webfeeds. In this view, the Webfeeds are organized broadly by topic area and are more related to general and commercial webfeeds. However, a user may create a personal portal and create a list of personally organized subscriptions. For example, one might choose to subscribe to newsfeeds that relate to educational blogging or technology; thus, every time the individual logs into the site, he or she can choose to view new posts only within educational blogging and view new posts only from a specific feed, as opposed to all subscribed feeds.

Usually, additional search features allow for text based search queries on the aggregated content. Regardless of the various design strategies used for Webfeed reader software, these clients all aim to support users who want to monitor and read potentially large numbers of Webfeeds. Webfeed readers query all RSS user subscriptions and automatically pull new content into the Webfeed reader. Desktop-based Webfeed readers also allow their users to browse these content collections offline.

The advantages for users are quite apparent - that is, there is no need to browse large numbers of Webpublishing projects, like personal Weblogs, manually in order to check for new content. Their Webfeed reader software queries all of the subscribed feeds following a single command and notifies the users of all new content items that have been published since its last query. This new content includes a growing

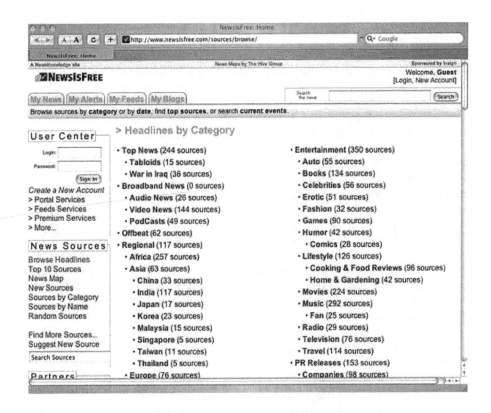

Fig. 6. A categorical view of an aggregator

numbers of traditional mass media publications such as online newspapers, discussion board contributions (Yahoo groups, for example), continuous search queries, audio enclosures, video clips, and digital photo archives, to name a few.

In the context of Weblog authors who are trying to engage in conversational exchanges with other authors (or their content), Webfeed readers are the most popular means to follow the visible portion of the ongoing Weblog authoring activities of a selected group of authors. Subscribing to the Webfeeds of those Weblogs that exhibit consistent levels of quality on a topic of a personal interest, can allow other individuals to scan the aggregated content for possible triggers for further engagement and exchange. A combination of content aggregation and editing features allows for a rather seamless (re-)publishing cycle, making it possible to publish a commentary in a matter of a few clicks.

Because of this ongoing syndicating, aggregating, monitoring, and (re-) publishing of content, a particular economy of attention and a Web of conversational exchanges can emerge and self-organize. The dynamics of these conversational relations are often invisible to the occasional reader of Weblogs and are hard to monitor and track from the outside. This is partly the result of the highly distributed nature of Weblog conversations, the technical limitations and current tools and practices, and the individual workflows and preferences of Weblog authors. Though there are some generic action patterns and conventions that could qualify as the core of current Weblog authoring practices, the individual's freedom for combining available tools with personal preferences of information processing, meaning making, and communication produce a considerable variability of visible outcomes.

Furthermore, it is important to keep in mind that conversational exchanges that are triggered through Weblog authoring tend to be continued or transferred to other media like instant messaging, phone, email, and face-to-face, as Nardi et al. (2004) were able to document in their ethnographic study on Weblog authoring. Efimova & de Moor (2005) reported similar results.

However, building publicly accessible personal content repositories on the Web and coupling these technologies with the ecology of RSS encoded content flows, offers anchors to trigger and develop conversational exchanges with others.

6 Constraints of Weblog Authoring in Meaning Making

Though Weblog authoring has to be considered as a major emergent practice of personal information gathering and management on the Web, tools and formats that are currently in use show some apparent limitations and constraints, especially after extended periods of content creation and publication. We identify five major limitations that constrain the representational activities required for higher-level meaning-making activities.

Limited organizational means. We have described general organizational principles of current Weblog authoring solutions earlier in this text. Both RSS encoded Webfeeds and the HTML rendered homepages of Weblogs are organized in a reverse-chronological manner, and current Weblog software applications offer very simple categorization schemes. Many of the RSS elements that could provide additional metadata on the level of individual posts are optional and are used inconsistently.

Lack of permanence. The focus on the most current content means that items gradually disappear from Weblog homepages and Webfeeds. After posts have dropped off the "window of attention" that the Weblog format provides they generally get buried in chronologically organized archives and are difficult to retrieve to support ongoing meaning making activities.

Lack of output control. Most Webfeeds are automatically produced via Weblog authoring solutions. Unfortunately, contemporary Weblog authoring solutions provide limited means for controlling the output of Webfeeds. In general, all content published on a Weblog homepage is also RSS encoded. Some software applications allow for additional category-based Webfeeds that contain all posts that were categorized accordingly by the author, or Webfeeds that contain all comments that have been written in response to posts published in a Weblog. Particular posts or small collections of posts are normally not easily encoded and published in RSS.

Fragmented conversations. One prevalent problem with Weblog based conversations is the highly fragmented nature of their occurrence. These exchanges can stretch over lengthy time periods and different Weblogs, each running its own flavor of content management system. This fragmentation and distribution makes it difficult to monitor referrers to a particular item (Efimova & de Moor, 2005).

Lack of explicit relations between posts. Relations between various posts that belong to a single Weblog project remain largely invisible, as long as the authors do not create explicit hyperlinks between these items. However, published Weblog posts are rarely re-edited by their authors, because this practice is considered to run counter to Weblogging conventions established in recent years. Once content is published, authors are rarely cognizant of where content is aggregated and cited. Any major edit would therefore change the original information source to the disadvantage of these authors and their readership. Also, Weblog authors generally do not tend to re-work their published content to make emerging relations more explicit. Though Weblog authors have been quite successful in establishing a number of shared practices and norms, there are no standard procedures and formats available that would regulate the cross-linking of Weblog posts after they have been published.

7 Concept Mapping to Make Sense of Weblog Representation

While Weblog authoring supports the initial logging and archival of information, our focus is also on identifying mechanisms for making meaningful connections between the logged information. Novak (1998) suggests that making meaningful connections within knowledge in a new domain can be difficult, especially when knowledge is poorly organized. It is in this second area that concept maps can be used as representational tools to structure and explicitly link the archived information generated via Weblogging. For example, if we consider blog posts to be records of events or artifacts resulting from an activity, they can be used as data to generate principled links and knowledge claims (Novak, 1998). Earlier, we mentioned that representation in the context of self-organized learning should be capable of displaying hierarchy and relationship of elements within a system of meaning. While Weblogs support the spontaneous expression of thought and feeling in specific instances of time, concept maps support a second level of representation by allowing the individual to relate individual items and construct patterns of intentionality and meaning among the separate elements.

Concept maps can serve to explain the conceptual and propositional structures that people use to explain events. Within self-organized learning, the structuring of knowledge is governed by an unknown and potentially infinite process of knowledge acquisition. Meaning building in this context is guided by the "...unique concept and propositional frameworks of the learners, but also varying approaches to learning and varying emotional predispositions" (Novak, 2002, p. 555). Caravita and Hallden (1994) suggest that learning consists not only of individual conceptions of events (for example, the weblog posts) but also the refinement, organization, and differentiation among the different contexts, which is supported through the use of concept mapping techniques. Apart from the construction of relations between individual blog posts, concept maps can also act as a form of meta-representation where learners can

Web of Blogs #

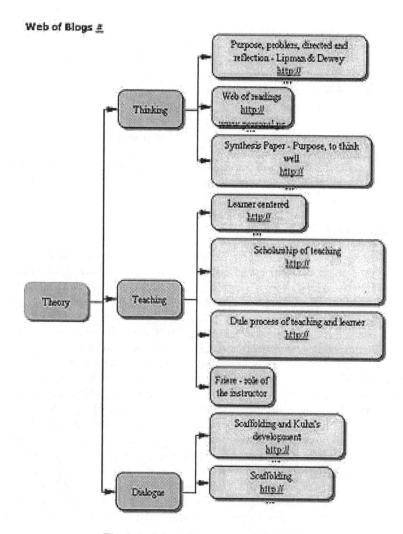

Fig. 7. Sample initial concept map of Weblog conten

represent knowledge in different ways and gain new insights into their processes of knowledge construction (or metacognition) (DiSessa, 2001).

Concept maps can also be used to evaluate the quality and structure of meaningful propositions within a known domain, as well as to iteratively identify new areas of understanding and inquiry within a new domain (Novak, 2002). Thus, mapping existing Weblog posts can provide an initial structure of knowledge, and at the same time identify areas where information is unknown and needed within the context of specific meaning construction activities. However, the task of creating an appropriate map of the posts is not easy. Concept maps require creative organization of the map, including concept selection, construction and labeling of meaningful relationships between concepts, and the appropriate representation of connections among different sections of the map (Novak, 1998). Creating a good concept map is a significant learning experience in itself and as illustrated in other chapters in this book (for example, Alpert, and Tergan), concept maps can be very large and complex. The gap between archival (Weblogging) and creating a meaningful overview of relationships (mapping) is both a matter of practice and logistics. For example, Fig. 7 is a sample concept map of Weblog content. In this case, archived posts were organized using a personal desktop tool (Inspiration™, in this instance) and then reposted as a graphic post. This representation could be considered to be a first pass at creating a good concept map, a process that requires much time and effort (Novak, 1998). The challenges inherent in creating good concept maps are addressed in other chapters in this book as well as by Novak (1998) and we will not reiterate these aspects. However, in the context of Weblog technologies, the logistics of concept mapping merit some attention.

7.1 Initial Empirical Support for the Utility of Concept Maps

To examine the utility of concept mapping in the second stage of knowledge construction, we designed and implemented a learning intervention in a graduate level seminar within Penn State University. The seminar was aimed at doctoral and masters level students, who were in the process of establishing or refining a research agenda. Within the seminar, students were asked to develop a research framework or a literature review paper within their specific area of interest. Developing such a product is characterized by the need for students to engage in prolonged sense-making within an unstructured and extensive domain of literature. To delineate the scope of information, students needed to identify, gather, and organize resources. Simultaneously students would need to examine the resources to identify utility and applicability to their areas of research. The identified tasks called for high levels of reflection, self-organization, and meaning-making. To support the different levels of knowledge construction, we implemented individual Weblogs to support chronological organization of resources and concept maps for structuring thoughts and arguments. The Weblog posts and concept maps were to be used iteratively - i.e, logged content from the Weblog was to be captured within the concept maps and manipulated to identify structure of reasoning and argument. Knowledge or resource gaps that emerged as a process of sense-making through the concept mapping software were to form the impetus for further resource logging on the Weblogs.

Students used the Weblogs for approximately 12 weeks and created concept maps mid-way and again at the end of this time period. We interviewed all five students in the class to get their perceptions of the utility of Weblogs and concept maps. We also examined the concept map data and Weblogs as additional sources of data to identify student use of both types of technologies. Overall, students professed to the utility of Weblogs in collating their data. Although students initially struggled with the practice of logging daily and consistently, in interviews, four of the five students indicated that the Weblogs were useful in archiving information. An illustrative quote from one participant is as follows:

I would have to say that [the Weblog] helped me to identify how important it was to organize your thoughts in some way that you could go back and look at it and say, what's different, what should I change, what should I add on, what am I missing.

Weblogs initially became a resource bank for citations and bibliographic material and one participant appreciated its utility for keeping track of most recent developments on her personal work.

> Because my organization strategies were just horrible at that time, because I didn't really keep track of any of my papers, there were just different versions and different versions and I'd have to read through them. I used to use the Weblog as my way to look at the Weblog and then look at my paper and say, OK, this is the last one I posted.

Two of the students admitted that they noticed a change in their use of Weblogs over the course of the seminar, indicating a change from an information archiving approach to a more reflective, commentary-oriented approach to posting. Thus, in some sense, we feel that the Weblogs were basically useful as a resource bank. When asked about the utility of concept maps, 4 out of 5 students indicated that although they did not fully appreciate the use of concept maps during the seminar, they would definitely integrate them in future work. Here are some illustrative comments:

> ... if I were to map out the Weblog, I would have seen how the different levels, how it all breaks down by different levels and what should be grouped.... I would have actually had a structure for writing my paper and I could have actually, used that as an outline for writing my paper. So although I was aware of all this information, how it all fit together, I didn't see it in my paper. ...I just had to make a more detailed map and everything fit together and then I would have had a great paper. [Participant 2]

> I didn't see it [concept map] as an organization strategy. ... I didn't see... I didn't personalize it. I saw it as an assignment, turn in the product, just going through the motions ... whereas now I see it more as a personal kind of tool I can use to organize my thoughts. [Participant 3]

> I think there's a tendency, when you go to write, that you need to use everything. Everything I have in my web log. Because when you map it out it makes sense to you then, in mapping it out... [you find] that's not necessarily the case. [Participant 1]

It is interesting to note that most students initially found the construction of concept maps to be a chore - there was resistance to the strategy as well as a lack of clarity about its utility. However, in retrospect, when the amount of information became bigger and less manageable, students began to see the usefulness of concept maps in structuring an argument and identifying the key components and links. This sentiment is particularly well illustrated in the last quote. It also appears that students' usage of the concept maps (as well as the Weblogs) was initially driven by notions of accountability - that is, they were required by the course instructor and were thus important to use. From the interviews, it seems that students did not immediately perceive the value of Weblogs and concept maps in supporting their archival, organization, and meaning-making strategies. However, the execution of a synthesizing activity (in this case, the writing of a final paper) seemed to become a trigger for re-examining the utility of these strategies. Based on these initial data, it would seem that it is important to identify the purpose and utility of these strategies and technologies early in the cycle of use. It also seems important for early integration of activities that require overt archival and organization strategies and thereby alert students to the utility of these strategies and technologies.

Apart from issues of praxis, one participant mentioned the role of logistics in her lack of usage of the concept mapping techniques.

> ... however I think it [concept map] would have been more helpful if I would have gotten the links to work. I would have had to do that as an image map and I didn't do that.

This comment echoes our earlier discussion about the difficulties inherent in combining the two technologies to support meaning-making. To support the practices of self-organized learning that are initially facilitated by Weblogging, we see the need for a seamless technological extraction and visual mapping of Weblog posts. Earlier, we mentioned two mechanisms needed for self-organized learning - spontaneous expression of thought and action elements in multiple forms, and the ability for these elements to be viewed within the context of a hierarchy of relationship. Given that Weblogs allow for spontaneous, organic recording, we focus now on the technologies that can organize Weblog posts into a meaningful overview. Until recently, concept mapping applications were largely desktop-based, which means that the mapping of Weblog posts required one to: (1) copy important phrases or titles of individual posts into the concept mapping software, (2) map the existing nodes, and (3) re-post the graphic on a Weblog to make the process public. While this process is manageable with a small number of posts, the process becomes more complicated with larger numbers of posts.

8 Future Thoughts on Representational Levels

We see several possible paths for further development toward a seamless integration of Weblog authoring and visual mapping tools and practices. We have outlined a number of problems and limitations of the current practice of Weblog authoring if one intends to go beyond the mere creation and maintenance of personal content repositories. The re-organization, elaboration, and comparison of collected material, and the construction of new concepts and propositional links on a further layer of abstraction, could be greatly enhanced and augmented by visual mapping strategies. For this purpose, we would need a procedure for rapid extraction of the core elements of Weblog posts and the creation of a visual representation that could be published to a visual mapping plane. Since Weblog posts are commonly encoded and published in XML/RSS, and often aggregated via Webfeed reader software before they are edited and re-published via an adjacent Weblog editor, it would be conceivable to integrate visual mapping capabilities in this existing workflow. For example, once a particular Weblog post is present in a desktop-based Webfeed reader/editor, it could be "published" to a visual mapping pane (preferably living on the Web) according to predefined transformation rules.

As a starting point, such a technology should be able to extract at least the title of a Weblog post and its permanent link and to merge these elements into an active hyperlink placed into a visual mapping object (box, circle, etc.,) of some sort. In addition, we could imagine the entire content of a Weblog post becoming available on the visual mapping pane. Most likely, the content would only be accessible as a second layer that is made visible through some type of user action. Another feature could be a list of all hyperlinks contained within a particular post. However, once a selection of this transformed Weblog post is published to the visual mapping plane, users should be able to treat these objects like any other manually created object in their visual mapping environment. Carrying over the philosophy of individually addressable items of micro-content from the Weblog authoring realm, Web-based visual mapping environments should assign permanent links to all mapping objects to allow for their referencing in normal hypertext writing. At the same time an RSS encoded Webfeed of the change history of a particular visual map would be accessible through any standard Webfeed reader and once aggregated it would be open to editing and instant republication to a Weblog.

Webnote (http://www.aypwip.org/webnote/) is a prototype (see Fig. 8) of an open Web-based tool for visual note-taking that displays some of the features outlined above. Though its visual palette is currently limited to colored boxes that can be sized and moved freely on the page, Webnote offers an RSS encoded Webfeed of all notes that are created and changed. Users can also install a bookmarklet in their browser

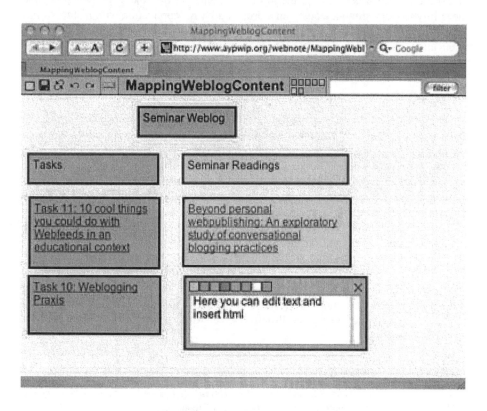

Fig. 8. A screenshot of the Webnote prototype interface

that allows them to mark text on any Webpage and automatically transform it into a Webnote object (colored box on the Webnote plane), which contains the selected text and a hyperlink to the source. The logical extension, in our view, is an RSS import filter as part of a tool like Webnote that would turn the items on a particular Webfeed into Webnote objects of a predefined format.

Another promising development is the focus of software developers on creating concept maps that can be shared and edited across the Web (see chapters on this topic in this book). This attribute is vital for continued shared dialogue with others in the context of self-organized learning. One such instantiation of the shared construction and peer review of propositions is the Knowledge Soup environment with *Cmap* for elementary and secondary school children (Cañas, Ford, Novak, Hayes, Reichherzer & Suri, 2001). In this environment, students can develop concept maps off-line, i.e., on their own personal machine, and then share specific propositions by uploading them to a server. By sharing propositions, individual students gain the ability to receive feedback from peers and the instructor. The type of interaction and interface promoted by this environment provides many of the conversational abilities that we would like to suggest within a visual mapping tool. For example, the ability to share propositions with a peer group, the ability to comment on others' propositions, and the ability to work simultaneously on a proposition. An application with features similar to CmapTools (http://cmap.ihmc.us/) and the added feature of RSS extraction and publication would be ideal in the context of visual mapping for Webpublishing.

9 Summary

In summary, Weblogs show great potential for becoming a mechanism for individual and shared dialogue in the context of self-organized learning. The practices developing around this technology promote individual expression and the development of a critical intellectual voice (Oravec, 2003), as well as engagement in critical dialogue with artifacts created by others. Both of these aspects map seamlessly into the requirements for self-organized learning, which we believe to be fundamental to learning and working in the information economy (see for example, Brown, 2000). However, to support the nascent meaning construction established by these practices, we anticipate the development of a specific set of visual mapping tools that will allow individuals to seamlessly extract Weblog material and construct a meaningful overview of the individual Weblog elements. Such organic practices of information archival and knowledge construction, we believe, will allow individuals to navigate vast amounts of information more easily, as well as allow them to gain better control of their learning and practices within ill-defined, real-world environments.

References

Berners-Lee, T. (2000). *Weaving the Web: the original design and ultimate destiny of the World Wide Web by its inventor.* New York: Harper Business.

Blood, R. (2002). Weblogs: A history and perspective. In J. Rodzvilla (Ed.), *We've got Blog: How Weblogs are changing our culture* (pp. 7-16). Cambridge, MA: Perseus Publishing.

Boud, D., Keogh, R., & Walker, D. (Eds.). (1985). *Reflection: Turning experience into learning*. London: Kogan Page.

Brown, J. S. (2000). Growing up digital. *Change, 32*(2), 10-21.

Cañas, A. J., Ford, K. M., Novak, J. D., Hayes, P., Reichherzer, T. R., & Suri, N. (2001). Online Concept Maps: Enhancing Collaborative Learning by Using Technology with Concept Maps. *Science Teacher, 68*(4), 49-51.

Caravita, S., & Hallden, O. (1994). Re-framing the problem of conceptual change. *Learning and Instruction, 4*, 89-111.

DiSessa, A. A. (2001). *Changing minds: Computers, learning, and literacy*. Cambridge, MA: MIT Press.

Downes, S. (2004). Educational blogging. *Educause Review, 39*(5), 14-26.

Efimova, L., & de Moor, A. (2005). *Beyond personal Webpublishing: An exploratory study of conversational blogging practices*. Paper presented at the 38th Annual Hawaii International Conference on System Sciences (January 3-6), Big Island, Hawaii.

Fiedler, S. (2003). Personal Webpublishing as a reflective conversational tool for self-organized learning. In T. N. Burg (Ed.), *BlogTalks* (pp. 190-216). Wien, Austria: Libri.

Halavais, A. (2002). *Blogs and the "social weather"*. Paper presented at the Internet Research 3.0, Maastricht, The Netherlands.

Harri-Augstein, E. S., & Thomas, L. F. (1991). *Learning conversations: The self-organized learning way to personal and organizational growth*. London, UK: Routledge.

Herring, S. C., Scheidt, L. A., Bonus, S., & Wright, E. (2004). Bridging the gap: A genre analysis of Weblogs. In R. H. Sprague (Ed.), *Proceedings of the 37th Annual Hawaii International Conference on System Sciences*. CD-ROM Edition. Los Alamitos, CA: IEEE.

Nardi, B. A., Schiano, D. J., & Gumbrecht, M. (2004). *Blogging as social activity, or, would you let 900 million people read your diary?* Paper presented at the ACM Conference on Computer Supported Cooperative Work, Chicago, IL.

Novak, J. D. (1998). *Learning, creating, and using knowledge: Concept Maps™ as facilitative tools in schools and corporations*. Mahwah, NJ: Lawrence Erlbaum Associates.

Novak, J. D. (2002). Meaningful Learning: The Essential Factor for Conceptual Change in Limited or Inappropriate Propositional Hierarchies Leading to Empowerment of Learners. *Science Education, 86*(4), 548-571.

Oravec, J. A. (2003). Weblogs as an Emerging Genre in Higher Education. *Journal of Computing in Higher Education, 14*(2), 21-44.

Schön, D. A. (1987). *Educating the reflective practitioner*. San Francisco: Jossey-Bass.

Sculley, J. (1991). The relationship between business and higher education: A perspective on the 21st century. In C. Dunlop, & R. Kling (Eds.), *Computerization and controversy: Value conflicts and social choices*. Boston: Academic Press.

Smith, P., & Ragan, T. (1993). *Instructional design*. New York: Macmillan Publishing Company.

Facilitating Web Search with Visualization and Data Mining Techniques

Young-Jin Lee

University of Illinois at Urbana-Champaign,
Champaign IL 61820, USA
ylee12@uiuc.edu

Abstract. Although conventional Web search environments are very useful for well-structured, closed-ended questions, they become less efficient in dealing with ill-structured, open-ended questions. This paper presents design rationales and implementations of an alternative Web search environment called Vis-Search. The VisSearch environment adopts visualization techniques to reduce various cognitive loads of iterative Web searches. It also employs a data mining algorithm to utilize Web search results of others. This paper describes in detail how these techniques can be used to facilitate efficient Web searches for ill-structured, open-ended questions, thereby fostering creation of a community of knowledge on the Web.

1 Introduction

Information and knowledge are growing at a far more rapid rate than ever before in the history of mankind. As Nobel laureate Herbert Simon put it, the meaning of "knowing" has changed from "being able to remember and repeat information" to "being able to find and use it" (Simon, 1996). Therefore, the goal of education is better conceived as helping students develop strategies to find useful information, and make sense of it, rather than helping them memorize and retrieve it. This new notion of "knowing" has become more important with the advent of the World-Wide-Web (Web) as it brings us a virtually infinite source of information with diverse qualities. Since the Web has been already used as a major source of information in many educational settings (National Center for Education Statistics, 2000a, b), it is important to help students find meaningful Web resources and make sense of what they have discovered. However, most of recent research have been focusing on the use of the Web as a virtual space that either allows people in different locations and at different times to collaborate (Pea, Edelson & Gomez, 1994; Songer, 1996), or enables them to share information and knowledge (Belll, 2002; Lamon. Reeve & Caswell, 1999; Linn, 2000; Scardamalia, Bereiter & Lamon, 1994). Although these projects reported successful Web uses in improving students' learning, they did not pay enough attention to the most common use of the Web. None of them provided an efficient way to find useful Web-based information; students were assumed to be able to locate useful resources on the Web for themselves or they used only limited amount of Web resources provided.

S.-O. Tergan and T. Keller (Eds.): Knowledge and Information Visualization, LNCS 3426, pp. 326–342, 2005.

Finding useful Web-based information is not an easy task. Of many difficulties in locating useful information on the Web, the size and the speed of growth of information in the Web are the most difficult ones. The Web has brought us a world of virtually infinite information. It contains diverse information in almost every area. Not only are there a great number of possibilities to choose, but they also vary very widely in quality. Evaluating all this information on the Web, therefore, would take nearly forever and finding meaningful Web-based information is getting more and more difficult. In an effort of alleviating this difficulty, graphical Web browsers such as Netscape or Internet Explorer have been developed and Web search engines such as Google[1] or YaHoo[2] have emerged. Although Web search engines and Web browsers, which are called conventional Web search environments in this paper, are fairly powerful, they have several serious shortcomings as they were not developed with instruction in mind (Soloway & Wallace, 1997). Next section discusses the shortcomings of conventional Web search environments in greater detail.

1.1 Shortcomings of Conventional Web Search Environments

Conventional Web search environments usually require people to express their information need as a text string, which is often called a *search query,* then compare the search query to their collection of Web pages, and finally return a set of Web pages satisfying a certain minimum threshold of relatedness, where relatedness of a Web page is usually determined by the number of occurrences and locations of the search query. However, many people have difficulties choosing appropriate search queries (Nordlie, 1999). Web search results thus usually contain lots of irrelevant information, and iterative processes to refine the search query and remove irrelevant information from the Web search results are crucial to acquire good quality Web-based information. Moreover, it is much more difficult to construct successful search queries for ill-structured, open-ended questions because such questions, e.g., "Describe how computers can affect the quality of our education." can be approached in many different ways unlike closed-ended questions such as "What is the capital of the United State?" The problem of conventional Web search environments is that they do not provide an efficient way to refine Web search results. In particular, people need to keep multiple Web browser windows open or use additional software, such as a word processor, to keep track of the refinement of their Web searches.

This problem becomes more serious when combined with the complexity of Web structures and the limited functionality of Web browsers. Many researchers have shown that people easily become lost in the hyperspace while navigating on the Web because of its high cognitive load[3] (Carroll, 1999; Hess, 1999; Nachmias & Gilad, 2002; Tauscher & Greenberg, 1997; Wallace, Kupperman, Krajcik & Soloway, 2000). In addition, people become often confused when they try to go back to previous Web sites with a backward navigation button of Web browsers as their mental model of the backward navigation button does not match the way it is implemented (Cockburn & Jones, 1996).

---

[1] http://www.google.com
[2] http://www.yahoo.com
[3] For overall discussions of cognitive load, see (Conklin, 1987; Norman, 1993; Sweller, 1988).

Another serious shortcoming of conventional Web search environments is that they do not provide effective ways to reuse useful Web resources people had found in the past. Most of conventional Web search environments employ bookmarks to increase reusability of useful Web resources identified. Although bookmarks are fairly convenient as they allow people to quickly return to useful Web sites, they do not sufficiently represent the contents of useful Web sites they are pointing to (Cockburn & Jones, 1996; Wallace et al., 2000). In other words, it is often practically impossible to figure out the real information contained in the bookmarked Web site only by looking at the title or its URL from the bookmark (Lee, 2004; Lee, in press, a, b; Tauscher & Greenberg, 1997). Furthermore, the size of the bookmarks grows so fast that they become easily unusable in practice (Abrams, 1998).

Finally, although it is quite common that many people search the same or similar Web resources (Markatos, 1999), conventional Web search environments are not able to take advantage of previous Web search results[4]. Many college students taking the same course, for example, would want to search the Web for their class projects, but conventional Web search environments do not allow them to utilize useful Web-based information other students had discovered. Moreover, it becomes even worse when we consider the fact that students who will take the same course in the future would be very likely to search the same or similar Web-based information again.

These shortcomings come from, in large parts, the *stateless* nature of the underlying HTTP (HyperText Transfer Protocol) used in the communication between a Web browser and a conventional Web search engine. A typical HTTP transaction used between a Web search engine and a conventional Web browser does not utilize any information about requesting clients. Thus, when a Web browser interacts with a Web search engine, each interaction (e.g., repeatedly requesting a Web search extended from previous ones) is completely separated from each other so that people have to either keep many Web browser windows open or use additional piece of software while extending or refining their Web search results. However, bookkeeping of multiple Web browser windows or switching between different software applications costs high cognitive load, substantially decreasing the efficiency of their Web search processes. Similarly, as Web search engines do not know if the same or similar Web searches had been performed in the past, people have to repeat the same or similar Web searches over and over again.

2   Architecture of VisSearch Environment

This paper presents VisSearch, an alternative Web search environment addressing the aforementioned shortcomings of conventional Web search environments. The VisSearch environment provides the solutions to those problems under the following two assumptions:

---

[4] Some Web search engines such as AskJeeves (http: //www. ask. com) and AltaVista (http://www.altavista.com) provide Web search queries other people had used. However, the quality of such information is very primitive (Lee, 2003).

1. Iterative Web searches are often required to find meaningful Web-based information[5].

2. There exist enough number of people looking for useful Web-based information on the same or similar topics.

It should be noted that these two conditions can be easily met in most of educational situations as many educational reform proposals have been emphasizing the importance of students' problem solving capability, especially for *open-ended questions;* and there already *exist* many people, such as college students taking the same course or professors having similar research interests, who would search the Web on the same or similar topics.

The VisSearch environment consists of three major components, VisSearch Client, VisSearch Server, and VisSearch Recommendation Engine. The VisSearch Client is responsible for providing most of user interfaces for searching and organizing useful Web-based information. It creates visual computational artifacts for various Web search processes, such as performing a Web search or creating a bookmark for a useful Web resource located, so that people can reuse the visualized artifacts when later they want to. The VisSearch Server collects Web search results from multiple VisSearch Clients and saves them into a central repository. Finally, the VisSearch Recommendation Engine compares all Web search results compiled in the VisSearch Server one by one to mine meaningful patterns in the Web search queries and the resulting useful Web-based information. The VisSearch environment adopts various techniques drawn from the results of Human-Computer Interaction (HCI) and data mining research to overcome the drawbacks of conventional Web search environments, which will be explained in great depth in Sect. 3 and 4, and in Sect. 5, respectively.

3 Creating Reusable Computational Artifacts

The information processing theory asserts that human memory consists of three different parts: sensory memory, short-term memory, and long-term memory. Sensory memory, which is connected to short-term memory, perceives auditory and visual information. Short-term memory, which is connected to both sensory memory and long-term memory, fetches auditory and/or visual information stored in sensory memory, makes sense of it and permanently stores the processed results into long-term memory. Although short-term memory is very efficient, ordinary people have only about seven chunks of short-term memory. Thus, it is important to effectively use limited short-term memory in order to achieve the best learning performance (Gagné & Glaser, 1987; Stuart, Moran & Newell, 1983).

This limitation of short-term memory is clearly applicable to iterative Web search processes. As people search useful Web-based information, especially for ill-structured, open-ended questions, they repeatedly need to: (a) find successful Web search queries; (b) evaluate (intermediate) Web search results; and (c) maintain useful Web resources obtained from multiple (intermediate) Web search results. Since each of these processes presumably takes up their short-term memory, their efficiency of

---

[5] It may not hold for simple, close-ended questions, and the VisSearch environment may not be appropriate for such questions.

Web searches will substantially decrease when their short-term memory is exhausted. The VisSearch environment allows Web searchers to maximize their short-term memory use by creating reusable computational artifacts from various Web search processes.

3.1 Search-Graph: Visualizing Web Search Results

While conducting a series of separate Web searches with conventional Web search environments, people create a single, reusable knowledge network, called a *search-graph* in this paper, with the VisSearch environment.

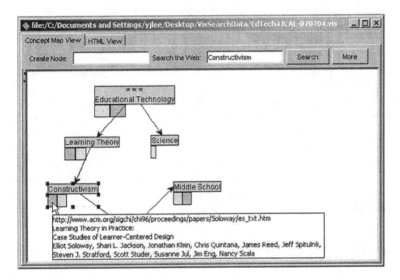

Fig. 1. An example search-graph consisting of six search query nodes, five relation links, and twelve visual bookmarks. It also shows a user comment attached to one of the visual bookmarks of the search query node, "Constructivism" in response to a mouse-hover action. One search query node and three visual bookmarks are behind the user comment displayed

In appearance, a search-graph looks similar to a concept map (see Fig. 1). It consists of several search query nodes and relation links, which represent all Web search queries to be used in an entire Web search session and the associations between pairs of Web search queries, respectively. In functionality, the search-graph visualizes the evolution of iterative Web search processes. As people continue to extend and refine their Web search results, more search query nodes will be created in the search-graph. A search query node (shown as a bigger rectangle with text in Fig. 1) takes two roles. First, it can be used as a building block to construct a Web search query. In the Vis-Search environment, people can search useful Web-based information by selecting appropriate search query nodes in the search-graph. For example, in the search-graph shown in Fig. 1, one can search useful Web resources about "constructivist learning theory" by selecting two search query nodes, "Constructivism" and "Learning Theory." Second, it can be used as a conceptual bin to hold useful Web-based information related to a particular concept represented as a search query node. When a good Web resource is found, users can associate it with a search query node by dragging-and-dropping it on top of an appropriate search query node. The VisSearch environment then creates a visual bookmark (shown as a small rectangle without text in Fig. 1) to visualize the useful Web resource found.

The search-graph approach is inspired by HCI research in which visual representations have been employed to facilitate efficient Web navigation (Ayers & Stasko, 1995; Cockburn & Jones, 1996; Hightower, Ring, Helfman, Bederson & Hollan, 1998). These projects provide a scrollable graphical overview of the Web pages people have visited earlier in order to help them situate themselves within hyperspace; they, for example, can avoid visiting the same Web sites by looking at the history of their Web navigation visualized. The search-graph approach extends this concept into iterative Web search processes.

3.2   Hit Browser: Visualizing History of Web Search Engine Hits

As briefly mentioned in the previous section, the VisSearch environment is equipped with its own Web search facility. People can specify their information need by selecting any number of search query nodes in the search-graph. The VisSearch environment constructs a Web search query by combining text of all selected search query nodes. After that, it requests a Web search to the Google Web search engine, receives Web search results, often called Web search engine *hits,* via Google Web API (Application Programming Interface) (Google, 2004), and visualizes them in its Hit Browser component.

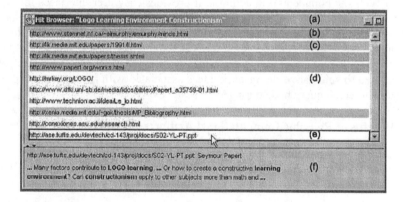

Fig. 2. The Hit Browser component of the VisSearch environment shows the search query used (a), the Web page on which a visual bookmark has been created (b), the Web page that has been visited (c), the Web page that has not been visited yet (d), and the Web page that is currently selected (e). In a color monitor display, the Web page on which a visual bookmark has been created and the Web page that has been visited are rendered in blue and gray, respectively. The Hit Browser component also shows the URL, the title, and the short description of the Web page currently selected at the bottom (f)

The Hit Browser component has two main roles. First, it shows Web search results with additional information. As shown in Fig. 2, the Hit Browser displays the search query used, the URL, the title, and the short description of the selected hit page at the moment. Second, it visualizes how Web search results have been used in the Vis-Search environment during iterative Web search sessions. Web search results displayed in the Hit Browser initially have a "white" background color. However, when a hit page is double-clicked, the Hit Browser changes its background color to "gray" (see Fig. 2) and displays its content in the VisSearch Web Browser (see Fig. 3), allowing users to read the contents of the double-clicked hit page without leaving the Vis-Search environment. Finally, when a hit page is drag-and-dropped onto a search query node in a search-graph, the Hit Browser changes its background color to "blue" (see Fig. 2), and requests the search-graph to create a visual bookmark of the drag-and-dropped hit page under the corresponding search query node.

3.3 Web-Site/Search-Query Comments: Visualizing Inspired Thoughts

When people find useful Web resources during Web searches, they often create bookmarks in order to reuse what they have discovered. Although the bookmarks of conventional Web search environments are fairly convenient, as they allow for easy return to useful Web-based information with a single mouse click, they suffer from serious drawbacks. People often have to go back to their book-marked Web pages before using them as the information bookmarks provide, such as the URLs and the titles of bookmarked Web pages, is insufficient to represent the actual contents of them (Cockburn & Jones, 1996; Wallace et al., 2000). In order to address this problem, the VisSearch environment allows for creating user comments on visual bookmarks (called Web-site comments). In addition, it provides easy user interfaces for creating and reusing them. User comments can be created by typing, copy-and-paste, or drag-and-drop of text, and easily accessed by just moving the mouse cursor to visual bookmarks (see Fig. 1). Furthermore, the VisSearch environment allows for creating user comments even on search query nodes (called search-query comments), which can be used to summarize the inspired ideas associated with a certain concept represented by a search query node during Web searches.

3.4 Benefits of Reusable Computational Artifacts

As discussed in the previous three sections, the VisSearch environment creates various reusable computational artifacts from Web search processes. The following subsections explain in detail the benefits of creating reusable computational artifacts.

Reducing cognitive load of maintaining multiple Web search results. As discussed in Sect. 1.1, conventional Web search environments require high cognitive load in maintaining multiple Web search results as they do not provide an easy way to chunk multiple Web search results. With the VisSearch environment, however, the cognitive load of maintaining multiple Web search results can be significantly reduced (Lee, in press, a, b) because multiple Web search results are visualized as a single search-graph whose nodes are search queries used and useful Web-based information found during iterative Web searches. Therefore, short-term memory of Web searchers can be freed from maintenance of Web search results and can be used for much more important tasks such as thinking about good Web search queries and evaluating search engine hit pages.

Replacing recall with recognition. Another benefit of creating reusable visual artifacts is that it can replace much of the need for user-centered *recall* with user-centered *recognition.* The efficiency of Web searches in conventional Web search environments substantially decreases as Web searches are conducted over the course of several days. For example, people frequently re-submit the same search queries as there is no easy way to remember their past search queries. People also often need to re-visit the Web sites they had created bookmarks on to refresh what they had discovered in the past (Lee, in press, a,b). With conventional Web search environments, it is nearly impossible to avoid these mistakes unless Web searchers somehow *memorize* what they have done during their previous Web searches. However, the reusable, visual artifacts, which can be saved and retrieved, allow to easily avoid this inefficiency in the VisSearch environment. By *scanning* the search query nodes in their search-graph retrieved, people can easily recognize their past search queries. By *reading* their Web-site comments associated with visual bookmarks in the search-graph restored, they can easily figure out the actual contents of visual bookmarks (Lee, in press, a,b).

Providing large computational offloading. Computational offloading is the cognitive load that can be relieved by an external representation while solving a given task. Previous studies have shown that visual representations generally provide substantial amount of computational offloading (Larkin & Simon, 1987; Scaife & Rogers, 1996). When iterative Web searches are considered as a problem-solving process, (intermediate) Web search results can be regarded as how people understand the problem at hand and what they have learned at the moment. As people continue their quest to solve the problem, their search-graph will be enriched with more search query nodes and visual bookmarks. Since the search-graph visually elucidates search queries tried (by way of search query nodes) and useful information discovered (by way of visual bookmarks and Web-site comments), its computational offloading can help people better perceive where they are in the whole problem-solving process, thereby increasing the overall efficiency of their Web searches.

Increasing reusability of Web search results. Most of conventional Web search environments provide bookmarks to help people better reuse meaningful Web-based information they had collected in the past. However, as explained earlier, the bookmarks of conventional Web search environments suffer from two shortcomings. First, they cannot sufficiently represent the contents of Web sites (Cockburn & Jones, 1996; Wallace et al., 2000). In order to address this problem, the VisSearch environment allows to create Web-site comments, user comments attached to visual bookmarks. The Web-site comments become more powerful when Web searches are carried out over the course of several days as they allow people to easily recognize the actual contents of useful Web sites found in the past (Lee, in press, a, b). In fact, this is a good example of the benefit of a history-rich object as Norman argues (Norman, 1988). According to him, when an object can have a history of its own, it can acquire new affordance and people can interact with such an object in new ways. Since Web-site comments can be saved and restored along with the search-graph they belong to, they can have a history of their own, thus acquiring new affordance that allows people to avoid unnecessary Web navigation.

The other problem of the bookmarks is that they grow so fast, as ordinary people rarely categorize their bookmarks, that they easily become unusable in practice (Abrams, 1998). In the VisSearch environment, however, every visual bookmark is *always* categorized (see Fig. 1) as the process of creating visual bookmarks and cate-gorizing them are combined into one single process; people have to decide the best search query node before drag-and-drop a URL of a useful Web site. Therefore, all visual bookmarks are always associated with at least one search query node, which can significantly increase the reusability of the visual bookmarks created (Lee, in press, a, b).

4 Reducing Cognitive Load of Interrupting Tasks

Finding useful Web-based information is rarely a one-shot process. As briefly ex-plained earlier, Web search results almost always contain lots of irrelevant informa-tion. Therefore, it is usually unavoidable to extend and refine Web search results until obtain satisfactory results. As Ellis (Ellis, 1989, 1997) described in his information seeking process model, which can be applicable to Web search contexts, information seeking can be best described as a complicated Web structure with many interrupting sub-tasks whose boundaries are not clearly defined.

Let's take an example of a person who has found a promising search query while reading a certain Web page. This person can then either stop reading the current Web page and start a brand new Web search with the inspired search query, or continue to read the current Web page while trying to remember the inspired search query. In both cases, the ongoing task (conducting a new Web search with the promising query or continuously reading the original Web page where the promising search query was encountered) will be interrupted by the other task (remembering where he or she was reading in the original Web page or making the inspired search query available until finish reading the original Web page). Furthermore, since these interruptions can hap-pen recursively, the whole Web search processes become even more complicated and the efficiency of Web searches gets substantially deteriorated. There is, however, no definite theory of how to efficiently support these complicated, concurrent processes except that (a) the number of tools required to accomplish a given task should be minimized; (b) spatial locations can be used as an effective memory aid in conducting concurrent tasks; and (c) multiple displays should be positioned to minimize informa-tion hiding (Kirsh, 1995, 2000; Miyata & Norman, 1986).

The VisSearch environment realizes these three design principles as follows. First, it provides an integrated Web search environment that enables people to conduct Web searches, view contents of Web pages, organize multiple Web search results, and utilize Web search results of other people without depending on any other external tools. The search-graph and the Hit Browser, described in Sect. 3.1 and Sect. 3.2, allow users to search the Web and organize useful Web-based information they found. In addition, the VisSearch Web Browser enables them to read the contents of any Web sites (see Fig. 3).

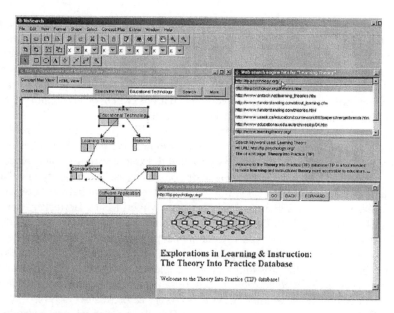

Fig. 3. Users can specify their search query by selecting search query nodes in the search-graph (left). The VisSearch environment lists potentially useful Web sites in the Hit Browser (top right) with additional information such as the title, the URL, and the short description of each hit page. The VisSearch Web Browser enables users to examine the content of a Web site of interest (bottom right)

Second, the VisSearch environment consistently places its components; the search-graph is always located at the left side; the Hit Browser, which shows the Web search engine hits, and the Recommendation Browser[6], which allows people to take advantage of Web search results of others, are always displayed at the top right side; and the VisSearch Web Browser is always shown at the right bottom side (see Fig. 3). Therefore, users can easily access the appropriate component they want to use.

Finally, the VisSearch environment carefully arranges its components so that none of them is hidden by others when each of them is needed. For instance, it keeps the search-graph, the VisSearch Web Browser, and the Web-site comment dialog box all visible while a new Web-site comment is being created. Users, therefore, can read the content of a Web site of interest (in the VisSearch Web Browser) and see the overall progress of their iterative Web searches (in the search-graph) while summarizing contents of a useful Web site they found (in the Web-site comment dialog box).

5   Utilizing Web Search Results of Others

It is quite common that many people search useful Web-based information on the same or similar topics (Abrams, 1998). For instance, college students taking the same course would search the Web for their term papers and professors having similar research interests would look for useful Web-based information for their research

---

[6] The Recommendation Browser is explained in Sect. 5.2.

interests. Just like a breakthrough research project would be frequently cited in many research papers, a useful Web-based information is very likely to be found commonly in many Web search results. Therefore, we can count how many times a particular Web site appears in the Web search results of people who share the same or similar interests when evaluating the quality of Web-based information. Having found such information, we can provide it as recommendations when other people who have similar interests are looking for useful Web-based information.

There have been several attempts to build a computer system that can enable us to take advantage of other people's work. Several computer systems, which are called *collaborative filtering* systems, have been developed to explore ways to match people with similar interests and to make recommendations on this basis. The majority of collaborative filtering systems use a correlation-based method to model similarities between users (Hill, Stead, Rosenstein & Furnas, 1995; Konstan, Miller, Maltz, Herlocker, Gordon & Riedl, 1997; Shardanand, 1995). In order to compare users' interests, correlation-based collaborative filtering systems typically require people to explicitly rate a finite set of information. However, the downside of this explicit rating approach is that unless they perceive some benefits for providing ratings, people tend not to rate the information requested. In such cases, it could result in lack of ratings, causing a serious impact on the performance of collaborative filtering systems (Avery & Zeckhauser, 1997).

In order to overcome this drawback, the VisSearch environment uses a data mining technique called an association rule, instead of correlations. When people finish or save their Web searches, their Web search results are sent to the VisSearch Server through a Web connection. The VisSearch Recommendation Engine then analyzes the Web search results compiled in the VisSearch Server to find frequent patterns in Web search queries and the resulting useful Web resources with an association rule data mining algorithm. The mined frequent patterns are then used to help other people when they search useful Web-based information later. Since the VisSearch environment does not require any extra work, such as explicit rating of search engine hits, the problem of explicit rating of conventional collaborative filtering systems is avoided in the VisSearch environment.

5.1 Association Rule Algorithm

The association rule data mining algorithm, first introduced to analyze the buying patterns of supermarket customers (Agrawal, Imielinski & Swami, 1993, 1998), can be formalized as follows:

1. Let $I = \{i_1, i_2, ..., i_m\}$ be a set of items, often called an *itemset.*
2. Let D be a set of transactions, where each transaction T is a subset of itemset such that $T \subseteq I$.
3. Let X be a set of items in I. A transaction T is said to contain X, if $X \subseteq T$.
4. An association rule is an implication of the form of $X \rightarrow Y$, where $X \subset I, Y \subset I$ and $X \cap Y = \emptyset$. X and Y are often called *antecedent* and *consequent,* respectively.
5. The rule $X \rightarrow Y$ has *support s* in transaction set D, if and only if $s\%$ of transactions in D contain X *and Y.*
6. The rule $X \rightarrow Y$ holds with *confidence c* in transaction set D, if and only if $c\%$ of transactions in D that contain X also contain Y.

As an example, let's consider an association rule, *pizza* → *soda* with support 30% and confidence 40%. This rule indicates that 30% of the supermarket transactions involve the buying of pizza and soda, and 40% of the transactions that involve the buying of pizza also involve the buying of soda. The association rule mining problem consists of discovering all association rules with support and confidence larger than some user-specified thresholds.

The association rule mining technique can be applied in the context of Web searches. The VisSearch environment seeks association rules such as "30% of saved search-graphs include a search query X and a useful Web site Y, and 40% of the search-graphs containing a search query X are also associated with a useful Web site Y." Once such an association rule is found, the Web site Y can be provided as a recommendation to other Web searchers who have just constructed a search query X. Since mining association rules is computationally intensive, the VisSearch environment implements an optimized association rule mining algorithm called the FPGrowth (Han, Pei & Yin, 2000).

5.2 Finding Association Rules from Web Search Results

As described in the previous section, the association rule algorithm requires a set of transactions, D, where each transaction T is a subset of the itemset I, and the itemset I is a set of unique Web search queries used and useful Web-based information found in the context of Web searches. The problem with conventional Web search environments is that they do not provide an easy way to collect this information; all search queries are discarded after use and no associative information between search queries and bookmarks is retained.

This information, on the other hand, is readily available in the VisSearch environment. From Fig. 4, for instance, we can easily construct four transactions, (e.g., $T_1 = \{Query_1 : URL_1, URL_2, URL_3, URL_4\}$), because every visual bookmark always belongs to at least one search query node. Since there are two types of item, search query or URL of useful Web-based information, the association rule algorithm described above can generate four types of association rules, *query* → *URL*, *query* → *query'*, *URL* → *query*, and *URL* → *URL'*, and mined association rules can be used for guiding other Web searchers as discussed earlier.

When Web searches are done, the VisSearch Client saves the Web search results, represented as search-graphs, into a central repository of the VisSearch Server. The compiled search-graphs are first preprocessed. During the preprocessing phase, all search queries are capitalized and all stop words such as articles, prepositions or interrogative pronouns are removed as they do not carry additional information. After that, the VisSearch Recommendation Engine applies the association rule mining algorithm to the preprocessed search-graphs, and mines frequent relationships among search queries and useful Web-based information. By default, when it starts, the VisSearch Client checks the mined association rules in the VisSearch Server and downloads them if necessary. The VisSearch Client notifies users by displaying an additional "star" icon, as shown in Fig. 5, when there is at least one association rule related to a search query node or a visual bookmark. As the number of stars in the star icon is proportional to the number of association rules relevant, it is easy to recognize which search queries had been more frequently used or which Web sites had been more commonly found in the Web search results compiled in the VisSearch Server. In addition, the VisSearch Client provides an easy user interface for accessing the information that the association rules recommend. Users can select the "View Recommendations..." contextual menu to bring up the recommended information in the Recommendation Browser component as illustrated in Fig. 5.

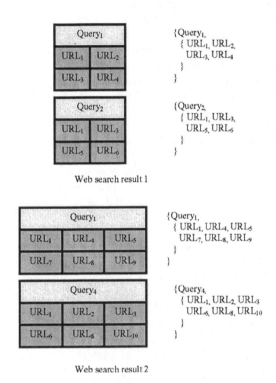

Fig. 4. Schematic representations of two Web search results (left) and their symbolic representations (right)

In the example shown in Fig. 5, the VisSearch environment recommends "EFFECTIVENESS" and "BENEFIT" as related search queries to the search query, "Educational Technology," which reflects the fact that many people who had searched the useful Web-based information about "Educational Technology" had often used "EFFECTIVENESS" or "BENEFIT" while refining their Web search results. The VisSearch environment also suggests five Web sites in Fig. 5, which means that many people who had searched meaningful Web resources with a search query, "Educational Technology," had often found some combinations of these five Web sites to be valuable to them.

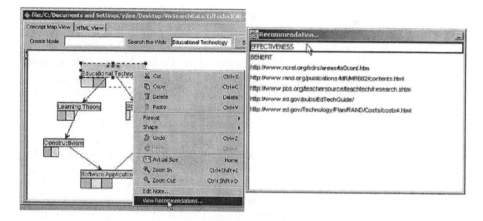

Fig. 5. The "View Recommendations..." contextual menu allows users to access the information recommended (left). In this example, the Recommendation Browser lists two recommended Web search queries and five useful Web sites with respect to the search query node "Educational Technology" (right)

6 Conclusions

This paper describes VisSearch, an alternative Web search environment capable of visualizing iterative Web search processes and utilizing Web search results of other people. In many educational situations, it is quite common to search useful Web-based information over the course of several days. However, due to the limitations of conventional Web search environments, many people are often overwhelmed and distracted by the amount of information, what is often called "information overload" (Conklin, 1987; Hess, 1999; Nachmias & Gilad, 2002). The VisSearch environment efficiently addresses this problem by (a) reducing cognitive load of iterative Web searches with reusable computational artifacts; (b) reducing cognitive load of concurrent tasks with an integrated Web search environment; and (c) utilizing useful Web search results of others with an association rule data mining algorithm.

In the VisSearch environment, reusable computational artifacts serve as short-term and long-term *externalizations* of intermediate Web search processes, replacing much of the need for user-centered *recall* with user-centered *recognition*. The VisSearch environment also provides an integrated Web search environment in which iterative Web search results can be efficiently organized as a single, evolving knowledge network similar to a concept map, and useful Web-based information can be searched and viewed without using any other external tools.

Although visualization techniques adopted in the VisSearch environment have many benefits over conventional approaches, they might be less useful for simple, closed-ended questions as conventional Web search engines could easily find the answers to such questions. In addition, the VisSearch environment, or visualization techniques in general, might be less beneficial to expert Web searchers; they may not want to learn a new approach as they have already developed their own efficient Web search strategies with conventional Web search environments.

In addition, although the VisSearch environment can reduce considerable amounts of complexities in organizing complicated, multiple Web search results, maintaining many search-graphs would cause a similar maintenance problem as with organizing bookmarks of conventional Web search environments. One of the possible solutions to this problem would be to create a *meta-search-graph*. The meta-search-graph can merge multiple search-graphs and visualize them as a single knowledge network whose node represents a unique search-graph, instead of a unique search query as in an ordinary search-graph. Just as user comments can be associated with search query nodes of an ordinary search-graph, they can also be attached to nodes of a meta-search-graph, allowing users to easily recognize the actual information contained in each node of their meta-search-graph. In that respect, the meta-search-graph is somewhat similar to *Topic Map* (Mason, 2002). Nodes of a meta-search-graph and visual bookmarks can be viewed as *Topics* and *Occurrences,* respectively as nodes of a meta-search-graph enable users to connect abstract knowledge to concrete Web-based information.

Finally, the VisSearch environment allows for utilizing Web search results of other people. It employs an association rule data mining algorithm to find frequent patterns in Web search queries and useful Web resources, and provides recommendations based on the association rules mined. One shortcoming of this approach is, however, that it is not easy to provide enough recommendations in the early stage until there are enough number of people sharing the same or similar interests. Although this problem, known as a *critical mass problem* of recommender systems, will disappear as the VisSearch environment acquires enough number of users, it can be addressed by utilizing index structures of existing conventional Web search engines such as YaHoo or Open Directory[7] in which every Web site added to their index structures is examined by human catalogers.

References

Abrams, D. (1998). Information Archiving with Bookmarks. In *Proceedings of the SIGCHI Conference on Human factors in computing systems* (pp. 41-48). Los Angeles, CA: ACM Press.

Agrawal, R., Imielinski, T., & Swami, A. (1993). Database Mining: A Performance Perspective. *IEEE Transactions of Knowledge and Data Engineering, Special Issues on Learning and Discovery in Knowledge-Based Databases, 5*(6), 914-925.

Agrawal, R., Imielinski, T., & Swami, A. (1998). Mining Association Rules Between Sets of Items in Large Databases. In *Proceedings of the 1993 ACM SIGMOD International Conference on Management of Data* (pp. 207-216). Washington, DC: ACM Press.

Avery, C., & Zeckhauser, R. (1997). Recommender Systems for Evaluating Computer Messages. *Communications for the ACM, 40*(3), 88-89.

Ayers, E., & Stasko, J. (1995). Using Graphical History in Browsing the World Wide Web. In *Proceedings of the 4th International World Wide Web Conference.* Boston, MA: O'Reilly. Available online: http://www.w3j.com/1/Contents.html#2.

---

[7] http://www.dmoz.org

Bell, P. (2002). Using Argument Map Representations to Make Thinking Visible for Individual and Groups. In T. Koschmann, R. Hall, & N. Miyake (Eds.), *CSCL2: Carrying Forward the Conversation* (pp. 449-485). Hillsdale: Lawrence Erlbaum Associates.

Carroll, J. B. (1999). Expert Internet Information Access. *Journal of Educational Computing Research, 20*(3), 209-222.

Cockburn, A., & Jones, S. (1996). Which Way Now? Analysing and Easing Inadequacies in WWW Navigation. *International Journal of Human-Computer Studies, 45*, 105-129.

Conklin, J. (1987). Hypertext: An Introduction and Survey. *IEEE Computer, 20*(7), 17-41.

Ellis, D. (1989). A Behavioral Approach to Information Retrieval System Design. *Journal of Documentation, 45*(3), 171-212.

Ellis, D. (1997). Modelling the Information Seeking Patterns of Engineers and Research Scientists in an Industrial Environment. *Journal of Documentation, 53*(4), 384-403.

Gagne, R.M., & Glaser, R. (1987). Foundations in Learning Research. In R.M. Gagné (Ed.), *Foundations in Learning Research* (pp. 49-83). Hillsdale: Lawrence Erlbaum Associates.

Google (2004). *Google Web API*, from http://www.google.com/apis.

Han, J., Pei, J., & Yin, Y. (2000). Mining Frequent Patterns Without Candidate Generation. In *Proceedings of the 2000 ACM SIGMOD International Conference on Management of Data* (pp. 1-12). Dallas, TX: ACM Press.

Hess, B. (1999). Graduate Student Cognition During Information Retrieval Using the World Wide Web: A Pilot Study. *Computers & Education, 33*, 1-33.

Hightower, R., Ring, L., Helfman, J., Bederson, B., & Hollan, J. (1998). Graphical Multiscale Web Histories: A Study of PadPrints. In *Proceedings of ACM Conference on Hypertext* (pp. 58-65). Pittsburg, PA: ACM Press.

Hill, W., Stead, L., Rosenstein, M., & Furnas, G. (1995). Recommending and Evaluating Choices in a Virtual Community of Use. In *Proceedings of ACM CHI '95 Conference on Human Factors in Computing Systems* (pp. 194-201). Denver, CO: ACM Press.

Kirsh, D. (1995). The Intelligent Use of Space. *Artificial Intelligence, 73*, 31-68.

Kirsh, D. (2000). A Few Thoughts on Cognitive Overload. *Intellectica, 1*(30), 19-51.

Konstan, J., Miller, B., Maltz, D., Herlocker, J., Gordon, L., & Riedl, J. (1997). Grouplens: Applying Collaborative Filtering to Usenet News. *Communications of the ACM, 40*(3), 77-87.

Lamon, M., Reeve, R., & Caswell, B. (1999). Finding Theory in Practice: Collaborative Networks for Professional Learning. In *Proceedings of 1999 Annual Meeting of the AERA*. Montreal, Canada: AERA Press. Available online: http://www.ikit.org/abstract/finding_theory.html.

Larkin, J., & Simon, H. (1987). Why a Diagram is (Sometimes) Worth Ten Thousands Words. *Cognitive Science, 11*, 65-100.

Lee, Y.-J. (2003). *Efficient Web Searching for Open-Ended Questions: The Effects of Visualization and Data Mining Technology*. Unpublished Doctoral Dissertation. University of Illinois at Urbana-Champaign.

Lee, Y.-J. (2004). Creating a Concept Map of Your Web Searches: A Design Rationale and Web-Enabled Application. *Journal of Computer Assisted Learning, 20*, 103-113.

Lee, Y.-J. (in press). The Effect of Creating External Representations on the Efficiency of Web Searching. *Interactive Learning Environments*.

Lee, Y.-J. (in press). VisSearch: A Collaborative Web Searching environment. *Computers & Education*.

Linn, M. C. (2000). Designing the Knowledge Integration Environment. *International Journal of Science Education, 22*(8), 781-796.

Markatos, E. (1999). *On Caching Search Engine Results*. ICS FORTH.

Mason J.D. (2002). *ISO/TEC 13250: Topic Maps*, from http://www.yl2.doe.gov/sgml/sc34/document/0322_files/isol3250-2nd-ed-v2.pdf.

Miyata, Y., & Norman, D.A. (1986). Psychological Issues in Support of Multiple Activities. In D.A. Norman, & S.W. Draper (Eds.), *User-Centered System Design* (pp. 265-284). Hillsdale: Lawrence Erlbaum Associates.

Nachmias, R., & Gilad, A. (2002). Needle in a Hyperstack: Searching for Information on the World Wide Web. *Journal of Research on Technology in Education, 34*(4), 475-486.

National Center for Education Statistics (2000a). *Students' Use of the Internet*. Washington DC: U.S. Department of Education.

National Center for Education Statistics (2000b). *Teacher Use of Computers and the Internet in Public Schools*. Washington DC: U.S. Department of Education.

Pea, R., Edelson, D., & Gomez, L. (1994). The CoVis Collaboratory: High School Science Learning Supported by a Broadband Educational Network with Scientific Visualization, Videoconferencing, and Collaborative Computing. In *Proceedings of 1994 Annual Meeting of the AERA*. New Orleans, LA: AERA Press. Available online: http://www.covis.nwu.edu/info/papers/pdf/pea-aera-94.pdf.

Nordlie, R. (1999). "User Revealment" - A Comparison of Initial Queries and Ensuing Question Development in Online Searching and in Human Reference Interaction. In *Proceedings of the 22nd Annual International ACM SIGIR Conference on Research and Development in Information Retrieval* (pp. 11-18). Berkeley, CA: ACM Press.

Norman, D.A. (1988). *The Psychology of Everyday Things*. New York: Basic Books.

Norman, D.A. (1993). *Things that Make Us Smart: Defending Human Attributes in the Age of the Machine*. New York: Addison-Wesley Publishing Company.

Scardamalia, M., Bereiter, C., & Lamon, M. (1994). The CSILE Project: Trying to Bring the Classroom into World 3. In K. McGilly (Ed.), *Computers as Cognitive Tools, Vol. 2: No More Walls* (pp. 201-228). Cambridge: Bradford Books/MIT Press.

Scaife, M., & Rogers, Y. (1996). External Cognition: How Do Graphical Representations Work? *International Journal of Human-Computer Studies, 45*, 185-213.

Shardanand, U., & Maes, P. (1995). Social Information Filtering: Algorithms for Automating "Word of Mouth". In *Proceedings of ACM CHI '95 Conference on Human Factors in Computing Systems* (pp. 210-217). Denver, CO: ACM Press.

Simon, H.A. (1996). *Observations on the Sciences of Science Learning*. Paper prepared for the Committee on Developments in the Science of Learning for the Sciences of Science Learning: An Interdisciplinary Discussion. Department of Psychology, Carnegie Mellon University.

Soloway, E., & Wallace, R. (1997). Does the Internet Support Student Inquiry? Don't Ask. *Communications of the ACM, 40*, 11-16.

Songer, N.B. (1996). Exploring Learning Opportunities in Coordinated Network-Enhanced Classrooms: A Case Study of Kids as Global Scientists. *Journal of Learning Sciences, 5*(4), 297-327.

Stuart, K. C, Moran, T P., & Newell, A. (1983). *The Psychology of Human-Computer Interaction*. Hillsdale: Lawrence Erlbaum Associates.

Sweller, J. (1988). Cognitive Load During Problem Solving: Effect of Learning. *Cognitive Science, 12*, 257-285.

Tauscher, L., & Greenberg, S. (1997). How People Revisit Web Pages: Empirical Findings and Implications for the Design of History Systems. *International Journal of Human-Computer Studies, 47*, 97-137.

Wallace, R. M., Kupperman, J., Krajcik, J., & Soloway, E. (2000). Science on the Web: Students Online in a Sixth-Grade Classroom. *Journal of the Learning Sciences, 9*(1), 75-104.

The Role of Content Representations in Hypermedia Learning: Effects of Task and Learner Variables

Jean-Francois Rouet, Hervé Potelle, and Antonine Goumi

Laboratoire Langage et Cognition, CNRS and University of Poitiers,
99 avenue du Recteur Pineau,
86022 Poitiers Cedex, France
{jean-francois.rouet, herve.potelle,
antonine.goumi}@univ-poitiers.fr

Abstract. We discuss the role of content representations in hypermedia documents. The phrase "content representation" covers a broad category of knowledge visualization devices ranging from local organizers, e.g., headings, introductions and connectors, to global representations, e.g., topic lists, outlines and concept maps. Text processing research has demonstrated that the principled use of content representations can facilitate the acquisition of knowledge from texts. As regards the role of global content representations in hypermedia learning, the effects vary according to individual and situation variables. We review empirical studies investigating different types of global representations in the context of comprehension and information search tasks. The evidence suggests that networked concept maps are most effective for users with some level of prior knowledge, in nonspecific task contexts.

1 Introduction

In order to be usable, information systems need to be organized according to standard patterns. For instance, textbook contents are normally structured into chapters, sections, subsections. In addition, the organization of information needs to be made visible to the reader, through the inclusion of content representations. Materials printed on paper include a broad range of organizational devices (see Goldman & Rakestraw, 2000, for a review). For example, most books include tables of contents, page headings, indexes and other local and global content representations.

New information systems deeply transform the way information is displayed. For instance, the use of frames and multiple windows in Web-based information challenges the notion of a "document page". This raises new challenges for information systems designers: How to represent the contents of vast information repositories so as to ensure easy navigation and effective learning by inexpert users? Ideally, such an endeavor should rely on explicit models of reading, comprehension and resource-based learning (e.g., Kintsch, 1998). So far, however, the design of information systems remains largely empirical, due in part to the lack of communication across research and design communities, but also to the lack of explicit models of the mental processes involved in complex information processing.

S.-O. Tergan and T. Keller (Eds.): Knowledge and Information Visualization, LNCS 3426, pp. 343–354, 2005.
© Springer-Verlag Berlin Heidelberg 2005

This chapter discusses the role of various types of content representations in hypermedia-based learning. We use the word hypermedia in a broad sense, comprising any coherent set of online documents involving verbal, pictorial, and/or diagrammatic information. The chapter contains three sections. In the first section, we review some models of complex information processing, focusing on the role of content representations. In the second and third sections, we review two studies examining the role of content representations in complex electronic documents. The first study (Potelle & Rouet, 2003) examined how hierarchical and networked concept maps influence university students' comprehension of a hypertext. The second study (Goumi, Rouet & Aubert, 2003) focused on the effects of concept maps vs. alphabetic lists as information search tools in an educational CD-ROM. In the final section, we discuss the implications of our findings for the design of complex information systems.

2   The Role of Content Representations in Text Processing

According to a widespread theory, comprehension involves the construction of a multilayered mental representation (Kintsch, 1998; Kintsch & van Dijk, 1978). The first level of representation is called a surface representation. It consists in encoding the explicit form of the message: visual features, letters, words and sentences. During the reading process, the surface representation is quickly subsumed by a propositional representation, in which content words are connected into micro and macropropositions. Finally, propositions from the text are integrated with the reader's prior knowledge in order to form the situation model. Similarly, the mental model theory by Johnson-Laird (1983) assumes that readers form internal representations that share analogical properties with the objects and events described in the text.

Psycholinguistic research has pointed out the prominent role played by the structural properties of texts in the comprehension of texts. Texts are easier to understand if they are organized according to standard rhetorical schemata (Kintsch & Yarbrough, 1982; Meyer, 1985). The rhetorical organization of a text is usually represented in the text itself, through e.g. the order of sentences, introductions, connectives (Spyridakis & Standal, 1987). A text's organization can also be made explicit through the use of local and global content representations. Local representations (e.g., headings) convey the topic and organization of the subsequent passage of text. Global representations (e.g., tables of contents, concept maps) convey the content and organization of a set of passages.

2.1   Effects of Local Content Representations on Comprehension

Text comprehension researchers have extensively studied the effects of headings on readers' comprehension and memory for text. Early studies demonstrated that, in some cases, headings are absolutely necessary for the reader to make sense of the text (Brandsford & Johnson, 1972; Dooling & Lachman, 1971). In more common cases, headings, introductions and connecting statements improve comprehension and memory for text. Poorly designed headings can even focus the reader's attention on detail information (Kozminsky, 1977). Headings, however, will not be effective if their wording is unfamiliar to the reader (Spyridakis & Standal, 1987).

Several interpretations have been proposed to explain the facilitative effects of content representations. In their seminal studies of text comprehension, Kintsch and his colleagues argued that readers use initial information as a foundation for the propositional textbase (Kintsch, Kozminsky, Streby, McKoon & Keenan, 1975; Kintsch & van Dijk, 1978). Incoming propositions are connected to the initial proposition set through referential and coherence links. Thus, the propositional contents of the title or initial sentence can influence the formation of a textbase (Kieras, 1980). However, other researchers have suggested that the presence of headings and other structuring materials triggers a "structure strategy" on the part of the reader. The structure strategy consists in attempting to retrieve the conceptual structure that connects ideas together (Lorch & Lorch, 1996). Thanks to textual organizers, the visual structure of a text would act as a system of "processing instructions" telling the readers how the materials should be connected (Goldman & Rakestraw, 2000).

Headings may also influence text comprehension through low-level word identification mechanisms. Using difficult and ambiguous texts, Wiley and Rayner (2000) found that headings decreased the frequency of regressive eye fixations and the duration of "wrap up" pauses observed at clause boundaries. Further experiments indicated that headings speeded up the activation of word meanings from memory, suggesting a clearly bottom-up influence. Van den Broek and his colleagues (van den Broek, Virtue, Gaddy Everson, Tzeng & Sung, 2001) have proposed a similar interpretation of the role of text organizers in text comprehension, through a set of neo-connectionist activation rules.

The propositional, strategic, and bottom-up interpretations of the effects of headings are not mutually exclusive. The respective processes may apply in parallel, with different strengths depending on text, reader, and task variables.

2.2 Effects of Global Content Representations on Comprehension

So far, the scientific literature is much less informative as regards the effect of more complex organizers, e.g., tables of contents, concept maps and flowcharts. The lack of evidence contrasts with the pervasive use of such these devices in real-life expository materials, such as textbooks, manuals or encyclopedia. Experimental research, however, tends to focus on simple, well controlled materials and situations. Most research studies conducted until now also used very basic task settings, e.g., asking participants to read or order to memorize or to prepare for a comprehension test. These tasks are much simpler than the activities performed with texts in naturally-occurring contexts: Readers or textbooks, manuals or encyclopedia most often have to make their way through dozens of pages before they can access and read relevant materials. And these materials often take the form of a collection of texts, often accompanied by pictures and diagrams, and structured through various types of content representations. In such situations, text processing strategies strongly rely on the readers' purposes and on their ability to make use of complex content representations.

Some evidence suggests, nevertheless, that content representations are also essential in helping readers make sense of complex texts. For instance, in a study by Glenberg and Langston (1992), a flowchart diagram helped readers construct a mental model of a procedure described in a text (e.g., "how to write a scientific paper"). Rouet, Vidal-Abarca, Bert-Erboul and Millogo (2001, experiment 2) found that the inclusion of an explicit table of contents at the top of a lengthy scientific text presented online increased text review, and facilitated the location of key information while searching. And Mannes (1994) found that an outline introducing a lengthy expository text, but with a slightly discrepant structure, promoted deep comprehension of the materials, as evidenced in a diagram drawing task and in a pair relatedness judgement task.

Thus, the type of symbol used to represent the contents of hypermedia documents might deeply affect the readers' strategies and their actual learning from the materials. In the remaining of this chapter we review two of our recent studies investigating the role of concept maps in hypermedia comprehension and information search, respectively.

3   The Role of Concept Maps in Hypermedia Comprehension

3.1   The Representation of Hypermedia Contents

Menus, concept maps and other types of content representations play an essential role in hypermedia usability (Nielsen, 1999). There is no agreement, however, as to which type of representation better suits which type of users. McDonald and Stevenson (1998) showed that navigation aids facilitate low prior knowledge readers' comprehension. Psychology students read a hypertext on the topic of discourse production. The hypertext was presented either with a navigational aid (i.e., a network concept map or a simple list), or without such an aid (i.e., only as a set of hypertext nodes and links). Both types of aids lead to better comprehension, but only in low prior knowledge students. Moreover, the time needed to answer questions was shorter when using a concept map than a list. Another study by Hofman and van Oostendorp (1999) tried to assess the effects of content representations on several representation levels as a function of readers' prior knowledge. Undergraduate students with high vs. low prior topic knowledge were asked to study a science text on sun radiation and health. The text was presented either through a network concept map showing various types of relationships between ultraviolet radiation and skin cancer, or through an alphabetic topic list (i.e., without explicit high-level relations). Structural levels of text information (i.e., microstructure vs. macrostructure questions) as well representations levels of text (i.e., textbase vs. situation model questions) were manipulated so as to produce four types of comprehension questions. Contrary to previous results, Hofman and van Oostendorp found that the concept map hindered the situation model construction of the low knowledge students. They concluded that the concept map had diverted readers' attention from more appropriate levels of processing. For readers with little prior knowledge, simpler representations, e.g., content lists or hierarchical maps, may be more productive than complex network representations.

3.2   Prior Knowledge and Content Representations: An Empirical Study

Thus, even though concept maps are usually thought to be beneficial, there is quite some discrepancy between the results of past studies. Potelle and Rouet (2003) attempted to clarify the picture by suggesting that hierarchical representations may help low knowledge (LK) students, whereas network representations may be more beneficial to high knowledge (HK) students. They argued that hierarchical maps may facilitate the construction of the hypertext macrostructure in LK students (Dee-Lucas & Larkin, 1995; Shapiro, 1999) because they display basic global relationships among the topics dealt with in the text (Lorch & Lorch, 1996). Reading a hierarchical map may help the LK students to build a mental representation organized with categorical /thematic links. On the other hand, a network map could hinder LK students' construction of the macrostructure because of its too complex semantic links (Hofman & van Oostendorp, 1999).

Potelle and Rouet (2003) designed a simple hypertext made of seven content cards about various aspects of "social influence", a core topic in social psychology studies. They designed three content representations of the hypertext (Fig. 1). The *hierarchical map* was organized with superordinate and subordinate links from the most general to the most specific topics about social influence. The *network map* was organized by connecting the main topics with semantic links. The relevant links were identified in a pilot study involving ten PhD students who were asked to draw connections between two parallel lists of topics. Finally, the *alphabetic list* presented the topics in alphabetic order, without explicit connections.

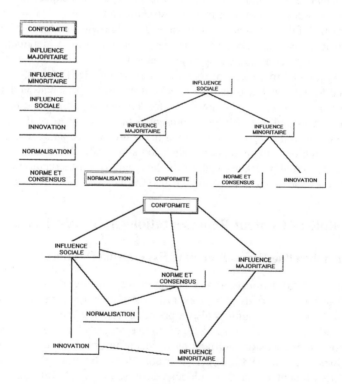

Fig. 1. The three content representations used in the study by Potelle and Rouet (2003). Alphabetic list (left), hierarchical map (center), and network map (right)

Potelle and Rouet hypothesized that the hierarchical map would function as a structural cue for all the readers, which would improve comprehension, especially at a macrostructural level. The network map, however, was based on implicit semantic relations generated by expert students. Understanding these relations (e.g. "minority influence - innovation") requires some prior knowledge of the domain. Thus, having to study this type of overview might be detrimental to novice readers. Forty seven students participated in their experiment. Subjects were categorized as novices vs. specialists based on the median split of a knowledge pre-test. They had to study the hypertext for a period of 20 minutes, with an explicit comprehension objective. Comprehension was assessed through a 16-item multiple choice questionnaire, and a summary task. The participants were also asked to draw a map of the hypertext from memory.

Comprehension was positively related to prior knowledge, and microstructure questions were better answered than macrostructure questions. An interaction between prior knowledge level and the type of content representation was found. Low knowledge students had better scores when using the version of the hypertext with a hierarchical map than with the other two formats. For the more expert students, the type of content representation had no significant impact. As expected, the effect was stronger for macrostructure than for microstructure questions, even though the three-way interaction failed to reach significance. Low knowledge students also included more thematic ideas in their summaries when reading from a hierarchical map. Finally, they drew more accurate map of the hierarchical hypertext than of the other two systems. Again, no difference was found for high knowledge students.

Potelle and Rouet concluded that the effects of content representation depend in part on the reader's prior knowledge level. As for any text organizer, the reader must be able to recognize and use the signals presented in a content map. If the map is ambiguous, or uses unfamiliar symbols, then the result will be an added burden on the reader, with dubious effects on comprehension and recall. When designing hypertext systems, care should be taken to adjust the level and type of structural information to the capabilities and needs of the user (see also Carmel, Crawford & Chen, 1992).

4   The Role of Content Representations in Search Tasks

4.1   Comprehending Versus Searching Hypermedia Documents

Searching for information is a very common way to interact with complex documents. Searching occurs as part of everyday activities, e.g., travelling, cooking, or setting up devices. Searching is also a prevalent reading mode in occupational activities (Guthrie & Kirsch, 1987) and, of course, in learning. There is evidence that reading for comprehension and reading to locate information are two rather different activities (Guthrie, 1988; Rouet & Tricot, 1996; Rouet, et al., 2001). Searching requires the student to have an objective, or search goal. Information found in documents is not processed according to its importance in the document, but according to its relevance with respect to the person's goal. While searching, the reader must retain and update her/his representation of the goal, assess the relevance of the information categories available, make selections and extract relevant information from the contents found. Then, s/he must also integrate the information selected to her/his representation of the task.

4.2   Effects of Three Types of Interfaces on Search: An Empirical Study

Quality instructional multimedia resources should allow students to locate contents of interest quickly and accurately. Currently such databases, whether online or on CD-ROM, use a variety of content representation techniques and search tools, ranging from alphabetic indexes to concept maps and keyword search engines. The respective effectiveness of these interfaces for naturalistic search tasks has seldom been investigated.

In order to build an appreciation of the potential and limits of different interfaces on information search, one must bear in mind the specific processes that characterize information search (Guthrie, 1988; Rouet & Tricot, 1996). The information searcher must construct and update a representation of the search goal, assess the relevance of the information categories available, make selections and extract relevant information from the contents found. Then, s/he must also integrate the information selected to her/his representation of the task. According to Guthrie's (1988) model, searching a document requires five distinct steps: forming a goal (e.g., understanding the requirements of a question), selecting a category (e.g., selecting a column in a table), extracting information (e.g., locating a figure within a column), integrating new information with previously extracted information, and recycling through the first four steps until a satisfactory answer can be provided.

Goumi et al. (2003) investigated the effects of different types of interfaces (an alphabetic index, a concept map and a hybrid interface) on the selection phase. The search task was performed by two groups of students (basic and advanced students) using an instructional multimedia database. They had to answer a 12-item questionnaire during two experimental sessions (6 questions per session). Goumi et al. hypothesised that different content representations (e.g., alphabetic lists vs. concept maps) would have a specific impact on the selection phase of the search process, i.e., the phase where the searcher tries to match his/her search goal with the available categories. More precisely, they suggested that a concept map may require the searcher to guess what the knowledge area relevant to the question is while a list of keywords may encourage the searcher to perform a piecemeal matching task.

Two groups of participants were recruited. The first group was made of 18 students preparing their second year in a basic technical program (BTS, basic students). The students participated as part of a class assignment. The second group was made of 9 voluntary students, in their first year of a specialised training program (IUT, advanced students). The students in both groups participated voluntarily as part of an optional practice session.

The experiment used a prototype CD-Rom multimedia database, "Electronics in Questions", designed by a group of instructional researchers at the Ecole Nationale Supérieure des Télécommunications (ENST, Paris, France, http://www.cript.enst.fr). The database contains 90 multimedia articles each presenting a notion or a problem in the domain of electronics. Example of article topics are "What types of transistors does one have to use to design a ROM memory unit?", or "You were asked to design the Cosine function of a calculator with ten significant decimals. What are the options?" Individual articles are accessible through three distinct interfaces: A concept map, an alphabetical index and a hybrid interface including both types of representations (Fig. 2).

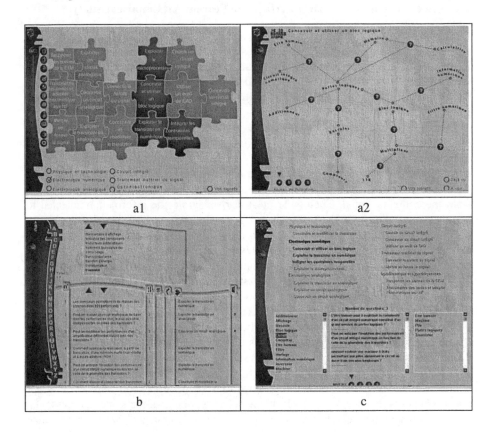

Fig. 2. The three interfaces included in the prototype CD-ROM used in the Goumi, Rouet and Aubert (2003) experiment. a- concept map (a1 = main level, a2 = subordinate level); b- alphabetic index; c- hybrid interface with hierarchical content list (upper part of the screen) and alphabetic index (lower part of the screen)

A paper questionnaire of 12 questions was designed for the experimental task. Each question corresponded to specific information in one of the database articles. The number of mouse clicks needed to access relevant information was equivalent in each of the three interfaces. For some questions, the information appeared literally in one of the database articles, while for the others, the student needed to drawn inferences or to perform simple computations from the information available. In addition, a questionnaire entitled "Please give your opinion" assessed users' perceptions of the three interfaces. Students were asked about the perceived difficulty to access to and comprehend the content of the articles for each question, the advantages and disadvantages of each interface, and which interface they had preferred.

The students participated in two sessions of two hours each, spaced out of a week, in groups of 2 to 12 participants. Each participant worked individually on a standard PC. The three interfaces were introduced and demonstrated at the beginning of the first session. Then the students had to perform six search tasks corresponding to 6 of the 12 questions. The interface to be used was specified for each question, so that each student performed two search tasks with each interface. A time limit of 10 minutes was roughly set up to complete each question. Students' selections in the CD-Rom and search time was recorded for each question. The order of presentation of the questions as well as the interface used were counterbalanced across students.

During the second session, the students were asked to complete six more search tasks, again using each of the three interfaces and according to the same procedure. Finally, students were asked for their subjective opinion about the interfaces, by means of a questionnaire. The session ended with a short explanation about the objectives of the study.

The study's main result was an interaction of student groups with interface type of information access. For students in the basic program (BTS), the index was the most effective interface: When searching with the index, the students found the target-article in a smaller number of clicks. Advanced students (IUT) needed a smaller number of clicks to access relevant contents. For this group, the hybrid interface required less clicks than the other two interfaces, even though the difference between the "hybrid" and "index" interface was not significant.

Qualitative analyses showed that differences across groups when using the hybrid interface were due to the fact that basic level students used it more as an index than as a map. Advanced level students understood better the functionalities of this interface, and the fact than it combines the two other interfaces. More specifically, advanced students used the upper part of the screen (structured table of contents) in order to preselect relevant areas of knowledge, before making selections in the index (lower part of the screen).

The concept map was described as "difficult to use and complicated, with too many choices (too large)" whereas the index, according to the same students was "easy to use". The seemingly more seductive aspect of the concept map turned out to be a barrier to fast and easy access to content information. Another question asked the students which of the three interfaces they preferred and why. Both groups of students preferred the alphabetic index over the other interfaces (six advanced students and ten basic students) because of its easiness of use and, again, because of its alphabetic order. Nevertheless, 3 advanced students and 8 basic students preferred the hybrid interface. None of the students preferred the concept map.

5   Conclusions

The number of online resources available for learning is increasing exponentially. So far such resources (e.g., Web sites and other e-learning materials) include a large variety of content representations, ranging from content pages with embedded links to concept maps leading to specific sections, or to menu lists arranged in alphabetic order. There is no consensus over when and for whom these interfaces are most effective. In this chapter, we have tried to argue that an answer to these questions has to take into account the type of user the resource intends to help, and the type of task that it is intended to support. Concept maps, despite their popularity, are not always the most effective way to represent contents in a hypermedia document. For tasks that involve browsing and comprehending the document contents, concept maps are useful only to the extent that the user can interpret the symbols used to represent different types of information units and different types of links. As a consequence, simple menu list or hierarchical diagrams often prove more productive for inexpert users.

Concept maps also seem better suited to exploratory learning tasks than to directed search tasks. Most learned tend to have an analytic approach when searching for specific information. As a result, alphabetic lists may allow faster access to relevant contents than more elaborate representations. However, as mentioned above, the evidence available so far concerns only a limited range of materials, students and tasks. Thus, no universal design standards can be drawn from it.

The works reviewed in this chapter suggest that a reflection about knowledge representation should take into account the type of knowledge being conveyed and the status of pre-existing information (texts, documents). Maps are found in extremely different contexts. In some cases, they are constructed from scratch as a communication process among members of a learning community. In other cases, maps are found by the user of a pre-existing learning resource. The map is then used in order to figure out the structure of the resource, and to select relevant contents within that resource.

Finally, there is a difference between maps that are built as a part of a knowledge construction activity (whether individual or collaborative) and maps that are used as artifacts conveying meaning. In the former case there is evidence that map construction is an effective activity (see Dansereau, Jonassen, this volume). In the latter case, the evidence is mixed. We found that list-based interfaces were sometimes as good as complex graphical representations. Consequently, map authors who don't have an opportunity to make the rational behind their design decisions explicit to the user should be extremely considerate to their cognitive characteristics as well as the contexts that surround their uses.

References

Brandsford, J.D., & Johnson, M.K. (1972). Contextual prerequisites for understanding: Some investigations in comprehension and recall. *Journal of Verbal Learning and Verbal Behavior, 11,* 717-726.

Carmel, E., Crawford, S., & Chen, H. (1992). Browsing in hypertext: A cognitive study. *IEEE Transactions on Systems, Man, and Cybernetics, 22*(5), 865-884.

Dee-Lucas, D., & Larkin, J.H. (1995). Learning from electronic texts: Effects of interactive overviews for information access. *Cognition & Instruction, 13*(3), 431-468.

Dooling, D.J., & Lachman, R. (1971). Effects of retention on the comprehension of prose. *Journal of Experimental Psychology, 88,* 216-222.

Glenberg, A.M., & Langston, W.E. (1992). Comprehension of illustrated text: pictures help build mental models. *Journal of Memory and Language, 31,* 129-151.

Goldman, S.R., & Rakestraw Jr., J.A. (2000). Structural aspects of constructing meaning from text. In M.L. Kamil, P.B. Mosenthal, P.D. Pearson, & R. Barr (Eds.), *Handbook of reading research, Vol. III* (pp. 311-335). Mahwah, NJ : Lawrence Erlbaum Associates.

Goumi, A., Rouet, J.-F., & Aubert, D. (2003). The effectiveness of three types of interfaces on information access in an educational CD-Rom. *Paper presented at the European Conference for Research on Learning and Instruction. Padova, Italy, August 26-30.*

Guthrie, J.T. (1988). Locating information in documents: examination of a cognitive model. *Reading Research Quarterly, 23*, 178-199.

Guthrie, J.T., & Kirsch, I. (1987). Distinctions between reading comprehension and locating information in text. *Journal of Educational Psychology, 79*, 210-228.

Hofman, R., & van Oostendorp, H. (1999). Cognitive effects of a structural overview in a hypertext. *British Journal of Educational Technology, 30*, 129-140.

Johnson-Laird, P.N. (1983). *Mental models.* Cambridge, MA: Cambridge University Press.

Kieras, D.E. (1980). Initial mention as a signal to thematic content in technical passages. *Memory and Cognition, 8*, 345-353.

Kintsch, W. (1998). *Comprehension: A paradigm for cognition.* Cambridge, MA: Cambridge University Press.

Kintsch, W., Kozminsky, E., Streby, W.J., McKoon, G., & Keenan, J.M. (1975). Comprehension and recall of text as a function of content variables. *Journal of Verbal learning and Verbal Behavior, 14*, 196-214.

Kintsch, W., & van Dijk, T.A. (1978). Toward a model of text comprehension and production. *Psychological Review, 85*, 363-394.

Kintsch, W., & Yarbrough, J.C. (1982). Role of rhetorical structure in text comprehension. *Journal of Educational Psychology, 74*, 828-834.

Kozminsky, E. (1977). Altering comprehension: the effect of biasing title on text comprehension. *Memory and Cognition, 5*, 482-490.

Lorch, R.F., & Lorch, E.P. (1996). Effects of organizational signals on free recall of expository text. *Journal of Educational Psychology, 88*, 38-48.

Mannes, S. (1994). Strategic processing of text. *Journal of Educational Psychology, 88*(4), 577-588.

McDonald, S., & Stevenson, R.J. (1998). An evaluation of the effects of navigational tools and subject matter expertise on browsing and information retrieval in hypertext. *Interacting with Computers, 10*, 129-142.

Meyer, B.J.F. (1985). Prose analysis: purposes, procedures, and problems. In B.K. Britton, & J.B. Black (Eds.), *Understanding expository text* (pp. 11-64). Hillsdale, NJ: Lawrence Erlbaum Associates.

Nielsen, J. (1999). *Designing Web Usability: The practice of simplicity.* Indianapolis: New Riders.

Potelle, H., & Rouet, J.-F. (2003). Effects of content representation and readers' prior knowledge on the comprehension of hypertext. *International Journal of Human-Computer Studies, 58*, 327-345.

Rouet, J.-F. & Tricot, A. (1996). Task and activity models in hypertext usage. In H. van Oostendorp, & S. de Mul (Eds.), *Cognitive aspects of electronic text processing* (pp. 239-264). Norwood, NJ: Ablex.

Rouet, J.-F., Vidal-Abarca, E., Bert-Erboul, A., & Millogo, V. (2001). Effects of information search tasks on the comprehension of instructional text. *Discourse Processes, 31*(2), 163-186.

Shapiro, A.M. (1999). The relationship between prior knowledge and interactive overviews during hypermedia-based learning. *Journal of Educational Computing Research, 20*(2), 143-167.

Spyridakis, J.H., & Standal, T.C. (1987). Signals in expository prose: Effects on reading. *Reading Research Quarterly, 22*, 285-298.

van den Broek, P., Virtue, S., Gaddy Everson, M., Tzeng, Y., & Sung, Y. (2001). Comprehension and memory for science texts: Inferential processes and the construction of a mental representation. In J. Otero, J.A. Leon, & A.C. Graesser (Eds.), *The Psychology of Science Text Comprehension* (pp. 131-154). Mahwah, NJ: Lawrence Erlbaum Associates.

Wiley, J. & Rayner, K. (2000). Effects of titles on the processing of text and lexically ambiguous words: Evidence from eye movements. *Memory and Cognition, 28*, 1011-1021.

Supporting Self-regulated E-Learning with Visual Topic-Map-Navigation

Andreas Rittershofer

Dietrich-Bonhoeffer-Gymnasium, Öschweg 21,
72555 Metzingen, Germany
andreas@rittershofer.de

Abstract. Teaching and learning at school is changing: students are expected more and more to organize their learning by themselves and also to be responsible for their learning progress by themselves. This creates new demands on the materials and media used to teach and learn. Fixed linearity is blocking, flexibility a great advantage - but it should not lead to missing structure. Topic maps offer the chance to guide the students through huge amounts of information with a carefully measured mixture of freedom and guidance. Topic maps are a rather abstract idea for the average user, so a way to make them usable with ease has to be found. A visualisation of the relevant parts of the topic maps realizes this in an intuitive usable manner. This lead to the development of the LmTM-server http://www.LmTM.de/, an e-learning-server for students at school. The navigation is realized completely via topic maps. The information stored in the topic maps can be extracted in several ways, for a text-based navigation, a graphical navigation, an alphabetical list of topics and a link list in the page footer. The combination of all these variants gives the user a very comfortable means at hand to explore the information on the LmTM-server.

1 Introduction

Teaching and learning at school is changing - not only due to the PISA-study. Lessons have had one main actor for a long time: the teacher. The students played the most part a more passive role. Today they are expected to be active, to plan and organize their learning and also to be responsible for their learning progress by themselves. This makes new demands not only on the students - but also on the teachers and the materials for teaching and learning too. The teacher is no longer the primary information broker in the classroom. He plays now the role of a moderator for information and knowledge. He therefore needs teaching and learning materials which are very flexible in their usage. The advantages of an increasing usage of the so-called new media is obvious. The "classical" lessons are very teacher-centric, the content is ordered in a strictly linear way and it is the same order for all students. Most times the order is given by the book used. This fixed linearity is a block for self-determinated learning. Every student should have the possibility to manage the given contents in his own order - an order he likes. There is one risk at this point: the loss of any structure. Students need some orientation, some guidance to big amounts of information or

S.-O. Tergan and T. Keller (Eds.): Knowledge and Information Visualization, LNCS 3426, pp. 355–363, 2005.

they get lost. Without knowledge they cannot cope with lots of information, so they cannot transform information to knowledge - a vicious circle.

2 Topic Maps

Topic Maps are an ISO-standard (ISO13250). First the notation was only in SGML (Standard Generalized Markup Language), later a XML based notation (eXtensible Markup Language) followed. Topic maps in XML notation are called XTM: XML Topic Maps.

This is not the place for an extensive course of XTM, but the most important things should be mentioned: "The purpose of a topic map is to convey knowledge about resources through a superimposed layer, or map, of the resources. A topic map captures the subjects of which resources speak, and the relationships between subjects, in a way that is implementation-independent. The key concepts in topic maps are topics, associations, and occurrences. A topic is a resource within the computer that stands in for (or "reifies") some real-world subject. Examples of such subjects might be the play Hamlet, the playwright William Shakespeare, or the "authorship" relationship. Topics can have names. They can also have occurrences, that is, information resources that are considered to be relevant in some way to their subject. Finally, topics can participate in relationships, called associations, in which they play roles as members. Thus, topics have three kinds of characteristics: names, occurrences, and roles played as members of associations. The assignment of such characteristics is considered to be valid within a certain scope, or context." (http://www.topicmaps. org/xtm/index.html).

Sometimes you can read of the Tao of topic maps: Topics, Associations, Occurrences. (Tao is a philosophy based on Lao Tse.)

3 LmTM – Lernen mit Topic Maps (Learning with Topic Maps)

3.1 Introduction

The new demands of today's lesson at school lead to the development of the LmTM-server http://www.LmTM.de/. The most important requests to realize are:

- Topic maps should be the base for navigation.
- Topic maps should lie as an abstract layer over the materials.
- Topic maps and materials can be on different physical machines.
- Topic maps should be usable textually and graphically.
- The navigation should give orientation and guidance to the student, but not restrict him. So the topic maps have to be designed in a way that they give some structure but leave enough freedom for different ways of approach to the information.

These goals could be achieved with XTM, without using all features XTM are offering.

3.2   Textual Navigation

The textual navigation is the navigation variant without visualisation - as the name indicates. So there are no special requirements for the hard- and software of the user, a frame-capable browser is a standard nowadays. The information extracted out of the topic map is shown in the left frame, the right frame is reserved for the occurrences of the topics. An example is shown in a screenshot (see Fig. 1).

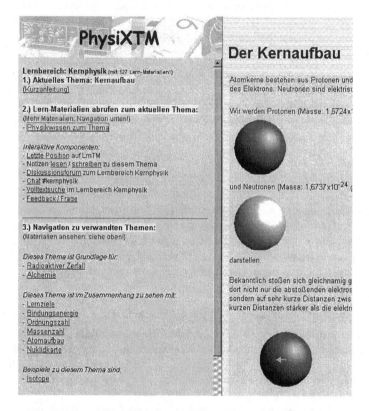

Fig. 1. Text-based navigation in the left frame, occurrence in the right frame (shown partially)

In the first line the current field of knowledge is mentioned ("Lernbereich: Kernphysik" in this example), followed by the number of occurrences (here 127 occurrences) to give some idea of the size of this field of knowledge. The rest is divided into three parts from "1.)" to "3.)".

- "1.)" shows - in green letters - the actual topic ("Kernaufbau") and thus the actual position in the topic map; the technical term "topic" is translated into "Aktuelles Thema".
- "2.)" lists all occurrences of the actual topic; the technical term "occurrence" is translated into "Lern-Materialien abrufen zum aktuellen Thema". In this example there is only one occurrence: "Physikwissen zum Thema". (Additionally you can

see some links to some interactive components outside of the topic map.) A click on an occurrence in the left frame opens this occurrence in the right frame, a small part of the right frame is shown in the screenshot.

- "3.)" shows all associations in which the actual topic is involved; the technical term "association" is translated into "Navigation zu verwandten Themen". A click on an association in the left frame changes the actual topic and thus the actual position in the topic map to the topic just clicked on. The contents of the left frame changes accordingly, this means a new actual topic ("Aktuelles Thema") with its occurrences and associations. The contents of the right frame is erased if some occurrence was shown there and if JavaScript is enabled.

The translation of the technical terms from the topic map standard to colloquial terms was absolutely necessary. The users should be able to use the LmTM-server without knowing technical things behind the surface, without some knowledge of topic maps.

At the very first use of this navigation variant a short time of adaption to this new navigation paradigm is necessary because of the strict separation of contents in the right frame and navigation in the left frame and also the strict separation of walking through the topic map via associations and calling up occurrences.

3.3 Graphical Navigation

The graphical navigation is the gem of the LmTM-server, but it makes some requirements on the software of the users computer: Its WWW-browser must support SVG (SVG: Scalable Vector Graphics, a W3C-standard). Browsers like Konqueror under Linux or some Mozilla-builds (Linux, Windows) are able to handle SVG on their own, in other cases there is a plug-in from Adobe that can help (http://www.adobe.com/svg/viewer/install/). Hopefully all browsers will have native SVG-support in the near future.

The actual relevant part of the topic map is visualised as a map, an example is shown in a screenshot (Fig. 2). This map lets the user navigate in the given information. The actual topic and thus the actual position in the topic map is shown in the center of the map, here it is the "Huygenssches Prinzip". All occurrences of this topic are listed in blue letters below the topic name. A click on such an occurrence opens it in a new window.

The actual topic shown in the centre is associated with other topics via associations. These associated topics are shown around the actual topic. A click on such a topic shows a new map, dynamically created out of the topic map, with the topic just clicked on as the new actual topic in the centre. Associations in topic maps have no direction, but the topics of an association are playing roles in the association. Obviously this gives some reading direction of the association implicitly, which the user has to interpret by himself.

The use of the graphical navigation is rather intuitive: walking through the topic map via the associations just needs a click on them, calling up occurrences in a new window also just needs a click on them. The occurrences are shown in a new window in order not to lose the map, the visualization of the actual position in the topic map. So when you close an occurrence window you find yourself back in the map.

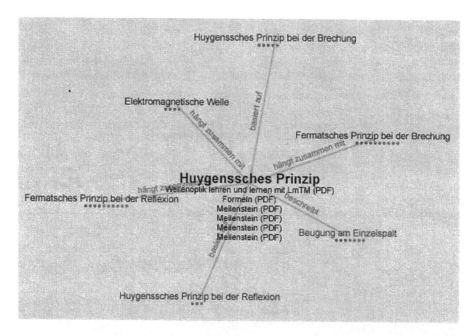

Fig. 2. Graphical navigation with only the next neighbours shown. The actual topic is in the centre, below the actual topic its occurrences are listed. All topics associated with the actual topic are placed around the actual topic

In the screenshot above you can see the occurrence "Meilenstein" four times because there are four occurrences of this type. On the one hand it is not too nice to have the same identifier four times for four different occurrences of the same type, on the other hand the topic map would have to be blown up enormously when a different identifier is used for each distinct occurrence of the same type. It seems to be a reasonable compromise to use the same identifier for different occurrences of the same type.

The actual SVG standard does not have any automatic line break in long text lines. In the next version this will be possible - very nice for long topic identifiers, see screenshot above.

Very helpful while navigating is the possibility to estimate the relevance of an associated topic before clicking on it and so making it the new actual topic. This is achieved with the red and blue dots. Each blue dot stands for a topic which is associated with the topic concerned. A lot of blue dots under a topic thus means: This topic is involved in a lot of associations with other topics - so this topic seems to be an important topic. Each red dot stands for one occurrence which the topic concerned has. A lot of red dots under a topic thus means: This topic has a lot of occurrences, a lot of learning material to read.

There are two variants of graphical navigation on the LmTM-Server. Above we discussed the first variant where only the next neighbors of a topic were shown in the visualization of the relevant part of the topic map. The second variant also shows the

next but one neighbors, see screenshot (Fig. 3). For this variant of graphical navigation the display size and display resolution are the limiting factors. Some information
is hidden, for example the identifiers of the associations, the red and blue dots, the
associations between topics in the second level. Nevertheless the visualization is
rather confusing to read.

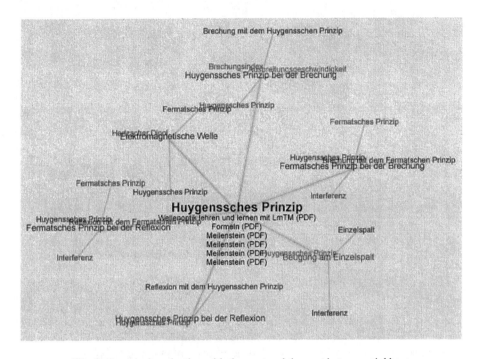

Fig. 3. Graphical navigation with the next and the next but one neighbors

3.4 Alphabetic List

Additionally all topics of a topic map can be shown in alphabetic order, this list is dynamically created out of the topic map. This list has the character of an encyclopedia
and is very useful for fast look-ups, when some basic knowledge is already present.

The topics are listed in italics (see Fig. 4) behind blue icons, below each topic in a
smaller font the corresponding occurrences are shown behind a red icon, if present. A
click on a topic shows the corresponding part of the topic map in the right frame, not
shown in this screenshot. This way the visitor can easily explore the neighborhood of
each topic and see the associated topics. A click on an occurrence shows this occurrence in the right frame, also not shown in this screenshot - so this is like an encyclopedia: you click on a key word and get the explanation.

The use of this navigation variant is very easy and straight forward, but the user
needs some basic knowledge of the actual field of interest the actual topic map covers.

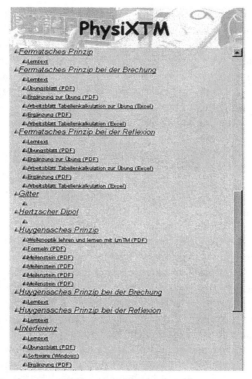

Fig. 4. Alphabetic list

3.5   Links in the Page Footer

Each web page with learning materials of the LmTM-Server has in its page footer additional information, dynamically extracted out of the topic map and included via SSI (Server Side Includes, a web server technique): all occurrences of the actual topic and all associated topics are listed in the page footer (see Fig. 5).

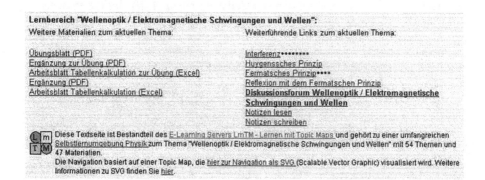

Fig. 5. Links in the page footer: occurrences are listed in the left column, associated topics in the right column

This screenshot shows in the left column five additional occurrences ("Übungs-blatt", "Ergänzung zur Übung", "Arbeitsblatt Tabellenkalkulation zur Übung", "Er-gänzung", "Arbeitsblatt Tabellenkalkulation"), in the right column three associated topics ("Interferenz", "Huygenssches Prinzip", "Fermatsches Prinzip", "Reflexion mit dem Fermatschen Prinzip") and below these some links to interactive components outside the topic map. With this information and links in the page footer it is possible to navigate through the topic map and to explore the field of interest without making use of the textual or the graphical navigation.

4   Experiences from Practical Usage

The LmTM-Server is used by the author in everyday lessons at school and the log files are showing intense use from other schools. The navigation on the LmTM-server is rather different in comparison with other web servers: The web pages with the learning texts doesn't have any intrinsic navigation, the navigation is realized com-pletely via a superimposed topic map. This is a new paradigm in using and navigating web pages. At the first moment visitors aren't used to navigate this way, eventually they tend not to accept this new navigation paradigm and leave the server. So it is a good idea to give new users a short introduction in the navigation of the LmTM-server. This is no problem for the usage at school, but difficult for users coming over some links, for example from search engines.

At school the teacher using the LmTM-server in his lessons should give the stu-dents some short introduction in using the navigation of the LmTM-server, either the textual navigation or the graphical navigation or both. The experience shows that the students learn and accept the principles in a few minutes and then navigate on the LmTM-server without problems.

But what about the other users? Most internet users don't want to read any manual. The careful analysis of click-streams in the servers logfiles pointed out things to im-prove and to simplify the navigation, but more fine tuning concerning the navigation seems to be necessary and possible. The visitors of the LmTM-server can discuss these topics online (http://www.lmtm.de/w-agora/index.php? bn=lmtm_lmtmforum).

In most cases the navigation the students in a classroom are using is via the topics, the identifiers of the associations are regularly not noted. Typically the students are using the first visualization variant with only the next neighbors shown. Often used - especially by visitors coming to the LmTM-server via search engines and directly en-tering an occurrence - are also the links in the page footer. After working some time in a field of knowledge the alphabetic list is used more often in a way like an ency-clopedia.

Not all students are on the same level in planning and organizing their learning by themselves and to be responsible for their learning progress by themselves. It is very important to consider these different skill levels in order to lead the use of the LmTM-server to success. If not sure it is a good idea (for the teacher) to assume lower skills in this techniques. The "Meilensteine" (milestones) are developed and integrated in the LmTM-server to help teachers and students using the server. They help in using the LmTM-server successfully by offering a step-by-step guide.

Asking the students after having finished a course with self-regulated e-learning using the LmTM-server the students were always very satisfied with this way of learning, they also would prefer learning this way in the future. This demonstrates that the ideas that lead to the development of the LmTM-server are valid and stable: Give the students as much freedom as possible but also offer them a guide through lots of information, so that they are able to transform them to knowledge by themselves.

In general the size of the display and its resolution can't be big enough to show as much information as possible without scrolling. A perfect solution would be a two-screen usage: The visualized topic maps on one display and the learning materials - the occurrences of the topics - on the other display.

5 Ideas for Further Development

In order to estimate the relevance of a topic before clicking on it red and blue dots are shown below the topics. It is planned to show some short text as a compressed abstract of the main occurrence of the topic while the mouse is over the topic in the SVG-visualization.

The reading direction of the associations could be symbolized via a small arrow on the association line.

It would be desirable that every interested teacher has the possibility to use the LmTM-server and its navigation technique for his own learning materials and field of knowledge. This isn't too easy though. The main task is to create the topic map. The average user has to learn first some basics of the topic map paradigm before being able to create his first topic map. Additionally there aren't really good tools for creating topic maps. The computer scientist will use a validating XML-editor and the XTM-DTD, but this is surely not the right tool for the average user.

The semantic web project of the W3C also copes with the task to represent information and knowledge and the associations in between in an abstract notation. So it is possible to create an OWL-ontology - also in XML-notation as the XML topic maps. But dealing with ontologies isn't easier then dealing with topic maps. A prototype of an e-learning platform based on ontologies instead of topic maps is available under http://www.OntoLearn.de/.

References

http://www.topicmaps.org/xtm/index.html
http://www.adobe.com/svg/viewer/install/
http://www.lmtm.de/w-agora/index.php? bn=lmtm_lmtmforum

Information and Knowledge Visualization in Development and Use of a Management Information System (MIS) for DaimlerChrysler

A Visualized Dialogue and Participation Process

Hans-Jürgen Frank[1] and Johannes Drosdol[2]

[1] Lindenschmitstr. 30, 81371 München, Germany
frank@dialogarchitect.com
[2] DaimlerChrysler AG, Corporate Service Center RMI/X,
70546 Stuttgart, Germany
johannes.j.drosdol@daimlerchrysler.com

Abstract. The contribution outlines the process and the results of the development of a computer system for DaimlerChrysler. The task was to create a Management Information System (MIS) for the leaders of the department of research and technology responsible for technical innovations and the management of technology. The MIS was conceived as a tool for strategic decision making, for sharing experiences, as a knowledge and information repository, and as a dialogue platform for opening up possibilities for continuous collaboration and dialogue about task-relevant information, operating data, and knowledge for directing research and development projects. The contribution focuses on how the dialogue and participation process of different partners as well as the results of the development process are visualized and integrated into the system.

1 Introduction

Managers and decision-makers are confronted with a mass of information and data. Information visualization (IVis) is the first step towards selecting information and making it available. Knowledge visualization (KVis) helps to create meaning from this information to facilitate decision-making and to generate new knowledge as a basis for improvement, innovation and change. Both perspectives (IVis and KVis) are key to and necessary for the success of the Management Information System (MIS) developed in this project. This was possible only by creating a synergy between IVis and KVis. The presentation outlines how knowledge and information in the dialogue and participation process of different partners as well as the results of the development process are visualized and integrated into the system.

The purpose of this article is to describe how visualization can take the role of a facilitator for the creation of new knowledge and new processes and show the synergy potential between IVis and KVis in a concrete project example from business. The

S.-O. Tergan and T. Keller (Eds.): Knowledge and Information Visualization, LNCS 3426, pp. 364–384, 2005.
© Springer-Verlag Berlin Heidelberg 2005

experience of this project demonstrates that it is not sufficient to see IVis and KVis as only the design of pleasant forms, nice structures or beautiful colors. It takes a stand against the opinion of some people who see IVis or KVis as a superficial design activity with the aim of making dull information a little less ugly only by dressing it up in a nice outfit.

The authors' intention is to document how IVis and KVis are used for the solution of specific problems in the work environment of a big company and how IVis and KVis can play a crucial role in changing the work flow and in designing new processes for sharing and decision-making. This article deals with a development and utilization process applying visualized storytelling and sharing between information experts, users, developers and decision-makers, which creates a living bridge between IVis and KVis. It shows how visualization is applied as a tool to accelerate dialogue and knowledge sharing.

2 Vis and KVis: Understanding of Terms

The terms IVis and KVis in this article are based on the following understanding:

Information visualization (IVis) means collecting data, documentation of abstract database data, for example business data etc., automatic visualization of big data masses and large quantities of information, helping to distribute data.

Information visualization used by information experts often does not provide user-friendly navigation or interfaces showing the underlying information structure. Data representation in simple lists or data sequences is often considered sufficient. Sometimes only part of the list is shown in detail on the screen.

Knowledge visualization (KVis) means the result of transformation from information to knowledge, representation of connections and links, designing the space between information elements, development of meaning, creating meaningful structures fitting the contents, helping to generate new knowledge which can be used by people, staff, leaders, decision-makers.

For certain tasks like for some cognitive or creative processes and for decision-making IVis is not sufficient, but KVis is necessary. Users who are not as familiar with the represented content as information providers or experts need a meaningful transformation from IVis to KVis. Sequential content structure has to be transformed into a meaningful (KVis) network of knowledge elements.

3 Client and Project Aims

DaimlerChrysler is one of the leading companies in the automotive industry with 362,100 employees worldwide (at the end of 2003). DaimlerChrysler's product and service portfolio ranges from passenger cars and commercial vehicles to financial and other automotive services. The task was to create a Management Information System (MIS) for the leaders of the department of research and technology. This is Daimler-Chrysler's central function for technical innovations and the management of technology. At several locations in different countries around the world approximately 28,000 employees work in the field of innovation. The MIS was conceived as a tool for strategic decision-making, for sharing experiences, as a knowledge and information repository, and as a dialogue platform for a continuous dialogue about task-relevant information, operating data, and knowledge for directing research and development projects. This is the basis for new products and processes as well as for strategies in technology. For managing the department as well as for directing research and development projects it is important that relevant, up-to-date and consistent information is quickly available to leaders. This information should be easy to find and to present. Content has to be identical for all the users.

The aim was to create a Management Information System with high up-to-dateness and flexibility, suiting the users' needs, processes and visions as far as possible. The basic idea was to develop not only a tool with a control function, but also a general homogenous information and dialogue platform with intuitive qualities and to create a knowledge and information space.

4   IVis and KVis in an Intercultural Dialogue Process

Our clients and our users are not bothered about the discussion of information specialists concerning the difference between IVis and KVis. However, they are obviously concerned about the non-usability of some data visualization sources and the illegibility of certain IVis outcomes (making experts necessary for understanding) as well as the advantage of user-fitting KVis structures. This shows the necessity of bringing together experts for IVis and of KVis. The distance between IVis and KVis is filled in this project by a dialogue process linking both. This is realized by the participation of human actors representing IVis and KVis (experts from IVis as well as from the field of KVis). This procedure of personification by real individuals introduces human factors and makes it possible to come to a living synergy between IVis and KVis in business reality.

4.1   Visualizing the Dialogue Process

The visualization of the dialogue process is realized at different levels:

- between IVis and KVis and their personal representatives;
- between information suppliers, knowledge transformers, process experts, managers and users;
- between the human utilization processes and the technical computer structures (with its KVis surface linking both).

At each of these levels we are challenged by an exchange between different cultures. The condition for the successful realization of this intercultural exchange process in this project is the application of specific visualization tools which are able to represent in real time all the content brought in by different dialogue partners. "Knowledge architecture" and tools, methods and experiences of the Dialogarchitect® made it possible to realize this intercultural dialogue in an operational and effective way within the actual business environment of the client company.

4.2 The Role of the Dialogarchitect®

In order to visualize the dialogue and participation process as well as to represent the network of knowledge and information relevant for users a powerful visualization tool has to be used. The Dialogarchitect® (registered trademark of Hans-Jürgen Frank) develops and uses images and space structures for improving effectiveness and for facilitating dialogue and the creation of good intentions between different cultures by designing and simulating win-win situations. Dialogue between different cultures does not only mean between different nationalities, but also between different professional languages and professions, between different hierarchical levels and groups of different interests as well as between technical and personal processes which often seem to represent conflicting cultures. One of the particular services of the Dialogarchitect® is to build up a visual "Project Space" or a "Knowledge Space" which can be used for dialogue and for creating a "Project Memory" or a "Common Brain" for a team or a company.

The toolbox of the Dialogarchitect® contains different manual and computer-generated instruments for visualizing and facilitating dialogue, for working with a large number of content elements, highly complex information structures and large knowledge networks. The Dialogarchitect® facilitated this development process and visualized the different content and experiences brought in by users, content providers, internal or external experts, decision-makers, the board and by developers. Thus, images were created in real time during workshops in a process which is similar to the drawing of storyboards in filmmaking. The resulting visual modules were organized in a knowledge space (see Fig. 2, 3 and 5-8) showing the overview and the relationships of all collected inputs during the dialogue (see below: KVis level 1). The Dialogarchitect® created a stage for dialogue between all the participants of the project and set up a dynamically growing "Project Memory" (see Fig. 2, 3 and 5-8).

After that development work the Dialogarchitect® accompanied the software programming to make sure that the user requirements and the intentions of the decision-makers were truly respected in the software and database programming. This was realized on the basis of the visual briefing documents (see below: KVis level 1). Then it was the task of the Dialogarchitect® to design the interface of the system accordingly to the underlying information network and to the navigation structure facilitating the utilization process (Fig. 9– 11) (see below: KVis level 2). The transparency at all content levels and the result of harmonizing the internal system structure and the structure of screen and navigation (see below: KVis level 2) have turned out to be an important factor for the success of the MIS.

5   The Development and Utilization Process

5.1 Work Steps Between IVis and KVis

Repeated feedback between IVis and KVis in the development as well as in the utilization process with ongoing dialogue and improvement also after the implementation of the MIS created a process beyond traditional requirements engineering. Visualization tools used for the exchange between IVis and KVis (Fig. 4) facilitated the dialogue and made all steps visible and transparent "building bridges" between these two visualization cultures.

To create this synergy between IVis and KVis the development was realized in continuous dialogue with the users. This process can be represented in a spiral climbing step by step to a higher level of added value. Fig. 1 shows the actions spiral consisting of a number of steps which are situated between the outcoming results of knowledge visualization (focusing on the user process and requirements) and the incoming results from information visualization (expert visualization / automatic data visualization from different sources).

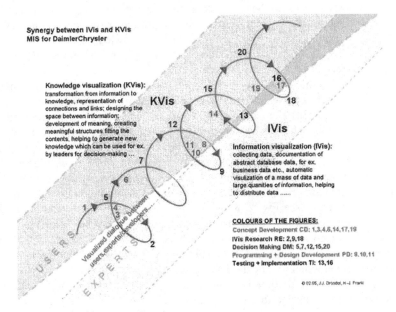

Fig. 1. Visualization of the development process aiming at the realization of a Management Information System (MIS)

We do not want to show an elaborated, methodical or scientific approach (in Fig. 1). But it was extremely interesting for us to review the process and to visualize it in order to make it visible for others. Trying to find appropriate ways for visualizing the process made it a more conscious structure for ourselves. First of all, it was our feeling that the dialogue process between IVis and KVis could be demonstrated best in a spiral connecting both. We had the impression that these two different cultures were approaching each other more and more during the process and that around the steps 8 and 10 a kind of overlap was happening between IVis and KVis.

The crossings of the spiral seemed to be the right places to situate the decision-making steps (5, 7, 12, 15 and 20). Then the steps of IVis research (2, 9, 18) seem quite far from each other. We recognized that the dialogue with IVis representatives was frequent, but less intensive than dialogue on KVis side. Even if we did not attribute a specific number for IVis work steps the spiral was connected frequently with the IVis field.

Distributing the work steps quite spontaneously around the spiral several other observations were interesting for us: It seemed obvious to situate testing and implementation (steps 13 and 16) in the overlap between IVis and KVis. The concentration of work steps for concept development (steps 1, 3, 4, 6) close to decision- making (step 5) showing very intensive conceptual work was leading to a concentration of the steps for software programming and design development (steps 8, 10, 11). This clear separation between conceptual work and realization as well as the frequent steps of early decision-making were important reasons for reducing cost by avoiding changes in the final software tool.

5.2 Outcomes of the IVis Work Steps

At different stages results from information visualization (IVis) came into the project work (Fig. 1). Data availability and quality of automatic data visualization from different sources were reviewed and visually summarized in the project space (see Fig. 6, pinboards in the background: showing the required content structure in the form of knowledge visualization). Results from IVis were visualized on post-its and joined to the corresponding images of the KVis structure. This led to the realization of the knowledge network for the future MIS.

IVis first offered an overview of available data and examples of automatic data visualization from different sources. This was completed more and more during the development process in line with user requirements. In the following utilization process IVis research had an important role in the realization of new user requirements and in the integration of new user groups.

5.3 Outcomes of the KVis Work Steps

The development of the requirements was visualized for the different phases of the project and discussed in dialogue between users, developers and decision-makers (Fig. 1). Two levels of KVis were created: KVis level 1 and KVis level 2. KVis Level 2 has been built on the results of KVis level 1.

KVis level 1 represents the requirements which are important for the development of the MIS. Images and visual pattern show information on a higher reality level than words and texts. They introduce this higher degree of reality even to abstract knowledge. This creates some kind of incentive and pressure for participants and decision-makers to give input and to make early decisions in a project phase which (without visualization) very often seems not concrete enough for achieving decisions and high effectiveness of collaboration.

KVis level 2 is the representation of the MIS content network on the screen and of the different possibilities for utilization processes in the navigation structure of the interface. The crucial point is that the content structure and the utilization process are perfectly harmonized with the representation of knowledge and the navigation dynamics on the interface. Thus, KVis level 2 focuses on interaction design between MIS and users.

Knowledge visualization of dialogue (KVis level 1): The "Project Memory". The KVis level 1 of the dialogue process focuses on the development of the "Project Memory". From the start of the project a dynamically growing "Project Memory" has been built up in a "Project Space". Here we collected step by step all relevant KVis representations (Fig. 2-7) which described at an abstract level user requirements as well as inputs from experts, decision-makers and the board in the form of images and patterns drawn in workshops and during the development process. Thus, drawings were used as KVis tools (KVis level 1) in this space representing a kind of common brain and a platform for dialogue.

After some months of development all the participants in the dialogue process were invited for a walk through this "Project Space" reviewing the different stages of work. This took place at a meeting we called "Peer Review". "Peer Review" was the outcome of knowledge visualization and the basis for feedback and decision-making before realization, testing and implementation.

Until the "Peer Review" meeting took place (step 12, Fig. 1) the "Project Memory" reached a level of completeness which represented the whole MIS in a kind of simulation including sketches of the interface (KVis level 2) fitting the collected requirements (see Fig. 7).

It was a simulation at an abstract level of the Management Information System showing the content structure, the user's vision for an improved work flow (KVis level 1) and the resulting navigation visualization on the MIS screen (KVis level 2) as well as the different steps leading to these results (KVis level 1). Through this visualization in the space we achieved a much higher level of reality than we could have got by a briefing text or a verbal formulation. This higher reality level created pressure for early decision-making and increased the speed of the project.

The walk through the visual space took place between the development work and the starting utilization process - just before the user test and implementation. It offered the possibility to compare the simulation (visual documents on the pinboards from KVis level 1) with the first pilot of the MIS (on the computer system from KVis level 2). Now the users had the possibility to test the system. We visualized their ideas for improvement and joined it to the existing drawings and patterns (KVis level 1) showing the user requirements on the pinboards in the project space. At the end of the "Peer Review" all inputs and decisions had been reviewed, completed and concluded. This completed the MIS simulation and made all necessary information and decisions visible and available for the completion of the realization of the MIS.

The following six phases were reviewed and discussed in the "Peer Review". Every phase contained one or several work steps (see Fig. 1).

Overview of the six phases in the "Peer Review"

Phase 1: Visualization of the aims and the necessity of the project
See Fig. 1: Step 1 KVis: Visualization of the necessity and the aims
and Fig. 2: first perspective in the "Project Space"

Phase 2: Visualized dialogue about user needs and information context

See Step 2 and 3 in Fig. 1:

Step 2 IVis: First ideas about data sources (Fig. 2) and

Step 3 KVis: Workshops: Visualized dialogue between users, developers, decision-makers and experts (Fig. 3)

Phase 3: Striking clusters showing the whole spectrum of the different user needs highlighted by visualized decisions

See Step 4and 5 in Fig. 1:

Step 4 KVis: Striking clusters and

Step 5 Decisions about MIS qualities and work flow

Phase 4: Visualization creating an overview of the whole information structure including the patterns of decisions and the outcoming instructions for programming

See Step 6-10 in Fig. 1:

Step 6 KVis: Visually condensed pattern showing the desired network of knowledge

Step 7 Decisions about

Step 8 KVis: The visualization of the decisions in Step 5 and 7 as a basis for the database and software programming

Step 9 IVis research: Finding the desired information

Visualized instructions for Step 10: Programming of the database

Phase 5: The computer screen matching the information structure and the utilization process

See Step 11 in Fig. 1:

Step 11 KVis: Development of the computer interface

Phase 6: Visual dialogue generating added value by all inputs during the "Peer Review" for completion and improvement

See Step 12 in Fig. 1:

Step 12 KVis: "Peer Review" - event reviewing the development work

The following text offers a more detailed description of each of these phases:

Phase 1: Visualization of the aims and the necessity of the project . The first step in every bigger project is to ask the managers of the firm about the current aims of the company. On this basis the aims of the project are developed. Some flipcharts summarize the patterns of the statements and the reasons why the project is necessary. This visualization helps to introduce the participants to the project within a few minutes. This is a very effective way of starting the dialogue between users, developers, decision-makers and experts at a common information level. At the same time, this promotes a way of developing a common perspective.

Fig. 2, 3 and 5, 6, 7 are photographs from different perspectives of the work space which was used as a visual "Project Memory" with images, drawings and screenshots on pinboards. This "Common Memory" visualized the dialogue between the different stakeholders, users, developers, decision-makers and experts. It was a dynamically growing visual platform for dialogue during the development process.

Fig. 2. First perspective of the visual "Project Memory" in the "Project Space" showing the aims of the project (based on the aims of the company) and the story which led to this development work

Phase 2: Visualization of the dialogue about user needs and information context. After having introduced the project aims and necessities we asked clients and users about needs and requirements, hopes, expectations and fears concerning the work with the future software tool as well as about their visions for an improved work flow.

The discussion has two main focuses:

- the content elements with their relationships and
- the work flow during the utilization process

We asked the following key questions concerning work flow and content:

Questions about work flow:

- How do you make decisions?
- Describe the steps of your work and of your decision-making process?
- When do you like to work alone? When do you need input? When is it helpful for you to be in dialogue with others?
- In what way would you like to work with the new Management Information System?
- What are the positive aspects in your current work? What should be improved?
- Do you see a vision for future work flow and for an ideal future work situation?

Questions about content:

- Which information do you need for decision-making? What kind of information do you need? How do you recognize that information has the quality you need for your decision-making process?
- How are the different information elements connected to each other?
- What are the main subjects and key issues? Can you imagine the knowledge as a network of connected elements? What does this network look like?

Fig. 3. Second perspective of the "Project Memory": pinboards showing user needs, inputs from decision-makers and experts

The images (Fig. 4) were drawn during development workshops representing user needs, requirements, expert ideas and input from decision-makers and formed the KVis structure on the pinboards. They were condensed in different ways leading to visual patterns which were the basis for decision-making and for the programming of the software and the database. This road map for realizing the MIS had two perspectives: the users' description and vision concerning the utilization process and pattern showing the content structure of the future MIS as a network of knowledge modules with their relationships. Results of the IVis research were joined on post-its on the KVis representation of the content structure.

Every request and answer is visualized by real-time drawings in one independent information module. Each module contains an image and the key words explaining the statement. These visual modules are distributed at once in the space (on pinboards) and form the visual "Project Memory". It offers a surface which shows the overview of all statements of the users. It was completed with the input of decision-makers, developers and experts.

This procedure is the basis for patterns describing the new software tool perfectly fitting user needs and business processes. It offers the chance for all participants to bring in their experience in a very effective visible way at the right moment and in the right place. The participants "star in their show" with their images. Experts are asked with regard to missing aspects. They complete this overall image by bringing in current and future trends as well as visions for collaboration and decision-making.

During the "Peer Review" a walk through the images of the user interviews showed the presence of all the ideas collected during the dialogue until that moment. The users understood that all their concerns had been taken into account seriously. It was interesting for us to hear the reaction of certain users. One of them said proudly: "Oh, it's really incredible what interesting ideas we already had a year ago."

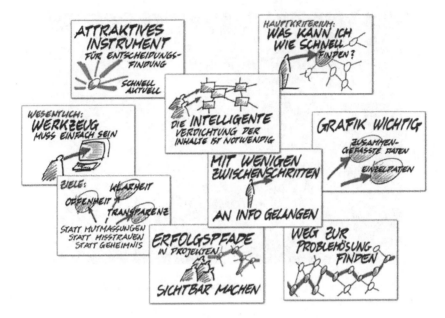

Fig. 4. Some examples of KVis modules (from the pinboards) drawn in dialogue workshops with users, decision-makers, experts, information providers (KVis level 1)

Fig. 5. Important perspective during the walk through the "Project Memory" with intense dialogue about the striking clusters summarizing the whole spectrum of user requirements

Phase 3: Visualization of the different user needs. The outcome of this dialogue process was a large number of visualized requirements and aspects concerning the content and the utilization process of the future Management Information System (Fig. 5). Many of the collected needs were very divergent and different or even contradictory, conflicting and opposite. We formed clusters out of these information modules focusing on the most important user perspectives. These patterns made the whole spectrum of user needs visible and showed why certain wishes could not be realized.

This was convincing for the users. They saw the divergence of their wishes in the wide range of the visualized clusters and they understood that it was not possible to realize all their demands. It was visible that some of their requests were too far away from the center of the clusters. The honesty and the openness about the requirements we did not realize created an atmosphere of complete confidence. We overcame even skeptical voices and the project became more and more "the baby" of most of the users.

Fig. 6. The content space showing all information elements, their relationships and the themes of the different main content fields (knowledge clusters)

Phase 4: Visualization creating an overview of the whole information structure (Fig. 6). Phase 4 aims at creating an overview of the whole information structure including the patterns of decisions and the outcoming instructions for programming of software and database. Continuing the walk of the "Peer Review" we find in another corner of the visual space the patterns for the information structure which was condensed out of the visualized user statements: apart from the information elements their relationships and their connections are presented as well as the higher level structure of the themes. This visual pattern had been specified in a workshop with the information suppliers and data experts. The outcome of IVis research was visualized on post-its and incorporated into these KVis patterns.

Phase 5: Visualization of the computer screen. The aim of the visualization of the computer screen and of the design for interaction was to make the overall content structure of the database visible for the users on every system screen. We wanted to create a visual surface realizing two criteria:

- showing the whole information structure at any time
- representing a navigation surface harmonized with the concept of an improved work flow and decision-making process.

Fig. 7. Screenshots on pinboards explaining the main principles of the navigation screen and the interaction design of the interface (KVis level 2)

The idea was to learn from principles of "self-similarity" (in German "Selbstähnlichkeit") in nature (see the similarity of a leaf with a shape corresponding to the form of the whole tree, or fractals showing the same structure on the microscopic level as well as on a macroscopic scale). Thus, the result of this development process was a navigation structure corresponding exactly to the pattern of the improved utilization and decision-making process and of the content structure. The visualized computer screen matches the information structure and the utilization process. This structure was integrated into a knowledge landscape exactly fitting the knowledge network corresponding to the database structure (Fig. 7).

Phase 6: Visual dialoguing. All the steps described above have been reviewed during the walk in the visual "Project Memory". This happened during the "Peer Review" in dialogue with users, decision-makers and the member of the board concerned. During this dialogue session the users also had the possibility to test the new MIS tool with its different functions developed up until then.

The "Peer Review" was not a project presentation we are normally used to for introducing a new computer tool. It was designed and realized as a visualized dialogue corresponding to the atmosphere of dialogue characterizing the whole process as well as to the dialogue quality of the resulting product and process design. In this spirit we visualized during the "Peer Review" all the inputs, critical remarks and positive reactions of our dialogue partners as well as their ideas for improvement and further development. The resulting visual wall of ideas was summarized and discussed with our interlocutors at the end of the meeting. Together with them we decided on the focuses and key pattern of the next steps for further development.

Fig. 8. Summary of inputs and ideas for improvement collected from participants in the walk during the "Peer Review" and decision for next steps of improvement, for critical points to examine during the user tests and for finishing work before implementation

For the member of the board and for the decision-makers this was proof that they had the possibility to direct the project perfectly corresponding to their aims. To do this they needed a very small amount of time: one hour at the start of the project and about one hour after one year in the "Peer Review". Visualizing and dialoguing was the key for the economy and the success of this dialogue process. It was important to visualize the key questions and the critical points together with a competent person from the firm before we did workshops with groups. In this way it was possible to create the right atmosphere and to come to the key questions and to the crucial points without losing time. This made it possible to keep the time schedule for every meeting.

In the "Project Memory" space the first prototype of the new MIS with its KVis interaction screen design was tested after the first development phase in the context of the visual collection of requirements and discussed with users and decision-makers Fig. 8 is a visualization of the results of the discussion.

Visualization of design for interaction (KVis level 2). The screen was designed focusing on two main aims - corresponding

– to the content structure and
– to the utilization process.

One of the challenges for managers is to find at once the right information even in a discussion in a meeting. In dialogue with colleagues it is important that every participant has access to the same database to explain his/her concerns. For facilitating common dialogue and decision-making, sharing of the same current knowledge is necessary.

Fig. 9, 10 and 11 are computer screenshots showing the first version of the final visual KVis interface of the MIS which was resulting from this development process.

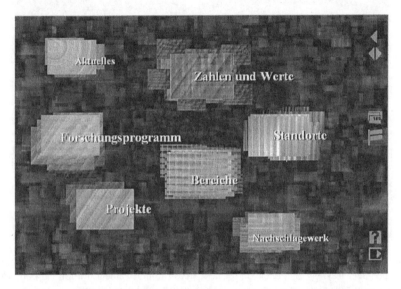

Fig. 9. Screenshot showing the overview of all the main themes contained in the MIS

Fig. 9 shows the overview of all the main themes contained in the MIS: "Current, Numbers and Values, Research Program, Locations, Reports, Decisions, Reference Book". This navigation landscape is the first screen shown to the user after having logged in. It opens access to the information. Here the user chooses (by clicking) the content field (s)he wants to visit. The different subjects are characterized by different colors and by different structures. These distinguishing marks help to remember where certain information can be found and realize an important user requirement to make it easy to find information and to come back to knowledge elements. In tests users easily remembered this content structure even without seeing the titles of the different subjects. We created in some way a spatial structure (even if it is not real 3-D) following the experience that elements located in certain positions in space remain present easier in users' heads. These effects have been confirmed during last year's utilization process.

Our purpose for including these screenshots is not to present a novel form of interface design but to document how the result of the dialogue process and the testing by users led to a structure which exactly fits in with the utilization process and which perfectly represents the underlying information structure. This transparency of the knowledge structure and of the utilization process were consequently resulting from dialogue during the development process and are visible in any screen of the MIS. The continuous overview of all the content fields seems important for decision-making because users in these processes do not always know what they are looking for. Very often the visual presence of content leads to the idea to look into information fields which decision-makers had not thought of before. It is like a walk through the countryside when we discover different things on the way which we had not planned to see.

Fig. 10. Navigation landscape showing the content of "Numbers and Values" with the overview of the whole content of the MIS on top on the right

After a click on "Numbers and Values" the user enters the next lower level of the content structure. Again (s)he finds a navigation landscape with the clusters of subjects belonging to this content level. The whole background of the screen is characterized here by color and structure in accordance with the representation of this information field in the screen before (Fig. 10). It is important that the backgrounds of all content fields are well distinguished from each other so that users can recognize on any screen which content field they are looking at.

As it was important for the users not to lose the overview of the whole knowledge structure of the MIS as soon as they access a lower information level the main content fields of the initial navigation landscape stay present in a reduced form in the right upper corner of the screen. In this way, the reduction of the initial navigation landscape is present at every level and in every system screen. From here the users can access every main theme and every "place" of the system with ONE click. Here again we do not just want to achieve a nice design of form or colors, but the systematic fitting of every screen to the users' content and process requirements.

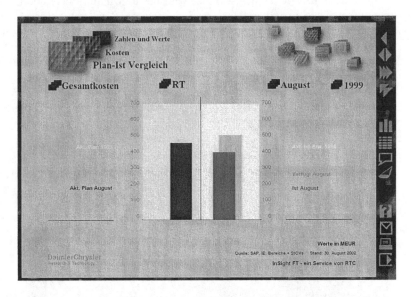

Fig. 11. Screenshot of a deeper content level showing the navigation landscape (on top on the right) and the level of information depth (on top on the left)

After a click on "Kosten" and "Plan-Ist Vergleich" we enter one of the subcontents belonging to "Numbers and Values". Again we find the same navigation principles we saw on the other content levels (Fig. 11:):

- the specific color and structure of the background belonging to the corresponding content field,
- the reduced navigation landscape in the top right corner.

Moreover, the user can see what detail level of the knowledge structure the current screen belongs to. This is visible in the top left corner of the screen by the representation of the number of levels which are shown one behind the other. Even if the main space of the screen (below the navigation fields) is representing a very detailed content level, this part of the knowledge structure (like any other extract) is situated in a larger context within the whole MIS structure.

This navigation system is not presented here as a model of navigation design or an example for other projects. Our message for developers of computer systems and interaction design is to profit from realizing an intensive and open dialogue with the users about structure and quality of content as well as about their experience and their visions concerning improved work processes. Visualization tools can be used to steer this dialogue and realize a development process full of effectiveness in collaboration, to recognize responsibility in a wider context and create pleasure in personal work and collaboration.

6 Overview of the Steps of the Whole Development and Utilization Process

Dialogue and synergy between IVis and KVis were realized in successive work steps (see Fig. 1). In the work steps we distinguish different kinds of content visualized by manual drawings (IVis and KVis level 1) or visualized on computer screen (KVis level 2): Research (RE), Concept Development (CD), Decision-making (DM), Software Programming and Design Development (PD), Users' Testing and Implementation (TI).

1) KVis (level 1) (CD): Visualization of the project context, of the necessity and the aims of the project (Fig. 2: aims on top, in the center of the photograph, context and necessity of the project on the pinboards in the middle of the photograph).

2) Ivis (RE): Collecting first ideas about data sources and availability of information (Fig. 2: on the pinboards at the right side of the photograph).

3) KVis (level 1) (CD): Workshops: manually visualized dialogue between users, developers, decision-makers and experts, (see Fig. 3: information modules on pinboards representing requirements and input from the different participants, overview of the whole collection of content elements and their connections, of focal points concerning the different topics and subjects).

4) KVis (level 1) (CD): Striking clusters condensing the whole spectrum of the different user requirements, visions and wishes for the future work flow (Fig. 5 see the four pinboards on the right).

5) Decisions (DM) about MIS qualities and work flow on the basis of the KVis striking clusters (see Step 4, Fig. 5) summarized in visual knowledge modules (Fig. 8 on the right of the door).

6) KVis (level 1) (CD): Visually condensed pattern showing the desired network of knowledge in the future MIS in a spatial structure built with pinboards (Fig. 6 in the background), visualization creating an overview of the whole information structure.

7) Decisions (DM) about content on the basis of the KVis pattern showing the desired network of knowledge (see Step 6, Fig. 6 in the background). The decisions were visualized on post-its fixed to the corresponding images.

8) KVis (level 1) (PD): The visualization of the decisions in step 5 and 7 (see also Fig. 8) is the basis for the database and software programming and guarantees the realization of the patterns describing content (see Fig. 6 in the background) and work flow (Fig. 5).

9) IVis research (RE): Finding the desired information within the mass of automatically visualized data from different available sources: where, in which form and format, in which quality, generated with which focus, perspective and interest (visualized on post-its on the corresponding images on the pinboards (Fig. 6)).

10) Programming of the database (PD): making available information from IVis research following the instructions developed by KVis (level 1: visualization during the development process) and being the content basis of KVis (level 2: visualization used as interface on the computer screen of the MIS).

11) KVis (level 2) (PD): Development of the computer interface (see Fig. 9-11) matching the information structure and the utilization process i.e. corresponding to the decided knowledge network and work flow (see also screenshots showing the principles of the interface design Fig. 12 on pinboards in the "Project Space").

12) KVis (level 1 + 2) (DM): "Peer Review" - meeting reviewing the development work: Walk together with users, decision-makers, board member and developers through the whole network of KVis visualizations (KVis level 1) which were created during the different steps of the MIS development process by then.

This walk was not realized in the form of a presentation, but as a dialogue process collecting and visualizing feedback from participants and ideas for improvement. Fig. 2–8 show the different perspectives of the visual "Project Space" which created a kind of "Project Memory" and a simulation of the future Management Information System at an abstract visualization level. In this visual space all user needs were visible as well as information elements, modules and their connections for the required MIS content structure.

In this context the first MIS prototype with its pilot interface (KVis level 2) was tested and discussed with users and decision-makers.

13) User testing (TI) of the first MIS pilot in the field.

14) KVis (CD): Visual collection of users' ideas and wishes for improvement.

15) KVis (DM): Decision and visual summary of selected improvement ideas to be realized (KVis level 1).

16) Implementation (TI) of the MIS into business reality (into the workspaces of managers): MIS ready for use: with database, software and navigation screen visualizing the meaningful network of knowledge elements; designed for the concept of an improved work flow - all possible user functions in a perfectly fitting interface for an effective and inspiring dialogue between users, user groups and the system – the MIS is accompanied by the visualized development story and the summary of decisions.

17) New information requirements (CD): KVis visualization (KVis level 1) of new user wishes for additional information fields and collection of user ideas for improvement.

18) IVis research (RE): Finding the desired, additional information within the mass of automatically visualized data from different available sources: where, in which form and format, in which quality generated with which focus, perspective and interest.

19) KVis (level 1) (CD): Development of a meaningful knowledge network with the new content modules integrating the new information fields and information modules into the existing knowledge structure.

20) Decision (DM) about alternative possibilities shown in KVis of step 19.

21) KVis (level 2) (PD): Design for the visualization of the new content structure on the computer screen.

22 ff) Programming (PD) of software and database, testing (TI), implementation (TI)

23 ff) New user wishes: Continuous improvement process (CD), (DM), (PD), (TI) - from time to time input from users and content team: new ideas and demands for ad-

ditional information etc. visualized in the "Project Space" as basis for project decisions (KVis level 1 and 2) caused by continuous change in company environment,
market context and work processes.

24) IVis research (RE): Finding the desired additional information within the mass of
automatically visualized data from different available sources: where ? in which form
and format ? in which quality ? generated with which focus, perspective and interest ?

25) KVis (level 1) (CD): Development and visualization of operational key patterns
showing new situations, opportunities and challenges in company environment, market context and work processes.

26 ff) KVis (level 1) (CD): Development for integrating the new knowledge network
and the latest pattern of work processes, decision about alternatives (DM).

27 ff) KVis (level 2) (PD): Design for additional navigation modules and visual surface pattern on the computer screen, decision (DM), realization (PD), testing (TI),
implementation (TI).

28) A new user group joining with specific needs for knowledge and work flow.

29) IVis research (RE): Finding the information desired by the new user group within
the mass of automatically visualized data from different available sources: where ? in
which form and format ? in which quality ? generated with which focus, perspective
and interest ?

30 ff) KVis (level 1) (CD): Development of a meaningful knowledge network and
work flow pattern for the new user group, decision about alternatives (DM), testing
(TI), implementation (TI).

31 ff) KVis (level 2) (PD): Design for the visualization on computer screen fitting the
content structure and the work flow for the new user group, decision about alternatives (DM), testing (TI), implementation (TI).

32 ff) IVis and KVis: Continuous improvement process (CD), (RE), (DM), (PD), (TI)
between IVis and KVis (level 1 and 2) for updating content and process structures.

7   Conclusion

The aim of the project was to create a Management Information System (MIS). The
MIS was conceived as a tool for strategic decision-making, for sharing experiences,
as a knowledge and information repository, and as a dialogue platform. It was demonstrated how IVis and KVis can join together to form a unity in one continuous process
instead of being isolated activities. The crucial linking factor for creating this synergy
was the active involvement of users who were highly motivated because they recognized a personal interest through this process. The application of KVis tools in the
dialogue between IVis and KVis created high energy concerning the visualization
process. Operational models became visible and enhanced effectiveness for continuous learning, for working with information and for generating new knowledge as well
as for communication between different interests and views. Visual continuity and
sustainability were of central interest. The Management Information System was implemented in 1997. Its structure was still in use at the time when this article was writ-

ten in February 2005. Its utilization during the past seven years with the same basic structure is a rich experience concerning the synergy between IVis and KVis and a sign of success in the context of quick change in the software world. During the development and the utilization process of the system we have learned that participation and dialogue with the users is a crucial factor for success. This process reaches a new level of quality in achieving concrete, visible and materialized outcomes which were realized through the use of visualization tools.

Several qualities make this project sustainable. These are:

- openness, transparency and goodwill in a process of visualized dialogue making users and decision-makers really part of the project
- introduction of a lot of relevant knowledge and experience available in the company by the involvement of the people concerned
- similarity (in German: "Selbstähnlichkeit") of methods, processes and qualities at different levels of the project:
  - the development process visualized as a "Project Memory",
  - the MIS tool itself and the utilization process continuously using the same spirit of intercultural dialogue,
  - the same quality of overview and transparency offered by the visualizing methodology in all work steps and their results
- the flexibility of the system for incorporating feedback, improvement ideas and new user needs
- the continuity of dialogue, involvement and participation which is especially important when people leave their position and when new people join.

An important potential of knowledge visualization is to generate new knowledge and to transform masses of information into meaningful content. Profiting from these possibilities and its potential for facilitating dialogue visualization can become a key driver for designing and realizing the space between different cultures, different professional fields and different interests. Visual dialogue can make the discipline of visualization the core of change processes in industry, public services, politics and global life. The tools and methods of the Dialogarchitect® offer new operational ways to realize this perspective. This leads to a relevant positioning of information and knowledge visualization facing more and more urgent needs for change in our world.

Author Index

Lecture Notes in Computer Science

For information about Vols. 1–3464

please contact your bookseller or Springer